The Concept of Water

R. D. V. GLASGOW

Published 2009 by R. Glasgow Books

The Concept of Water

© R. D. V. Glasgow

Contact: roopglasgow@hotmail.com

Typeset by Inma Grau

Cover design by www.pulgon.com

(Kike de la Peña and Pepa Aoiz)

First edition

ISBN 978-0-9561595-0-2

for my father,
Wilfred Glasgow,
1924-2006

CONTENTS

PREFACE

Water seems to be on everyone's lips at the moment, even if only metaphorically. The years 2005-2015 are the United Nations' second Decade for Water, and the city of Zaragoza in Spain has just hosted an international exposition with water (and sustainable development) as its central theme. Many books are now appearing on the politics and ecology of water, and Philip Ball's *H₂O: A Biography of Water* (Weidenfeld and Nicolson, 1999) provides an excellent scientific overview. At the same time, water is still seen by many as a non-subject. It is boring, wet and often just a pain in the neck, connoting never-ending rain and ever more frequent floods. Its availability in wealthy nations is taken for granted. For those with guaranteed access to it, it lacks the party-time associations of other drinks and tends to be dismissed as tasteless, colourless and devoid of interest.

The aim of *The Concept of Water* is to bring together the various aspects of our complex relationship with water, providing a systematic account of its symbolic and philosophical significance. This involves looking at how water has been understood and the role it has played in everyday thought, mythology, literature, religion, philosophy, politics and science, both across cultures and through history. Such a flagrantly cross-disciplinary approach reflects the conviction that no single discipline is watertight enough to be considered in isolation: water ends up dripping across boundaries and limits and getting everywhere. The structure of the book is based on four underlying themes associated with water, which correspond to the four main chapters (water as origin, water as flow, water as death and the depths, water as purity and panacea), each divided into four subsections.

I have used footnotes rather than endnotes in order to keep the basic flow of the argument as simple as possible while allowing the reader easy access to narrative diversions, meanderings and the odd oxbow lake. In addition, the footnotes are intended to provide useful background information where necessary, and indicate sources, referring the reader to the full bibliography at the end of the book. For the sake of brevity, the footnotes only cite book titles when the first reference is made; subsequently, just the surname of the author is given. If the bibliography contains two or more works by the same author, the reference is of course made explicit.

Concerned as it is with our *ideas* about water rather than with the substance itself, *The Concept of Water* is particularly indebted to a number of works by contemporary writers cited in the footnotes and bibliography. The books by Philip Ball, Maggie Black, David Blackbourn, Julian Caldecott, Roger Deakin, Tim Ecott, Iris Fry, Robert Kunzig, Mark Kurlansky, Fred Pearce, Robert Macfarlane, Clive Ponting, Tom Standage and others have all influenced this one. I have also consulted not only conventional encyclopaedias such as the *Encyclopaedia Britannica* and our endearingly clueless family *Chambers* dating from 1950, but also *Wikipedia*, which in my opinion – for all its flaws and vulnerabilities – continues to be thoroughly admirable as a work in progress. But my indebtedness is above all personal. My mother and family and my friends in Zaragoza and elsewhere have constantly supported me with their generosity and kindness. Special thanks go to Inma Grau in Zaragoza for setting the text and to Kike de la Peña and Pepa Aoiz in Madrid for designing the cover. The book is dedicated to the memory of Wilfred Glasgow, my father and brilliant friend.

Rupert Glasgow
Zaragoza, December 2008

Chapter One
Water as Origin

1

The Birth of Philosophy

According to most accounts, the history of Western philosophy begins with
Thales of Miletus, who lived some 26 centuries ago. Thales, it is said, was
the founder of philosophy, the proto-philosopher. These same accounts
then explain that Thales's most renowned credo was that everything is
made of water. As Bertrand Russell puts it, this is "discouraging to the
beginner, who is struggling – perhaps not very hard – to feel that respect
for philosophy which the curriculum seems to expect."[1]

    The modern-day reaction may be to dismiss Thales, philosophy
and water alike as worthy of no further attention. Yet there might remain a
suspicion that both the proto-philosopher and his subject matter go rather
deeper than it appears at first sight. The following pages are based, fairly
obviously, on the conviction that they *do* go deeper and *are* worthy of
further attention. The image we have of all three – water, philosophy and
a man called "Thales" – is notoriously protean[2]: in important respects,
they are what you make of them. The nebulous figure of Thales, as
delivered down to us by second- or third-hand accounts written centuries
after his death, himself embodies a fundamental ambiguity that hovers
between craftiness, wisdom and brilliance on the one hand and hopeless
impracticality on the other.

    For a start, he was one of the Seven Wise Men of the ancient
Greeks. He seems not only to have been an astute politician, but more
famously is said to have predicted an eclipse of the sun in 585 BCE that
cowed the warring Lydians and Medes into ending their conflict (though
this prediction is generally regarded as more of a lucky guess based on
what he had learnt from Babylonian priests than a rigorously mathematical

---

1. Russell, *A History of Western Philosophy*, 43.
2. On philosophy as protean, see Glasgow, *The Comedy of Mind*, 3-8.

achievement). He is also credited with introducing Egyptian geometry into Greece, expounding a theory that explained the annual inundation of the River Nile, and discovering how to calculate how far a ship is out to sea.[3] Equally remarkable, if the historian Herodotus is to be believed, was his practical skill in hydraulic engineering, exemplified during the war between the Lydians and the Persians, when the Lydian troops under Croesus found themselves unable to cross the River Halys and Thales dug a diversion in such a way that both the channels became fordable.[4] This, it has to be said, sounds more like one of Heracles's hydraulic feats[5] than the work of a philosopher. But it does suggest that Thales knew a thing or two about water.

Yet this multi-faceted and mercurial figure, who is even said to have made a small fortune with some timely speculation in the olive market, is also traditionally held up as the archetypal egghead. Most celebrated is the episode of star-gazing Thales tripping into a well – to the amusement of a "clever, witty" Thracian maid. According to the account given by the equally impractical Socrates in Plato's *Theaetetus*, the reason for the maid's mirth was that the philosopher had been "so eager to know what was going on in heaven that he could not see what was before his feet. This is a jest which is equally applicable to all philosophers." Such a man, Socrates goes on, "is the jest not only of Thracian handmaids but of the general herd, tumbling into wells and every sort of disaster through his inexperience."[6] Apocryphal or not, the anecdote has been passed down, repeated and modified through the centuries, as generations of philosophers have confronted the spectre of their own congenital uselessness, sometimes omitting the presence of the female onlooker, sometimes changing her gender, and sometimes keeping her quiet.[7] The original Aesopian version mentioned neither the sex nor the laughter of the passer-by, whereas for

3. Burnet, *Early Greek Philosophy*, 39-46.
4. Barnes (ed.), *Early Greek Philosophy*, 62.
5. On Heracles, see below, chap. I.4.
6. Plato, *Theaetetus*, 174A-C.
7. For a full account of the anecdote's history, see Blumenberg, *Das Lachen der Thrakerin*. Given the moral and theological implications of falls in conjunction with the anatomical associations of holes and shafts, a carnal subtext – implying either sexual incompetence or fleshly sinfulness – is rarely too far from the surface. As far as Thales's own inclinations are concerned, the best-known anecdote has it that when asked why he did not get married, his stock response tended to be: "It's too early," until the day came when he changed his tune and replied: "It's too late." See Barnes, 66.

a philosophical tumbler such as Martin Heidegger the laughter of the uncomprehending non-philosopher became a definitional feature of the true philosopher's essential vocation. Given Thales's pronouncements on the nature of the world, the fact that Thales finds himself irresistibly drawn back to water, albeit at the bottom of a well, seems too much of a coincidence to be passed over in silence.

Many philosophers, of course, have preferred to dissociate Thales from his pratfall and focus on his claims about the material substratum of the world. The authoritative voice of Bertrand Russell proclaimed that Thales's assertion that everything was made of water was to be viewed as "a scientific hypothesis and by no means a foolish one," and when the modern-day scientist Lewis Wolpert speaks of Thales's "wonderful leap," he is referring not to his feats of acrobatic tumbling, but to an even more spectacular leap into empirical science and the idea of the underlying unity of nature, a shift from mythological explanation to explanations that were "self-consistent and open to critical analysis." It was, says Wolpert, "one of the most exciting and important ideas in the entire history of mankind."[8]

With the benefit of hindsight, the choice of water appears inspired enough. Today's schoolchildren learn that a water molecule is not an element, but a compound comprising one atom of oxygen and two of hydrogen (the Frenchman Antoine Lavoisier, the founder of modern chemistry, having coined the termed *hydrogène* to mean "producer of water"[9]), and this hydrogen – so essential to water – is not only the most abundant element in the universe and the first to be formed from the Big Bang, but also the simplest, consisting as it does of just one proton and one electron. As late as the early 19th century, chemists were speculating that atoms of the heavier elements (i.e. of everything else) were produced by conglomerations of hydrogen atoms, thus making hydrogen the "first matter" or ultimate constituent of matter in general.[10] Even now, scientific attempts to find the "ultimate building blocks" of everything that exists have failed to come up with a satisfactory conclusion, delving beyond subatomic protons, neutrons and electrons into an even more arcane realm of quarks, leptons and bosons, but in the end leaving us with a dizzy sensation of infinite regress or circularity.

From Thales's perspective at least, water certainly seemed the most

8. Russell, 44; Wolpert, *The Unnatural Nature of Science*, 35-38.
9. This connection is reflected not only in the Romance languages and English, but also, for example, in German, where the word *Wasserstoff* speaks for itself.
10. Ball, *H₂O: A Biography of Water*, 10.

obvious candidate. For a dyed-in-the-wool traveller, who had voyaged to mainland Greece, Egypt and Babylon, it was natural for the sea to be endowed with geographical or even cosmological primacy, for it formed the link or medium taking seafarers from the long familiar to the newly known, then leading on to the as yet unknown. Unfathomable in depth and boundless in expanse, oceans exude a sense of the infinite, always seeming to stretch *beyond* whatever limits one might set. Today it is known that over two thirds of the planet's surface is submerged in liquid water, and another twentieth is covered by ice. Then there are the springs and geysers that come gurgling up from the bowels of the earth. In Aristotle's account, Thales accordingly conceived of the earth itself as floating like a log upon an immense expanse of water. His trips to Babylonia and Egypt might well have influenced him in this.

Water also has more immediate physical properties that may have contributed to Thales's view. First, it displays the unique capacity to exist in more than one physical state – solid, liquid or gas – under the conditions that generally hold on our planet. Unlike virtually everything else on Earth, we encounter water not only in liquid form, but also solidified as ice or snow and vaporized as clouds, steam, mist or fog. For the thinkers of the time, it was as though water had the capacity to transform itself into something akin to earth or metals – characterized by hardness and solidity – on the one hand, and with the attributes of air on the other.

Yet this is not all. The great majority of the other liquids that we come across in our everyday dealings – fruit juice, wine, milk, blood, urine, saliva – are themselves, in the words of Philip Ball, but "tainted water, full of dissolved or suspended substances,"[11] illustrating water's remarkable ability to carry or "contain" other matter, whether as solutions or suspensions.[12] Thales will doubtless have been aware of the wealth of fertile alluvial silt disgorged by the annual floods of the River Nile; ancient Egyptians called the river *Ar* or "black" on account of the colour of its sediments when in flood. Indeed, the mud of the Nile is black enough to have given the country itself its oldest name, *Kem*, which also means

11. Ibid., 154.
12. Modern-day river scientists in fact distinguish a river's dissolved load (where the particles of the solute are of molecular size and completely dispersed among those of the water) and its suspended load (of silts and clays) from the saltated load of larger particles such as sands, gravels and very small stones, as well as the tracted load of pebbles shunted along the river bed. See Nagle, *Rivers and Water Management*, 24-27.

"black." It was as though the land itself had emerged from the innards of the flowing waters. It has even been surmised that alchemy – and thus chemistry itself – may have not only their historical but also their etymological origins in the bounteous silts of this black land of *Al-Kemia*: "alchemy" would best be understood as the "Black Art," the "Egyptian Art" or the "Science of the Nile."[13] The waters of the Nile are responsible not only for belching out the dark, fertile land of the delta, but for spawning the art concerned with understanding such transformation.

Water's capacity to contain – and then ultimately dump – a whole range of other stuff perhaps explains one of the more eccentric ideas expressed by Plato, who in the *Timaeus* describes gold as an especially dense form of water. There are primarily two kinds of water, he says, one being liquid, the other "fusible" in nature. The former includes such liquids as sap, wine, oil and honey, while the latter is divisible into gold, adamant and copper.[14] Plato was not alone in entertaining such notions. Aristotle followed him in associating metals with moisture (rather than heat and dryness), while Aristotle's successor in charge of the Peripatetic School in Athens, Theophrastus, regarded metals such as silver and gold as coming from water, as opposed to the earth from which rocks and stones proceeded.

Such ideas on the watery origins of metals may have had their roots in observations of precipitates deposited at the mouths of hot springs and of the gold that nestled in certain streams and river beds. The traditional extraction of gold from the River Rhine – flushed down from Switzerland – was one of the river's most enduring occupations, going back to the Celts in the 3rd century BCE, and it was only with the "rectification" of the river in the mid-19th century that the phenomenon of "Rhine gold" and the "gold-washers" who made their living from it vanished from sight.[15]

---

13. See Gilchrist, *The Elements of Alchemy*, 3; Ball, *The Devil's Doctor*, 152; Marshall, *The Philosopher's Stone*, 139. As Marshall and Ball point out, the Egyptian god of wisdom Thoth, known as Hermes to the Greeks, later came to be regarded as the founding father of alchemy, giving his name to the Hermetic tradition of esoteric wisdom.
14. Plato, *Timaeus*, 58D-59C.
15. The Romans are said to have shipped so much Rhine gold back to Italy that they caused the price to sink. As late as 1838 there were still hundreds of gold washers plying their laborious trade; by the 1870s they had been rendered completely obsolete by the speeding-up of the river flow. On Rhine gold and its decline, see Blackbourn, *The Conquest of Nature*, 98-100.

Even earlier, the ancient Greeks had latched on to the trick of submerging their sheepskins in flowing water as a way of filtering out the tiny flecks of gold.[16] In fact, every cubic kilometre of ocean contains roughly a million dollars' worth of gold, amounting to a global value of some $300 trillion, though sifting it out would be a rather sheep-intensive way of earning a livelihood or boosting the national reserves.[17] In the 1670s, moreover, the German alchemist Hennig Brand tried to prove that gold could be distilled from the water that we pass, perhaps misled by a certain similarity of hue that nowadays finds its echo in the concept of the "golden shower." Though he unsurprisingly failed to extract gold, he did succeed in transforming his urine samples into a strange substance that on occasion glowed or burst into flame and is now known as the element phosphorus.[18]

As an empirical conjecture, Thales's claim that everything is made of water was not only open to corroboration (of sorts) in such everyday observations relating to the substance's physical characteristics, but has even been defended in a more modern, proto-scientific framework. The great physician and alchemist Paracelsus himself, writing in the early 16th century, regarded water as the first substance, the *prima materia* from which everything else emerged: "When the world was still nothing but water, and the Spirit of the Lord moved upon the face of the waters, the world emerged from the water; water was the matrix of the world and of

16. See Rupp, *Four Elements: Water, Air, Fire, Earth*, 323. Indeed, she suggests, the resultant golden fleeces may have inspired the tale of the one pursued by Jason, although strictly speaking this one came from the back of a flying ram that once belonged – as it happens – to Hermes.

17. Research has been done in the matter. Between 1925 and 1927 the German ship *Meteor* made a number of crossings of the Atlantic for the purpose of studying ocean chemistry. In particular, one of its tasks was to ascertain whether seawater would yield enough gold to pay off the country's crippling debts. See Broad, *The Universe Below*, 252-53. Today, metallic nuggets called manganese nodules, or more accurately polymetallic nodules, are known to be present across vast reaches of the world's seabed. First discovered in the 19th century, these nodules composed of elements such as manganese, iron, nickel, cobalt, copper and lead are formed by the gradual deposition of minerals around a small object. In one part of the central eastern Pacific there are believed to be between eight and 25 billion tons of polymetallic nodules. At present, the costs of mining them would be prohibitive, but interest has increased in recent decades. See Pernetta, *Philip's Guide to the Oceans*, 152-53. See also Broad, 255-57.

18. In chemical terms, the explanation is that urine contains phosphates (such as sodium phosphate), which under strong heat relinquish their oxygen atoms to leave phosphorus in its elemental form.

all its creatures."[19] There were, he wrote, "many thousand kinds of water in the element aqua," each giving rise to different objects, whether stones, corals or aquatic animals. Plants, according to Paracelsus, were "growing water."[20]

Just over a century later, a Flemish alchemist and disciple of Paracelsus by the name of Jean Baptista van Helmont – today regarded by some as the father of biochemistry – likewise took up the ancient Ionian idea that there is but a single underlying substance, i.e. water. "All earth, clay, and every body that may be touched," he wrote, "is truly and materially the offspring of water only, and is reduced again into water, by nature and art."[21] What made van Helmont stand out from the other alchemists of his day was his use of quantitative experimentation to try to answer biological questions, even though his experiments did tend to be designed to confirm his hypotheses rather than test them with a view to possibly modifying them. In his famous "willow tree experiment," conceived to prove that wood derives from the element of water, he planted a five-pound willow sapling in a pot with two hundred pounds of earth dried in a furnace, watered it assiduously for five years, and at the end of this time again weighed both the tree and the soil: while the earth had lost just two ounces of its original weight, the tree had gained 164 pounds, which van Helmont – unaware of photosynthesis and the part played by carbon dioxide in the production of the tree's cellulose tissues – confidently assumed could only have come from the water he had added. The only other element in van Helmont's aqueous universe was air, but this he regarded as inert and consequently rather uninteresting, as it never changed its form.[22]

Once again, van Helmont was not alone in harbouring such ideas. The 17th-century Anglo-Irish natural philosopher Robert Boyle, himself widely considered the first modern chemist, cheerfully accepted van Helmont's belief in the elemental nature of water:

> I will begin by reminding you of the experiments I not long since related
> to you concerning the growth of pompions, mint and other vegetables

19. Quoted in Ball, *The Devil's Doctor*, 263.
20. Ibid., 266.
21. Quoted in Ball, *H₂O*, 121. The following account is indebted to ibid., 120-25; on van Helmont's attitude to Paracelsus, see *The Devil's Doctor*, 390-94.
22. Van Helmont differentiated between air and water vapour, which could be changed back into water in its liquid state. In fact, he also detected the presence of other air-like substances, which were nonetheless neither air nor water vapour, and to which he gave the name *gas*, from the Greek *chaos*.

out of fair water. For by these experiments it seems evident that water may be transmuted into all the other elements.[23]

Boyle's observation of the formation of kidney and bladder stones in people who were feeding "but upon grass and other vegetables that are perhaps but disguised water"[24] led him to conclude that water could congeal to form minerals, and he also gave an account of its conversion into earth. This transformation of water into earth was a generally acknowledged "fact" of the time, accepted as such by Isaac Newton, who noted in his *Opticks* that "Water by Frequent Distillation Changes into fix'd Earth, as Mr. *Boyle* has try'd."[25] Well-acquainted with the work of both van Helmont and Boyle, Newton himself envisioned water as a universal substrate, porous and transmutable. In his own words,

> that rare substance water can be transformed by continued fermentation into the more dense substances of animals, vegetables, salts, stones and various earths. And finally by the very long duration of the operation be coagulated into mineral and metallic substances. For the matter of all things is one and the same, which is transmuted into countless forms by the operations of nature.[26]

Notably, Newton understood the transmutability of water into its infinite material manifestations as unidirectional: once transmuted, it would not turn back. In order not to dry out as it used up its waters for vegetation, the Earth thus required an extraterrestrial source of water, which Newton conjectured was provided by comets, in particular the vapour in their tails.[27]

*　*　*　*　*

23. Quoted in Ball, *H₂O*, 124.
24. Ibid.
25. See Schechner Genuth, *Comets, Popular Culture, and the Birth of Modern Cosmology*, 144-45; quotation, 145.
26. Quoted in ibid., 144.
27. See ibid., 145-49. In the *Principia*, comets are described – like the seas they replenish – as "absolutely necessary for [the] watering of the earth, and for the production and nourishment of vegetables" (quoted in ibid., 145).

Despite such scientific evidence for the elemental or universal nature of water, not everyone has been willing to see Thales's ideas in a merely empirical light. Although – in the manner of scientific hypotheses – his few assertions did provoke counter-hypotheses such as Anaximenes's declaration that the underlying substance was not water but air, some historians of ideas have insisted on the metaphysical or ontological quality of what Thales said, i.e. his concern with what "is" and the nature of this "is-ness." Boyle's term "disguised water" itself implies that reaching the truth involves a process of going beneath the surface of things, of going "deeper" to unmask deceptions or rupture illusions: the world may *seem* to consist of bricks, bats, pots and pans (not to mention human beings, fruit flies and cucumbers), but in fact all the physical objects everywhere around us are *really* water. It is as though they are just *pretending* not to be.

That the first counter-suggestion to Thales picked out *apeiron*, "the boundless," as its primary entity may likewise be taken as hinting at something beyond the purely physical. This concept was proposed by Anaximander, reputed among other things to be the world's first ever cartographer,[28] and it represents the equally impressive insight that if the multitude of particular entities in the world is made of one underlying substance, then this substratum cannot be identified with any one of these particular entities. Nowadays, this too would generally be regarded as a philosophical as opposed to a purely scientific argument.

In fact, the question of whether Thales was doing science or philosophy is as anachronistic as it is irrelevant. What is clear is that he was in some sense attempting to go "deeper" or "beyond" what was obvious or apparent.[29] Other pronouncements that are ascribed to Thales support the view that he was not making a merely materialistic affirmation. According to the doxographer Aetius, for example, Thales believed a divine power to be inherent in water, endowing it with movement, while Aristotle

---

28. Diogenes Laertius, *Lives of Eminent Philosophers*, I.130-31. As such, Anaximander should take credit for taking a huge step forward in the world of seafaring and navigation, i.e. humankind's attempts to "negotiate" the waters.
29. This is something that can be taken as common to philosophy and science. One distinction between the two is that if a redefinition of what is the case is made possible by greater technological precision, with the accompanying increase in the accuracy or complexity of computation, calibration and observation, then it is science. If it involves a purely conceptual move, it is philosophy. The great insights, say, of Newton or Einstein straddle the boundary between the two disciplines.

attributed to him the further claim that "all things are full of gods." Cicero declared that Thales believed in a divine mind that fashioned all things out of water.[30] In his capacity as one of the Seven Sages, moreover, Thales was associated with the adage that "water is best."

All in all, Thales thus proves to be as enigmatic and protean as ever. Yet this is perhaps appropriate for the *proto*-philosopher, the Herculean hydraulic engineer who searched for the underlying unity or deeper source of things, and whose search ended up turning him into a figure of fun at the bottom of a well. Indeed, wells were the perfect place for exploring the depths: the telescopic benefits of their narrow apertures for star-gazing were common knowledge at the time; they were ideal places for becoming intimately re-acquainted with water; and – as Democritus is famously reputed to have opined – they were ultimately where the truth was to be found.[31]

In his search for the origin of things, Thales found in water – as we shall see – the most protean of entities: it was its protean nature that enabled it to be everywhere. Both the original philosopher and the origin he posited, in other words, are shadowy shape-shifters, fleet-footed and fluid. As with the nebulous quarks, leptons and bosons now posited as the ultimate particles that make up the stuff of the universe, any attempt to pin down such an elusive origin can only be a process of enthusiastic but ultimately self-defeating tail-chasing. Yet whether Thales is to be credited with making an acrobatic leap into empirical thought or with stumbling like an arch-buffoon into new depths of metaphysical insight or obfuscation, what is undeniable is that before him there were others who observed, speculated and performed similar conceptual gymnastics. The origins of *Thales*'s thought in turn lie elsewhere. The following section will focus on myths of creation, where the idea of a primal ocean in some sense preceding everything else (i.e. preceding creation itself) proves to be as universal as the water it presupposes.

---

30. Burnet, 48-51.
31. See Glasgow, *The Comedy of Mind*, 336-37.

2

The Origins of Being

It has been widely supposed that Thales was influenced in his ideas by the ancient Greek cosmogonical stories of Oceanus and Tethys. In the *Iliad*, Homer had recounted how all the gods and living creatures originated from the waters of Oceanus, which girdled the world, and that Tethys – sea-goddess and creatrix – was the mother of all his children.

There were many variations on the theme. One of them, the Pelasgian creation myth,[32] describes how Eurynome, a goddess of the waters like Tethys, emerged naked from the chaos and, finding nothing to rest her feet upon, divided the ocean from the sky and danced upon its waves. The wind caused by her movements generated a giant serpent, Ophion, who coupled with her and got her with child. Or rather, got her with universe. Assuming the form of a dove, Eurynome laid a cosmic egg, which hatched to produce everything that exists. When Ophion proceeded to vex Eurynome by claiming authorship of the universe, she wisely "kicked his teeth out" and banished him to the caves beneath the earth.[33]

These Greek myths were in turn antedated substantially by other water-based creation myths proceeding from the ancient civilizations of Mesopotamia. The best-known and most complete of these is the Akkadian *Enuma Elish*,[34] the present form of which is generally believed to stem from 1100 BCE but which may date from as far back as 1900 BCE. According to this tale, prior to the formation of the skies above and the earth below, all that existed was the god Apsu (god of the primeval fresh waters) and the goddess Tiamat (goddess of the primeval salt waters). These two original deities came together, and as their offspring were born the world began to take shape. With the passing of time, however, tension arose between the inert ancient gods and the restless, active younger ones,

32. *Pelasgian* is the name used by ancient Greek writers to denote the inhabit-ants of pre-historic or pre-Hellenic Greece. It has been conjectured that one of the word's meanings is "from the sea," possibly sharing its etymology with the English *pelagic* ("relating to the open sea").
33. Graves, *The Greek Myths*, I.27. In the Olympian creation myth, by contrast, Oceanus and his sister-consort Tethys were two of the twelve Titans produced by the union of Mother Earth, Gaia, and Uranus.
34. See Dalley (trans.), *Myths from Mesopotamia*, 228-77.

whose energy and exuberance disturbed the peace of Apsu and Tiamat. Against Tiamat's will, Apsu plotted to wipe out the young gods, but Ea, the most cunning of the new generation, easily foiled his progenitor's plan, lulling him to sleep, seizing his cloak and crown, and surreptitiously slaying him.[35] Having overcome Apsu, crafty Ea now presided over the vast underground reservoir of fresh water, which was also known as *apsu*. Retiring to his temple with his consort Damkina, Ea fathered a child who was to become the mighty warrior-king Marduk.

The intergenerational conflicts were not yet over. Now it was the four winds that created the disturbance and Tiamat who was moved to take action. Annoyed by the sea-storms that the winds were churning up, the other gods taunted Tiamat for failing to avenge the death of her husband, and eventually she agreed to destroy the young Marduk. This time Ea proved too weak to vanquish Tiamat, and it was left to Marduk himself to assume authority over the other gods and defeat the raging sea-goddess, forcing the winds in through her open mouth to inflate her belly and then splitting her down the middle with a volley of skilfully directed arrows. Sliced in two like a flatfish, the top half of Tiamat's enormous body became the heavens, while the lower half was used by Marduk – not unlike the Jehovah of the Old Testament – to fashion the earth with its seas and oceans.[36] Knowing which side his bread was buttered, he also enlisted Ea's help to invent a miserable creature called Man who would have to do all the dirty work while the gods relaxed and roistered.[37]

The *Enuma Elish* shows how Marduk is granted leadership of the pantheon and authority over the universe for defeating the forces of primordial chaos embodied in Tiamat: the heroic struggle with the primal waters is a first step in a more general process of establishing cosmological, social and political order. Indeed, there is a sense in which the *Enuma Elish* is a work of propaganda, a paean to the local Babylonian god Marduk as a shaping deity, an agent of order and structure. It is but one in a whole range of closely related such tales that were told among the various peoples of ancient Mesopotamian civilization. Again, it was by no means the first.

In particular, the cosmology and cosmogony of the Babylonians owed a great deal to Sumerian mythology, which was then duly modified to give a theological justification to the precedence of their own god Marduk.

35. Ibid., 234-35.
36. Ibid., 255-57.
37. Ibid., 260-61.

According to an earlier Sumerian tale, the goddess of the primeval ocean, here called Nammu, herself spontaneously generated a male sky and a female earth.[38] The consummately practical Sumerian god Enki, who as lord of the *apsu* presided over the life-giving fresh waters beneath the earth, prefigured the Babylonian divinity Ea, and it was he who established order in the world. Particularly significant was the association of Enki with semen, amniotic fluid and thus with fertility in general: the Sumerian word for water, *a*, also denoted semen or conception, an identification that has recurred in diverse mythological traditions right through to modern times.[39] Not only did Enki bless such cities as Ur and Dilmun with bountiful crops and abundant livestock, but he organized the rivers, clouds and rains, and gave rise to the rivers Tigris and Euphrates by filling their beds with the flow of his seed. Like Ea after him, Enki – the creator of forms – then had the common sense to invent mankind to do the donkey work of digging the elaborate system of irrigation canals that allowed the region to prosper.

The Greek and Mesopotamian myths make it clear that water – which sometimes even precedes the "creator" gods themselves – embodies a radical duality. On the one hand, it is a metaphor for formlessness or chaos, for the primordial soup that antecedes individuation, differentiation, separation, shape, order and hierarchy. On the other hand, it manifests the fertility or creativity that itself *gives rise to* everything that follows.

As a symbol of formlessness, water is clearly not unique. The chaotic state of the primal condition can also be envisioned as swirling fog or as darkness. Space, void, the yawning abyss, chaos or even "nothingness" or "nothing" (which are conveniently enigmatic as concepts and doggedly defy any attempt at visualization) are in themselves equally suitable metaphors for this vacuity, conceptualising it as an absence of form, of differentiated matter, or of the light that allows such differentiation

38. Notably, the Sumerian narrative seems to dispense with the element of heroic struggle or a battle for mastery and control. As Dalley points out, it is impossible to speak of "the Mesopotamian view of creation" as though this were a single, unified tradition. Whereas the *Enuma Elish* featured fresh water and sea water as its primal forces, in the *Theogony of Dunnu* from the early second millennium BCE it was Plough and Earth that gave rise to creation and begot the Sea (ibid., 278-81).

39. See Eliade, *Patterns in Comparative Religion*, 190. Eliade cites a number of examples, including the Pima Indians of New Mexico, according to whose mythology a beautiful woman (Mother Earth) became pregnant when a drop of water fell upon her from a cloud.

to be perceived. On occasion, indeed, these varying metaphors may be interchangeable or coexistent.[40]

The ancient creation myth of Hermopolis,[41] for example, devotes considerable detail to describing what occurred *prior to* creation. According to this account, the *Ogdoad* or "Group of Eight" comprised four male and four female deities who dwelled in the primordial waters before time began and who in their pairs were taken to represent four distinct aspects of the pre-creation scenario. There was Nun and his consort Naunet, who embodied the original formless waters; Huh and Hauhet, who symbolized infinite space; Kuk and Kauket, who personified darkness; and Amun and Amaunet, who represented hidden power, or the void. These four pairs were incorporeal and in a sense lifeless, yet at the same time the sexual division among them expressed the *potential* for life. At a certain point in this infinite ocean of non-activity, the two sexes were irresistibly drawn together, producing what modern science has come to call the Big Bang – and the ensuing universe.[42]

Despite its inevitable limitations, the great advantage of water as a metaphor for primordial chaos is its capacity for overcoming its own shapelessness, or for "containing" within itself the seeds of future life or fertility. At the same time, the primacy of water means that the original chaos remains present *as a threat* in the event of future misdemeanour. If creation is but a blip in the watery infinite, then it will only take a small amount

40. This comes to light in the Vedic tradition of ancient Indian thought, where water is the wellspring of everything that is: as one text puts it, "water, thou art the source of all things and of all existence!" (*Bhavisyottarapurana*, 31.14, quoted in Eliade, *Patterns in Comparative Religion*, 188). One of the hymns of the *Rig Veda*, which date back possibly to 1200 BCE, adopts a particularly interrogative mode, recounting how "darkness was hidden by darkness in the beginning; with no distinguishing sign, all this was water." There was neither "non-existence nor existence" at this point. Yet even water is called into question: "Was there water, bottomlessly deep?" In this most tentative and subtle of hymns, darkness, non-existence and even the primal waters are all invoked but also ultimately transcended as images for the time before time. Indeed, we learn, even "the gods came afterwards, with the creation of this universe." See *The Rig Veda*, 25.
41. Hermopolis, the City of Hermes (or Thoth), is the site of ancient Khmunu, now Al-Ashmunayn, in central Egypt.
42. Scott Littleton, *Mythology*, 15-16.

of divine wrath to wash it away with a timely deluge. Of course, the gods themselves generally avoid the effects of such castigatory re-immersion.[43]

Precisely how the transition from watery chaos to irrigated order is achieved varies from culture to culture. In the case of the *Enuma Elish*, the shift from disorder to order involves battle, with first Ea and then the Babylonian warrior-god Marduk imposing themselves over the aqueous world parents Apsu and Tiamat. A parallel military or martial achievement seems to have been involved when Baal,[44] the Canaanite fertility god and Lord of Rain and Dew, vanquished the ancient sea-god Yamm. In many cases, such myths may have also reflected local tribal conflicts and rivalries.

A second set of images for enacting the move from all-pervading watery nothingness to a world of – wet or dry – "things" incorporates wind or some form of spirit or breath. It was the wind caused by Eurynome's dance that brought swaggering Ophion into being and set the ball rolling in the Pelasgian creation myth. According to the ancient Hindu mythological text *Markandeya Purana*, the creator god Brahma started out as a pure sound vibrating through the nothingness; when this sound echoed back on itself, it became wind and water, and it was the interplay of these two elements that gradually gave rise to the misty matrix of the world.

Yet it is the Biblical Genesis that displays some of the most remarkable wind and water symbolism, the Hebrew word *ruah* – like the Greek word *pneuma* – denoting "wind," "spirit" and "breath." The Biblical account of creation relates that in the beginning, when the earth was "without form" and darkness was "upon the face of the deep," the *ruah* of God moved "over the face of the waters." It was this divine breath or spirit that created light, separated the light from the darkness, day from night, and subsequently brought the firmament into being to divide "the waters

43. Such deluges, as we shall see, have been commonplace in the world's mythologies. Take the case of Viracocha, the creator divinity and water-god of pre-Incan and Incan mythology, who was widely believed to have emerged from Lake Titicaca. The Incan creation myth told how prior to humankind Viracocha had fashioned a race of giants who had failed to live up to expectations and were duly swept away by a cataclysmic flood. And that was that.

44. Baal was a supreme king of gods and a vitally important fertility deity – the arch-enemy of death and drought – for many ancient Middle Eastern communities. He became a bugbear to the Israelites in the 9th century BCE, when Jezebel attempted to introduce the Phoenician worship of Baal as opposed to the official cult of Yahweh.

from the waters,"[45] i.e. that turned the world from watery chaos into a state of individuation and order. Only after completing the difficult process of splitting the waters could God turn his attention to creating the earth.[46] According to Jewish legendary tradition, "there are two things which were not created: wind and water. They were there from the very beginning."[47]

A similar process takes place in the *Popol Vuh*, the sacred text of the ancient Quiché Maya of Central America. This begins with nothing existing, i.e. nothing but the sea, infinite peace, and the great expanse of the sky: "Whatever there is that might be is simply not there: only the pooled water, only the calm sea."[48] Creation comes about only when the sky-gods and the sea-gods enter into dialogue (by contrast with the Biblical monologue), thinking, worrying and coming to an agreement. The words are spoken, the waters are divided, and the earth emerges from the primordial ocean: "The channels of water were separated; their branches wound their ways among the mountains. The waters were divided when the great mountains appeared."[49] While the Mayan imagery suggests a process of ritual sacrifice,[50] the process of separation and individuation may also be considered a matter of *work*, a labour that involves shaping and crafting the cosmos from the immense and silent waters, giving form to what has been formless.[51] If the results are unsatisfactory, moreover, it is a

45. Genesis 1:1-9. I quote throughout from the Revised Standard Version.
46. In the legends of the Jewish *midrash*, the waters themselves resisted this separation, making the second day the day of God's cosmic struggle and almost bringing Him to resolve the whole of creation back into chaos. Seeing the divided waters weeping on account of their forced separation, God was saddened, and this was the one day He did not approve as "good." See Ginzberg, *The Legends of the Jews*, I.14-15; also Illich, *H₂O and the Waters of Forgetfulness*, 26.
47. Quoted in Biedermann, *Dictionary of Symbolism*, 383.
48. *Popol Vuh* (trans. D. Tedlock), 64.
49. Ibid., 66.
50. As Dennis Tedlock explains (ibid., 227), the terms used imply that the separation of the mountains from the water was "an act resembling the extraction of the heart … from a sacrifice."
51. Nowhere is the element of sheer *effort* more evident than in the most common of the Chinese creation myths, which dates from about the 3rd century CE. The Chinese envisioned the primal chaos as a vast cloud of moist vapour, it being the productive energy of the creator Pan Gu, armed with chisel and axe, that turns the original chaotic unity into the duality of *yin* and *yang*, separating sky and earth, night and day, valleys and mountains, and eventually –after a period of 18,000 years– creating a world that is ordered and differentiated. Such were his efforts that on completing his task of cosmic separation an exhausted Pan Gu lay down and died. His huge body transformed itself into the features

labour that can easily be undone: the possibility of a return to formlessness in the guise of a universal deluge represents a constant threat.

A different approach to describing the transformation from formlessness to order focuses more on its self-generating nature. The change, in other words, comes from *within* the water (although in some cases outside help may also prove necessary). This innate fertility is clearly present in the case of the Sumerian god Enki, for whom water is semen and semen is water (the creative ambiguity of such wordplay paralleling the polysemy of the Hebrew and Greek winds). Observing the fecund, life-giving, alluvial silts that were deposited when the annual flood of the Nile receded, the Egyptians too surmised that creation had begun in this way, as a single, fertile mound emerging from the primordial waters. This mound lay at the heart of all the Egyptian creation myths. The first thing engendered by the tumultuous coming together of the four pairs of gods of the Hermopolitan *Ogdoad* was just such a mound, which contained the cosmic egg from which the sun would hatch out. At Heliopolis,[52] where a group of nine instead of eight gods was worshipped (the *Ennead*), it was actually on the mound that the first god, Atum, came into being "of himself." To mitigate his loneliness in the watery infinite, Atum then proceeded to ejaculate the twins Shu (Air) and Tefnut (Moisture) into existence (theologians later attributing female qualities to Atum's hand).[53] A variation on this myth ascribes an active role to the *benu* or heron, who hovers above the primal waters and whose occasional cries create a disturbance that initiates the process of creation: when the heron then alights on the primal mound, it lays the cosmic egg from which the sun god emerges.

Many myths, indeed, feature one or several protagonists from the (still to be created) natural world who serve as agents or catalysts in the emergence of this mound. Most frequent is the Earth Diver, an animal such as a water bird, muskrat, beetle or crayfish, who plunges into the primal depths to fish up the land that will later expand to become the world. Many

---

of the Earth as we know it: his breath became the winds, his sweat the rains, and his blood the rivers and streams that quicken the Earth. His fleas were turned into humankind.

52. The ancient site of Heliopolis is located not far from what is now Greater Cairo.

53. See Scott Littleton, 12ff. Shu and Tefnut in turn engendered Geb (Earth) and Nut (Sky), who then produced Osiris and Seth and their consorts Isis and Nephthys.

North American Indian cultures recounted tales of how the world rose from the waters thanks to the magical intervention of such diving animals. The Huron and Iroquois tribes from the region around the Great Lakes, for example, told the story of the mother-goddess Ataentsic who, seduced and impregnated by a nameless being, found herself cast out from heaven and tumbling down through space with nowhere to land. When she eventually reached the watery wastes below, Turtle obligingly arose from the depths to give her a place for her lying-in, while Muskrat and Otter fetched up solid ground that would become the earth.[54] Ataentsic duly proceeded to give birth to twins, the evil spirit Hahgwehdaetgah and the benevolent creator god Hahgwehdiyu, who would shape and order the world as it was known. For the Cherokees, by contrast, the successful Earth Diver was a water beetle, while the Chickasaws gave the credit to a crayfish. The turtle plays a relatively constant role in such tales, supporting the whole world on his back and floating peacefully in the boundless waters. Ancient Chinese cosmology envisions a primeval sea-turtle, Ao, fulfilling a similar cosmic function.[55]

The Earth Divers are typically at home both in water and air, while the turtle has both aquatic and terrestrial attributes. In this sense, they clearly symbolize an ability to rise above or go beyond one's watery origins. Yet magical animals or deities will also do the trick. According to the creation myth of the Yoruba people of Nigeria, when the great sky-god Oloron looked down from on high and saw nothing but the immensity of the oceans, he summoned his two sons, Obatala and Oduduwa, to rectify matters, providing them with a bag of sand and dirt, a magical hen, a chameleon, and a great palm tree to shin down. While Obatala opted to make a strong wine from the tree's sap and drink himself into a stupor, his assiduous brother Oduduwa busied himself sprinkling the sand and the dirt over the waters, getting the slow chameleon to test whether it would hold (it did) and the hen to scatter it further afield. Such were the origins of the great continent of Africa. The Shinto creation story recounts how when the god Izanagi, accompanied by his consort Izanami, ventured onto the floating bridge of heaven – a rainbow – and prodded his bejewelled spear into the restless brine below, he stirred up the lumps of mud that

---

54. Eliot, *The Universal Myths*, 16.
55. Emerging gently from the watery depths, chelonians seem to have been an archetype of benevolent stability and universal structure. Kurma the Tortoise was the second *avatar* or manifestation of the great Hindu god Vishnu, likewise functioning as a sort of cosmic prop.

were to become the islands of Japan.

One recurrent agent of order and fertility comes from the plant kingdom. In ancient Egypt the lotus occurs in various of the creation myths. Legend had it that its blossoms originated on the muddy primordial waters of Nun, and its calyx brought forth the sun god Re, the supreme deity (for much of Egypt's history) responsible for introducing order into the universe and making life possible. Closing its petals at night and reopening them at sunrise, the lotus symbolizes the overcoming of darkness and the emergence of light from the watery primal ooze.[56] In ancient India, the lotus was intimately associated with the conceptual realm of water, fertility and with the creator god Brahma.

There are a great number of Hindu creation myths, many of which involve Brahma, seen as the embodiment of the all-encompassing spirit or universal consciousness known as *brahman*. Brahma also went by the name of Narayana, which means "supreme divinity" but can equally be understood to denote his association with the infinite waters. According to the early Hindu legal text *The Laws of Manu*, the universal spirit *brahman* willed first the waters into being and then an egg – floating on the surface – from which after a year Brahma-Narayana hatched forth to produce the sky, the earth and the rest of creation. In this capacity, the deity Narayana represents both the infinite waters and the energy that moves within or upon them and gives rise to creation.[57] In Indian mythology, the image of Narayana floating peacefully on the primal waters is a recurrent symbol of the cosmic stillness that precedes creation.

As the god of creation, Brahma takes pride of place in the Hindu *trimurti*, the triad of Brahma, Vishnu and Shiva. He has seldom been worshipped, however, and his significance has diminished over the centuries, as followers of Shiva have proclaimed the primacy of Shiva, and followers of Vishnu have asserted the pre-eminence of Vishnu. Indeed, it is Vishnu who is now most widely associated with Narayana and the creation of the world. In one of the foremost stories told by Vaishnavites,

56. In Memphis, the lotus god Nefertum was one of a triad of deities, along with the creator god Ptah and his consort the goddess Sekhmet. At Heliopolis, Nefertum, meaning "young Atum" and signifying the sunrise, had earlier represented the youthful form of the original creator god (who was subsequently subsumed within the sun cult as Atum-Re).

57. In the form of Apava, moreover, Brahma is the "water-mover" or "the one who sports on the waters": according to this tradition, Brahma is said to have split into two forms, the first male and the first female, in turn begetting the first man.

Brahma is merely the creative aspect of the more all-pervading Vishnu, now seen as the personal form of the *brahman* that existed before anything else. According to this myth, the first thing Vishnu does is engender a vast primal ocean, and having achieved this, he takes a breather (to sleep or meditate) on the back of the 100-headed serpent Ananta-Shesha, the symbol of eternity. As Vishnu reclines in thought, his creative energy is bodied forth in the form of a beautiful lotus blossom emerging from his navel. Cradled in the calyx of the flower is Brahma, who then creates the universe and generates order.

The significance of the lotus or water-lily also extends to the level of personal as well as cosmic edification. Rooted in mud and water, the lotus blossom floats on the surface as a symbol of beauty and non-attachment to which the human being – it is claimed – would do well to aspire. In Buddhist thought too, the lotus represents the state of those who float free of ignorance and attain enlightenment. Human beings, so the argument runs, are "like lotuses in a pool": "all are rooted in mud; most are swamped below the surface; but a few are struggling to the light and some have already blossomed."[58] The origins and roots of human beings in slime and watery sludge are the focus of the following section.

3

The Emergence of Life

Not surprisingly, creation myths have often conceived of men and women as being fashioned from something rather more solid – more manageable or tractable – than just water, such as clay or mud. The Biblical creation of the first man from earth and mud (just after the ground had been given its first watering)[59] clearly echoes the ancient Egyptian tale of the ram-headed god Khnum, associated with the soil and fertility of the Nile, who fashioned the first human beings from clay on his potter's wheel: the

---

58. Bowker (ed.), *The Oxford Dictionary of World Religions*, 169.
59. Genesis 2:6-7. Isaiah (45:9; 64:8) also uses the image of clay-making to describe the relationship of man to Creator: "we are the clay, and thou art our potter."

Hebrew word *adam* denoted "red clay."[60] It also recalls the Sumerian story of Enki, lord of fresh waters and divine ceramist, who – keen to invent some mug to do life's dirty work – moulded the first 14 men and women in a process patently modelled on brick-making.[61] In Islamic tradition, Adam is created from dust,[62] while the ancient Greeks attributed the creation of man to Prometheus, who used clay. According to a legend dating from the Chinese Han Dynasty (206 BCE – 220 CE), the mother deity Nü Wa – overwhelmed by loneliness on confronting her reflection in a pond – took hold of a fistful of mud from the water's edge and kneaded it into a human shape, forming a tiny body that leapt into life when she put it down. As this proved a rather slow way of doing things, she took a rope, dipped it into the mud and swung it around her head to send the mud flying and scatter the primordial humans far and wide.[63]

The use of mud or clay in fact implies a *mixture* of earth with water, which is associated with fertility and growth. In some myths of creation, however, the first people emerge more directly from water. In one of the accounts of Brahma's act of creation, as we have seen, it is Brahma-Apava – the one who sports on the water – who splits into male and female before begetting Manu, the first man. For the Chibcha people of what is now Colombia, the origins of man went back to a time shortly after light had been created, when the tribe's founding mother Bachue ("Big-Breasted") – the goddess of springs, streams and sources of water – emerged from Lake Iguaque carrying her three-year-old son in her arms. Having duly populated the Earth and educated their progeny, Bachue and her son-consort once more felt the call of the sacred lake from which they

---

60. A similar understanding links the words *human, humus* and *humble*, which derive from a root suggesting not only what is "lowly" or "of the ground," but also "wetness" – as in the original sense of the word *humour* (cf. humid). See Logan, *Dirt*, 15: "Both people and humus are wet inside."
61. See Dalley (trans.), *Myths from Mesopotamia*, 14-17; cf. 36-37.
62. Qur'an, 3:59. On another occasion the creation of man is said to have arisen from "dust, then a drop of fluid" (22:5). I quote throughout from the translation by M. A. S. Abdel Haleem (Oxford: Oxford University Press, 2004).
63. According to the *Popol Vuh* of ancient Mayan civilization, by contrast, the gods' earliest attempts to use such materials to bring forth a creature reflecting their glory were a spectacular failure. Their mud people simply fell apart, while the minds and hearts of their wooden people remained devoid of thoughts and feelings. For their final, successful attempt to create satisfactory human beings, the gods used ground maize and water.

had first appeared, changing into serpents and slithering back into the waters. Such conceptions of humankind's aquatic origins were frequent among the indigenous peoples of South America. According to Inca mythology, Manco Capac – the first ruler of their kingdom and founder of their dynasty – likewise emerged from the waters of Lake Titicaca together with his sister-wife Mama Ocllo.[64]

While giving man a relatively dry, dusty or loamy start in life, the Qur'an does trace the origins of *life itself* – i.e. the other species – back to a watery beginning, with "every living thing" being made "from water."[65] The Biblical Genesis, moreover, gives clear *chronological* priority to the creatures of the sea (and the firmament), producing a palaeohistorical narrative that is not completely out of step with more modern theories of evolution: while the host of aquatic creatures and great whales make their appearance on the fifth day, it is not until the sixth that the cattle, beasts and creeping things of the earth come into being, followed not too long afterwards by man and woman.

The early Greek thinkers too intuited the importance of water in the evolution of life. According to Anaximander, living creatures first arose from the moist element, and humans evolved from fish.[66] The puzzling fact that humans require such an extended period of infant nursing (which raises the question of how the *first ever* person actually survived babyhood) is resolved by proposing that we were originally incubated inside fish-like creatures. In the words of one commentator from the 3rd century CE, Anaximander believed "that there arose fish, or animals very like fish, that humans grew in them, and that the embryos were retained inside up to puberty, whereupon the fish-like animals burst and men and women emerged already able to look after themselves."[67] The notoriously enigmatic Heraclitus of Ephesus was said to have written: "for souls it is death to become water, for water death to become earth; but from earth

---

64. See Scott Littleton, 584-85.
65. Qur'an, 21:30.
66. See Barnes, 72-73: according to Hippolytus, Anaximander said that humans "originally resembled another type of animal, namely fish."
67. Ibid. In the words of Plutarch, Anaximander had said that "at first men came into being inside fish and were nourished there – like sharks – only emerging and taking to the land when they were able to look after themselves."

water comes into being, from water soul."[68]

More modern scientific orthodoxy would agree with Anaximander that life started in the seas. But for all the progress that has been made in tracing our evolution, precisely how life itself got going is still largely a mystery. For most of western history, the origin of life was in fact "explained" either in terms of divine creation, which implied that it was none of science's business, or spontaneous generation, which held that living organisms such as plants, worms or insects could arise *just like that* from mud, slime, excrement or decaying matter, given appropriate conditions of heat and moisture. It was only with the rise of Darwin's evolutionary worldview in the 19th century that the question of life's origins could extricate itself from the clutches of Christian theology and Aristotelian natural philosophy; from this point on, it could be conceived instead in terms of gradual, continuous evolutionary processes involving specific physicochemical mechanisms responsible for the self-organization of lifeless matter into the first living systems. The scientific consensus now is that there is no unbridgeable gap or discontinuity separating inanimate matter from living organisms; the emergence of life cannot be attributed either to chance or to the miracle of divine intervention.[69] Yet within the great diversity of origin-of-life theories and their many empirical divergences, the universal precondition common to all of them is the presence of liquid water, generally in the form of some hot, cold or lukewarm but above all aqueous primordial soup.

Charles Darwin himself insisted that his own work had "nothing to do with the origin of life."[70] Darwinian theory focused on the origin of species through natural, material mechanisms, but not on the *original* origin, i.e. that of the first species from which all subsequent species evolved. Not surprisingly, however, Darwin did devote some thought

---

68. Ibid., 121. Socrates is famously said to have commented that it would take a Delian diver to get to the bottom of Heraclitus's writings (pearl hunters from the island of Delos being renowned for their prowess in diving). Again, the watery depths are where the truth lies. Ironically, Democritus's celebrated dictum that the truth is to be found at the bottom of a well has on occasion been mistakenly attributed to Heraclitus: see Rabelais, *Oeuvres completes*, 291, 500.
69. See Fry, *The Emergence of Life on Earth*, 1-8.
70. Quoted in ibid., 55.

to the matter.[71] In a letter from 1871 he tentatively envisioned a "warm little pond" containing ammonia and phosphoric salts, which under the influence of light, heat and electricity might form "a protein compound … ready to undergo still more complex changes."[72] Despite Darwin's public asseverations, the materialistic implications of Darwinian evolution were that life was originally generated from inorganic matter through natural processes in the primordial waters.

One of the first prominent post-Darwinian theories posited the existence of a primordial matter or *ur*-slime said to have given rise to organic life in its entirety.[73] This seemed to find empirical corroboration with the discovery by the British biologist T. H. Huxley of a gelatinous ooze that had been dredged up from the seafloor by a telegraph survey ship a few years earlier. Huxley called this primal slime *Bathybius haeckeli* in honour of the eminent German biologist and philosopher Ernst Haeckel, who had originally propounded the idea of a pulsing mass of *Urschleim* as the ancestral mother of all living creatures, forming the missing link between inorganic matter and organic life. Huxley speculated that the deep-sea *Bathybius* formed a carpet of living protoplasm that covered the whole of the ocean floor. Yet this primeval goo proved to be the mother only of red herrings: it had in fact been produced by a reaction between the mud of the seafloor and the alcohol in which it had been bottled, and was nothing more interesting than a precipitate of calcium sulphate. Huxley was quick to recant; Haeckel was more reluctant to relinquish his *Urschleim*.

The problems associated with the protoplasmic theory induced many leading scientists of the day – including Lord Kelvin and Hermann von Helmholtz – to adopt a dualistic approach known as panspermia, according to which life and matter were two timelessly distinct categories. Life, they felt, was simply too complex to have originated from a random association of inanimate matter. Rather, the "seeds of life" had been brought to Earth on meteorites from elsewhere in the universe. To make a claim such as this, however, was to re-consign the mystery of life's origins

---

71. In a poem entitled *The Temple of Nature*, his grandfather, Erasmus Darwin, had referred to the spontaneous generation of the "first specks of animated earth," which took place "beneath the waves" of the primordial seas: "From Nature's womb the plant or insect swims, / And buds or breathes, with microscopic limbs" (I.249-50) (available online at Project Gutenberg, www.gutenberg.org).
72. Quoted in Fry, 56.
73. On the protoplasmic theory espoused by Huxley and Haeckel, see ibid., 57-59.

to a realm of unknowability conveniently beyond the reach of science.[74] It was not until the publication in the 1920s of two separate papers – one by Alexander I. Oparin, the other by J. B. S. Haldane, and both entitled "The Origin of Life" – that evolutionary materialism recovered its momentum.[75] Common to both scientists was the idea that an essential step in the emergence of living systems was the synthesis of increasingly complex organic compounds such as sugars and proteins in the primordial seas, forming what Oparin visualized as a colloidal solution in which coagulation would occur and what Haldane described as a "hot dilute soup." The primordial ocean, according to Haldane, was a "vast chemical laboratory."[76]

Under the influence of the Oparin-Haldane hypothesis, the question of the origin of life – previously regarded by many as an untouchable taboo – became a "legitimate scientific problem, open to research."[77] Since the middle of the 20th century, scientists have tried to simulate the primeval soup, reproducing the conditions in which the first living organisms somehow hoisted themselves into existence in the early days of the Archean Eon some 3.8 billion years ago. Stanley Miller and Harold Urey inaugurated the field of "experimental prebiotic chemistry" in an acclaimed experiment in 1953, when they concocted an atmosphere of methane, ammonia and hydrogen, together with a pool of water, and used an electrical discharge to imitate the primal thunderstorm. After a few days, they found that their pool of water had turned reddish and contained certain of the complex chemical compounds essential to life such as amino acids (the building blocks of proteins). Later experiments gave rise to purines and pyrimidines (the building blocks of DNA and RNA).

For all the encouragement such experiments have offered, however, they remain a long way from explaining the formidably complex proteins or the self-replicating molecules such as DNA and RNA that are the basis for all life on Earth. One particular problem is thrown up by water itself, moreover, in the form of the chemical reaction known as *hydrolysis*. This

---

74. On panspermia, see ibid., 59-62.
75. On the Oparin-Haldane hypothesis, see ibid., 65-78.
76. Ibid., 72. Oparin and Haldane did have different conceptions of what constituted a living organism: for Oparin it was a complex metabolic system; for Haldane it was a self-replicating genetic system. The divergence between metabolic and genetic approaches has been one of the most constant and fundamental divisions in origin-of-life work: see ibid., 86, 150, 184.
77. Ibid., 65.

is the reverse of the *dehydration synthesis* that links chains of monomers together and in so doing spits out a water molecule: hydrolysis *uses* a water molecule to split the chains up. Such a process critically hinders the progress from relatively small monomers to the chain-like polymers, i.e. from amino acids to proteins, and from nucleotides to DNA and RNA. In the words of one expert, water's tendency not to link amino acids and nucleotides into chains but rather to split them up means that "water-based life must ... fight a constant battle against destruction."[78] Other problems associated with the Oparin-Haldane hypothesis include the diluteness of the prebiotic soup (the sheer *unlikelihood* of the life-building reactions taking place) and doubts regarding the composition and nature of the primordial atmosphere.[79]

In view of these difficulties, some theorists have proposed that the massive, exogenous delivery of water and organic compounds by meteorites and comets might have been a major source of the prebiotic materials required for life to ensue.[80] Others have opted for the extreme conditions that would have existed in the vicinity of underwater hydrothermal vents.[81] These are exceedingly hot, deep-sea geysers spouting water that is especially rich in minerals, ammonia and carbon-based compounds such as methane. Such vents are now known to be relatively rich in a compound called hydrogen sulphide, moreover, which may well have provided the first living organisms – heat-loving microbes – with the hydrogen atoms needed to convert carbon dioxide into the sugar glucose and in turn provide the chemical energy necessary for powering their cells. The hypothesis of submarine volcanism suggests a scenario of infernal discomfort (infernal for us, that is, but home and hearth for the primordial hyperthermophiles): the waters in which life evolved would have been characterized by high acidity, blistering heat, crushing pressure and perpetual darkness.

Another alternative – of particular resonance given the venerable religious and mythological traditions of Khnum, Enki, Adam and others –

---

78. Planetary scientist Christopher Chyba, quoted in ibid., 245.
79. Both Oparin and Haldane assumed a "reducing" atmosphere rich in hydrogen-containing gases such as methane, ammonia and hydrogen: other scientists have suggested that the atmosphere may have consisted mainly of carbon dioxide, nitrogen and water. A "non-reducing" atmosphere of this sort makes it much more difficult to account for the accumulation and chemical evolution of organic compounds.
80. Ibid., 115-17.
81. Ibid., 117-23.

has been to suggest that the chemical evolution that led to living systems did not take place in the churning seas but on the surface of clay minerals. As William Bryant Logan puts it in *Dirt*,

> there was not enough motherly repose in the open sea, nothing to enfold, contain and order. This is exactly the function of a clay. Formed by water, it is the seat of a wild, capacious order. ... The clays, unlike their parent rocks, have no inaccessible interior, but instead a very large reactive surface. They unlock the potential waiting in raw matter. Clays stack, wrap, pile, and exfoliate, like leaves or sheaves of paper. In fact, experiments have shown that a single gram of a clay powder can have a total surface area larger than a football field.[82]

In its scientific form, the idea goes back to the work of J. D. Bernal, who in the 1950s suggested that clay minerals – by adsorbing and concentrating the organic molecules on their surface – would counter both the excessive diluteness of the primordial soup and the tendency for hydrolysis to occur rather than dehydration and polymerization. A more recent and more radical version of the idea, propounded by the chemist Graham Cairns-Smith, has been that the first "organisms" themselves *consisted of* mineral crystals such as clay, rather than proteins or nucleic acids.[83] Characterized by their exquisitely hydrated complexity and plasticity,[84] clays do seem to share some of the properties of life itself. And like living systems, they are deeply dependent on water.

* * * * *

82. For a persuasive paean to clays in general see Logan, *Dirt*, 123-32; quotation, 124-25.
83. Cairns-Smith speaks of self-replicating "crystal genes": the information they embodied would have taken the form of electrical charges on their surface, produced by structural irregularities. In the course of the process of evolution, the clay genes would have "learnt" how to synthesize organic compounds on their surface, providing organic life with a mineral scaffold which could subsequently be discarded. Cairns-Smith's ideas have recently been applied to the hydrothermal vent scenario.
84. Clays are composed of infinitesimal sheets that slide over one another, "held loosely in place by intervening layers of chemically combined water" (see Logan, 130).

By hook or by crook, life had emerged *within* the primordial waters. But it had not yet emerged *from* those waters. The story of life, writes Logan, is the story of bodies that have "learned to contain the sea." Some time over three billion years ago, an accumulation of chemical compounds "threw an envelope around itself and began to live. It now had an inside and an outside. The envelope regulated the flow of salts from one to the other, and back again, making the selective work of digestion possible." The intervening eons have seen a steady progression towards what biochemists know as "osmotic independence," as living systems have acquired and developed an ability to carry these salty fluids around inside themselves without drying out.[85] Terrestrial endotherms, including humans, have left the medium in which their ancestors originated, while keeping its salty and thermally stable essence internalized as blood. Others, including the cetaceans, have returned to their watery roots. Our emancipation from the primordial matrix, it seems, can only be contingent and provisional. In evolutionary terms it has depended upon an extraordinary combination of circumstances.

Perhaps the most momentous step of all was the emergence of photosynthesis around three and a half billion years ago, when enlightened cyanobacteria hit upon the idea of using water – the medium in which they lived – rather than hydrogen sulphide as the source of the hydrogen atoms that would turn low-energy carbon dioxide into energy-rich organic compounds (with the help of the energy of absorbed sunlight). The monumental significance of this development cannot be overemphasized. At one fell swoop, water ceased to be a mere medium and became a nutrient. The water molecules were absorbed, the hydrogen atoms used for energy-creation, and the oxygen dumped as waste.

For the world as it existed at the time, this was a grave development. While the cyanobacteria prospered from the abundance of water, the oxygen they blithely excreted was a corrosive toxin that unleashed unprecedented environmental carnage and rearranged the planet's whole biosphere. It was only with time that oxygen-breathing organisms evolved. Such creatures provided a counterbalance to the process of photosynthesis in the form of the "aerobic" respiration that used oxygen to burn up carbohydrates to carbon dioxide and water, releasing heat-energy as it did so. A pivotal result of the victorious emergence of photosynthesis, moreover, was not only the production of oxygen but also – once a certain *level* of oxygen was reached, possibly within the last billion years – the formation of a

85. Ibid., 11-12.

layer of ozone, which protected the Earth from the ultraviolet radiation that would have otherwise disarranged the macromolecules of any living organism. Whereas life's origins had been confined to a medium – water – that provided an effective shield from the Sun's ultraviolet light but at the same time let in the wavelengths needed for photosynthesis, the appearance of the ozone layer allowed life to emerge from the seas and colonize dry land.

This too was a slow process, as living systems gradually developed in complexity. The Cambrian Period (542-490 million years ago) was characterized by an extraordinary increase in the diversity of marine animals and plants, yet the land remained barren. The great watershed in evolutionary history that marks the split from a purely aquatic biosphere into one that was both aquatic and terrestrial is thought to lie in the Ordovician Period some 450 million years ago. It was plants that first took the plunge, or belly flop, into life on dry land: "no fish stood to gain by dragging itself on ill-adapted fins over the mud," writes Philip Ball, "unless there was food to be had there. Before animals could colonize the land, plants had to get there first."[86] To start with, there will have been mats of algae near shores; then liverwort-type plants evolved. Animals followed suit within the next 50 million years: at first probably tiny crustaceans resembling modern woodlice; later, about 370 million years ago, the first four-legged amphibians; then reptiles evolved in the course of the Carboniferous Period some 355-298 million years ago.[87] Rather less than a tenth of the history of life on Earth, it seems, has featured actual landlubbers as well as water-dwellers.

86. Ball, *H₂O*, 217.
87. Italo Calvino provides a whimsical variation on this account of the first movement of life from the oceans onto dry land in his short story "The Aquatic Uncle," which turns the juxtaposition of the aquatic and the terrestrial to comic account. The tale is set in the Carboniferous Period – a time, in Calvino's words, when "the first vertebrates ... abandoned aquatic life for terrestrial, descended from the osseous, pulmonate fish whose fins were capable of rotation beneath their bodies and thus could be used as paws on the earth" (*Cosmicomics*, 71). The narrator, Old Qfwfq, has proudly left the sea behind him in the name of progress, and is rightfully embarrassed by his great-uncle N'ba N'ga, a cantankerous, retrograde old fish who simply refuses to renounce the aquatic world. So imagine poor Old Qfwfq's dismay when his first love, the delightful, highly terrestrial Lll, swaps allegiances, jilts her stick-in-the-mud suitor, and slips back into the waters to join N'ba N'ga and "bring still more fish into the world" (ibid., 81).

As things stand, scientific orthodoxy thus assumes an ancestral lineage leading from the first prevertebrate chordates just after the Cambrian Explosion (more precisely, a worm-like sea creature called *Pikaia*, endowed with a notochord or stiffened dorsal rod that would evolve into our spinal column) to the first true vertebrates, which were jawless fish that appeared in the Middle Ordovician, and on via amphibians, synapsids and cynodonts to the placental mammals that were to keep a very low (shrew-sized) profile for the millions of years that the dinosaurs ruled the planet. Eventually this lineage leads us to the primates, a type of placental mammal that includes monkeys, apes and human beings.

Right through to seven million years ago, in fact, it is agreed that we share a common heritage with chimpanzees. At this point there appeared on the scene a hominid species called australopithecines, which emerged from the tropical forests of Africa on to the open savannah and walked upright instead of swinging from the trees. From here onwards, the experts find it impossibly difficult to agree with one another. While the savannah hypothesis keeps our ancestors very much on dry land, an attractive conjecture known as the "Aquatic Ape Theory" (AAT),[88] commonly rejected by most palaeoanthropologists, affirms that our pre-human ancestors evolved – at least for a certain period of time – in an aquatic or semi-aquatic environment.

Specific characteristics of the modern human body, claim adherents to AAT, reflect adaptations to this marine setting. It explains, for a start, why we are relatively unhairy; in this respect we show a greater resemblance to aquatic whales or dolphins or semi-aquatic wallowing animals such as hippopotamuses or pigs than to our hirsute fellow-primates such as chimpanzees or gorillas. It sheds light on the design of our kidneys, which is unique among primates, yet universal among marine mammals. It may also provide an explanation for our bipedalism (waist-deep water being naturally conducive to bipedal locomotion) and our innate podginess (which recalls the layer of subcutaneous fat or blubber in certain aquatic mammals much more than the scragginess of chimpanzees). It could likewise account for the fact that we weep in situations of emotional distress

88. The idea was conceived separately by the marine biologist Alistair Hardy in 1930 and by the German anatomist Max Westenhöfer, who in 1942 proposed the notion in his book *Der Eigenweg des Menschen* (*The Unique Road to Man*). More recently Elaine Morgan has popularised AAT in a series of books on the subject, such as *The Aquatic Ape* (1982) and *The Aquatic Ape Hypothesis* (1997). For an account see also Caldecott, *Water: Life in Every Drop*, 43-49.

(like seals, sea otters and the now extinct Steller's sea cow, but unlike any other primates, or any other terrestrial mammal except elephants); that we mate the way we are traditionally supposed to (aquatic mammals also opting for the style of missionaries rather than doggies; bonobos and orang-utans do likewise but are exceptions in this respect); and that we have voluntary control over our respiratory system (allowing us to dive out of the way of danger). This conscious control of breathing, it has been suggested, is not only of vital importance to diving animals, but possibly played a key role in the development of our ability to produce a complex and varied range of vocal sounds and thus use speech to communicate with one another.

Our marine origins are even reflected, it is claimed, in an affinity for water that is often described as *natural.*[89] Unlike scrawny chimps, for example, who tend to sink on the spot,[90] our layers of blubber make it relatively easy for us to keep afloat. This is something that comes intuitively to babies, who can swim long before they can sit up or crawl and who never try to breathe underwater but paddle to the surface to do so, instincts that non-swimmers subsequently lose as they grow older. Seen in this light, drowning itself may be considered *unnatural* (unless caused by injury, cold, exhaustion or polluted water). The trick to keeping afloat, it is said, is to "be oneself": to drown is to do something to the water.[91]

While most primates give water as wide a berth as possible, moreover, for modern-day humans it represents a context and a pretext for sporting and cavorting, swimming, surfing and snorkelling, for fishing, boating and indulging in idle reverie. Summer holidays are spent getting toasted in the sun so as then to be able to cool off in it. It evokes freedom and fun, and provides a welcome release from the constraints of gravity. The expression used by the ancient Greeks to refer to the three R's – the

---

89. See Rupp, 62-63, on both our aquaphilia and its limits.
90. Not all other primates are such hopeless land-lubbers, though. Witness the amphibious sporting of crab-eating macaques. In fact, most animals – even cats – can swim *after a fashion* if push comes to shove. Giraffes are perhaps the most natationally challenged mammals on account of their tendency to capsize. Elephants are among the best swimmers, but like humans they too are thought by some to have evolved as aquatic creatures (see Deakin, *Waterlog: A Swimmer's Journey through Britain,* 161-62).
91. See Farber, *On Water,* 143-44. Farber is quoting the Polish writer Jerzy Kosinski, in conversation with a Buddhist monk.

rudiments of any education – was "the alphabet and swimming."[92] For the supporters of AAT, this age-old attraction to water is an expression of our evolutionary memory.

However, there are limits to our proficiency and our well-being in marine environments, and they are in fact rather low. Despite being less dense than water, there are plenty of humans who would unhesitatingly describe themselves as non-swimmers. Cultural and historical factors have here played an important part. From Late Antiquity on, Christianity broadly discouraged bathing, which it associated with the sinful dissolution of Romans and, later, Moors. From the 14th century on, the Plague reinforced the view of water – especially when warm or hot – as an enemy, seen as opening the pores of the body and allowing death and disease to enter. More recently, industrialization has further ruptured our union with watery nature, reducing it to an adversary to be tamed and exploited.

The Romantic response has been to lament this loss as the product of an aquaphobic "civilization" that pampers and spoils us and alienates us from our *own* watery nature. Yet while the western world has thus unlearnt the innate aquaphilia of its ancestors, there are other cultures said to maintain this unity. Observing the natural affinity for water of the Polynesians, Herman Melville wrote: "No wonder that the South Sea Islanders are an amphibious race when they are thus launched into water as soon as they see the light. I am convinced that it is as natural for a human being to swim as it is for a duck, and yet in civilized communities how many able-bodied individuals die like so many drowning kittens from the occurrence of the most trivial accidents."[93] Be this as it may, even the very best of our species – the Polynesians and the Greeks of old, the Mark Spitzes and Michael Phelpses of today – are hopeless slowcoaches compared to fish, dolphins or whales. There is simply too much drag, and we are too inefficiently streamlined. Turtles swim five times faster than we do.[94] If there were an aquatic Aesop, Achilles and the turtle would swap

92. Levinson and Christensen (eds), *Encyclopedia of World Sport*, "Speed Swimming," 383. The Greeks were serious swimmers. The historians Herodotus and Thucydides wrote of the importance of swimming, and swimming races were held in honour of the god Dionysus.
93. Quoted in Deakin, 148.
94. It has been suggested that the sign of a genuinely aquatic mammal is that it "progresses not by paddling but by movements of the tail or sinuous movements of the body" (Deakin, 162). This clearly includes whales, seals and dugongs, but leaves humans dog-paddling in their wake. Mind you, turtles are hardly models of sinuousness.

roles, and Zeno the philosopher would have to reformulate his paradox to show that the swift turtle can never catch up with ponderous Achilles's lumbering crawl.

All this, of course, by no means disproves the Aquatic Ape Theory. Indeed, the fact that today's top competitive free divers can reach depths as great as 80 metres without any assistance and go down over 200 metres when using a weighted sled to aid the descent has been seen as providing further support for the hypothesis. Even though we cannot breathe in water and are not equipped to bear the increased pressure, the so-called "mammalian diving reflex" – which we share, albeit in a less developed form, with the genuinely marine mammals such as seals and whales – induces among other things a drop in the heart rate (bradycardia) and a restriction of the blood flow to the extremities (peripheral vasoconstriction), which allow us to survive longer without oxygen under water than we would in similar circumstances on dry land.[95] Humans are perhaps not as different from whales, dolphins and porpoises as has generally been assumed.

The main problem for the AAT is the lack of direct fossil evidence. Opponents have attacked the theory vehemently as a fanciful conjecture.[96] However, the fossil record in general is hopelessly patchy, and the palaeoanthropologists of the world present anything but a united front. Scientific disunity notwithstanding, it appears to be the case that some time over a million years ago there arose species such as *Homo erectus, Homo heidelbergensis* and *Homo antecessor*, hominids that gradually learnt to use fire and complex tools and to hunt animals, as well as tend the weak and infirm. And there is a reasonable degree of consensus that modern human beings – *Homo sapiens sapiens* – began to put in an appearance some time over the last hundred thousand years or so.

Whether our ape ancestors really went through an aquatic phase or not, however, our *deeper* origins are certainly water-based. To most

95. On the diving reflex and its relatively poor development in humans, see Ecott, *Neutral Buoyancy: Adventures in a Liquid World,* 307-8.
96. For a thorough attack on its lack of scientific rigour, see Gee, *Deep Time,* 97-99. Dismissing such narrative-based scenarios for their speculative nature, Gee ascribes them "the same validity as a bedtime story." They are "amusing, perhaps even instructive, but not scientific" (ibid., 114). In terms of scientific minimalism, Gee is perhaps right. As part of our self-image, however, the AAT does seem to be endowed with a special resonance. Like many of the bedtime stories we like to tell ourselves about ourselves, it is both instructive and stimu-lating.

modern-day comparative anatomists, geneticists and embryologists it is plain that we are all – as Neil Shubin puts it – "modified sharks." Deeper still, we're all modified pond scum.[97] And a lot of our design flaws stem from these aquatic origins and from the modifications of modifications that have gone on ever since:

> Take the body plan of a fish, dress it up to be a mammal, then tweak and twist that mammal until it walks on two legs, talks, thinks, and has superfine control of its fingers – and you have a recipe for problems. We can dress up a fish only so much without paying a price. In a perfectly designed world – one with no history – we would not have to suffer everything from hemorrhoids to cancer.[98]

We humans are souped-up fish, suggests Shubin, the "fish equivalent of a hot-rod Beetle."[99] The parts don't quite add up, and our bodies end up doing weird, impractical things like hiccoughing and having hernias.

Equally certain, moreover, is that human beings have what might be called their *ontogenetic origins* in an aqueous environment. Watery origins are common to the evolution of the species and the development of the individual, a link that has led to scientific and narrative parallels being drawn between the individual and the collective / evolutionary past we unconsciously embody.[100] The water in question here is the amniotic

97. Shubin, *Your Inner Fish*, 90, 178.
98. Ibid., 185.
99. Ibid. On hiccoughing as a product of the history we share with fish and tadpoles, see ibid., 190-92; on hernias as a consequence of "taking a fish body and morphing it into a mammal," ibid., 193-96.
100. Witness the popular 19th-century theory, most famously expounded by Ernst Haeckel but now largely discredited, that "ontogeny recapitulates phylogeny": i.e. the development of the individual embryo repeats the same path as the evolutionary history of the species. According to such a view, the human embryo thus passes through fish, reptile and mammal stages. J. G. Ballard's 1962 novel *The Drowned World* also explores this parallelism between our individual and our evolutionary past. Just as our individual unconscious goes back to the waters of the maternal womb, so too the collective unconscious is deeply aquatic. In Ballard's tale, the "drowned world" of the title – a consequence of melting ice caps and rising sea levels produced by an increase in solar radiation – results in a collective regression to the deep past we all have within us, plunging society back into the "archaeopsychic past [and] uncovering the ancient taboos and drives that have been dormant for epochs": the civilized world reverts, literally and figuratively, to a Triassic swamp. As one character explains, "[e]ach one of us is as old

fluid that surrounds and supports a growing foetus in the uterus from around two weeks after fertilization until the "waters break"[101] with the onset of childbirth. These waters, which by the twelfth week contain proteins, carbohydrates and lipids, also provide the foetus with buoyancy, absorb jolts like a cushion, and permit changes of posture. As parturition approaches, the growing foetus imbibes several litres of the waters each day. In the process of evolution from amphibians to reptiles, it was the amniotic fluid encased in shells of mineralised protein – amniotic eggs – that permitted reptiles to keep their as yet unborn offspring out of water without them drying out: for our reptilian ancestors, egg-shells were evolution's way of bringing the sea onto land with them.[102]

As a natural consequence of the aquatic circumstances of the human foetus, the process of giving birth in a tub of warm water – known as water birth – has recently undergone considerable growth in popularity. The idea behind it is that since the foetus has just spent nine months in the watery liquid of the amniotic sac, giving birth into a similar environment is gentler and less stressful for the baby. There are also believed to be a number of potential benefits for the mother: water is soothing and relaxing, and has been observed to increase the mother's energy; the buoyancy of the water facilitates movement; it seems to promote the production of pain-inhibiting endorphins; and the perineum becomes more elastic. As yet, there has been relatively little research done on possible risks.

* * * * *

Both for the individual human and for living organisms in general, water was involved at life's very inception. It has been both a medium and a nutrient. For most of life's history – indeed for all of the history of most life – water has been the matrix that has supported and sustained it; at the same time, it has been an essential raw material, fuelling the photosynthesis

---

as the entire biological kingdom, and our bloodstreams are tributaries of the great sea of its total memory. The uterine odyssey of the growing foetus recapitulates the entire evolutionary past" (ibid., 44).

101. The use of the term "waters" to denote the amniotic fluid is not confined to English. Spanish *aguas* and French *eaux* perform the same function, while German has the more graphic notion of *Fruchtwasser* or fruit waters.

102. Ball, *H_2O*, 219.

which produces high-energy carbohydrates for plants and which we – the animal kingdom – effectively reverse with our energy-creating combustion of carbohydrates. Its double nature as both medium and matter in a sense reflects its metaphorical duality as formlessness and fertility.

Irrespective of how far we consider ourselves to be *aquatic*, therefore, it is plain that we are also fundamentally *aqueous* in nature. Water is what our bodies are made of. It is the major constituent of all living matter, amounting to between 50 and 90 per cent of the weight of any living organism: newborn babies are almost 90 per cent water; adult human beings are roughly three quarters water; as venerable wrinklies we are still more than half water. Even our brain, commonly considered the very core of our identity as thinking beings, can be as much as 85 per cent water. Our food likewise tends to be predominantly watery, watermelons averaging 97 per cent water, potatoes 80 per cent, steak 65 per cent, and even bread 35 per cent.[103]

Of course, water is not the *only* substance necessary for our continued existence as human beings. While we can go for days without drinking water before our bodies start to fall apart at the seams, an absence of oxygen rapidly – within minutes – induces brain damage, coma and death. Further, it is more common to refer to life as we know it as "carbon-based" rather than "water-based"[104] in deference to the carbon atom's capacity for hooking up with other atoms (including other carbon atoms) to form the interminably long macromolecules characteristic, for example, of proteins and DNA. Carbon has thus been described as "shamelessly promiscuous" and "the party animal of the atomic world,"[105] and its shameless promiscuity is certainly essential to our genetic and metabolic constitution. Yet carbon atoms are much less plentiful in the human body than the hydrogen and oxygen atoms of water and amount to less than a tenth of the total.

In comparison to oxygen and to carbon compounds, moreover, the various "waters" of the human body are heavily charged with symbolic significance. Though the body is a naturally waterlogged vessel, it is considered vital that we should not leak, drip or overflow indiscriminately,

---

103. See Shapiro, *Suckers: How Alternative Medicine Makes Fools of Us All*, 226; also Rupp, 60-61.
104. Sometimes the term *carbaquist* is used to denote an approach that does justice to life's dependence both on liquid water and carbon compounds. See Fry, 243.
105. Bryson, *A Short History of Nearly Everything*, 309.

and activities and processes associated with the expulsion or exudation of our liquids have tended to be carefully regulated by social norms and traditions and often considered taboo. Even semen (Enki's water) and milk (the maternal water), which signify fertility and nourishment, are as a rule kept well out of public view by the dictates of decorum and propriety, while saliva, menstrual blood, urine and sweat have all generally been regarded with a mixture of disgust, anxiety and amusement.[106] The tears of laughter or distress underline this bond between leakage and the limits of our identity.

It is our blood – our lifeblood as it is often known – that tends to be identified as the deepest source of our vitality, watering us as the Earth's rivers irrigate the land or coursing through us as the oceans flow with the rhythm of the tides. This timeless analogy between the body's blood and the waters of the planet, between man and the macrocosm, was most famously formulated by Leonardo da Vinci, who wrote in his *Notebooks*: "while man has within him a pool of blood wherein the lungs as he breathes expand and contract, so the body of the earth has its ocean, which also rises and falls every six hours with the breathing of the world; as from the said pool of blood proceed the veins which spread their branches through the human body, so the ocean fills the body of the earth with an infinite number of veins of water."[107]

Such notions are anticipated in mythological imagery. One of the Chinese myths of creation told the story of Pan Gu, who was so worn out after 18,000 years spent separating the primal unity that he lay down and died, his vast body being transformed into the structural features of the world, and his blood into the rivers and streams that water it. When the primeval giant of Norse mythology, Ymir, was slain by younger gods, his flesh was likewise turned into earth, his bones into rocks, his brains into clouds, and his flowing blood into lakes and seas. According to the *midrash*, the body of man is "a microcosm, the whole world in miniature": "the hair upon his head corresponds to the woods of the earth, his tears to a river, his mouth to the ocean."[108]

---

106. On the ambiguous reactions provoked by the body's winds and waters, see Glasgow, *Split Down the Sides*, 160.
107. Leonardo da Vinci, *Notebooks*, 45-46.
108. Ginzberg, I.49. According to Aristotle, Empedocles by contrast likened the oceans not to blood but to the sweat "exuded by the earth when the sun heats it." This, he felt, accounted for its saltiness (see Aristotle, *Meteorology*, 353b11). Aristotle objected to this metaphor, considering it "merely poetical."

Blood is the body's transport mechanism. It conveys the oxygen and nutrients necessary for cellular metabolism and carries away the waste products. As a suspension of cells within a liquid matrix (plasma), our blood clearly betrays its descent from the salty seawater that served as the source of vital nutrition for primitive organisms: the underlying chemical composition of plasma is remarkably similar to that of seawater. In addition to its water and dissolved salts (sodium, potassium, chloride and bicarbonate ions), however, blood also contains the oxygen-bearing haemoglobin that gives it its ruddy colour, as well as other nutrients (such as sugars and vitamins), wastes and hormones.

For all its symbolic import, blood is not the only aqueous solution responsible for our body's haulage requirements. We also contain lymph. A relatively unsung hero, lymph is a pale, watery fluid that flows through the body in a secondary circulatory system, bathing the organism's tissues and removing unwanted bacteria. Derived from blood plasma but without the red blood cells, its primary components include lymphocytes (a sort of white blood cell), which chemically neutralize invading microorganisms, and macrophages, which – as their name implies – eat them up. Lymph is an essential constituent of our immune system. No less vital is the cytoplasm, the watery fluid *within* each individual living cell, which makes up more than two thirds of our body water. Described as a heady cocktail "spiced with proteins and DNA, sugars, salts, fatty acids, seething with hormones,"[109] this "water" is no *mere* vehicle or medium:

> It is all too tempting to regard the relationship of this fluid to the biomolecules it contains like that of the paper of this page to the words printed on it: as a carrier, a bland background on which the important business is displayed. But this won't do. Water plays an active role in the life of the cell, to the extent that we can consider water itself to be a kind of biomolecule. Without it, other biomolecules would not only be left stranded and immobile, like beach whales – they might no longer truly be biomolecules, unravelling or seizing up and losing their biological function in the process.[110]

While modern molecular biology might *seem* to be about proteins and DNA, writes Ball, it is really about the interactions of these molecules "in and with water."[111]

109. Ball, *H₂O*, 231.
110. Ibid., 231-32.
111. Ibid., 232.

That water is more than just a lubricant and means of transport is further exemplified by the active part it plays in the metabolic breakdown of vital molecules such as proteins and carbohydrates. This process, known as *hydrolysis*,[112] allows proteins to be decomposed to amino acids, fats to fatty acids, and starches and complex sugars to glucose and fructose: in the process of digestion, for example, enzymes secreted by the digestive tract thus catalyse the breakdown of complex molecules into simpler forms that can be assimilated by the body. Moreover, the energy released inside cells as a result of the hydrolysis of the molecule adenosine triphosphate, or ATP, is used by enzymes and proteins to perform the work the cell needs to be done. Every hour, something like a kilogram of ATP is hydrolysed to generate the energy that keeps us alive and kicking.

It is evident that for life – or at least life as we know it – to have come about water had to be endowed with some remarkable properties. Fortunately for us (i.e. for all living systems), water is inherently *weird*: scientists credit it with more than sixty anomalies that seem to defy the dictates of molecular physics.[113] For its role as the body's conveyor belt, its paramount feature is its very fluidity: it is crucial that water should be endowed with the structured mobility of a liquid under the conditions that obtain on Earth. That it does so is in itself an oddity. Molecules with the structure of water – comprising two atoms of hydrogen and one of oxygen – would not as a rule be expected have such high freezing and boiling points and thus be in a liquid state at such elevated temperatures (up to 100°C). The closest comparable compounds, hydrogen sulphide and hydrogen selenide, boil at less than –50°C and are gases at room temperature.

In our terrestrial environment, this makes it a prime challenge to avoid getting frozen. Failure to keep our body fluids such as blood,

112. We have already encountered hydrolysis as a possible stumbling block as life was in the process of hoisting itself out of non-existence from the prebiotic soup: hydrolysis is the reverse of the dehydration synthesis that allows the monomers of organic compounds to join up to form polymers, instead breaking polymers down to form monomers.

113. One such anomaly is the so-called Mpemba Effect, according to which hot water sometimes freezes more rapidly than cold, a phenomenon observed by Aristotle, Francis Bacon and Descartes. Although numerous explanations have been proposed, none has yet gained universal acceptance. See the chapter on *Wasser* in Passig and Scholz, *Lexikon des Unwissens*, 237-44, to which Bart Simpson provides the epigraph: "Water doesn't obey your 'rules'. It goes where it wants to. Like me, babe."

lymph or cytoplasm in a liquid state not only puts a spanner in the body's hydraulics – "like frozen pipes in a central heating system or frozen diesel in a lorry" – but causes irreparable and irreversible damage to our cells.[114] While flowing water is understood as a symbol of life and its presence a precondition for habitability, ice thus represents a suspension of animation at best and death more generally. There is plenty of frozen water elsewhere in our solar system, but this can by no means be equated with conduciveness to life.[115]

The anomalously high freezing and boiling points of water are produced by the characteristic molecular structure of H_2O. On account of a phenomenon called "hydrogen bonding," the hydrogen nuclei from one water molecule are attracted not only to the oxygen atom of that particular molecule, but also to the oxygen atoms of adjacent water molecules. These intermolecular links, which are roughly a tenth as strong as the bonds between the hydrogen and oxygen *within* the molecule, not only account for the molecules' reluctance to evaporate into the chaotic gas state (i.e. to boil), but also give water the stickiness or viscosity that holds raindrops together, allows small insects to walk on the surface of puddles, and enables sap – the lifeblood of plants – to get to the top of trees more than 200 feet tall. Like carbon, therefore, the behaviour of the hydrogen atom has lent itself to imagery of extramolecular infidelity, promiscuity, flirtatiousness and bigamy,[116] but the result is that water is in fact much

114. Ball, *H_2O*, 195. Some animals succeed in staying alive slightly below 0°C by a variety of strategies. Either they can depress the freezing point of their body fluids by filling them with certain solutes called cryoprotectants; they can manufacture protein molecules that stop ice from forming and keep the blood in a "supercooled" state; or they can develop what is known as "freeze-tolerance," which involves ensuring that only the extracellular fluid as opposed to the fluid inside their cells is allowed to freeze. Land-hibernating frogs do this. See ibid., 195-99.

115. The permafrost on Mars is not promising: temperatures even at the height of Martian summers rarely scrape above freezing point. Nor are the moons of Jupiter and Saturn that have permanent ice ages regarded as likely habitats for living organisms. Only on one, Europa, which is believed to harbour a briny ocean a long way beneath its icy surface, is there considered to be a small chance that humans might one day find extraterrestrial life. Despite surface temperatures of around –160°C, it is thought that mineral-rich hydrothermal vents produced by tectonic activity could be nourishing life within a subglacial ocean.

116. See Bryson's description of carbon as a "party animal." The adherents and opponents of the theory of "hydrogen bonds" in its early days referred to hydrogen's "bigamy." See Ball, *H_2O*, 140-68, for a full account of water's weirdness.

more highly structured than other liquids, comprising as it does an intricate nexus of interconnecting hydrogen bonds. A certain amount of extramarital "bonding" there may be, but the promiscuity is hardly disorderly.

These hydrogen bonds also account for another feature that is indispensable for water's role as the medium of the body's freight transport: thanks to its ability to form hydrogen bonds with solutes, water is a near-universal solvent,[117] dissolving an abnormally wide range of substances, in particular salts, sugars and amino acids. Without this quality, water would be a non-starter when it came to transporting the necessary nutrients from one place to another and carrying off the wastes: the exchanges and transactions necessary for life would simply be unthinkable. It is the capacity of water to contain dissolved gases, moreover, that allows aquatic animals such as fish to get their metabolic energy by using oxygen from their environment to burn carbohydrates, i.e. to breathe.

Water has further anomalous qualities as a result of its hydrogen bonds: its high *heat capacity*, for example, means not only that it takes more heat to warm water by a certain amount than is required to warm other substances, but also that the water then hangs on to this heat, as it were refusing to cool down. This is of prime importance for the blood in our bodies, which maintains a relatively constant temperature in spite of the ups and downs of the outside world; it also allows our baths to stay nice and warm for a reasonably long time (though never long enough, it seems). On a global level, one of the main consequences of water's high heat capacity is that the water of the planet's oceans and lakes retains the heat it absorbs from the sun, acting as huge reservoirs of stored-up warmth.[118]

Yet another of the eccentricities caused by water's hydrogen bonding is that it expands on freezing into ice, which is why pipes burst in winter, but also why ice – quite bizarrely[119] – floats on water. This too has

---

117. Nowadays, the term "universal solvent" is indeed commonly applied to water. Traditionally, it referred to the *alkahest* pursued by alchemists, i.e. the hypothetical liquid said to be able to dissolve *all* substances. The drawback of this liquid philosopher's stone, of course, would have been the impossibility of finding a vessel to keep it in.

118. In turn, this means that ocean currents such as the Gulf Stream can keep Northern Europe as much as 22°C warmer than it otherwise would be by obligingly conveying heat up from the tropics.

119. It is only habit that allows us to take it for granted. We would never expect a lump of solid metal to float on a puddle of the molten metal.

been indispensable for the development of life on Earth. Because oceans, lakes and ponds – when they freeze – do so from the top down, the thick layer of ice and snow on the surface functions as an extremely effective insulating lid or blanket, keeping the residual heat in and protecting the resident flora and fauna beneath. If these bodies of water were to freeze from the bottom up (as they apparently "ought" to), the exposed surface of the water would keep on losing energy, and more and more ice would amass until the whole ocean was completely solidified. Such a white, ice-bound planet, moreover, would further reflect away solar heat, making it increasingly difficult ever to thaw out again.

Scientists have long been struck by these weird properties of water and how vital this weirdness has been to our existence as aqueous beings. In the second decade of the 20th century, biochemist Lawrence Henderson drew attention to water's remarkable "fitness" for the development of life as we know it: "the properties of matter and the course of cosmic evolution," he wrote, "are now seen to be intimately related to the structure of the living being and to its activities."[120] For Henderson, the very structure of the universe – as exemplified by the anomalous properties of water – was geared to the generation of life. The universe, he felt, was essentially biocentric.

Such ideas lead to what is known as the "anthropic principle." According to the weak version of this principle, "the observed values of all physical and cosmological quantities are not equally probable but they take on values restricted by the requirement that there exist sites where carbon-based [and water-based (R.G.)] life can evolve and by the requirement that the Universe be old enough for it to have already done so." In other words, "those properties of the Universe we are able to discern are self-selected by the fact that they must be consistent with our evolution and present existence."[121] This translates into the less intimidating counterfactual: "if the universe were not as it is (observed to be), we would not be here to observe it." And this in turn presents us with the truism that if water were different in character from what it is, we would not be here to observe it.

Hidden within the weak anthropic principle, however, there may be stronger implications. For Henderson, the biocentric universe signified that water (as well as other strange phenomena) was "deliberately" pre-

---

120. Quoted in Davies, *The Mind of God*, 198. See also Gribbin, *In the Beginning*, 174-75.
121. Barrow and Tipler, *The Anthropic Cosmological Principle*, 16.

designed *for the sake of* the emergence of life. And this he took as an argument for the existence of God. Others have eliminated deity from the equation and seen human life as the ultimate purpose of cosmic evolution – not so much as some sort of pinnacle of creation, but as representing the possibility of the universe's self-observation. For certain interpretations of the principle, observers are required in order to bring the universe into being.[122] In this sense, it might be claimed, water possesses the properties it does in order to be able to observe itself through us (and thus come into genuine existence). But here we have smuggled in metaphysical presuppositions that are not present in the anthropic principle in its weaker, purely logical form.

This raises the further question of the extent to which we are being anthropocentric and geocentric in our conception of life as carbon-based and aqueous. Life "as we know it," to be sure, is patently based on a conjunction of liquid water and the biogenic elements, especially carbon. But does life have to be like this? To what extent is our idea of life restricted by the limits of our own empirical and conceptual framework? Even to ask this question is to confront these very limits. For a start, as Stephen Jay Gould pointed out, while experimental science is dependent upon repeatability and actual repetition, "all life on earth – the only life we know – represents, for all its current variety, the results of a *single experiment*, for every earthly species evolved from the common ancestry of a single origin. We desperately need a *repetition* of the experiment."[123]

Given at least the *possibility* of extraterrestrial life that is radically different from ours (which would provide the repetition – the second experiment – for which Gould yearns), some scientists, such as Robert Shapiro and Gerald Feinberg, have viewed the *carbaquist* approach to life as deeply misguided.[124] Their idea is that until we come across a different

---

122. Ibid., 21-22. Such interpretations have been proposed by some quantum physicists, for example, as a way of coping with certain counter-intuitive implications of quantum theory.

123. Gould, "War of the Worldviews," in *Leonardo's Mountain of Clams and the Diet of Worms*, 339-54; quotation, 353

124. For a discussion of Shapiro and Feinberg, see Fry, 238-49. Defining living systems above all in thermodynamic terms (as "a highly ordered system of matter and energy characterized by complex cycles that maintain or gradually increase the order of the system through an exchange of energy with its environment"), Feinberg and Shapiro propose conceivable alternative life-forms that de

form of life, say, from an extraterrestrial origin, we cannot *know* what is contingent and what is necessary for life to come into being: we cannot *know* that all life necessarily depends upon water and carbon. It could be the case that other elements or compounds will do just as well. But what would such life-forms be like? As so often where our conceptual limitations are at issue, the argument tends toward circularity,[125] for how would we even recognise any other form of life *as* life unless we knew what we were looking for – i.e. unless it had certain features in common with what we understand to be life?

As watery organisms, it is perhaps only natural for us to be aquacentric. Yet it is not merely out of chauvinism, insists Iris Fry, that most modern-day researchers regard carbon-based compounds in a liquid-water medium as providing the best foundation for the emergence of life, wherever it may be. There are sound physical and chemical reasons that justify the carbaquist position. A fully rounded conception of living systems as "complex, self-organized, self-maintaining, and self-reproducing systems that are the products of evolutionary processes" calls for molecules that are "large, complex, stable and varied,"[126] and the properties of water and carbon – as well as their cosmic abundance – certainly provide the best-known basis for any such system. Of course, we can "conceive" of life-forms based on a combination, say, of silicon and alcohol – a *silicoholic* approach – but only in a vacuous sense that flies in the face of chemical plausibility. By the same token, we can "conceive" of a world in which the atoms themselves have different chemical properties. But what is certain is that such a world would not be *our* world, and *we* would not be there to wonder at its existence or make friends with its inhabitants. It is difficult to get round the absolute necessity of liquid water and carbon compounds for life as we know and understand it.

Of course, we cannot jump over our own shadow: not only is life or mind a single, as yet unrepeated experiment, but *we* are that experiment. Given the limitations of our perspective, we cannot *know* whether we (life

---

pend not on water and carbon, but on ordered flows of liquid ammonia or liquid silicates (at the appropriate temperatures) or even solid hydrogen. But a merely thermodynamic definition of life (involving an open, self-organizing system and a flow of energy) is perhaps too loose, for it also applies to non-living systems (i.e. "dissipative structures" such as vortices of water).

125. See Fry, 240.
126. Ibid., 248.

or mind) are a serendipitous by-product of water's weirdness or a necessary stage in the realization of its inherent potential; nor can we *know* whether water is necessary to life and mind or just one of a number of possible media. Yet the nature of water does seem to have lent itself *intrinsically* to the emergence of life and – by extension – to the evolution of water-based organisms who can reflect on it.

This multi-layered image of "reflection" is a revealing one. The myth of Narcissus ostensibly tells of a beautiful youth who falls in love with his own reflection in a pool. Born of a river-god and a nymph, however, Narcissus is himself a creature of the water, and his self-infatuation also represents *water*'s self-infatuation: water charmed by water.[127] Seen in these terms, the myth narrates the split implied by self-reflection (or self-knowledge) and a yearning for renewed unity. As Narcissus pines away, water laments its lost innocence. Perhaps it even regrets its life-fostering weirdness.

4

The Fountainhead of Civilization

"Life on Earth may have begun in water," writes Rebecca Rupp. "If so, most of it certainly stayed there. Water, as environments go, is prime real estate, the pick of the biosphere."[128] It is also, in many senses, the easy option. The fact that human beings are among those creatures whose distant ancestors hundreds of millions of years ago were bold enough to take to the land is estimated to mean that some 99.5 per cent of the planet's habitable space by volume is effectively out of bounds to us.[129] Terrestrial life has also required a considerable range of adaptations: for bearing the organisms' body weight in air; for locomotion by means of limbs as opposed to fins; for inhaling oxygen directly from the air instead of filtering it from the water; and for dealing with the much more extreme range of temperatures that occur on land. Having successfully negotiated the transition to a terrestrial habitat with all the adaptation this entailed, it

127. On Narcissus, see below, chap. II.2.
128. Rupp, 79.
129. *New York Times Book Review*, "Where Leviathan Lives," 20 April 1997, p. 9, quoted in Bryson, 295.

is hardly surprising that only a few groups of mammals have ventured back to a marine environment. These include whales, dolphins, porpoises, seals and sirenians such as the dugong and the manatee, as well, more recently, as the marine otter and the polar bear, which still have the mammalian characteristic of hair rather than the subcutaneous blubber of the "true" marine mammals.

Over 90 per cent of the world's biomass is said to inhabit the sea. This includes a good deal of plankton, but also representatives of every known phylum of the animal kingdom, ranging from sponges, cnidaria such as hydras, jellyfish, sea anemones, sea pens and corals, annelids such as ragworms and sea mice, arthropods such as lobsters, crabs, shrimps and water fleas, molluscs such as clams, cockles, mussels, cuttlefish and octopuses, echinoderms such as starfish, sea urchins and sea cucumbers, through to the chordates, which include fish, amphibians and marine mammals such as the above-mentioned cetaceans.

Unsurprisingly, the few of us who have followed the path taken by Calvino's Old Qfwfq and gone terrestrial have tended to stick as close to water as possible. At present, over two-thirds of the world's cities with more than a million inhabitants are located on the coast, and many more are beside rivers. Our bodies are simply too dependent on water for us to let it out of our sight for long. Just as medieval communities needed a regular supply of water for their flour mills and tanneries, for their forges, potteries, fulling mills and sawmills, for brewing and cooking, watering and washing, so modern-day humans use it not only for sustenance and sanitation, but for recreation, irrigation and a host of industrial processes including power generation, papermaking, cement hydration, and textile manufacture, processes in which it functions as a coolant, diluting agent, solvent, suspending agent and a source of hydrogen. Its protean nature is reflected in its unrivalled multi-functionality. Water is society's factotum.

This dependence goes back to the very roots of human society. The earliest groups of hunter-gatherers had no choice but to stay close to springs, rivers or lakes to make sure that they had a reliable source of freshwater: storing it or transporting it was not an option. The transition to agriculture and a sedentary lifestyle seems to have been a gradual process of diffusion and adaptation, made possible by the gentler and more stable climate that followed the retreat of the last ice age. At all times, however, the need for a dependable supply of easily available drinking water remained an underlying assumption. Proximity to the River Jordan was the basis for the first known permanent human settlement at Jericho, a village comprising some 300 inhabitants, which flourished around 9,500 years ago.[130] Even after nine and a half millennia, Jericho's stone tower, thought to be the oldest man-made structure in the world, is still standing, and the nearby spring – which appears in the Bible as Elisha's Spring[131] – still provides a steady 76 litres of water every second.

Jericho's early inhabitants continued to hunt and gather seeds in the surrounding area, yet domesticated barley and wheat were also cultivated in small fields. By 6000 BCE agricultural societies had sprung up across much of south-west Asia, and it was here – more specifically in the flood plain of the Rivers Tigris and Euphrates in the area formerly known as Mesopotamia and now as Iraq – that "civilization" is commonly considered to have first emerged. In fact, Mesopotamia was not settled until relatively late – around 5700 BCE – on account of the tough climate and the difficult farming conditions it presented, difficulties that called for flood control, irrigation and high levels of co-operation between large numbers of farmers. Civilization depended not only on water, in other words, but also upon a *concerted* human effort to tame it and turn it to account. The earliest agricultural communities were large kinship groups of around a thousand people, and by 3000 BCE the Sumerian city of Uruk in the far south had a population of some 40,000.[132]

The world's oldest civilizations all sprang from the fertile flood plains of major rivers: while Mesopotamia was born on the banks of the Tigris and the Euphrates, and Egypt emerged from the alluvial silts of the Nile, the cities of Mohenjo-Daro and Harappa flourished on the banks of the Indus in what is now Pakistan, and ancient Chinese civilization sprang up beside the Yangtze and Yellow (Huang He) Rivers. By 2500 BCE the Sumerians, the Egyptians, the Chinese and the Dravidians of the Indus Valley had all developed sophisticated systems of dams and canals to impound their flood waters and irrigate their lands throughout the dry season.

The concept of "civilization," of course, is notoriously resistant to definition and tends to come laden with ethnocentric ideological baggage: *we* are civilized and therefore define what counts as civilization; *you*

130. On the transition to agriculture, see Ponting, *A New Green History of the World*, 36-46, especially 45-46 on Jericho. See also Pearce, *When the Rivers Run Dry*, 211.
131. See II Kings 2:19-22.
132. On the emergence of civilization in Mesopotamia, see Ponting, 54-59.

fail to meet our criteria and are therefore uncivilized.[133] In the case of the Mesopotamians, civilization came to be epitomized by the benefits of agriculture and the consumption of beer and bread it made possible. For the first time in human history, the pre-eminence of plain water as the fundamental beverage on which man depended for survival was challenged by a novel drink produced when the newly cultivated cereal grains were left to soak in water. This drink was not only rich in nutrition and safer to drink than water (having been boiled), but also endowed with seemingly magical properties of intoxication. As Tom Standage puts it, beer was "one of the things that distinguished [the Mesopotamians] from savages and made them fully human," associated as it was with a "settled, orderly lifestyle, rather than the haphazard existence of hunter-gatherers."[134] As with irrigation and flood control, civilization was inextricably bound up with a process that involved making water safe or user-friendly.

In etymological terms, "civilization" denotes first and foremost the emergence of life in towns or cities. In fact, archaeologists have generally focused on three indicative features: towns with a high population density, monumental buildings such as palaces and temples, and the existence of writing. The Sumerians had all three, yet while the ancient Egyptians – like the Mayan civilization of Central America – had no major cities, and the Incas have not left permanent written records, they have tended to be regarded as civilizations on the basis of their level of social complexity and technical attainment.[135]

What emerges in each case, however, is that for "civilization" to develop, one of the essential preconditions was a conjunction of social organization and hydraulic skill that allowed groups of people to control and channel their freshwater supplies and in turn generate an agricultural surplus. Stockpiled food could then provide these societies with the economic base required for supporting non-food-producing specialists such as kings, bureaucrats and priests, in turn leading to a more stratified social structure and facilitating the construction of temples and palaces. These new non-food-producing specialists would further be able to spend their time in novel activities such as imposing taxes, devising dogmas, justifying wars, writing documents and inventing things. As a consequence,

---

133. Gandhi was alluding to this when, asked what he thought of Western civilization, he replied that he thought it would be a good idea.
134. Standage, *A History of the World in Six Glasses*, 27. On the emergence of beer, see ibid., 9-23.
135. See the discussion in Renfrew, *Before Civilization*, 212-13.

by 3000 BCE – and rather later in the case of India, China and the Americas – the societies of Mesopotamia and Egypt had developed into complex, hierarchical, militaristic structures "ruled by religious and political elites with immense powers of control over their populations."[136] This radical transformation, together with all the cultural and technological innovation it made possible, was unthinkable without the controlled use of water to foster agricultural development and generate a surplus of food.

It has been conjectured that large-scale irrigation and hydraulic management thus provided the basis not only for the emergence of civilization, but for the creation of the *states* and *empires* of the ancient world. The abundant evidence of monumental waterworks in the world's oldest civilizations in Mesopotamia, Egypt, China and India led the historian and sinologist Karl Wittfogel to argue that the centralization of political power was *founded upon* the massive-scale engineering that harnessed the rivers. The question, of course, is whether these awesome hydraulic feats were the cause or merely an effect of state formation.[137] Whatever the case, they were the work (and death) of many thousands of slaves, who sacrificed their lives to the greater hydraulic good. Managed by bureaucrats, they reflected the glory of despotic rulers and legitimised their tyranny. In this sense, the control of water became tantamount to the control of life – not just one's own, but that of one's subjects.

Water is inextricably tied up with power, therefore, its history inseparable from manifestations of might. The origin of civilization is also the origin of war. Between 3000 BCE and 2300 BCE the city states of Sumer were constantly at war for control of the water resources upon which they relied: Lagash and Umma were at loggerheads for a century and a half over a boundary dispute involving irrigation waters.[138] More recent conflicts between Israel, Jordan and Syria (over the waters of the

---

136. Ponting, 64.
137. In *Guns, Germs and Steel* (282-84), Jared Diamond argues against Wittfogel's "hydraulic theory" of state formation, instead proposing such factors as population density or population size as decisive. Diamond notes that – while small-scale irrigation systems commonly preceded the rise of states – in many cases the construction of large-scale networks of hydraulic management did not take place until considerably *after* the formation of states. What seems clear is that while some form of hydraulic co-operation is necessary for civilization to be possible, the relationship between massive-scale water management and centralized macro-civilizations (i.e. states) is contingent: there is no reason why hydraulic co-operation should not remain small in scale or decentralized.
138. Ponting, 57-58.

Jordan), Syria, Iraq and Turkey (over the Euphrates) and Egypt and Sudan (over the Nile) are perpetuating an age-old tradition. The *mafia* has its origins in the struggle for control over sources of water in drought-ridden Sicily.[139] The word *rival*, meaning "one who shares the same stream or river," underscores the recurrent choice between conflict and co-operation. To the extent that war, conflict and coercion are put above co-operation, the very concept of "civilization" undermines itself.

Megalomanic hydraulic schemes, imposed from "above" by totalitarian authority or despotic whim, are tantamount to a form of war waged against one's own people. Here too, "civilization" contradicts itself. As early as the 7th century BCE, the unsuccessful attempt to construct a canal running from the River Nile to the Red Sea under King Necho II of Egypt accounted for the lives – according to Herodotus – of some 120,000 Egyptians.[140] Today the costs tend to take the form of massive population displacements and environmental carnage. Estimates of the number of people displaced by large dams in India over the last 50 years vary from 21 to 55 million people.[141] It is believed that the Sardar Sarovar Dam on India's River Narmada will displace more than 200,000, reducing a largely indigenous population to voiceless, rootless destitution and destroying a landscape of inexpressible symbolic importance. Arundhati Roy has spoken of weapons of mass destruction deployed by a state to subjugate its own population.[142]

In the case of the Narmada, the police brutality inflicted upon anti-dam activists has included rape, assault and the death of a 15-year-old boy. In 1958, the suppression of Tonga resistance to the enormous Kariba Dam on the Zambezi in Zambia left eight dead and 32 injured.[143] Among

139. See Munda, *Social Multi-Criteria Evaluation*, 666.
140. See also Brown, *The Story of Maps*, 119.
141. See Leslie, *Deep Water*, 24, and in general, 13-103, on the popular resistance to the dams under construction in the Narmada Valley; also *New Internationalist*, no. 336, July 2001, pp. 18-19. The World Commission on Dams has put the worldwide figure for displacement caused by large dams at between 40 and 80 million, although it could well be much higher than this. See Leslie, 142; Black, *The No-Nonsense Guide to Water*, 58. Jacques Leslie estimates that the figure for the number of people living *downstream* whose livelihood has been seriously harmed by large-scale dam construction is probably hundreds of millions, "at least three or four times the forty to eighty million upstream dam-affected people" (158).
142. See Roy, "The Greater Common Good," in *The Cost of Living*, 101.
143. See Leslie, 23, 123, 207.

the most notorious enactments of this systematic nullification of human dignity and life were the Chixoy or Río Negro Massacres that took place in Guatemala in the early 1980s, when over 400 indigenous Mayans – including 107 children – who refused to leave their home village of Río Negro prior to its scheduled inundation by the Chixoy Reservoir were raped, tortured and murdered by the country's military officials. The Three Gorges Dam project in China will involve the resettlement of at least one and a half million.[144] Here too opposition is repressed.

Similar forces continue to threaten Europe. In Spain, the right-wing *Partido Popular* recently sought to bulldoze through a "National Hydrological Plan" which would have transferred 1,050 cubic hectometres of water per year over 400 miles from the emblematic River Ebro in the north of Spain – the river from which the Iberian Peninsula itself takes its name – to the south-eastern regions of Almeria, Valencia and Murcia. Conceived ostensibly in the name of "progress," the Ebro diversion formed part of a mega-project designed first and foremost for the benefit of the south-east's booming tourist industry, its unsustainable intensive agriculture, and the constructors, engineers and speculators who thrive on laying concrete.[145] In cases such as this, vested interests in conjunction with a technocratic ideology turn nature into an enemy and ride roughshod over local communities, environmentalists and international directives. The question then becomes: progress of what sort, for whom, and at what price?

The question goes back to the very roots of society. "Civilization" is now almost universally assumed to be linked with "progress" as an implacable march forward towards some unspecified state of ideal wellbeing. Yet there is in practice no reason to equate civilization with a necessary movement "forward" except in the empty sense in which time itself is visualized as a unidirectional arrow from past to future.[146] Even

---

144. See for example Pearce, 176-79. Other sources put the figure much higher.
145. Hundreds of thousands turned out in a series of demonstrations in Zaragoza and Barcelona, and thousands of people from Aragon and Catalonia (and elsewhere) made the trip to Brussels to voice their dissent. Fortunately for the wetlands of the Ebro Delta, which would have been ravaged, there was a change of government.
146. Of course, humankind has progressively increased its overall technological control over the environment: the advances of science, spectacular as they are, represent an increased ability to modify and manipulate the world around us. Yet paradoxically this *gain* in control has been shadowed by a parallel, progressive

the very first transition from "pre-civilization" to "civilization" – the shift from societies based on hunting and gathering to a settled agricultural lifestyle – cannot unambiguously be applauded as an *advance*. As Clive Ponting has argued, the combination of hunting animals and gathering foodstuffs which provided humans with their sustenance for hundreds of thousands of years prior to the emergence of agriculture was "without doubt the most successful and flexible way of life adopted by humans and the one that caused least damage to natural ecosystems."[147] The vast majority of humankind since the emergence of agriculture, by contrast, has lived an existence "under the constant threat of starvation and in the face of the daily reality of an inadequate diet and malnutrition."[148]

This is not to deny the role of skilful water management in helping overcome drought, control flooding and generate well-being and wealth. Not surprisingly, feats of hydraulic genius have been duly celebrated and exalted, and the benign rulers or wise engineers who oversaw them have been revered as gods and heroes. In the 3rd century, the people of Sri Lanka extolled their monarch King Mahasena as divine for supervising the construction of the great artificial lakes that were to save them from famine and drought.[149] The mythological tradition of China focuses at its origins upon the immense works of hydraulic engineering and flood-control that were undertaken along the country's major rivers and the figures responsible for them. One of the central such characters was the historical-mythical flood-tamer and saviour-hero Ta Yü (ca. 21st century

---

loss of control, manifest in an increased capacity to render the planet uninhabitable, whether by design or carelessness. The defining progression has been one of scale, as the global population has risen from some four million 12 millennia ago, to 50 million in 1000 BCE, increasing to 250 million by 200 CE and now to well over six billion and still rising (Ponting, 36): civilization can thus best be equated either with a purely mathematical progression or a vacuously chronological progression.

147. Ponting, 17. Far from leading lives that were "nasty, brutish and short," new evidence suggests that hunter-gatherers enjoyed nutritionally varied diets and still had plenty of time for leisure and ceremony. See ibid., 18-23.

148. Ibid., 108.

149. Black, *The No-Nonsense Guide to Water*, 13. In the same spirit of beneficence, a 12th-century successor of his, Parakrama the Great, decreed: "Not a single drop of water received from rain should be allowed to escape into the sea without being utilized for human benefit."

BCE), who as emperor was said to be the founding father of China's first dynasty, the Xia Dynasty. The historically much better-attested figure of Li Bing, who flourished in the 3rd century BCE and whose system of dams and channels for flood-control and irrigation turned eastern Szechwan into the "Land of Abundance,"[150] has since assumed some of the magical qualities of his mythical predecessor. In ancient Greece it was the heroic figure of Heracles whose prowess and valour was epitomized by spectacular exploits of hydraulic engineering: his fifth labour, for example, was to clean out the filthy cattle stables of King Augeias, which he accomplished by diverting the flow of two neighbouring rivers; his second labour – overcoming the many-headed Hydra – was understood by commentators as a feat of flood control; and his defeat of the shape-shifting river god Achelous was commonly interpreted in terms of the dyking, draining and subsequent cultivation of a low-lying tract of land around the River Achelous.[151]

Even in cases such as these, however, the underlying concept has been of civilization "doing battle" or "at war" with water and with nature, which are phenomena to be "tamed" or "subjugated" or "overcome": instead of acknowledging water as its foundation and fountainhead, civilization has tended to define itself in terms of an implacable *opposition* to water.[152] In a comprehensive act of self-deception and repression, civilization thus prefers to understand itself as emerging *in spite of* water rather than as inextricably dependent upon it. Yet in viewing itself as a work of man conquering nature and water, it conveniently ignores that man himself is nothing but nature and is mostly water. Water's fluid ambiguity – as formlessness and order, destruction and the possibility of creation – does not fit easily into stable categories of meaning and identity. Civilization, with man as its agent and voice, duly steps in to appropriate the positive values (structure and stability) and give itself airs.

Nowhere is this dualism (man vs. water) more evident than in civilization's tireless efforts over the last 300 years to reclaim marshes and fens, drain moorland, rectify rivers and construct ever bigger dams. Until the last few decades, the consensus throughout was that nature –

---

150. On Li Bing, see Kurlansky, *Salt: A World History*, 23-26, where he is described as "one of the greatest hydraulic engineering geniuses of all time."
151. See Graves, II.107-10; 116-19; 190-95; see also Scott Littleton, 199-200.
152. Related viewpoints continue to crop up in a variety of contexts and assume a number of forms. Witness, for example, the claim that "building is a battle against water": *Bauen ist Kampf gegen das Wasser* (Bernd Hillemeier, professor of construction materials, quoted in Passig and Scholz, *Lexikon des Unwissens*, 141).

with water as its most powerful symbol – was an enemy to be overcome, shackled, and reduced to servitude. As the scientific worldview spread its wings, humankind's technological mastery over nature was a cause championed by the progressive, who saw it as signalling moral advance and the promise of a better future.[153] Instead of fighting one another, man was to take up arms against a common adversary, watery nature. As the Scottish philosopher James Dunbar wrote in 1780, "let us learn to wage war with the elements, not with our own kind; to recover, if one may say so, our patrimony from Chaos, and not to add to his empire."[154] Taming a river or reclaiming land thus took on a holy or godlike dimension: to cultivate crops where once a watery waste had prevailed was to repeat the act of Creation, turning disorder and chaos into a fertile land of abundance and prosperity.

This conception of the progress of civilization as a struggle with or a war waged on water was pervasive. The 19th-century hydraulic expert Johann Gottfried Tulla – according to whom "cultural improvements and the securing of property depend heavily on hydraulic and hydro-technical undertakings" – is still commemorated in his birthplace Karlsruhe as "The Man Who Tamed the Wild Rhine."[155] His expertise in controlling the flow of water turned Tulla into a sort of *Kulturbringer*, a bringer of cultivation and culture alike. In "rectifying" or "correcting" the Rhine, Tulla was putting nature in its place, which was of course at the service of civilized humankind. The sphere of dam-construction made the martial metaphor even more explicit. In the words of the pioneer of German dam-building, Otto Intze, "it is necessary when dealing with rivers that carry large masses of water … to present the water with a battleground so chosen that the human comes out the victor. This battleground against the forces of nature should be the creation of large reservoirs."[156] There was a clear visionary element in this war on water. The dams were to generate power, irrigate fields, store drinking water, facilitate inland navigation and provide protection from floods. A river in shackles seemed essential to the creation of a better society.

---

153. See Blackbourn, *The Conquest of Nature*, 3-8.
154 .Quoted in ibid., 64. Thus Walter Benjamin's lament in the aftermath of the First World War: "instead of draining rivers, society directs a human stream into a bed of trenches" (quoted in ibid., 4).
155. Ibid., 78, 96.
156. Ibid., 203.

Projects to drain marshland – such as the Fens in England or the Oder Marshes in Prussia – were likewise spoken of in terms of military conquest over watery wastes or worthless, inhospitable wetlands. Frederick the Great held that "whoever improves the soil, cultivates land lying waste and drains swamps, is making conquests from barbarism."[157] Colonization was civilization. But as David Blackbourn has shown, "the human domination of nature has a lot to tell us about the nature of human domination."[158] For not only did the colonization of reclaimed land increase productivity, reduce malaria and turn watery wilderness into agricultural granary, it also conveniently did away with areas intrinsically associated with lawlessness and disorder: places of darkness and dankness, decay and miasma, havens for subversives, bandits and deserters. Swamps were considered home to "semi-amphibious marsh-dwellers," a benighted, backward, barbaric people who stood in the way of enlightened progress and whose resistance – fierce riots in the Fens or sabotage in the Oderbruch – was as irrelevant as the protests in modern-day China or India.[159] In the first half of the 20th century, the dehumanization of water- or river-people was perpetuated in the Pripet Marshes, the largest wetlands in Europe, which cover what is now southern Belarus and northern Ukraine: while the Germans saw themselves as *Kulturbringer* or cultivators, the Slavs were denigrated as archetypal swamp-dwellers, a term with marked connotations of depravity and vice. The widespread cliché of the "Slav flood" further contributed to the combination of alarm and animosity they provoked.[160]

Again, this is not to question the many palpable benefits of irrigation, dam-building, flood control or land reclamation. It is undeniable that in the course of the relentless rise in world population over the last century, irrigation emerged as a foundation for global food security. However, as Maggie Black and others have reported,[161] large-scale watercourse

---

157. Ibid., 41. Characterizing Frederick the Great, Blackbourn writes of "the anti-water prejudice of an extreme, incorrigible landman," who once complained "that even taking the waters at a spa made him feel *deplaciert*: water was best left to the eels, flounders, pike and ducks" (see ibid., 31).
158. Ibid., 6.
159. On the prevalent view of marshes and marsh-dwellers, see ibid., 40-46.
160. See ibid., 239-96; esp. 244-45. The "marshy district" was a term for prostitution; "flowers of the marsh" were prostitutes.
161. See Black, *The No-Nonsense Guide to Water*, 54-67, and Pearce, 153-61; also Blackbourn, 218-23.

systems based on dams and irrigation are proving inherently problematic, leading not only to the social unrest associated with mass population displacement and to environmental destruction and the accelerated extinction of animal species (not to mention the threat this poses to the livelihood of riparian communities), but also to the waterlogging and increased salinity provoked by over-irrigation. Accumulations of silt in many dams are drastically reducing storage capacity and efficiency, while the artificial blockage of the flow of silt downstream lessens the fertility of flood plains (in turn making it necessary to apply chemical fertilizers, with their own destructive side-effects) and leads to the erosion of river banks and coastal deltas. Further, the hubris of attempting to "tame" Europe's major rivers has come to light in the once-in-a-century floods that are no longer restricted to one a century: the image is of angry rivers "rattling their chains," and of civilization's belated attempts to appease the river spirits awakened by rectification. With EU support, river floodplains and wetlands are now being restored and reopened, creating flood retention basins that hand the rivers back at least some of the freedom they had been denied.[162] Wetlands are being positively reappraised for their role in flood control, the biodiversity they harbour, and the wealth of social, environmental and economic benefits they bring.[163]

A civilization that defines itself by its *opposition to* water – like a mind at war with its own body – condemns itself to a repressive or schizoid dualism that can ultimately turn pathological. There is a growing awareness, indeed, that water has been inherently linked not only to the birth of civilizations but also to their death and the ensuing dusty oblivion. Over the course of time, increased salinity caused by inefficient drainage systems came to ruin the once abundant lands of southern Mesopotamia, and by 1700 BCE harvest yields dwindled to just a quarter of what they had been, leading to the irreversible decline of the great Sumerian cities that had depended upon them.[164] The downfall of the great Indus civilization is believed in part to have been caused by a series of devastating floods that left the area vulnerable to the havoc wreaked by waves of Indo-Aryan raiders.

162. Blackbourn, 331-48.
163. See Nagle, 45-58. Signed by more than 60 countries, the Ramsar Convention (1971) has laid the foundations for international cooperation in the conservation of wetlands, adopting notions of "wise use" and "sustainable utilisation."
164. On the decline of Sumer, see Ponting, 69-72; Pearce, 212-13. As Arundhati Roy expresses it, an irrigation network without adequate drainage is like a body with arteries but no veins (Roy, 88).

Most famous perhaps is the rise and fall of the exceedingly prosperous Sabaean or Sheban civilization of the first millennium BCE, a civilization based on a high degree of hydraulic know-how and a complex system of water management and that reached a pinnacle with the construction of the great Marib Dam in what is now Yemen.[165] Commonly regarded as an engineering marvel of the age, the collapse of this dam in the 6th century CE signalled a decline in the region's hydraulic prowess and marked the end of a mighty civilization. The flooding that ensued was duly pounced upon by the Qur'an, which considered it a punishment inflicted upon the people of Sheba for not paying enough attention to God.[166]

*   *   *   *   *

The cautionary tales of Sumer and Sheba illustrate the close link between water and wisdom or knowledge. This link finds itself reflected, first of all, in such figures as Enki and Ea, the ancient Mesopotamian gods of water and wisdom associated with the creation of civilization out of the primal oceans. As the patron of divine learning, moreover, Ea sent seven sages to teach humankind the arts and skills of civilization, the first of whom – called Uan or Adapa – was responsible for inculcating the rites of religious observance (though after somehow displeasing Ea he was expelled from earth and returned to the fresh waters of the Apsu).[167] Subsequently given the name Oannes by the Babylonian writer Berossus, Uan is thought to have been represented as a composite half man, half fish, who would emerge from the Persian Gulf to impart his learning, culture and wisdom. Even the word for sage, *apkallum*, is believed to contain this link with water: for the Mesopotamians, the ocean was "the home of wisdom."[168]

165. In fact, Sheba was doing very nicely even before the dam was built. The visit paid by the extremely wealthy Queen of Sheba to Solomon in Jerusalem took place a couple of centuries prior to its construction in the 7th century BCE. Sheba was a rich trading nation that benefited from a first-rate strategic location.
166. Qur'an, 34:15-16.
167. On the story of Adapa or Uan, see Dalley (trans.), 182-88.
168. Eliade, *Patterns in Comparative Religion*, 202. A similar association between ancient wisdom and water exists in the *Popol Vuh*, which refers to its original hieroglyphic source as "The Light That Came from Beside the Sea" (see *Popol Vuh*, 63, 179-80; also 51, 219). This place "beside the sea" was where the first Quiché lords were said to come from.

In ancient Egypt, Osiris – as the god of death and rebirth – was seen as responsible for the annual renewal of the crops produced by the floodwaters of the Nile: by extension, he was also a water-god and cultivator, credited with teaching humankind the arts of agriculture and civilization. In Hinduism the figure of the river goddess Sarasvati, in later writings usually considered the consort of Brahma,[169] is widely venerated as the patron of eloquence, learning and the arts. Generally depicted as fair-skinned and beautiful, she is regarded as the personification of the sacred river Sarasvati,[170] the banks of which proved fertile soil for the hymn-making and ritual of Brahmanism. She is even identified with Vach, the Vedic goddess of speech and personification of sacred utterance, and is said to have invented Sanskrit.

Of course, it is not only water that tends to be associated with wisdom and civilization. According to the famous Greek legend of Prometheus, it was the gift of fire – stolen from the heavens – that made possible the birth of civilization. Fire is the archetypal *shaping* element; it provides light, warmth and protection and through its use in cooking may well have transformed the human diet in ways that played a significant part in human evolution.[171] The light produced by fire, moreover, is conceptually bound up with vision not only in its physical sense, but with ideas, enlightenment, illumination and all forms of clarification: i.e. with civilization in what are commonly seen as its most noble and highest forms.

An ancient treatise pseudonymously attributed to the Greek writer Plutarch explicitly weighs up "Whether Water or Fire Be Most Useful," successively presenting the advantages of the two opposing elements. Here it is water – in the form of the oceans – that emerges as the primary civilizing force:

169. One legend has it that originally Vishnu had three wives – Sarasvati, Lakshmi and Ganga – but the three of them got on so badly that Vishnu gave Ganga to Shiva and Sarasvati to Brahma.
170. Water in general and rivers in particular are sacred among Hindus, but there are seven rivers that are the object of special veneration: the Ganges (Ganga), Yamuna, Narmada, Sarasvati, Godavari, Kaveri and Sindhu. The word "Hinduism" itself derives from the Persian word *hindu* (cf. the Sanskrit *sindhu*, "river"), meaning "of the Indus Valley." Etymologically as well as historically, rivers lie at the very wellsprings of Hindu belief and Indian civilization.
171. See Rupp, 228-30.

this element united and perfected our manner of living, which before was wild and unsociable, correcting it by mutual existence, and creating community of friendship by reciprocal exchanges of one good turn for another. And as Heraclitus said, if there were no sun, it would be perpetual night; so may we say, if there were no sea, man would be the most savage and shameless of all creatures.[172]

Oceans are thus associated with distance, travel and broadened horizons, as well as with the concomitant possibilities for commerce and the exchange of ideas. Of course, the waters of the ocean separate (and thus protect) as much as they connect. A nation of seafarers can either be a nation of explorers and travellers or a nation of colonizers and conquistadors (and is most likely to have elements of both).[173]

Yet this does not invalidate Pseudo-Plutarch's point. In ancient historical practice, there is abundant evidence of the spread of cultures *by sea* from one territory to another, frequently bringing together adjacent coastlands within a shared cultural heritage. For the earliest human settlers on the Atlantic shores of the European continent in the Mesolithic period between 10,000 and 4,000 BCE, it was clearly easier to travel by sea than negotiate mountains or the swampy and heavily forested landscapes further inland. Far from being the case (as often assumed) that the seas divided and land united, the Tardenoisian culture that came to Cornwall, north-eastern Ireland and the Isle of Man from western Brittany and the Atlantic coast of France seems to have taken advantage of the western seaways virtually as soon as the conditions permitted, blazing a trail that was to be taken up both by the Maglemosian people of the Neolithic Age and the Christian pilgrims of the Age of the Saints. In the words of E. G. Bowen, "there is much to be said for the view that it was along these western sea-routes that the elements of civilization first reached the far distant fringes

---

172. [Plutarch], *Moralia XII*, 7.
173. See Edward W. Said's definition of the intellectual as "like a shipwrecked person who learns how to live in a certain sense *with* the land, not *on* it, not like Robinson Crusoe whose goal is to colonize his little island, but more like Marco Polo, whose sense of the marvelous never fails him, and who is always a traveler, a provisional guest, not a freeloader, conqueror, or raider" (*Representations of the Intellectual*, 44).

of the continent."[174] Even today, the inhabitants of the Hebrides off the west coast of Scotland speak of being *joined* by the sea to the other islands and to Ireland, rather than separated from them.[175]

Water travel need not only be a matter of open seas or oceans. For many centuries, rivers rather than roads were the most crucial thoroughfares and networks of communication and commerce. In the early part of the 17th century, London – with its population of a quarter of a million – had no less than 3,000 watermen who rowed for hire on the Thames: the river was considered a safer and more convenient highway than seedy streets that harboured hidden perils. By the end of the 18th century the figure was estimated to have risen to some 12,000. The industrial revolution saw the construction of some 4,000 miles of canals in Britain before the railways came to dominate freight transport, and in rapidly developing Germany inland shipping more than held its own with rail transport right through to the early 20th century.[176] Navigating a flow of water was an essential aspect of mobility, communication, transport and trade. Perhaps as a reflection of its origins, the technology of modern-day communications still uses navigational or aquatic imagery: while Spanish-speakers "navigate" the Internet for information or entertainment, English- or German-speaking cybernauts surf it.[177]

On top of such pragmatic considerations, water travel has also embodied a search for origins. Seneca enigmatically claimed that "when you have come to understand the true origin of rivers, you will realise that you have no further questions."[178] Such a search is typified by the River Nile with all its connotations of esoteric, alchemical wisdom. Fascinated by its strange behaviour, the ancients believed that its source was to be found at the centre of the world or on the inaccessible Mountain of the Moon;

174. Bowen, *Britain and the Western Seaways*, 26. See also p. 12: "As in the Mediterranean, so on the Atlantic seaboard, there were times – such as, for example, during the 'Megalithic Age', or in the Early Christian period – when the whole length of the coastlands of the Atlantic fringe were united in a common cultural inheritance dependent upon intense maritime activity."
175. Deakin, 244-45.
176. Ackroyd, *Thames: Sacred River*, 104-5, 167; Black, *Water: Life Force*, 76, 81; on Germany, see Blackbourn, 204-5.
177. While "naut" has its roots in the Greek *naus* (ship), "cyber" goes back to the Greek *kubernetes*, a steersman or helmsman. The hidden implication that cyberspace is a watery place captures its protean nature as a flow of information.
178. Quoted in Ackroyd, 36.

discovering the springs from which it flowed represented the ultimate challenge. Caesar is said to have offered to abandon his wars in return for a glimpse of them, a quest that continued right through to the fearless explorers of the 19th century.[179] In the same spirit, intrepid sea-travellers searched for the fabulous paradises of folk tales and fable. The legendary 6th-century seafaring abbot Saint Brendan – "Brendan the Navigator" – was said to have voyaged to a "promised land of the blessed," interpreted by some as a pre-Colombian discovery of America,[180] by others as an equally appetizing trip to the Canaries.

The wind-powered sail was the motor behind the European age of discovery and invasion, taking venturesome seamen such as Vasco da Gama, Christopher Columbus and James Cook to places as far afield as India, America, Tahiti and Australia and the expedition of Ferdinand Magellan all the way round the world. Conversely, a reluctance to pursue such maritime expansionism was the reason why China – in the early 15th century arguably the most highly developed civilization in the world – would subsequently undergo a steady relative "decline."[181] In its heyday between 1405 and 1433, the Chinese navy under Admiral Cheng Ho – an eight-foot-tall eunuch (so it was said) – undertook a series of seven official long-distance overseas expeditions consisting of hundreds of ships and tens of thousands of sailors. Apart from engaging in trade and displaying Chinese might, these highly successful expeditions "swelled the emperor's coffers with pearls, coral, ivory, gemstones, and rare woods, and added to his private zoo lions, leopards, ostriches, zebras, an oryx, and a giraffe."[182] Yet the 1433 expedition was to be the last of them; three years later the construction of seagoing ships was banned by imperial edict, and soon another order outlawed ships with more than two masts. Cheng Ho's great vessels were allowed to rot away. Confucian conservatism – the mandarin bureaucracy's dislike of warfare, trade and commerce – led China to turn its back on the world and ignore the potential for overseas expansion, allowing the smaller ships of Europe to conquer, colonize and (in their own eyes at least) "civilize" the world.

As the striving of European countries to rule the waves and the scholarly abstention of Ming China makes clear, the mastery of water – or

179. See Ball, *H₂O*, 36-39, on the River Nile.
180. See Biedermann, 185-86.
181. On the technological precocity of early Ming China and its subsequent decline, see Kennedy, *The Rise and Fall of the Great Powers*, 5-10.
182. Rupp, 180.

"the waters" – has proved to be a central motor driving the progress of civilizations (measured in terms of commercial, economic and military might). Such advances were further reinforced by another line of water-based developments as fundamental to the emergence of industry as irrigation had been to the origins of agriculture: the use of water for power-generation. The idea of utilizing the natural force of water as a source of power – as a way of driving machines – goes back to antiquity. The use of the bucket wheel as a means of exploiting the flow of a river to haul water upwards (for distribution) could be found in ancient Egypt, Mesopotamia and China, while the idea of using the waterwheel for grinding grain and making flour first developed with the ancient Greeks and was subsequently adopted in the greater part of ancient and medieval Europe. By 1086, when the Doomsday Book was compiled, well over 5,000 water mills were recorded in England, and further uses for water power – such as fulling cloth, tanning leather, sawing wood, driving forges and making paper – gradually emerged over the centuries. Indeed, flowing water remained civilization's major source of power well into the industrial revolution, as the newly developing alternatives struggled to become more efficient. As late as the early 1860s Prussia still had one water mill for every thousand inhabitants; in 1875 water power continued to generate more energy than steam in the state of Württemberg; and in the United States many industries – including textile manufacture – relied upon a flow of water for their energy until into the 1880s.[183]

Yet arguably the most radical change came with the development of an alternative form of water-based power, the steam engine: i.e. a heat engine that converts the thermal energy that exists in steam into mechanical work. Steam power was the driving force behind the later part of the industrial revolution, and it would profoundly transform society and culture. The steam engine too, of course, had its roots in the past. The first steam device, the aeolipile, had been invented as a toy by the Greek engineer and geometer Heron of Alexandria in the 1st century CE. But it was not until the 18th century that significant work was done to refine the basic principle of exploiting the heat energy of steam by permitting it to expand and cool in a cylinder equipped with a movable piston. Newcomen's "atmospheric engine," designed in 1705, was capable of pumping water from coal mines; Cugnot had devised the first functional self-propelled steam vehicle by 1769; Trevithick's self-moving railway steam engine – the steam locomotive – appeared in 1804; while Watt's

183. See Ponting, 273-75; Blackbourn, 195.

steam engine represented another huge step forward in efficiency later in the 19th century. In the course of the industrial revolution, steam power effectively displaced the water power of mills and the muscle power of horses and humans as the major source of industrial power. As Paul Kennedy describes the transformation:

> What industrialization, and in particular the steam engine, did was to substitute inanimate for animate sources of power; by converting heat into work through the use of machines … mankind was thus able to exploit vast new sources of energy. The consequences of introducing this novel machinery were simply stupendous: by the 1820s someone operating several power-driven looms could produce twenty times the output of a hand worker, while the power-driven "mule" (or spinning machine) had two hundred times the capacity of a spinning wheel. A single railway engine could transport goods which would have required hundreds of packhorses, and do it far more quickly.[184]

By 1870, the capacity of Britain's steam engines amounted to some four million horsepower, a measure of power that would have required 40 million men to generate it – yet this many men would in turn have needed more than three times the country's total annual wheat output for sustenance: "The use of inanimate sources of power," writes Kennedy, "allowed industrial man to transcend the limitations of biology and to create spectacular increases in production and wealth without succumbing to the weight of a fast-growing population."[185]

In the course of the industrial revolution, the momentum of flowing water was gradually replaced by the combustion of fossil fuels in conjunction with new, steadily improving steam engines that could turn this heat energy into mechanical work. Yet interest in flowing water as a major source of energy was renewed with the advent of electricity. In 1884, the Irish engineer Charles A. Parsons invented the turbine, a device that – in effect honing the ancient idea of the waterwheel – could convert the energy of a moving stream of water, steam or wind into electrical energy by passing this stream through a system of fan-like blades that are thus caused to rotate. Today the flow of (usually falling) water through rotating turbines attached to turbo-generators provides almost a fifth of the world's electricity.

184. Kennedy, 186.
185. Ibid., 188.

At various times in the 20th century, hydroelectric power has aroused considerable fervour on account of its seeming inexhaustibility and renewability. German pioneers at the turn of the century hailed it as "white coal" or even as the "true Rhine Gold."[186] It was seen as cheap and clean: the very embodiment of progress. There are now tens of thousands of hydroelectric dams throughout the world. The enormous dam at Itaipu on the River Parana, which supplies Rio de Janeiro and São Paulo, can generate as much as a dozen conventional power stations; the Three Gorges dam in China will have an even greater capacity.[187] Yet there is an increasing awareness of the drawbacks associated with such dams: the trauma of mass displacement, the environmental destruction they cause, their inefficiency and inadequacy in terms of power generation, irrigation and flood control.

Yet even apart from hydroelectric power, water remains essential to the powering of "civilization," whatever that is. Most electricity is generated utilizing the kinetic energy of a flow of steam produced when either fossil fuels or nuclear reactions heat water. Notably, it is the steam turbine that makes it possible to harness nuclear energy for useful work: the nuclear reactor in itself does not generate either mechanical work or electrical energy, but simply boils water. The turbine then converts the kinetic energy of pressurized, superheated steam into the rotary motion that drives the electrical generator. Once again, it is water's protean nature – as a jack of all trades – that allows it to perform the not inconsiderable task of energizing a civilization that would otherwise soon judder to a halt.

186. Blackbourn, 206-10.
187. Pearce, 156; Black, *Water: Life Force*, 59.

Chapter Two
Water as Flow

1

Water and Fire

Most of the world's electricity is generated when turbines are caused to rotate by the kinetic energy of a jet of steam or the pull of gravity on water. Tidal power generators harness the force exerted by the moon on large bodies of water, while wave power generators unlock the power stored in water by the action of wind. Yet water does not have a monopoly when it comes to powering modern civilization. Turbines may be caused to rotate by wind as well as steam or water. Solar power plants use the photovoltaic effects of semiconductor technology (e.g. "waste" silicon from the computer chip industry) to generate electricity directly from sunlight. Wood, peat and fossil fuels such as coal can all serve as sources of energy. Air, fire and earth – to fall back on the classical elements – can each play their part.

By the same token, water is not the only substance to have been regarded as the substratum underlying the diverse phenomena of the world. We have already seen that the ancient Greek philosopher Anaximander disagreed with his master Thales in postulating "the boundless" rather than water as the indestructible, eternal cause and origin of all things. The third of the great Ionian philosophers, Anaximenes, claimed that it was air, not water, that underlay the diversity of the universe. Fire, he argued, was air in its rarefied state, while wind, clouds, water, earth and stones were air in progressively more condensed form.[188] Air also incorporated *pneuma*, the breath that informs the soul of the individual person and that permeates the world as a whole.[189]

188. This is according to Hippolytus, quoted in Barnes, 77.
189. Ibid., 79.

While the Ionian moralist and poet Xenophanes subsequently attributed primordial status to earth,[190] Heraclitus – the philosopher of transience and change – opted for fire as the primal state from which all things come and to which all things will return. For Heraclitus, the universe itself had its origins in fire, which turned into water and then into earth, before being converted back to water and then fire in a never-ending cycle.[191] The human soul he viewed as a composite of fire and water, the former elevating man to higher goals, the latter dragging him back down to baser passions. He consequently suggested that we do well to avoid dampening our soul unduly with alcoholic beverages.[192] By a quirk of philosophical irony, water-despising Heraclitus himself came to be plagued by water when he contracted dropsy at the age of 60. According to legend, he tried to dry himself out by getting his servants to plaster him with cow-dung while he lay in the sun, but "being unrecognisable when so transformed, he was devoured by dogs."[193]

It was Empedocles in the 5th century BCE who reached the compromise of allowing these four substrata – water, air, earth and fire – to exist in conjunction with one another. At this stage, they do not yet go by the name of "elements," but are referred to as *rhizomata*, or roots, and are associated with four divinities, "shining Zeus, life-bringing Hera, Aidoneus and Nestis, whose tear-drops are a well-spring to mortals" (Nestis being the name of a Sicilian water-goddess).[194] These four roots are eternal, indestructible, unchangeable and irreducible, ultimately accounting for all things that exist in the world. Yet they are not the whole story, for the different forms produced by their intermingling and separation in turn require the influence of two active principles, love and strife. The function of love is the generation of union (or attraction between opposites); of strife, the disruption of union. At times, however, Empedocles attributes causal powers to the roots themselves: fire is understood to divide and separate, water to be "adhesive and retentive, holding and gluing by its moisture." This, said Plutarch, was why he also referred to fire as "cursed

190. Ibid., 97. Some say that Xenophanes held both earth and water to be first principles.
191. Ibid., 107, 122.
192. Burnet, 152.
193. Diogenes Laertius, II.411-13.
194. Burnet., 264. There is some doubt as to which of the other divinities corresponds to which root. Burnet associates Hera with earth, Zeus with air, and Aidoneus with fire. Others have identified Hera with air, Aidoneus with earth, and Zeus with fire.

Strife" and water as "tenacious Love."[195]

In the words of Bertrand Russell, "the chemistry of the ancients stopped dead at this point. No further progress was made in this science until the Mohammedan alchemists embarked upon their search for the philosopher's stone."[196] In fact, Empedocles's fourfold scheme was to exert a profound and lasting influence not only on chemistry, but also on medicine, psychology and the cultural imagination in general. The Greek physician Hippocrates – commonly regarded as the father of medicine – founded his theory of bodily humours or fluids on the idea of the four underlying elements, and building on Hippocratic conceptions in the 2nd century CE, Galen categorized the varieties of human temperament and personality in accordance with the predominance of a particular humour. Earth was associated with the black bile and a melancholic disposition; fire with the yellow bile and a choleric temperament; air with the blood and a sanguine personality; while water corresponded to the phlegm and a character that tended towards the phlegmatic. Emotional health depended upon equilibrium among the four bodily humours. An ideal temperament would result when the four humours – the four elements – were present in equal proportions. An excess of one or another would give rise either to bodily ailments or to a personality that was one-sided and dominated by a single trait. Too much bodily fire would make you petulant and irascible; too much water dull and lymphatic.

Galen's theory of personality types dominated Western medicine for 14 centuries and beyond.[197] The French royal physician André du Laurent wrote an authoritative dissertation on the humours in the 17th century in which he describes phlegmatic people as lazy, sluggish and backward, with the higher qualities of the soul sunk in torpor. They lack acumen or nobility of spirit and should be "banished to dining-rooms and kitchens."[198] The great German philosopher Immanuel Kant did not agree. In his *Anthropology* he recognized both the negative and positive aspects

195. Barnes, 176.
196. Russell, 62.
197. It even formed the basis for the comic theory of Ben Jonson (1572-1637), whose theatre drew its laughter primarily from characters dominated by a single passion or fixation. The idea was that obsession, monomania and one-sidedness, with the behavioural repetition and predictability they entail, are inherently funny. Comedy of character in general – focusing, say, on a person's fiery irascibility or watery dullness – uses the same principle of reiteration and recognition.
198. Quoted in Screech, *Montaigne and Melancholy*, 27.

of the phlegmatic humour: a tendency to indolence or apathy on the one hand and equanimity and constancy on the other. The man of phlegm, he wrote, is not on that account a sage, but is more likely to become one.[199] Perhaps Kant was here seeking to do justice to the wateriness in his own disposition.

Empedocles's theory of the four roots was also taken on board by philosophers. Democritus incorporated the four elements into his atomic theory, according to which the universe comprised an infinite number of miniscule, indivisible, irreducible atoms in constant motion within empty space. The atoms of the distinct elements possessed different physical qualities that accounted for their properties: fire atoms, he said, were spiky and painful, while water atoms were smooth and pearl-like. In *Timaeus*, Plato too adopted and modified the four "roots" of Empedocles, understanding fire, air, water and earth not as simple, basic substances but as geometrical structures. In Plato's scheme, fire atoms are four-sided tetrahedrons (their acute angles making them the sharpest of the elements), whereas water atoms are icosahedrons, the most bulbous and least pointed of the structures, composed of 20 sides.[200] It was Plato who first used what was to become the standard term *stoicheion* – the Greek word for the letters of the alphabet – to denote the elements. Plato also broadly embraced Hippocratic pathology, explaining disease as an excess or deficiency of one of the four elements that constitute the body (though regarding bile and phlegm not as normal ingredients of the organism but as products of an indisposition).

Aristotle too incorporated the theory of the four *stoicheia*, but as with Plato they were not the ultimate foundations of reality.[201] Aristotle believed in a single underlying substance – *prote hyle* – that gave rise to the four elements in accordance with the presence or absence of four qualities, which consisted of two pairs of opposites: hot and cold, and wet and dry. The idea was thus that each element constituted a combination of two qualities: fire, for example, was hot and dry; water, cold and wet. While for Plato the four elements could be transmuted into one another by a geometrical process of rearranging the triangular faces that made up the polyhedral atoms, therefore, for Aristotle they could be converted

199. Kant, *Anthropologie in pragmatischer Hinsicht*, 195-96, 239.
200. Plato, *Timaeus*, 55A-B. See 82A-83C for his ideas on humoral pathology.
201. In fact, he added a fifth element for good measure, the ether. But this was divorced from worldly matters, instead belonging to the heavenly realm.

into one another by interchanging the appropriate quality. By cooling air, which was hot and wet, one could convert it to water, which was cold and wet. Water could in turn be converted to cold dry earth by removing its moisture.

The Aristotelian conceptual framework was to dominate European ideas on the nature of matter for some 2,000 years. As Philip Ball writes, however,

> [a]lthough Western culture has come to regard the Aristotelian fourfold categorization of the elements – earth, air, fire, water – as the canonical pre-scientific classification of matter, it was by no means unique: many others have been proposed at various times from the earliest of recorded history to the advent of modern chemistry. Common to nearly all such schemes, however, was water. So was fire: fire and water were indispensable to any culture, so their primacy is not hard to understand. We can see readily how this dualism might have been emphasized by the natural associations with the Sun and Moon respectively.[202]

Ancient Chinese symbolism accordingly opted for a cosmos founded on five elements: earth, metal, wood, fire and water, as well as the two underlying principles of *yin* and *yang*. For Taoist and Confucian tradition, indeed, five was a sacred number: these five elements corresponded to five points of the compass (four plus the centre), five primary colours (yellow, blue, red, white and black), five planets (Mercury, Venus, Mars, Jupiter and Saturn), and so on. While fire was associated with the south, red, Mars and the phoenix, water was paired with the north, black and Mercury, as well as with cold, fluidity and the tortoise. Along with the moon, the pine, the bamboo tree and the plum, it was also one of the five pure things.[203] Indian symbolism originally recognized three elements – fire, water and earth – but later added air and, like Aristotle, the rather foggy notion of *akasha*, the ether.

Further west, the intellectual stagnation that followed the decline of ancient Greece did not extend to the Arab world, which added new ingredients to the conception of elements. The 8th-century Arab alchemist Jabir ibn Hayyan (Geber) laid the emphasis on sulphur and mercury as the two underlying elements of which all metals were composed, and the following century the Persian physician Al-Razi (Rhazes) was to turn Geber's

202. Ball, *H_2O*, 109-10.
203. Biedermann, 133.

fundamental duality into a trinity, proposing that all solids were composed of combinations of sulphur, mercury and salt, signifying combustibility, volatility and substance respectively.[204] Creatively combining the Greek and Arabic systems in the 16th century, the Rabelaisian figure of Paracelsus came to the conclusion that while all matter was indeed composed of air, fire, earth and water, these were in turn founded upon a threesome of mercury, sulphur and salt. Mercury he associated in particular with water, sulphur with fire, and salt with earth.[205]

Geber's original duality of sulphur and mercury was to exert a great influence on the alchemical tradition as a whole, corresponding to the time-honoured duality of fire and water, and signifying the combustible and the volatile. This was further reflected in a system of dualities of sun and moon, male and female, and active and passive. The reconciliation of these opposites came to be seen as a central task in the process of spiritual perfection: the philosophical stone required a marriage or wedding or "conjugal bathing" of mercury and sulphur, of quicksilver and brimstone, of watery matter and fiery spirit. A similar system of associations pervades ancient Taoist thought, where it is yin and yang that represent the underlying cosmic duality: yin symbolizes the feminine, the passive, water, cold and the north, whereas yang represents the masculine, the active, warmth, light, dryness and the south. In theory they are equal in status, and mutually dependent.[206]

Mercury is the embodiment of the protean spirit of alchemy, the volatile and elusive transforming agent essential to the alchemical process. Indeed, the feminine mercurial principle represents fluidity and the power of transmogrification, and is often identified with the philosopher's stone, not as a substance but as a process, as alchemy itself.[207] Intrinsically connected with mercury (its kindred spirit in protean volatility), water

---

204. See Rupp, 21-22.
205. See Ball, *The Devil's Doctor*, 261-70, on the inconsistencies within Paracelsus himself.
206. Taoist alchemy thus also sought a wedding of fire to water, using techniques in breathing, yoga, gymnastics, dietetics and meditation to achieve a stable equilibrium between the house of fire (the heart) and the house of water (the lower abdomen).
207. Roob, *Alchemy and Mysticism*, 26; Gilchrist, *The Elements of Alchemy*, 43ff.

likewise assumes central importance in alchemical thought.[208] Yet the water to which the alchemists refer is no more a simple matter of good old H_2O than "philosophical" mercury or azoth corresponds to the element Hg, and when there is reference to "our water," it is water in an obscure, metaphorical sense. The same goes for "sweet water," "Pontic water,"[209] "water of the wise," "mercurial water" and "white water." Similarly, "royal water" (*aqua regia*) – which the 13th-century magus Roger Bacon believed capable of dissolving gold to produce the elixir of life – was in fact a mixture of three parts concentrated hydrochloric acid to one part nitric acid. Nitric acid was itself known to the alchemists of the 8th century as *aqua fortis*, or strong water, and is still employed to incise a design into a metal plate in the process known as etching.

There is one kind of water above all, however, that is endowed with special significance in alchemical texts. From time immemorial, dew has been conceived as celestial moisture endowed with revitalizing and rejuvenating qualities. The ancients believed the morning dew to be tears left behind by the dawn-goddess, Eos, and Pliny the Elder had described it as a true medicine and heavenly gift for eyes, ulcers and intestines.[210] In alchemical thought it further became a symbol of the philosopher's stone in embryo, simultaneously incorporating the vitality of the plants on which it settled and beneficial celestial influences from on high. In the *Zohar*, the most influential text of medieval Cabbalistic mysticism, dew is thus endowed with holy attributes: "this dew is the manna on which the souls of the just nourish themselves. The chosen hunger for it and collect it with full hands in the fields of heaven."[211] There is a famous plate from the *Mutus Liber* ("The Silent Book"), dating from 1677, which shows a male

208. This is echoed in etymology. The obsolete name for mercury, *hydrargyrum*, from which the modern-day element's chemical symbol – Hg – is derived, reflects its perceived wateriness as well as its perceived silveriness, compr nding the hydrous and the argentine. As another of mercury's traditional names reminds us, mercury is silver that is quick as opposed to dead or lifeless. The arcane term *azoth* was coined by Paracelsus from the first and last letters of the Latin, Greek and Hebrew alphabets to express that mercury represented the beginning and the end (see Roob, 308; Marshall, 296-97).

209. In Greek mythology, Pontos was a pre-Olympian god of the sea, born of Gaia and Aether or – according to Hesiod's *Theogony* (line 116) – of Gaia alone.

210. Biedermann, 95.

211. Quoted in Roob, 375. For the *Mutus Liber*, see ibid., 374-392. The harvesting of dew is shown on 380.

and a female alchemist wringing out the dew they have collected in sheets exposed to the air, with the sun and the moon looking on from above.

The 17th century saw the decline of alchemy as a form of spiritual or empirical enquiry and the gradual emergence of modern-day chemistry. By the second half of the 18th century chemists had isolated the two components of water, oxygen and hydrogen; in the 1780s the notoriously reclusive figure of Henry Cavendish recombined them to synthesize water. Yet the idea that water was not an irreducible element but a compound of two gases was slow to gain acceptance. Many of the leading scientists of the day railed at the "arch-magician" Antoine Lavoisier for imposing upon their credulity.[212] With time, however, the Frenchman's ideas came to hold sway. According to his *Elementary Treatise on Chemistry*, dating from 1789, there were 33 known elements. Eight of these have since been shown to be compounds, and two – heat and light ("imponderable fluids," as he referred to them) – have also been removed from any such classification. The remaining 23 included metals such as gold, silver, copper, iron, mercury, tin and lead, non-metals such as carbon, phosphorus and sulphur, and the three gases hydrogen, nitrogen and oxygen. He missed only three of the elements then known to exist.

Today there are believed to be 92 naturally occurring elements and another 24 that can only be made by artificial means (on this planet at least). The original four have now been shown not to be elements at all, but a mixture of gases (in the case of air), a conglomeration of soils and rock particles, a process of combustion, and a chemical compound. Water has been well and truly ousted from its elemental position in the make-up of the world. Yet even though the classical elements play no role in modern chemistry, air, earth, fire and water – the latter two in particular – have continued to structure our imaginative experience and shape our vision of the world. The following section will look at the fluid nexus of associations shaped by this opposition between fire and water, and at some of the links with what is considered high or low, spiritual or base.

* * * * *

Fire is the element of passion and erotic, spiritual or insurrectionary fervour; a fiery temper is one that is easily or quickly roused; and ardent

212. See Ball, *H₂O*, 135.

love is characterized by its all-consuming intensity.[213] Water by contrast has the deflating effect of wet blankets, damp squibs, and drips. A slight shift in emphasis occurs when the contrast is phrased in terms of heat and cold. While heat is linked even more directly to lust and the joys of rutting, and a heated discussion is one with raised voices and frayed tempers, coldness may imply – depending on the context – frigidity, heartlessness or dispassionate neutrality. Cool adds a more positive, contemporary twist, suggesting composure and effortlessness. The old opposition between a phlegmatic and a choleric disposition finds itself echoed in such dualities.

In the form of a divine spark, however, fire also represents the human soul and its higher aspirations. Just as the process of combustion produces not only an increase in temperature but also the emission of light, so the metaphor of fire may be bound up not only with heat but also with illumination, clarification and spiritual or intellectual enlightenment. Light has been one of the quintessential symbols of divinity, and the opposition of light and darkness a fundamental metaphysical duality. Traditional Manichean systems of thought associate light with truth, and darkness with untruth and ignorance; patriarchal ideology takes light to be a masculine force, moreover, and darkness feminine. In such binary systems, darkness thus represents a state of non-differentiation akin to the primeval waters prior to creation. Yet as many mystics and heterodox believers down the ages have known, absolute light and absolute darkness are in practical terms indistinguishable. Determinate knowledge and recognition always depend on a chiaroscuro or interplay of light and dark.[214] At the same

213. The metaphor of burning passion was parodied by the 17th-century states-man and poet Buckingham in his burlesque *The Rehearsal*, where Prince Pretty-man uses the metaphor of fire in comically literalistic terms to describe the incendiary – indeed incineratory – nature of love: "All hearts turn ashes which her eyes controul: / The Body they consume as well as Soul." Not to be outdone, Prince Volscius counters that his passion has not a consuming but a refining effect: "Amidst the flames they ne're give up the Ghost / But, with her looks, revive still as they roast" (Act 4, scene 2).
214. See, for example, Edmund Burke's *Philosophical Enquiry* (1757), 73-74. Misquoting *Paradise Lost*, Burke describes "a light which by its very excess is converted into a species of darkness." This idea, he continues, is "not only poeti-cal in an high degree, but strictly and philosophically just. Extreme light, by overcoming the organs of sight, obliterates all objects, so as in its effect exactly to resemble darkness." Hegel wrote: "Pure light and pure darkness are .

time, any mystical awareness of the absolute tends to transcend light and darkness, just as it by-passes the associated dichotomies of good and bad, knowledge and ignorance, male and female, heaven and earth, high and low, sun and moon, fire and water.

Despite the mystical or Hermetic awareness that wisdom lies in an overcoming of duality or a wedding of opposites, the fiery sun and its light has consistently been paired with the masculine, paternal, active, spiritual and elevated half of the equation, and watery darkness with the feminine, maternal, passive, bodily side of things, as well as with the inconstant moon.[215] In these terms, therefore, there is clearly a close network of associations between water and "woman" as stereotyped and typecast by male-dominated ideology. According to Paracelsus, himself anything but misogynistic, water was "the matrix of the world and of all its creatures"[216]: even today, the waters of the ocean lend themselves to imagery of a primordial womb. "What causes the sea to rise?" asks Paracelsus. "Just as the sea expels things and falls, one may understand woman as a mother of children. The sea is the mother of water. Because woman is a mother, she produces such rivers in herself, which rise up and flow out every four weeks."[217]

Yet the womb can signify not only maternal care and creative fertility, but also a more threatening female sexuality with its subversive power and fickle faithlessness. The timeless male ambivalence towards woman, womb and water finds modern-day expression in the attitude of the old Spanish-speaking fisherman in Ernest Hemingway's *The Old Man and the Sea*. Whereas Spanish-speakers usually refer to the sea in its masculine form, as *el mar*,[218] the old man preferred *la mar*,

---

two emptinesses which are both the same." See his *Wissenschaft der Logik*, in *Werke*, 5.96.

215. See Eliade, *Patterns*, 155: "from the earliest times, certainly since the Neolithic Age, with the discovery of agriculture, the same symbolism has linked together the moon, the sea waters, rain, the fertility of women and of animals, plant life, man's destiny after death and the ceremonies of initiation."

216. Quoted in Ball, *The Devil's Doctor*, 263.

217. Ibid., 281.

218. Although Spanish usually prefers *el mar* and reserves *la mar* for more poetic or elevated usage, there is a special use of *la mar* to mean "a lot" or "very" in such phrases as *la mar de guapa* (exceedingly pretty) or *la mar de contento* (extremely happy).

which is what people call her in Spanish when they love her. Sometimes those who love her say bad things of her but they are always said as though she were a woman. Some of the younger fishermen ... spoke of her as *el mar* which is masculine. They spoke of her as a contestant or a place or even an enemy. But the old man always thought of her as feminine and as something that gave or withheld great favours, and if she did wild or wicked things it was because she could not help them. The moon affects her as it does a woman, he thought.[219]

In general, bodies of water seem to be simply too protean to be pinned down by any single gender. While the French have *la mer* but the masculine *l'océan* and the Germans *das Meer* and *der Ozean* but *die See* (as well as the masculine *der See* for lakes and lochs), in Hebrew and Arabic the words for sea and rivers are masculine.[220] While most rivers in Germany are feminine (*die Ruhr*, *die Mosel*, *die Donau*), perhaps the mother of all German rivers is famously masculine (*Vater Rhein* or Father Rhine), as are most non-German ones (*der Nil*, *der Ganges*) unless they happen to end in an –a or an –e (*die Wolga*, *die Loire*, *die Themse*). French too allows orthographic considerations (the presence or otherwise of a mute –e ending) to determine river gender: *le Rhin*, but *la Seine* and *la Tamise*, albeit with enough exceptions to induce quiet desperation (*le Rhône*, *le Danube*, *le Tibre*). In England, only the Derwent is unambiguously masculine.[221] The Thames seems particularly at sea as regards its gender. In its upper reaches – where it is still known as Isis – its waters are certainly feminine, but after the confluence or marriage of the Isis and the Thame at Dorchester the river adopts a masculine identity, perhaps suggesting that it is fierce, strong or grubby. Even though the Germans and French – unlike the Spanish (with *el Támesis*) – feminize him as *die Themse* and *la Tamise*, there can be little doubt that the big, ugly, malodorous Father Thames of the 19th century was very much a Real Man along the lines of Father Rhine.

Where waters are wrathful, savage or feral, there is a greater tendency to call them male. Towards the climax of *Moby Dick*, the narrator refers to the "masculine sea" with its "strong, troubled, murderous

219. Hemingway, *The Old Man and the Sea*, 19-20.
220. See Farber, 43.
221. Ackroyd, 29. On the nuptials of Isis and Thame, as depicted in Spenser's *The Faerie Queene* and elsewhere, see ibid., 28.

thinkings."[222] Where seductive and treacherous, it is the feminine that is more commonly evoked. Above all, water transgresses the categories: it is best understood as bisexual or perhaps trisexual or possibly even polymorphous in its sexuality, a site of pure potential. Yet this transgressive unpredictability returns us to the stereotype of female inconstancy and the threat of subversion. Like Mother Nature in general, women and water have persistently represented flux and instability, the enigmatic and the unfathomable. The problem is pinning them down, fixing their position and controlling or stemming the flow. Obsessed with mastery, the language of early modern science was dominated by imagery that presented Mother Nature – and by extension the waters that pass through her – as a seductive but ultimately vexatious female, to be unrelentingly pursued, harassed, laid bare, and finally vanquished and penetrated.[223] The same impulse is present in what has been described as "an almost Freudian fixation"[224] on the part of hydraulic engineers with "taming" the unruly flow of rivers by the construction of dams. The current preference for "soft engineering" – working *with* nature instead of trying to bridle or dominate her/it – is an echo of late-20th-century changes in sexual politics.

The intimate relationship between water and woman is reflected in deities such as Artemis and Aphrodite of the Greeks or the river goddesses of Hinduism. The link may likewise be perceived in Christianity, where God is patriarchal and luminous and the various Mary-figures are the closest we come to female deity.[225] The first such figure is the Old Testament figure of Miriam, sister of Moses, whose name is the Hebrew equivalent of the Greek *Maria* or *Mariam* (both of which occur in the Gospels).[226] The link with water is suggested by the very name, which has commonly been

---

222. Melville, *Moby Dick*, 505 (ch. 132). Here, notably, it is the air that is described as feminine. Perhaps it was in their capacity as air rather than as water that hurricanes were originally given women's names (such as Carol, Edna and Hazel in stormy 1954). As Robert Kandel puts it, however, "since 1979 gender equality in hurricane naming has supplanted the era of *femmes fatales* that began in 1953" (Kandel, *Water from Heaven*, 150). Famous male hurricanes of recent years include Andrew and Mitch.

223. See Midgley, *Science as Salvation*, 77.

224. See Pearce, 160.

225. As Elaine Pagels expresses it (*The Gnostic Gospels*, 71), Mary may be venerated as the "mother of God," but she is never "God the Mother," on a par with "God the Father."

226. Pelikan, *Mary through the Centuries*, 16, 28. On Mary and Miriam, see 23-25.

interpreted as containing the sea in the form of the Hebrew word *yam* and meaning "sea of sorrow" or "waters of bitterness" (referring to the bitter plight of the Israelites or the brackish waters of the desert). Other proposed derivations include "drop of the waters," "myrrh of the sea" or "mistress of the sea."[227] Indeed, water plays such a central role in the story of Miriam (who looks upon her brother Moses from the banks of the Nile, who leads the celebrations by the Red Sea, and whose well – Miriam's Well – was said by the *midrash* to have kept drought at bay during the Exodus) that she has come to be seen as the "embodiment" of water.[228]

Early Christian thinkers were keen to explore the Old Testament for parallels that foreshadowed or amplified the few data to be found in the New, and the name they had in common made Miriam the most obvious prototype of Mary. Augustine accordingly interpreted Miriam's song of celebration at the Red Sea as prefiguring Mary "the leader of the heavenly choir" in praise of the Almighty.[229] The Qur'an actually conflates Mary and Miriam, referring to Mary the mother of Jesus as the "sister of Aaron."[230] A link with water underscores this conflation: just as Miriam was famously associated in Jewish thought with the well that bore her name and accompanied the Israelites during the Exodus, the Qur'an describes how the Lord provided Mariam in labour with a stream of water at her feet.

With time, moreover, a quirk of etymology lent the connection between Mariam (i.e. Mary or Miriam) and the waters of *yam* a further, nautical dimension that neatly accorded with the Christian notion of the ship of faith. Speculating on the name's roots, the 4th-century Church Father Jerome interpreted the Hebrew name *Miriam* to mean "drop of the

---

227. The etymologies are contentious. Further derivations link her to "rebelliousness" or being "well-nourished."

228. On Miriam see Exodus, 2:4, 15:20-21. On Miriam's Well, see for example Ginzberg, I.265.

229. See Pelikan, 28, 97.

230. In 19:28. Hostile Christians accused the Prophet of confusing Miriam and Mary – both of whom would have been called Mariam – even though the two women lived over a millennium apart. Muslim commentators have suggested that "sister of Aaron" simply means "of the tribe of Aaron" or "virtuous woman." Alternatively, the conflation of the two Mariams may be seen as signalling an intentional parallelism between Moses and Jesus, restoring Jesus to a succession of prophets that included Abraham, Moses and Mohammed himself. See Pelikan, 73-75. On the spring of water see the Qur'an, 19:24.

sea," which he rendered into Latin as *stilla maris*. By a slip of a scribe's pen, however, *stilla* (drop) was turned into *stella* (star), and Mary became the "star of the sea," the guide of mariners and the lodestar of voyagers, the Latin *mare* (sea) seeming to reinforce the link between Mary and the marine or maritime. This nautical metaphor reflects a timeless association of the sea with the unknown or unmapped, with uncharted waters both literal and figurative, and Mary the star of the sea came to represent not only navigational aid for sailors, but more general spiritual orientation through the stormy sea of life. Medieval poetry attached particular importance to this symbol of Mary as the lodestar of voyagers.[231]

That Christ himself was deeply associated with water on account of its symbolic powers of purification and regeneration[232] further influenced how the association of Mary with water was understood. Early Christians who sought to stress the divinity as opposed to the humanity of Christ argued that he had passed through the body of his mother Mary as water passes through a pipe: in these terms Mary was a mere medium or channel through which the divine water flowed.[233] On the other hand, her paradoxical status as the mother of God – a creature who begot her own Creator, *ouroboros*-like – led to appellations such as "the fountain from which the living fountain flows, the origin of the beginning."[234] In this sense, Mary was the very spring or source of the "living waters" that were Christ. In 19th-century France, the Virgin Mary became closely bound up with the miraculous waters of Lourdes, where she made a series of apparitions in 1858 and told the peasant girl Bernadette Soubiroux: "I am the Immaculate Conception."[235] If Rome is the head of the Roman Catholic Church, it has been suggested, then Lourdes – with its explicit Marian water-veneration – is its heart.[236]

231. Pelikan, 93-94. See also Stone (trans.), *Medieval English Verse*, 24, 28.
232. See below, chapter 4.
233. The early Christian heresy known as Docetism held that the humanity of Christ, his sufferings and death, were apparent rather than real. The idea was to exempt Christ from the abominations of carnality, epitomized by the processes of procreation and birth. The Church Fathers responded by emphasizing the *reality* of his birth from the Virgin Mary. See Pelikan, 50-52.
234. Ibid., 130.
235. See ibid., 182-84; on the doctrine of the Immaculate Conception, 189-200. The dogma of the Immaculate Conception, which refers to the question of whether or not Mary herself – not just Jesus – had been conceived and born in original sin, had been defined and imposed by the Roman Catholic Church just four years earlier.
236. Ibid., 184.

Theories linking Mary with the mother deities or water goddesses of paganism have tended to be dismissed as facile by Christian theologians,[237] yet there can be little doubt of the associations in the population imagination. Peter Ackroyd has argued for just such a correlation in the case of the Thames, the banks of which have more than 50 churches or chapels dedicated to Mary within a course extending just 215 miles. According to Ackroyd, Mary is just the most recent in a line of water goddesses that go back to the great mother goddesses of pre-Celtic belief and include the classical figure of Isis (the name given to the river's upper reaches). The river, he writes, "was in legend and superstition also associated with the virgin. Virgins would bathe in the Thames so that they might become fertile. ... So who better to bless the water than the Virgin herself?"[238]

Of course, the Virgin Mary or the Immaculate Conception is much too unambiguously *perfect* for any official or doctrinal association to have ever been possible: pagan goddesses of water or maternity were always more ambivalent figures. Yet the mother of God is by no means the only New Testament figure to bear the name Mary with its maritime associations. Interpreting the Virgin Mary and Mary Magdalene as complementary incarnations of the dual nature of femininity (virginity and harlotry, or motherhood and promiscuity), recent speculation has focused on the way Mary Magdalene – whose importance comes to light in the Gnostic texts – was subordinated to the blessed virgin as the archetypal feminine.[239] In the same way, the inconvenient idea that Jesus was married to Mary Magdalene – a wedding of male and female, light and water – is said to have been quietly swept under the theological carpet by early Christian misogynists. Reinforcing the link with water, popular legend has it that three Maries (including Mary Magdalene) fled to Gaul after the crucifixion of Jesus, emerging bedraggled from the Mediterranean Sea at what is now the town of Saintes-Maries-de-la-Mer in the wetlands of Provence.

In the orthodox Christian story the transgressive aspect of womanhood is played down, and the "other" Mary is only given a bit part. The association between water and female sexuality as a potentially threatening or subversive force has been much more in evidence in other

---

237. Ibid., 57-58.
238. Ackroyd, 93-94.
239. Medieval anti-Christian polemicists, by contrast, explicitly conflated the two Maries as a way of undermining the flawlessness of the virgin. See Pelikan, 73-74.

cultures. Take the ancient Greek figure of Artemis. Like her Roman counterpart Diana, Artemis was the goddess not only of chastity, the secrets of womanhood, and the moon with all its menstrual connotations, but also the hunt, vegetation and fertility. This link with the moon endowed her with power over the sea (as mistress of ebb and flow), moreover, and she was generally attended by 60 Oceanids.[240] All over the Peloponnese, where she was known as *Artemis Limnatis* or Artemis of the Lake, she supervised waters and luxuriant vegetation, and in parts of the peninsula her dances were wild and orgiastic. Combining chastity and a much more lascivious sexuality, therefore, Artemis embodied a duality parallel to that of the two Maries taken together. The darker side of her personality also came to the fore in the tale of Actaeon, who happened to catch sight of her bathing in the forest waters and tarried to watch. Artemis changed him into a stag, and had him ripped to pieces by his own mastiffs.

Aphrodite, the Greek goddess of love and sexual desire known as Venus to the Romans, was also intimately bound up with the watery element. According to one popular version of her birth, she was the daughter of the ancient sky god Uranus and thus one of the most senior figures of the Olympian pantheon. When Kronos castrated his father Uranus, he cast the severed genitals into the sea, where Uranus's semen combined with the foam of the ocean to engender beautiful Aphrodite ("foam-born"). Gentle breezes brought her ashore naked on a scallop shell, an image famously captured in a 1st-century wall painting from Pompeii.[241] Untainted by sexual union, Aphrodite Urania symbolized sacred love. Another version of her origins, by contrast, portrayed her as the offspring of Zeus's profligacy, in this case his liaison with the nymph Dione, daughter of Oceanus and Tethys. This Aphrodite represented profane love and sexual passion.

Again, therefore, an aquatic goddess proves to be cleft by a profound ambiguity, personifying chastity and licentiousness, marriage and harlotry, in-your-face fecundity and restrained femininity. Notably, it was water

240. Graves, I.85-86, speculates that the name *Artemis* may itself be derived from *themis*, meaning water. The Oceanids were the 3,000 nymphs begotten by the Titans Oceanus and Tethys, each one the patron of a particular ocean, river, lake, spring, pond or cloud.
241. See Scott Littleton, 170. Sometimes Aphrodite is thought of as the daughter of Uranus with Thalassa, the primordial sea-goddess who personified the Mediterranean.

that allowed her to have her cake and eat it,[242] for like Hera – the wife of Zeus – Aphrodite took an annual bath to renew her virginity. Goddess of chastity as she was, she thus also managed to enjoy an impressive stream of lovers that included Ares (the god of war, known to the Romans as Mars), Hermes (the Roman Mercury, with whom she produced Eros and Hermaphroditus) and Dionysus (by whom she conceived Priapus, the god with the unfeasibly large plonker). When her husband the fire-god Hephaestus (the Roman Vulcan) caught her in bed with Ares, he cast a wire net over the two of them, a symbol not only of a cuckold's vain attempts to capture and control exuberant femininity, but also – as Robert Graves suggests[243] – of her role as goddess of the sea and fishing.

In Hinduism there is a parallel association between the holy rivers and the female deities that personify them, goddesses such as Sarasvati, who embodies the legendary river once said to have run through north-west India. The sacred River Ganges is incarnated as the goddess Ganga, while the Narmada – sent forth by Shiva to release the world from evil – is also worshipped as a female divinity. Dedicated to Narmada, the following lines from a traditional Indian raga again highlight the deep connection between flowing water and the seductive womanhood that distracts dry ascetics from their arid reflections:

> From Shiva's penance you became water.
> From water you became a woman
> So beautiful that gods and ascetics
> Their loins hard with desire
> Abandoned their contemplations
> To pursue you.[244]

Such ambivalence, anathema to Christianity, is absolutely fundamental. Even though the name *Narmada* itself means "whore" in Sanskrit, the river is considered the most sacred one in India: "Oh damsel of the beautiful hips, / Evoker of *Narma*, lust, / Be known as Narmada, / Holiest of rivers."[245]

242. The Spanish term for "having one's cake and eating it" – *nadar y guardar la ropa* (which amounts to swimming without getting wet) – is particularly appropriate.
243. Homer, *The Odyssey*, 130-33. See Graves, I.67-73. Tellingly, the sea-god Poseidon was the only one of the gods who was not shaking and booming with "uncontrollable laughter" at the sight of her humiliation.
244. From Mehta, *A River Sutra*, 259.
245. Ibid. See also 143-44.

While light may be a recurrent symbol or expression of godhead, therefore, a universal association with purification and regeneration invests *water* with an equally divine nature. Notably, this applies not only to polytheistic systems such as the Greek pantheon or Hinduism – where bathing in the Ganga can procure salvation, and the very sight of the Narmada is enough to purify and cleanse the beholder – but also the monotheistic and patriarchal structures of Judaism, Christianity and Islam, which likewise ascribe to water the power to cleanse and purify. There is in this sense no clear-cut symbolic opposition between light and water, for both elements are simply too fluid – too protean – to be pinned down, instead intertwining more on the model of yin and yang. The primeval waters prior to creation may resemble undifferentiated darkness, returning to wreak death and destruction in the guise of the deluge, yet the waters associated with Jesus are waters of healing, purification and life.[246] Light may be a manifestation of divinity, yet fire is inextricably bound up with conceptions of hell, the diabolical and an unpleasant smell of sulphur.

The conception of a fiery, mephitic hell is derived, at least partially,[247] from the Jewish Gehenna, a rubbish dump on the outskirts of Jerusalem where not only garbage but also the corpses of animals and criminals were thrown into fires that were kept constantly alight for hygienic reasons. The term *Gehenna* came to symbolize an unappealing place and was a curse, for ending up on that fiery rubbish tip indicated a life at odds with the laws of Yahweh.[248] The function of fire here is thus one of purification – in a certain sense analogous to water – and rooted in sanitary considerations. This becomes clearer with the later, Roman Catholic concept of Purgatory, which represents a process of refinement (in a metallurgical sense) or cleansing as a preparation for heaven. The fires of Purgatory are like those of Hell, but have the considerable advantage of not lasting for ever.

Among Biblical literature, the pseudepigraphical (i.e. non-canonical) Book of Enoch, known as First Enoch and believed to have been written in the 1st century by Jewish refugees in Egypt, describes hell as a decidedly fiery location: "I saw columns of fire fall, beyond all measure of height and depth. And beyond that abyss I saw a place which

246. See below, chapter 4.
247. Another influence was the observation of volcanoes, which were cited by Tertullian as proving that a subterranean hell does exist.
248. See Turner, *The History of Hell*, 40ff. In fact, Jewish thought did not tend to dwell on the question of an afterlife.

had no firmament of the heaven above and no firmly founded place beneath it. There was no water on it and no birds; it was a horrible wasteland" (1 Enoch 17). Second Enoch, by contrast, adds water – albeit in frozen form – to the infernal picture: "There was no light but that of murky fire. It had a fiery river and the whole place is everywhere fire, everywhere frost and ice, thirst and shivering, while the fetters are cruel, and the angels fearful and merciless, bearing sharp weapons and merciless tortures" (2 Enoch 12).[249] A similar conjunction of ice and fire is also present in the ancient Norse conception of *Ragnarok*, the Destiny of the Gods, which will begin with the frosts and snow of a terrible winter called Fimbulwinter, feature some almost farcically spectacular carnage as the warring gods go about massacring one another, and end in conflagration and flooding. The Christian Hell – though generally depicted, as in the Book of Revelations (21:8), as a lake burning with fire and brimstone – in fact owes its name to the Norse goddess of death Hel, whose underground realm was a place of cold.

The underworld of the ancient Greeks, Hades, was dark, dank, marshy and joyless rather than fiery, featuring the poisonous River Styx[250] (which means "hateful") as well as various ominous-sounding tributaries such as Acheron ("woe"), Phlegethon ("burning") and Lethe ("oblivion"). Nor did the punishments meted out to evildoers in the region of Hades known as Tartarus necessarily involve combustion: watery torments proved every bit as popular. While Ixion did find himself tied to a fiery wheel for killing his future father-in-law and attempting to rape Hera, Tantalus, guilty of filicide, was condemned to be immersed up to his chin in water that disappeared the moment he made to quench his thirst, and the Danaides, who had murdered their husbands with hairpins, were set the task of using sieves to fill a bottomless container with water. Even today, human malice uses water to create hell on earth, with torturers around the world employing methods such as the "water cure" (forcing the victim to ingest great quantities of liquid), a technique now known as "waterboarding"[251] (pouring water over the face of an immobilized victim

249. Quoted in ibid., 44-45. See also Ginzberg, I.132.
250. It was said to dissolve any material except horses' hooves. According to other accounts, however, it could also bestow immortality – as almost occurred with Achilles, whose immersion failed to incorporate his heel.
251 .This goes back to the Spanish Inquisition, when it was known as the *tormento de toca*.

to induce a sensation of drowning) and the "Chinese water torture" (a sustained dripping on the victim's forehead).

Water and ice can clearly be just as infernal as fire. And while fire may be associated with conflagration, destruction and pain, it may equally symbolize life, warmth, civilization, inspiration, literal and metaphorical illumination, and – like water – purification and the removal of sin. As with water, moreover, human beings exist in a relationship of utter dependence upon fire: without the light and heat of the sun, we would simply not be here. These two most fundamental elements seem to reflect and echo one another, therefore, not only as foundations – each of them necessary, neither in itself sufficient – for life and civilization, but as protean shape-shifters that defy binary schemes. Witness the ancient Vedic god of fire, Agni.[252] As the messenger of the gods, Agni mediates between the human and the heavenly, symbolizing not only the fire of the sun and lightning but also the sacrificial fire that is lit in the domestic hearth. He is depicted as seven-tongued, has a thousand eyes and flaming hair. He also has two faces, one benevolent, the other malevolent, and "personifies all the gods, the power of the divine, immanent in all things."[253] Combustible though he may be, in the *Rig Veda* Agni is explicitly identified with the Child of the Waters, a spirit born of the watery depths, who resides in the water and hides there when fleeing from other gods. As lightning is born of the clouds, and the sun is mirrored in water, Agni thus reflects the "dialectic conjunction of fire and water."[254] One of the hymns describes how "[t]he young women, the waters, flow around the young god, making him shine and gazing solemnly upon him. With his clear, strong flames he shines riches upon us, wearing his garment of butter, blazing without fuel in the waters."[255]

In chemical terms, water is born of fire: the process of combustion involves a conversion of a fuel and oxygen to carbon dioxide and water (plus light and heat). Water, in turn, can extinguish fire, but in some of its myriad guises it can also nurture it. The idea of inflammable water takes us back, perhaps, to the combustible waters passed by Hennig Brand in the process of discovering phosphorus. It also recalls the "burning water," or *aqua ardens*, that 12th-century Italian alchemists – following in Arabic footsteps – produced by distilling wine, a liquid that burst into flame when

252. On Agni, see *The Rig Veda*, 97-118.
253. Bowker, 30.
254. Wendy Doniger O'Flaherty, in *The Rig Veda*, 105.
255. Ibid.

lit, but was also found to produce considerable conflagration in the human gullet.[256] One of the modern Spanish terms for brandy, *aguardiente*, continues to betray the fieriness of such "waters." To set the Thames on fire is to pull off an unusually impressive exploit,[257] but it was one notably achieved by the *Luftwaffe* in September, 1940, when it targeted the nearby docks and warehouses and in the process released a film of burning oil and rum onto the waters of the river. Pollution has had a similar effect. In 1866 the British Royal Commission on River Pollution reported that the Bradford Canal was so contaminated it could be set on fire (as the local children were discovering to their delight), and the second half of the 20th century witnessed major conflagrations on the Iset in Russia (1965), the Cuyahoga at Cleveland in the United States (1969) and the Volga.[258]

Fire and water are both so notoriously protean that it is impossible to ascribe definitive priority to one over the other. As the alchemists knew, a marriage of the two is central to the pursuit of the philosopher's stone. According to legend, the 8th-century Sufi master Rabi'a was reputed to carry in one hand a bowl of water and in the other a bowl of fire. When asked why, she explained: "I want to pour water into Hell and throw fire into Paradise so that these two veils [i.e. obstacles to the true vision of God] disappear and it becomes clear who worships God out of love, not out of fear of Hell or hope of Paradise."[259]

256. See Standage, 98.
257. See Ackroyd, 391, on a possible derivation of the expression, involving a sieve or *temse* used for sifting flour: "It was believed that a vigorous workman could make it ignite with constant friction against the flour-bin, and of an inefficient workman it was said that 'he will never set the temse on fire.'" See ibid., 211-12, on the bombing of the Thames.
258. See Ponting, 357.
259. Smith, *Rabi'a the Mystic and her Fellow-Saints*, xxvii; see also 98-99. Fire and water imagery pervade the symbolism associated with Rabi'a. Even though fire was identified in Sufi thought with anger (the "fire of wrath" as opposed to the "light of mercy"), Rabi'a was herself described as being "on fire with love." At the same time, her oratory was said to be like a "swamp of water from her tears" [of penitence and contrition]. See ibid., 41, 56.

2

Shape-Shifting and Reflection

We have already encountered the deep-seated association between water and mercury, with all its associations of shape-shifting and mutability. Any conception of water as the origin or underlying substance of the world also implies a capacity for self-transformation: it suggests, in short, that water can (and does) assume *any* form. This attribute is embodied most famously in the water-god and archetypal shape-shifter Proteus, the prophetic old man of the sea and shepherd of the sea's flocks. Although he came to be regarded as subject to the great sea-god Poseidon, his capacity to assume whatever shape he pleased led some to see him as a symbol for the original matter from which all was created. Graves interprets his name to mean "first man," i.e. *proto-man*.[260]

Proteus knew all things – past, present and future – but would always try to avoid revealing what he knew. To extract a prophecy from him it was necessary to catch him unawares and tie him down during his early-afternoon siesta, but even then he would resort to his powers of self-transformation to try and escape. Only when vanquished would Proteus return to his proper form and provide the truthful answer his interlocutors were seeking.[261] In fact, Proteus was just one of four sea gods referred to by Homer as "Old Men of the Sea," each of them shape-shifters endowed with the gift of prophecy or truth-telling. Closest to Proteus in his associations is Nereus.[262] Born of Pontos – the personification of the sea – and Gaia, the sea god Nereus is famous for having wrestled in his myriad forms with

260. Graves, I.128.
261. In Homer's *Odyssey*, Menelaus relates how, with his ships becalmed on the journey home from the Trojan War, he was told by the sea-nymph Eidoethea that the solution was to capture her father Proteus, who would tell him how to raise the wind to enable him to sail home. Disguised as seals, Menelaus and his followers duly jumped the snoozing Proteus, who tried to break free by becoming a lion, a serpent and even a flowing stream. But it was to no avail, and Proteus had no option but to tell Menelaus the truth about the murder of his brother Agamemnon, the death of Ajax, the stranding of Odysseus, as well as the sacrifice that was necessary to appease the gods and whip up a wind. See Homer, 72-78.
262. The other two are Phorcys and Glaucus.

Heracles, who was seeking advice on how to obtain one of the golden apples kept at the world's end by the Hesperides.[263] Nereus's daughters by the Oceanid Doris were beautiful water nymphs known as Nereids, and one of these, Thetis, proved to be a chip off the old block. Assailed during her midday sleep by "noble" Peleus – whom Zeus had decreed she should marry[264] – Thetis turned successively into fire, water, a lion, a snake and a huge, ink-squirting cuttlefish. But Peleus refused to let go and eventually had his way. Achilles would later be the product of their union.[265]

Closely associated with meteorological phenomena, the ancient Vedic deities that preceded Hinduism in India likewise tended to be protean in character. This applied to Agni, god of fire and lightning, but also to Indra, the supreme deity of the Indo-Aryans, who not only dispensed rain and generated fertility and fruitfulness, but was a warrior god with countless forms, capable of assuming any shape he pleased. One such feat was to turn himself into the hair of a horse's tail in the process of slaying the demonic dragon Vritra, who had stolen all the water and prevented the monsoon from breaking: this releasing of the waters was considered the greatest of Indra's heroic deeds.[266] Another Vedic storm god was Rudra, who was commonly identified with Agni or Indra in the context of the monsoon rains. Like the meteorological phenomena he symbolized, Rudra too was an ambiguous figure, one side of his character signalling fertility, healing and life, the other side wrathful destruction.

With the emergence of Hinduism in post-Vedic times, Rudra in particular gradually came to be identified with the great Hindu deity Shiva, to whom he bequeathed his ferocity.[267] Shiva was originally one of the Hindu *Trimurti* or three forms of deity (Brahma embodying the force that creates; Vishnu the goodness that maintains equilibrium; and Shiva the fire that destroys), but to his followers he has come to embody all three

---

263. Graves, II.145-46. This was the eleventh of his twelve labours.
264. Graves, I.268-76. In fact, Zeus would have married Thetis himself, but the Fates had prophesied that any son born to Thetis would eventually become stronger than his father. Annoyed that she had rejected his advances, moreover, he decided that she should never marry an immortal.
265. Homer's *Odyssey* describes Thetis's grief when Achilles fell at Troy. She "came up from the sea with the deathless Sea-Nymphs, and a mysterious wailing rose from the waters," causing panic among the soldiers until they were steadied by wise words from Nestor. See Homer, 364.
266. *Rig Veda*, 148-56.
267. There is also believed to have been a continuity between Indra and Shiva.

aspects in one: he is creator, preserver and destroyer. While ostensibly symbolizing fire as Vishnu represents water, therefore, in fact both of them embody both. Above all, Shiva is a thoroughly complex deity, combining opposites such as sensuality and renunciation, fire and water, male and female, life and death. He may manifest himself accordingly as a reclusive ascetic, an erotic dancer, a fertility god, a benign protector or a fearsome destroyer. In one poem, the 12th-century Hindu reformer Basava, a devotee of Shiva as "Lord of the Meeting Rivers," refers to Shiva's eighty-four hundred thousand faces.[268] Shiva has especially close links with the holy River Ganges, which bestows *Svarga* – the paradise of Indra – upon those who bathe in it. The river is said to spring from the toe of Vishnu, and flow from heaven to earth through the matted hair of Shiva. Beautiful Ganga, the divine personification of the river, was initially a consort of Vishnu, but – according to one version of events – Vishnu's three wives bickered so much that Ganga was passed on to Shiva, and Sarasvati to Brahma. On the left bank of the Ganges lies the ancient holy city of Benares, formerly called Varanasi and said to be the home of Shiva, who is here worshipped as Visvanatha, the Lord of the Universe.

While Shiva's complexity stems in part from the apparently contradictory nature of his many roles, Vishnu's protean nature comes to light in his *avatars*, i.e. his earthly manifestations or incarnations. He is often depicted either as seated on a lotus blossom, or reclining on the 100-headed serpent Ananta-Shesha on the primordial waters, for this is the guise he assumes after the destruction of the universe and prior to its subsequent recreation. In a reflection of the evolution of life on earth, the earliest of Vishnu's ten avatars in the present age took aquatic form, saving humanity from watery chaos. The first was Matsya the fish-man, who rescued Manu, the father of the human race, from a great flood; the second was Kurma the tortoise, who played a pivotal role as a support in recovering the divine drink soma, or *amrita*, from the Ocean of Milk; Vishnu's third avatar, Varaha the boar, rescued the Earth from the bottom of the cosmic ocean, where it had been dragged by the demon Hiranyaksha. Later avatars took on human form, such as Krishna, the eighth avatar, and Gautama Buddha, the ninth. The tenth, Kalki, has yet to occur and will signal the end of the present age of the world.

268. *Speaking of Siva*, 81. Basava founded the reformist movement known as Virasaivism, which rejected all forms of inequality, violence, ritualism and taboo. In the words of Harihara, his 15th-century biographer: "Love of Siva cannot live with ritual." Quoted in ibid., 62.

There is clearly an important distinction to be drawn between the tricky, shape-shifting mutability of such figures as Proteus on the one hand and the multiple, contradictory facets of Shiva or the avatars of Vishnu on the other.[269] In fact, these different levels of proteanism echo and reflect different aspects of the mercurial nature of water. Of course, water is not the only one of the four traditional elements that is essentially protean. While water takes the shape of whatever vessel contains it, air is equally – if not more – adaptable. "Wind is almost anything you want it to be," according to Lyall Watson.[270] "There are few things as steady or as changeable, as fierce or as gentle, as unstable or as undeviating, as light or as bold, as wroth, as balmy, or as protean as wind." Fire is the epitome of the shape-shifter, the flicker of its flames as elusive in form as it proved enigmatic in composition. Yet it is the myriad or multi-layered nature of water's proteanism that sets it apart: its reflective proteanism.

In symbolic terms, for a start, there is its multivalence and polysemy: water can mean different things to different people or at different times: purity or contamination, birth or death, heaven or hell, thirst or drowning. In pragmatic terms, its multiple significance is reflected in its manifold uses in agriculture (irrigation), domestic activity (washing, cooking), leisure (swimming, fishing), and industry, where it has applications in areas as diverse as power generation, cement production, textile manufacture, paper-making, coal-slurrying, or the preparation of food and beverages. In conceptual terms, water's links with underlying origins as well with the unfathomed and unmapped depths of the ocean – i.e. with the hidden or unknown – have invited the human imagination to run riot and, traditionally at least, turned the uncharted sea into the perfect

269. There is another important divinity associated with water and rain who exhibits a protean nature characterized by contradictory manifestations. This is Quetzalcoatl, or Plumed Serpent, one of the most highly venerated deities in the ancient Aztec pantheon. He was not only worshipped as a creator god and – as Ehecatl – god of wind, bringer of rain, fertility, vegetation and regeneration, but under the name of Ce Acatl he was also identified as the Morning Star, the enemy of rain and the harbinger of drought. When the 16th-century Spanish conquistadors under Hernán Cortés entered Quetzalcoatl's sacred city, Cholula, the locals were convinced that the lord of waters would protect them, sending a flood to drown the invaders if they desecrated his temple. Under the subsequent influence of the Christian tale of death and resurrection, the Aztec belief in Quetzalcoatl's second coming led to his identification with Jesus. See Scott Littleton, 558-61.
270. Quoted in Rupp, 158.

dwelling-place for monsters and water-spirits, projections of a culture's fears, frustrations and desires. The *idea* of water, as we shall see, seems malleable enough to assume whatever shape we impose upon it.

In chemical terms, water's status as a near-universal solvent – the fact that so many substances dissolve in it – endows it with an unparalleled capacity for self-transformation, in turn inviting speculation on the mysterious or even miraculous curative properties it might possess. In physical terms, the fact that it is the only substance to occur at ordinary temperatures on Earth in all three states of matter – solid, liquid and gas – opens up a further realm of perpetual self-metamorphosis and motion. Its cyclical nature manifests itself most obviously in the hydrological cycle, i.e. the constant movement of water between the earth and the atmosphere, the endlessly self-repeating process of evaporation, atmospheric accumulation, precipitation, terrestrial flow and then renewed evaporation.[271] This, in turn, allows water to be associated equally with what is high and what is low, with up and down, deep and shallow – as well as all their symbolic connotations. In a different form, water's circularity comes to light as the thermohaline circulation, the flow of ocean currents driven by differential temperature and salinity levels, which constitutes a source of global heat redistribution as great as that of the atmosphere. The circular flow of our bodily sea-water – the blood circulation – likewise regulates the workings of the human organism.

Water's tendency to evaporate or to drip or flow away, moreover, endows it with a shape-shifting elusiveness seemingly purpose-made to frustrate human efforts to capture it or pin it down. The Spanish expression *echar agua en una cesta* – to throw water in a basket – denotes an activity considered hopeless, futile or to no avail, such as working on a holiday. It might also be used to describe the activities of water companies such as the English firm Wessex Water, which loses more than two billion litres a month in leaks (and attempts to compensate for this by pumping millions of litres of water from local rivers and aquifers). The water leaking from mains pipes in England would be enough to cover the needs of half the

---

271. The very existence of the hydrological cycle, writes Philip Ball (H_2O, 26), is due to the special capacity of water to occur equally well as a solid, liquid or gas under the conditions that obtain on our planet. In this, water differs from almost everything else on earth: virtually all the "non-aqueous fabric" of the planet's surface persists in the same physical state over time, gases (such as oxygen and nitrogen) remaining gases and solids (such as rocks and stones) remaining solid.

country's households.[272] By the same token, the amount of water that evaporates annually from Lake Nasser in Egypt, the second-largest man-made reservoir in the world, would suffice to fill every tap in England: it is estimated that between 10 and 16 cubic kilometres of water are lost each year from the water's surface, roughly a quarter of the average annual flow of the Nile into the reservoir.[273] By whatever means, water is constantly decamping – flowing out of reach, eluding classification, escaping use, transgressing national boundaries. And we are constantly chasing its coat-tails, for without it we wither, shrivel and die.

It is generally water in its liquid state – as a flow – that is most intimately linked with the possibility of life, both human and non-human. Yet water in this form is only part of the endless terrestrial cycle that includes glacial ice, snow and frost, hail and sleet, rain and drizzle, lakes and ponds, rivers and streams, wetlands and marshes, oceans and aquifers, clouds, fog, steam, water vapour and the early morning dew, not to mention the 1,000 cubic kilometres of water passing through the world's plants and animals at any one time.[274] All this water – solid, liquid or gas – is constantly assuming new shapes or guises, gyrating, eddying or flowing, finding a new vessel to fill or leaking from an old one. Its most impalpably protean form is as clouds, with their shadowy swathes of liquid or frozen water and an average life-span of no more than ten minutes. These nebulous apparitions may come as wraith-like cirrus or fluffy cumulus, threatening cumulonimbus or implacably dull stratus, yet – as cloud expert Gavin Pretor-Pinney points out – attempts at pigeon-holing anything so mutable and ephemeral will always tend to be self-defeating.[275] Cumulus clouds, he writes, are "shaped like elephants, cats, Albert Einstein and Bob Marley." The stratocumulus is "not unlike the pop singer, Cher, at the height of her costume-changing stage routines –

---

272. See Pearce, 26-30. In the dry summer of 2005, Thames Water – which supplies London – admitted that it was losing 100 litres a day for every home it supplied.
273. See ibid., 162-63. Russian hydrologist Igor Shiklomanov has calculated that worldwide a total of 350 cubic kilometres of water disappears through reservoir evaporation every year.
274. See ibid., 33. The flow of water through living organisms is itself mind-boggling. A single, sweaty oak tree transpires 200 to 300 gallons of water a day.
275. Pretor-Pinney, *The Cloudspotter's Guide*, 96-97: "clouds pay little attention to the rules of behaviour we presumptuously ascribe to them. Chaotic to their misty core, they do their best to confound our attempts at classification."

always nipping off stage to reappear in a more fantastical outfit."[276] And while clouds may be "expressions of the atmosphere's moods," which "can be read like those of a person's countenance," they also reflect the person viewing them: they are "the Rorschach images of the sky – abstract forms onto which we project our imaginations."[277]

Ice, by contrast, might appear the very opposite, seeming to hold on to its shape and freeze time in mid-flow. Glaciers can be virtually as old as the hills they plough through, and by drilling to great depths scientists have now recovered Antarctic ice that dates back at least 750,000 years.[278] Yet mountaineers, with their acutely developed sense of the aesthetics of ice, have repeatedly expressed their wonder at the myriad shapes and designs it can form. Marvelling at the landscape of "ice-buildings" among the Savoy glaciers of the Alps, Marc Bourrit wrote in 1774: "We only have to change our situation to make it resemble whatever we please."[279] Each traveller, in the words of the modern-day writer Robert Macfarlane, "saw what he chose to see in this visually biddable world. ... Ice could be sculpted by the sun and by the perceiving mind into almost any conceivable shape: a pagoda, an elephant, a fortress." Snow is characterised by a similar mutability. It is, notes Macfarlane, "the disguise artist of the mountains. It can rock benignly down through the air in flakes as big and soft as duck down, or be fired from the clouds in shotgun-pellets of hail. It can lie in neat windrows, or in irregular waves."[280] It also does a special line in transforming the landscape, creating a new, enchanted world, wiping out traces and footsteps, and generally helping people lose their bearings. In practical as well as aesthetic terms, moreover, ice is an unusually slippery customer, displaying a bone-breaking lack of friction that can nonetheless gives hours of pleasure to skiers, ice-skaters and tobogganists.[281]

276. Ibid., 10, 96.
277. Ibid., 11, 122.
278. See Macdougall, *Frozen Earth*, 177-78.
279. Quoted in Robert Macfarlane, *Mountains of the Mind*, 220.
280. Ibid., 217.
281. Ice offers 20-30 times less frictional resistance to motion than most other solids, lubricating itself with a microscopic film of water. Another aspect of ice's versatility is the variety of different crystal structures or polymorphs it exhibits. Whereas most solids may present two or three different structures at different pressures (the graphite form of carbon, for example, may at very high pressures be transformed into the denser, diamond form), scientists have already identified 12 distinct crystal structures on compressing ice. These are known as ice-I, ice-II, and so on. See Ball, *H_2O*, 181-88.

Water and ice also function as *agents* of change and transformation. In many parts of Europe, irresistible glaciers – or rather the rock debris embedded in their underbellies – were responsible for hewing out the contours of the landscape, carving out mountains and sculpting great U-shaped valleys with their arêtes, corries and cirques. Rivers too are incessantly wearing away at their beds, reshaping and fine-tuning the planet's topography. It is estimated that an average total of between 2.7 and 4.6 cubic kilometres of sediment weighing close to fifteen billion tons is carried from land to sea each year, an agglomeration of silts, clays, pebbles and stones that ceaselessly resculptures the landscape and can end up – given five or six million years – scouring out gorges as gargantuan as the Grand Canyon.[282] The world's waters are tirelessly transporting other substances too, whether as blood bearing oxygen to the cells of living bodies, sap taking dissolved minerals from the root system to the leaves of plants, or canals and rivers carrying human freight to its destination. As a near-universal solvent that is itself in permanent flux, water serves as the lubricant for what is known as "biogeochemical cycling," constantly conveying vital nutrients such as carbohydrates or nitrates from one ecosystem to another. Water, suggests Ball, is what ultimately "makes the world go round."[283]

Given its tendency to dissolve other substances, indeed, "pure" water is a rarity. The minerals that water picks up from soils and rocks as it journeys through and over the planet's lithosphere endow water with a thousand further faces – or tastes – often dissimulated by the medium's deceptive transparency. Captivated by the proteanism he saw in water, Leonardo da Vinci wrote:

> And so it is now sharp and now strong, now acid and now bitter, now sweet and now thick or thin, now it is seen bringing damage or pestilence and then health or, again, poison. So one might say that it changes into as many natures as are the different places through which it passes. And as the mirror changes with the colour of its objects so this changes with the nature of the place where it passes: health-giving, harmful, laxative, astringent, sulphurous, salt, sanguine, depressed, raging, angry, red, yellow, green, black, blue, oily, thick, thin.[284]

282. Nagle, 27. A quarter as much again is believed to be transported in solution rather than as suspended sediment.
283. See Ball, H_2O, 27.
284. Leonardo da Vinci, *Notebooks*, 21-22.

Sulphates, chlorides, bicarbonates of sodium or potassium, and oxides of magnesium or calcium are the most common solutes in the planet's surface and groundwater, yet domestic sewage and industrial wastes are making their presence ever more keenly felt. The range of mineral waters, each provided with its characteristic measure of mineral salts or gases that make it desirable for therapeutic or gastronomic purposes, testifies to the subtlety of water's multiple personality. Classified as alkaline or saline, arsenical or chalybeate, sulphurous or acidulous, each type has an identity and character of its own. The sheer variety of possibilities was famously captured in a legendary *Two Ronnies* sketch in which Ronnie Barker's pub landlord reels off a seemingly never-ending selection of waters that soon develops an alliterative rhythm of its own (Alpine mineral water, Ireland stream water, Windermere lake water, Canada dry water, Red Indian running water, French Perrier water, Yorkshire Terrier water) and becomes marginally less enticing (babies' hot water, babies' pot water, babies' bathwater, murky water, dirty water, squirty water …). He also has water on the rocks, on the knee and, not surprisingly, on the brain. Lager is used for washing the glasses.

Water has other, hidden faces. Many public supplies of drinking water contain not only chlorine for disinfection, but also fluorides, which are reputed to be good for the teeth. In excessive concentrations, however, fluorides can cause crippling deformation of the bones and eventual anaemia, kidney failure, muscle degeneration and cancer. Tens of millions of people are currently believed to be suffering from fluoride poisoning in India. Arsenic is another such cumulative poison, slowly killing millions of Bangladeshi people who have no option but to drink well water that is laced with it.[285] Duplicitous as it is, water can accommodate toxins and contaminants, carcinogenic minerals and corrosive acids; it can spread germs and provide a breeding ground for parasites. As Leonardo realized, water's amoral proteanism makes its role notoriously double-edged when it comes to human health.

For all its natural – at times treacherous – transparency, water's protean character also shows itself in the varieties of colour that can be associated with it. Maritime geography generally distinguishes four categories of region: along with riverine waters, these are the brown water of the littoral area, the green water further out to sea, and the blue water of the deep. It is because over two-thirds of the Earth's surface is covered by

285. See Caldecott, 161-63; Pearce, 72-78.

water that our planet – to a non-planet-dweller – is the blue planet. White water, by contrast, is a flow of water – such as rapids – characterized by its broken foamy surface; glacial melt-waters also tend to acquire a milky-white coloration on account of the rock flour they contain, the remains of stones and boulders triturated by the slowly moving ice; "white coal" has been a common term for the water used to generate hydroelectric power. Poets such as Pope and Spenser have traditionally lauded the "silver" Thames, an idealized association with pomp and magnificence that conveniently overlooked the cloacal brownness of its tributaries.[286] The Yellow River in China is named after the yellow-coloured silt that makes it the world's muddiest river. Roughly a million tons of the stuff flows down the river annually, making it 70 times more muddy than the Mississippi, which is itself affectionately known as the "Big Muddy."[287]

Black water rivers,[288] which move slowly through marshland or heavily forested areas, in fact tend to be tea- or coffee-coloured rather than black, acquiring their colour from the decaying, tannin-rich vegetation along their course. The Rio Negro, which feeds the Amazon, is the most famous such river,[289] while the black-sounding but relatively clear-flowing Niger is in fact a red herring – as indeed are both the Black Sea and the Red Sea, whose names have nothing to do with the colour of their water. (One conjectured etymology is that "black" and "red" in this case refer to the points of the compass, denoting north and south respectively.) The term "red tide" is also a misnomer, for the harmful algal blooms to which it is commonly applied are neither tidal nor necessarily red. However, blood-red water may be found wherever there is pollution from an iron mine. Our blood itself is essentially iron-tinted seawater, obtaining its

286. See Ackroyd, 337. Ackroyd's own description of the river's variety of hue includes its "silvery sheen," "deepest green," "muddy brown," "dark blue," as well as its "absolute clearness," its blackness or darkness, and an indescribable non-colour no-one has ever satisfactorily been able to name (ibid., 300-1).
287. See Pearce, 129-44, on the Yellow River. The Chinese, writes Pearce, have a phrase "when the river runs clear," which denotes that eagerly awaited time in the future when English pigs are also due to take to the air and Spanish frogs turn hairy.
288. Black water is also a term commonly used to designate heavily polluted domestic waste water. Its less contaminated counterpart is grey water, which proceeds from activities such as dish-washing and laundry.
289. There are also rivers called Rio Negro in Argentina and Uruguay. On the ecology of black and white rivers, see Caldecott, 91-93, 123.

colour from the protein haemoglobin which binds oxygen to its iron atoms and obligingly transports it around the body.[290] The Colorado River, which flows from the Rocky Mountains to the Gulf of California, takes its name from the Spanish *colorado*, meaning reddish-coloured and referring to the ruddy brown colour of the water's suspended mineral sediments. There are also a number of Red Rivers in the United States, while in Catalonia the blushing Llobregat derives its appellation from the Latin *rubricado*. In England, the Cornish town of Redruth (which is Cornish for "red ford") and the nearby Red River at Godrevy presumably owe their names to the region's traditional tin-mining industry and the toxic legacy of heavy metals that were flushed from its mines.[291] Particularly mysterious are the red rains – often as strongly coloured as blood – reported to have fallen on parts of the southern Indian state of Kerala in the second half of 2001, the origin of which has been the focus of ongoing speculation.

One of the most emblematic images of water's protean nature is the spectrum-spanning rainbow produced by the refraction and reflection of the sun's rays as they pass through rain or mist, in turn symbolizing nebulous or shimmering illusions. Iris, the ancient Greek personification of the rainbow, was said by Hesiod to be born of the sea-god Thaumas and the ocean nymph Electra. Often represented as supplying the clouds with the water required to irrigate the world, Iris was a messenger of the gods and as such closely associated with the figure of Hermes (or the Latin Mercury), who was also a divine messenger, as well as a trickster and patron of thieves.

Like water, shape-shifting tricksters defy the dictates of property and propriety, refusing to be pinned down and made to behave. In this

290. While vertebrate animals such as human beings use haemoglobin for oxygen transportation, other animals employ different carriers. Arthropods such as insects and molluscs have haemocyanin, which uses copper instead of iron and as a result is blue rather than red.

291. In the 1990s, the final demise of the industry gave rise to a further, spectacular episode of red-river pollution in Cornwall, when the closing of the mine at Wheal Jane, near Falmouth, left the Carnon River both red and dead. As Roger Deakin describes (*Waterlog*, 135-36), in two months over 10 million gallons of heavily contaminated water flooded down towards Cornwall's beautiful south coast. Besides copper, zinc, cadmium and arsenic, the waters included large quantities of iron, "which is what turned Restronguet Creek rust-red as the toxic flood bled iron hydroxide into the sea down the Carnon River." The only thing not to turn red, laments Deakin, were the faces of those responsible, who got off scot-free.

sense, they embody a deep, possibly anarchic freedom: the only laws they obey are the laws of their own dynamics. This is manifestly the case with rivers, which transgress national borders and cock a snook at administrative boundaries. Quietly unremitting in their flow, river waters epitomize the liberty of liquid. While land, fixed and stable as it is, has lent itself to being divided up and parcelled out as private property, running water – refusing to stay still – has traditionally resisted ownership and been regarded as a common asset exempt from individual claims to exclusive proprietorship. In an international context, where competing communalities may be invoked, problems seem inevitable: worldwide, some 269 river systems cross national frontiers, leading to hundreds of potential conflicts between the claims of upstream and downstream users.[292]

It was as an embodiment of freedom that rivers came to be viewed as something to be tamed, shackled and controlled.[293] Where the mastery of nature was the dominant ideology, the idea was that water was there to be put to use, whether for private gain or the public good. By association, water-people – people who worked or dwelled on rivers or marshland – were commonly considered to be naturally unruly or insubordinate, and likewise in need of "taming." From medieval times through to the 19th century, the boatmen of the Thames were renowned for their wild manners and colourful language: "water language" and "water wit" were terms given to the fruity vernacular of watermen, which could frequently

292. According to the United Nations, 158 international river basins could prove to be flashpoints for conflicts. See Black, *The No-Nonsense Guide to Water*, 19, 125-28. Disputes may be intranational as well as international, moreover, between upstream and downstream regions within a single nation.
293. The dialectic of flow and control is no straightforward matter. Romantic river-lovers and hardy outdoor swimmers may lament even the swimming pool as an artefact of control (a "machine for swimming in," as Iris Murdoch put it), fettering flow and making it safe and serviceable. They may deplore aquaculture, the farming of fish in cages, which now accounts for almost a third of the world's fish catch. Zealous technophiles, by contrast, may marvel at the ingenuity of civilization. Pragmatists are likely to acknowledge their functionality, perhaps sigh wearily, and accept them both as the most practical, utilitarian solutions currently available. Such pragmatism applies at best when the fish farming is organic and environmentally sustainable, and confining ourselves to the point of view of the species that we happen to be. On the destruction caused by non-organic, large-scale industrial fish farming – the massive quantities of pesticides, antibiotics, disinfectants and uric acid that are dumped in rivers and the sea – see Goodall, *Harvest for Hope*, 121-30. Not even pragmatists can justify this.

turn subversive and irreverent.[294] The river seemed to lend itself both to lawlessness and to periodic revelry and licence. As Peter Ackroyd explains, "the river actively worked against hierarchy and division of all kinds, particularly because water is a dissolving and unifying element.... All the divisions and distinctions of dry land are washed away and erased."[295] Further, river waters have enjoyed a timeless association with idling and reverie, i.e. with freedom from time and the workaday world. River banks remain the perfect place for day-dreaming and drifting, for allowing the mind to escape the shackles of logic and utility. Blurring fixed contours and distorting figures and forms, water itself is a dream-like element. Romantic thought conceived of genius as an untamed river, an exuberant flood or torrent, as opposed to the placid canals and rectified waterways of mediocrity.[296]

The oceans too have often been bound up with symbolism of freedom. To follow the sea has been to flee the burdens and bonds of life on terra firma. In the 19th century, the emergence of the seaside as an escape from drab city-life provided an opportunity for periodic liberation that found expression in marital indiscretion and naughty-but-niceness and was reflected in popular song: "You can do a lot of things at the seaside that you can't do in town."[297] The oceans themselves have traditionally resisted appropriation. The principle of the "freedom of the seas" was formulated in the early 17th century by the Dutch jurist Hugo Grotius, whose treatise *Mare Liberum* proposed that the high seas were an international domain, free to be used by any nation for purposes of seafaring trade, but belonging to none of them. According to this principle, territorial waters under the jurisdiction of a particular state only cover an area extending a specified distance from that state's coastline (traditionally a distance of three nautical miles, though now generally more); beyond this area lie international waters, which are open to nationals of any state for purposes of fishing and navigation.

Yet the concept of "freedom" is inherently vulnerable to abuse. In a maritime context, it has meant that seafarers could blithely plough

---

294. Ackroyd, 175-76.
295. Ibid., 117-19. On the drunkenness and sexual licence associated with the river, see 247, 259-60.
296. See for example Goethe's *The Sorrows of Young Werther*. In Werther's letter of 26 May (Book I), ditches and dykes symbolize the caution and control he associates with bourgeois dullness and complacency.
297. See Sprawson, *The Swimmer as Hero*, 29; also Staveacre, *Slapstick!* 142-46.

the seas massacring fish, whales or seals with no consideration of who
– if anyone – "owned" the resources in question. The result has been the
reckless desolation of fragile ecosystems in a realm seemingly beyond
public awareness, control or jurisdiction. Technological advances make
the threat more pressing than ever. In practice, maritime freedom has thus
signified the freedom to over-exploit what would now be regarded as "the
common heritage of humankind." Left to its own devices, freedom has
turned into a parody of freedom, and international regulation is necessary
to put a halt to the decimation of species and the wanton destruction of the
marine environment.[298]

The welfare of the planet's waters, with the freedom they
symbolize, is thus under threat from two directions: first, from a *lack* of
control when it comes to protecting marine life and the marine environment
or providing drinking-water and sanitation; and second, from an *excess*
of control when it comes to shackling rivers or draining wetlands. This
blind, bureaucratic faith in the fixity of concrete to regulate the protean
unpredictability of flow has led to an "orgy of dam-building"[299] that has
already lumbered us with some 45,000 large dams (dams at least five
storeys tall) and is believed by geophysicists to have altered "the speed
of the earth's rotation, the tilt of its axis, and the shape of its gravitational
field."[300] Yet the pathological fixation on the repression of flow is also
causing rivers – and displaced river-people – to rattle their chains in anger.
Just as a vacuous or amoral freedom ends up working to the detriment of
the defenceless and voiceless, a megalomanic obsession with controlling
and managing what is naturally fluid and protean – whether on the part
of politicians, bureaucrats or engineers – likewise proves destructive and
unsustainable.

298. A parallel degradation of the concept of "freedom" has characterized the provision of drinking water too, where the threat of lawlessness comes from an ideology that defines freedom in purely economic rather than moral, ethical, social or
political terms. In recent decades, the idea of drinking water as a communal asset
– freely available for everyone to satisfy their basic needs – has been undermined
by an ideology of globalized "free" trade for which water is just another private
good, to be extracted and traded with a view to making profits in accordance with
market forces. Freedom has been turned into a caricature of freedom.
299. Black, *The No-Nonsense Guide to Water*, 115.
300. Leslie, 4.

* * * * *

Leonardo saw that water's protean nature was not just a matter of shape-shifting elusiveness, but also to do with its mirror-like or reflective qualities.[301] This reflectiveness is not only to be understood literally, as its capacity to throw back an image, but also metaphorically, as its polymorphous receptiveness to the ideas and concepts, fears and hopes, that we project onto it. In consequence of water's deeper proteanism, there is a sense in which we see in water what we want to see in it. Just as we may project Bob Marley, Cher or a herd of elephants onto a passing cloud or a form carved out of ice, so the legendary creatures of the seas reflected man's aspirations and anxieties in the face of the great unknown, while the elevation of water to a panacea or a cure-all for the ills of civilization tells us as much about the ills of civilization and our perception of them as about water.[302]

A special feature of water, therefore, is that it also seems to imitate, echo or reflect some of humankind's own more special features. Many of water's qualities conspire to make it appear animated, imbued with vitality. Constantly in motion, it "speaks" or "laughs" or "makes music" as it dances along. It heals, cleanses, quenches thirst, and brings withered vegetation back to life. In more meditative moments, it reflects both the world and the reflective observer, who may in turn reflect on this reciprocated reflection. It may be all transparency and limpidity, yet on other occasions hide untold secrets in its murky depths. It has been likened to the human spirit or soul,[303] but is often associated with the self at its most soggily carnal and with its darkest, most hidden or taboo operations. The Uruguayan poet Juana de Ibarbourou wondered whether in an earlier life – prior to flesh and blood –

301. See Leonardo da Vinci, 21-22, 47.
302. The same presumably applies to this piece of writing, which may end up telling the reader as much about "R. G." – whoever he is – as about water. But I hope not.
303. See Theodor and Wolfram Schwenk, *Water: The Element of Life*, 11: "Many of water's qualities … show a distinct relationship to soul and spiritual attributes in human beings." For Shelley, the river is a natural image of human consciousness, fluid and free: "Rivers are not like roads," he writes, "the work of the hands of man; they imitate mind, which wanders at will over pathless deserts, and flows through nature's loveliest recesses" (quoted in Ackroyd, 343).

she had perhaps been a "cistern, spring or river."[304]

It is not surprising, then, that many advocates of water as a cure for spiritual or physical ills have tended to adopt imagery that is strikingly anthropomorphic. For the Austrian forest warden Viktor Schauberger (1885-1958), for example, water – when healthy – was a living organism, to which one could attribute such faculties as appetite, respiration, volition, memory and a temper.[305] Even more anthropomorphic is the outlook adopted by Masaru Emoto, whose books focus on the beauty of the crystals formed by frozen water. While well-formed and beautiful crystals are created when water is exposed to classical music by Beethoven, Chopin or Mozart, he claims, heavy-metal music causes the water to produce fragmented and malformed crystals. Water, we are told, likes to hear or be shown positive words such as "thank you" or "I love you," but seems to disapprove of pornography.[306] Given water's reflective proteanism, however, it is fair to conjecture that if the experimenter had had different ideas of what is morally and musically dubious, the water in question might not have come across as such an implacable goody-goody.

Water itself is intimately associated with music, its own musicality being reflected in the babbling of brooks, the whispering of rivers and the roaring of waves. Chopin, Debussy, Ravel and Vivaldi all composed music in imitation of water.[307] In ancient myth, rivers were "the voice of God."[308] The Hindu river goddess Sarasvati is the patron of eloquence, reputed to have created Sanskrit. Water, writes Peter Ackroyd, is "the presiding deity of flowing or fluid language, of language without break, of freely associative language, and of rhythmic or harmonious language."[309] The discourse of water is infinitely versatile; myriad are its voices.

304. Juana de Ibarbourou: *Acaso en otra vida ancestral, yo habré sido, antes de ser carne, cisterna, fuente o río.* This was quoted at the entrance to Expo Zaragoza 2008.
305. On Schauberger see Bartholomew, *Hidden Energies: The Startling Insights of Viktor Schauberger.* For examples of such anthropomorphism, see 106, 113, 136. This is not merely poetic self-indulgence. Even sober engineers are sometimes tempted to anthropomorphize water, referring to river-water without sediment as "hungry" on account of its tendency to corrode riverbanks in the search for a new load.
306. See Emoto, *The Hidden Messages in Water; The True Power of Water; The Secret Life of Water.*
307. Rupp, 51.
308. Ackroyd, 183.
309. Ibid., 183-84.

The fluid mutability of water's language is something which Hermann Hesse's Siddhartha comes to appreciate in the course of his spiritual enlightenment at the hands of a river and its ferryman Vasudeva: "Is it not true," Siddhartha asks Vasudeva, "that the river has very many voices? Has it not the voice of a king, of a warrior, of a bull, of a nightbird, of a pregnant woman and a sighing man, and a thousand other voices?" Quite so, agrees Vasudeva, "the voices of all living creatures are in its voice."[310] As Siddhartha learns, however, these thousands of voices are all expressions of an underlying unity. Losing his ability to distinguish the multiplicity of voices, he becomes aware of the oneness that holds them together: "the lament of those who yearn, the laughter of the wise, the cry of indignation and the groan of the dying" all intertwine to form an integral part of the "stream of events, the music of life."[311] Of course, not all water is either so loquacious or so heavily charged with deep, philosophical meaningfulness. Aware of its own lack of depth, the water in Christian Morgenstern's poem *Das Wasser* remains admirably tight-lipped:

> Without a word, without a word,
> Water runs along unheard;
> Because if not, because if not,
> The next few words would be its lot:
>
> *Beer* and *bread*, *kind* and *true*,
> And this is really nothing new.
> And so in sum, and so in sum,
> Water's better keeping mum.[312]

The association of water and music emerges particularly graphically with the sirens of antiquity, the cliff-dwelling sea nymphs whose seductive song – which Homer describes as "liquid" – was said to lure sailors to their destruction on the rocks below. As anyone who listens to their magical tones will be doomed, wily Odysseus makes his men plug their ears with wax and has himself tied to the mast so as to resist their charms. In Homer, the watery destiny awaiting those who

310. Hesse, *Siddhartha*, 86.
311. Ibid., 107.
312. The German (*Alle Galgenlieder*, 51) runs: *Ohne Wort, ohne Wort / rinnt das Wasser immerfort; / andernfalls, andernfalls / spräch' es doch nichts andres als: / Bier und Brot, Lieb und Treu, – / und das wäre auch nicht neu. / Dieses zeigt, dieses zeigt, / dass das Wasser besser schweigt.*

fall prey to the sirens' song is not identified as fatal pleasure, although subsequent Christian folklore has tended to interpret the episode in carnal terms and portray the sirens as *femmes fatales*, even confusing them – partly on account of their hybrid nature as birds and women – with the vindictive, grasping and repulsive harpies. In fact, as Cicero was keen to emphasize, the content of their song is the knowledge of past, present and future that is the privilege of those who are not subject to time. "We have foreknowledge of all that is going to happen on this fruitful earth," they sing to Odysseus.[313] Predictably enough, it was the fixation on morbid carnality that was to carry the day in the evolution of siren mythology.

The tale of Orpheus, whose name – according to Graves – may have meant "on the river bank,"[314] also brings together water and music in telling fashion. Born of a muse and a Thracian river king, Orpheus was endowed with superhuman musical ability: the overwhelming beauty of his art could charm wild beasts, inspire trees and stones to dance, arrest flowing rivers in mid-course, and move the very gods to acts of mercy. Famed as the music-making companion of the seafaring Argonauts, it was said that when Orpheus heard the sirens, he took out his lyre and played music even more beautiful than their singing, thus drowning out the seductive sound of their voices. During his journey to the underworld to try to bring back to life his young wife Eurydice, Orpheus's music had such a placatory effect on Hades that he won permission to restore his bride to the land of the living – under the condition that he did not look behind him until she was safely back in the sunlight. Look back he did, however, and in so doing he lost Eurydice for ever. Turning away from women and failing to worship his previous patron Dionysus, moreover, Orpheus was subsequently torn limb from limb by the wild Maenads, the female followers of Dionysus. His head was cast into the River Hebrus, but it floated – still singing – downstream to the sea and onwards to the island of Lesbos, where an oracle of Orpheus was established.[315]

313. Homer, 199. On the sirens, see Warner, *From the Beast to the Blonde*, 399-402.
314. Graves, I.114.
315. A mystery religion or movement based on Orpheus's lyrics and teachings is thought to have come into being by the 6th century BCE, although the actual evidence is scanty. Part of the Orphic ritual is believed to have entailed the simulated or real dismemberment of a Dionysus-figure, who was then seen to be reborn. There is clearly a close, but somewhat obscure association between Orpheus and Dionysus. Between them they embody two of the key elements – divine water and human blood / wine – that would later be brought together in another resurrection figure.

Like Proteus and Nereus, the sirens had knowledge of past, present and future; Orpheus's decapitated head was such an enthusiastic prophet that it virtually put Apollo's other oracles out of work[316]; the beguiling voice of water clearly has an innate tendency to indulge in sooth-saying. In conjunction with its transparency and related notions of "purity," water's reflective surface led to a tradition of oracles based on its alleged powers of prophecy and divination. It was as though the reflections furnished by bodies of water represented an "anti-world" or an alternative, deeper view of our own. Visionaries looked into water to disclose the misdeeds of the past or future, anticipating the crystal balls of later witches or wise women and the metal mirrors of Asian shamans. The custom of water divination, or hydromancy, has appeared in cultures as far afield as ancient and modern Europe, North Africa, the Near East, and North Asia. One technique involves casting three pebbles into the water and interpreting the play of concentric ripples that ensues. Another, known as water-scrying, entails approaching the river with a question and throwing in a piece of bread: if the bread sinks, the answer is yes; if it floats, it is no.[317]

In a similar spirit were the sinister water ordeals developed as a way of revealing divine judgement, or rather vindicating capricious human judgement. The old judicial ordeal of "swimming" witches (with their hands tied) to see if they floated was used in witch cases in England in the late 16th and 17th centuries on the principle that water, as the instrument of baptism, would reject those in league with the Devil: i.e. if they did float, they were guilty.[318] Based on a treacherous misuse of concepts of "purity," such immersion was sometimes viewed as a way of breaking the contract between witch and Devil. Women under suspicion of witchcraft often voluntarily submitted to it in the hope of clearing themselves of

---

316. Graves, I.113. Eventually Apollo had to come and tell Orpheus's head to button it.

317. See Ackroyd, 85-86.

318. See Thomas, *Religion and the Decline of Magic*, 146, 619, 658. Of course, water's proteanism is such that in the appropriate context "floating" may lend itself to the opposite interpretation: "walking on water" is a privilege of the godlike or godly. The 5th-century figure of St Piran, the most famous of the Irish saints who travelled to Cornwall, is reputed to have swum to the north coast of Cornwall with a millstone round his neck, placed there by a gang of heathen Irishmen before they hurled him into the stormy sea (see Halliday, *A History of Cornwall*, 86). Settled in Cornwall, St Piran built a chapel, preached the word of God, and indulged his fondness for a tipple.

long-standing aspersions.[319] Equally sinister is the ancient Celtic figure of the "Washer at the Ford." Commonly known in Irish Gaelic as a *bean sídhe* or banshee, this phantom-like apparition dwelt near fords or streams, disclosing to warriors which of them would fall on the battlefield that day: "My work is to haunt all the streams of Ireland," she would screech, "washing away all the sins of men."[320]

Protean in nature, the surface of water imitates or mimics what it reflects. In this sense, the reflecting surface of a body of water is the archetypal mirror, evoking the ancient belief that a person is magically linked to his mirror reflection. Yet mirrors are notoriously ambiguous in their associations. On the one hand, they signify the sins of pride, vanity and self-love; on the other, they represent the virtues of self-knowledge and judiciousness. The first aspect in particular is commonly understood to be epitomized in Greek mythology by the beautiful figure of Narcissus, the son of the river-god Cephisus and a nymph. According to Ovid, the seer Teresias predicted that he would live to a ripe old age provided that he never knew himself.[321] Heartlessly spurning all aspiring lovers, however, Narcissus was induced by the goddess of revenge, Nemesis, to fall hopelessly in love with his own reflection in a pool. Entranced at the sight of himself and unable to tear himself away, he languished and eventually died.[322]

The episode is generally interpreted as a cautionary tale warning of the effects of "narcissistic" self-absorption and self-infatuation. On a deeper level, however, it also brings to light the problematic nature of "self-knowledge" itself, to the extent that the act of reflective awareness or consciousness gives rise to an apparent split or disunity within the reflective self. By its very operation, reflection seems to produce two separate or independent entities – the observer and the observed, subject and object, mind and body – making self-awareness inherently schizoid.

---

319. Women were also vulnerable to another ceremony based on water's purifying qualities, the ritual of "ducking." Popular from the early Middle Ages through to the 18th century, this punishment was generally reserved for foul-mouthed or shrewish wives, who would be strapped to a "ducking stool" and immersed three times, often with fatal consequences.
320. Scott Littleton, 265.
321. Graves, 1.286-88.
322. On dying he was transformed into the flower that bears his name. In China, the word for "narcissus" means "water immortal," and is a symbol of happiness and fortune associated with the New Year. See Biedermann, 235.

Watery Narcissus may yearn for unity with his other self, but he is doomed to remain self-different and fragmented. One version of the tale has Narcissus fall into the pond and drown. Death here brings him the union impossible in life; water returns to water. Yet in both cases the reflecting surface of the water – which is both an entity in itself and the image of something else – reflects an inner disunity in the onlooker, a disunity only resolved (or dissolved) by death. The mirror of the water reflects the mirror that is our mind and the split it entails.

In practice, of course, reflection and meditation are vital to human well-being, and water and reflective contemplation are intrinsically bonded. Simply taking the time to stop and focus our attention on the movements of water in pools, lakes, rivers or oceans has the effect of calming the spirit and soothing the soul. Buddhists have often sought the company of water for their meditations, the still limpidity of a bowl of water or the tranquil flow of a brook or stream serving as a reflection of the meditating mind. Anglers have spoken of the peace and solitude conferred by their river-bank pastime, and of the benefits of a return to nature or the wilderness. "The greatest privilege of fishing," writes Jeremy Paxman, "is the obligation it puts upon you to be quietly part of a world we spend the rest of our lives trying to defy, control or ignore."[323] Water is felt to reflect deeper truths than mere sooth-saying. As an embodiment of flow, rivers – as we shall see below – have served as emblems of the transience of things and the constancy of change. Siddhartha's most important spiritual mentor is the river. "The river knows everything," says Vasudeva, "one can learn everything from it."[324] Or as Pooh puts it, there are times when "if you stood on the bottom rail of a bridge, and leant over, and watched the river slipping slowly away beneath you, you would suddenly know everything that there is to be known."[325] As an embodiment of flow, rivers stand for everything there is to be stood for.

Oceans too, which are themselves but a tangled mosaic of eddies, gyres, vortices, swirls and enormously powerful deep currents, can imbue the observer with a double-pronged sense of immensity and awed participation. Melville speaks of "ocean reverie."[326] What has become known as the "oceanic feeling" – a feeling as of "something limitless,

323. Paxman, *Fish, Fishing and the Meaning of Life*, 2.
324. Hesse, 84.
325. Milne, *Winnie-the-Pooh's Little Book of Wisdom*.
326. Melville, 21-22: "as every one knows, meditation and water are wedded for ever."

unbounded"[327] – has been interpreted as the underlying source of religious sentiments, i.e. of the elemental mystical energy that is subsequently seized upon, pinned down, dogmatized and domesticated by *institutionalized* religious or ideological systems. For Arthur Koestler, it was also the spur to the pursuit of scientific truth. "From the Pythagoreans onward," he writes, "through the Renaissance to our times, the oceanic feeling, the sense of participation in the mystery of the infinite, was the principal inspiration of that wingèd and flat-footed creature, the scientist."[328] The metaphorical connection between the sea and the infinite truth is one of mutual reflection: the truth is sea-like as much as the sea truth-like. Isaac Newton visualized himself as a boy looking for pebbles on the sea-shore with the "great ocean of truth" stretching out undiscovered in front of him.[329] In "The Prelude," Wordsworth portrays Newton as a Romantic explorer-hero, his mind "for ever / Voyaging through strange seas of Thought, alone."[330] Boundless are the uncharted waters that lie beyond the limits of the human intellect, where only an intrepid few make occasional incursions.

The aesthetic conception of the sublime gloried in the immensity and intensity of nature – whether desert or ocean, rugged precipice or rushing cataract – for the way it transcended the human urge to control, predict, classify and comprehend. In the oceanic feeling too, the human self is engulfed in, and willingly yields to, something immeasurably bigger than the merely individual, returning to origins as a wayward child might return to his mother or father, with a mixture of apprehension and trust, the "pleasing fear" felt by Byron as he wanton'd with the breakers.[331] In regressing to the watery, universal matrix, the finite self becomes one with its other, but in the process – given its puny insignificance – it may well "lose" itself, forfeiting distinctness and individuality. Deeply ambiguous as ever, water is where self coincides with other, the bounded with the beyond.

327. Freud, *Civilization and its Discontents*, in *Standard Edition*, XXI.64. Freud was in fact referring to feelings expressed by his friend Romain Rolland in correspondence. The supremely dry Freud goes on to admit that this "oceanic feeling" is not something he has been able to pinpoint in himself.
328. Koestler, *The Act of Creation*, 262-63.
329. The full quotation can be found in the second volume of David Brewster, *Memoirs of the Life, Writings, and Discoveries of Sir Isaac Newton*, 2 vols. (Edinburgh: Thomas Constable and Co., 1855), chap. 27.
330. Wordsworth, *The Prelude*, 103.
331. Lord Byron, "Childe Harold's Pilgrimage," Canto the Fourth, Verse 184.

3

Rivers of Time, Streams of Consciousness

Novalis famously described the human body as a "moulded river."[332] Like a living body, a river combines the preservation of form with an exchange of matter; it is a synthesis of stability and change, "channelling" the flux that provides its lifeblood. Such features have led certain scientists too to suspect that principles underlying the "secret of life" may be inherent in simpler examples of fluid motions. Essential to a thermodynamic definition of life is the *openness* of living systems to the environment, which makes self-organization possible through a flow of energy. This openness is a feature common to hydrodynamic systems and to living systems in general. The Nobel prize-winning chemist Ilya Prigogine himself uses the river analogy: "Not everything in a living system is 'alive.' The energy flow that crosses it somewhat resembles the flow of a river that generally moves smoothly but that from time to time tumbles down a waterfall, which liberates part of the energy it contains." Another Nobel laureate, Erwin Schrödinger, refers to a living organism's "astonishing gift of concentrating a '*stream of order*' on itself and thus escaping the decay into atomic chaos – of 'drinking orderliness' from a suitable environment."[333]

The human body is a river which requires a regular influx of water (among other things) and discharges a regular outflow. It is flux incarnate. The individuated self, by contrast, depends upon its sense of a fixed boundary between itself and what is not itself, i.e. between self and other. Our rational integrity is founded upon the principle of identity, which dictates that "I = I," or I am who I am, a constant in time. The contradiction

332. The description was taken by W. H. Auden as the epigraph to his poem "River Profile" and also appears as an epigraph in Theodor Schwenk's *Sensitive Chaos*.

333. Prigogine and Stengers, *Order out of Chaos*, 156; Schrödinger, *What is Life?* 77 (my emphasis). The problem with a *merely* thermodynamic definition of life, as we have seen, is that it may prove too wide, failing to exclude apparently non-living systems: i.e. other dissipative structures such as vortices of water or burning flames (see Fry, *The Emergence of Life on Earth*, 240). Those who stress water's own vitality or aliveness may not find this problematic: the poetic idea of having been a river in an earlier life runs along these lines.

runs deep: we are individuals made of water, yet the water of which we are made is trans-individual. It flows through the self, perforating the boundary between self and other and to this extent becoming the *deeper* boundary where self coincides with other, where I meet and overlap with what is not me. Water is the ultimate constituent of the self, but also its ultimate margin, the underlying mediator of self and non-self. Undermining our unity or identity, water is thus akin to a kind of unconscious that incorporates the leaky, muddy, bodily self that our "higher" faculties like to order, control and where possible ignore. Saliva, urine and semen are treated as taboo, and all bodily functions associated with them are to be strictly regulated. Failure to control these waters amounts to bodily pollution and is not to be tolerated.[334]

That water has indeed come to constitute a sort of *collective unconscious* throughout "civilized" Western society in general is reflected on a range of levels. It takes the form, as we have seen, of a repression of flow, a technocratic urge to shackle or tame rivers, construct dams, and drain marshland. It comes to light in our ignorance and fear of the oceans, humankind's "higher" aspirations sending us soaring towards the moon and the stars rather than down into the depths. As a rule, water is banished to underground conduits that bring it unfailingly to our taps and tactfully usher away what we have used and sullied. Symbolically, bottled mineral water companies have further "privatized" a naturally public good by capturing its flow in plastic receptacles, putting it on the market as a self-contained, static commodity, and making us pay through the nose for something which – like clean air – should be freely available to all alike.

This mistrust of "flux" (the very word implies not only continuous change and instability, but unwanted bodily discharges) is echoed on other levels. Western thought in general – embodied in its philosophical tradition – has commonly sought to arrest flow and overcome transience. The flux of the world has been deeply associated with the destructive aspect of time, the loss of things held precious, and thus with the worthlessness of what is impermanent. Ever since Plato, philosophers have pursued the timeless

334. Tears, it seems, are less likely to constitute such defilement. According to the anthropologist Mary Douglas, this is in part because of the limpidity that contrasts, for example, with thick nasal rheum or other bodily oozes. Moreover, she continues, "tears are naturally pre-empted by the symbolism of washing. Tears are like rivers of moving water. They purify, cleanse, bathe the eyes, so how can they pollute? But more significantly tears are not related to the bodily functions of digestion and procreation" (*Purity and Danger*, 155).

and the unchanging through the contemplation of divinity, mathematical truth, abstract ideas or the laws of nature. The flow of running water has symbolized the ephemerality that abstract thought has shunned in its yearning to overcome time.

There have always been dissident voices. Even before Plato, Heraclitus the Obscure is famously reputed to have said that "you cannot step into the same river twice."[335] This is usually taken to mean that reality is in unceasing flux and transformation: all things are flowing, *panta rei*. Yet as we have already seen, Heraclitus's writings are themselves murky waters, and Socrates advocated special diving skills in order to get the bottom of them. One version – "on those who enter the same rivers, ever different waters flow" – may be understood as saying that all is ceaseless change. Yet the very reference to "the same rivers" suggests a certain constancy, implying the persistence of identity *in spite of* change. Elsewhere Heraclitus writes: "We step and do not step into the same rivers, we are and we are not."[336] This beautifully enigmatic fragment not only compounds the ambiguity ("the rivers are the same, but then again..."), but also adds a further dimension: not only have the river waters changed, but so have we. Like rivers, *we* are waters subject to the ceaselessness of change.

The fleeting nature of the self has been a recurring thorn in a great deal of philosophical flesh. Trying to grasp the nature of himself *as a self*, the great Scottish sceptic David Hume found "nothing but a bundle or collection of different perceptions, which succeed each other with an inconceivable rapidity, and are in a perpetual flux and movement."[337] The search was thus launched for some sort of identity or unity on which the constant flow of our conscious experiences could be grounded, whether our psychological continuity (our memories and expectations), our physiological or spatio-temporal continuity (our body), or some sort of transcendental ego or subject that underlay all diversity. Relatively few have been the philosophers such as William James and Henri Bergson, who have accepted or stressed the primacy of flow as opposed to the static, discrete nature of our conceptualization of experience. In his *Principles of Psychology* (1890), James developed the concept of the "stream of consciousness" to describe experience, a stream in which "every definite

335. According to W. D. Glasgow, the Irish philosopher F. La Touche Godfrey used to make the point that in fact "you cannot step into the *same* river *once*."
336. Barnes, 116, 117.
337. Hume, *A Treatise of Human Nature*, 302.

image of the mind is steeped and dyed in the free water that flows around it." Consciousness, he argued, "does not appear to itself chopped up into bits," for it is "nothing jointed; it flows."[338] It is clear that the river-metaphor can apply to my conscious mind – the fugitive liquidity of spirit – as much as to the murky depths of the unconscious.[339]

The question of identity – of constancy in flux – is no idle one. I can remember nothing about the person I was when I was two, and share virtually none of my cells and few of my character traits with the lovely little boy I am said not to have been at the time. In pragmatic terms, however, few people would dispute that there exists some sort of identity between the earlier and later me. It is my sameness over time that forms the basis for all moral responsibility, as well as for the judicial convention that holds my present self accountable for my past transgressions.[340] By the same token, the Yellow River altered its course through China some 26 times between 600 BCE and 1949 CE, often by hundreds of miles and with cataclysmic consequences. Even its mouth has shifted vast distances up and down the Chinese east coast. Yet although its waters may have been different, and its course may have changed, no one would dispute that *one and the same river* has been responsible for wreaking this havoc over the centuries. Perhaps it is the origin or source that certifies its sameness, much as my birth certificate vouches for certain aspects of my identity (even though I can never actually remember where it is). Or perhaps it is simply the visible and identifiable *continuity* of its flow that yields the foundation from which its identity, such as it is, can be inferred.[341]

Yet in spite of the continuity of *my* public identifiability (the perceived external constants that provide my flowing waters with a *metaphorical* river-bed), there remains a sense in which I am *not* the same person I was a day ago, a year ago or twenty years ago, just as

338. James, *Principles of Psychology*, vol. 1, 255, 239.
339. By extension, it can refer to the collective as much as the individual consciousness. Our species as a whole suffers terminal logorrhoea. The history of ideas – of philosophical, religious, scientific or narrative thought – is best envisioned as a raging torrent or a river in spate, turbid and ungovernable. Each work of science, literature or metaphysics, however humble or wayward, is a whirling eddy or vortex within the Big Muddy of human cerebration.
340. See Glasgow, *Split Down the Sides*, 45-47.
341. Even when changing its course, the Yellow River does not just stop in its tracks and then turn up a few hours or minutes later in a different part of China. It flows there.

there is a sense in which I am not the same person I will be tomorrow, a year from now, or twenty years from now. Sooner or later, the constantly moving waters of the river I am at the moment will have all passed (I will have passed them), and my metaphorical river-bed may well have changed its course too (I may be unrecognizable to those who know me at present, including myself). I may dissociate from my past self (as an embarrassment or a liability) and my future self (as an irrelevance). In general, however, I keep such impractical attitudes and insights well and truly concealed within the junkyard of my unconscious (the kingdom of bodily functions and short-term pleasures), and give my existence meaning and consistency within the context of an ongoing narrative autobiography which incorporates my memories of the past me and my care for a future me.

For all the value I may ascribe to my continued existence, the onslaught of time is relentless, and one day the river that I am will dry up. Water and the fluidity that characterizes it is a particularly potent symbol of my own impermanence. In the face of death and transience, life is often felt to acquire significance through one's sense of having left some sort of a trace, somewhere, in someone or on something. Archetypally, such a trace has taken the form of a mausoleum, monument or tombstone, something big and *made of stone* that gives us the illusion of lasting for ever. Stone here represents a stasis and permanence – albeit only provisionally – that is seemingly the antithesis of watery flux. When the Romantic poet Keats famously asks for the words "Here lies One Whose Name was writ in Water" to be inscribed on his grave, there is irony and paradox in his request and its execution. Yet this is not surprising, for Keats is himself as protean as the shape-shifters of the sea. By his own admission, he is a "poetical character" in the sense of one who "is not itself – it has no self – it is every thing and nothing."[342] Like other protean poets, Keats combines the shapelessness of water with the stone-carved timelessness of the words he bequeathed to posterity.

The idea of time as flowing water is itself as old as the hills. The Roman stoic Marcus Aurelius picked up on Heraclitus's image in his *Meditations*, writing that "the age and time of the world is as it were a flood and swift current, consisting of the things that are brought to pass in the world. For as soon as anything hath appeared, and is passed away,

342. Keats, *Letters of John Keats*, 157. In the same letter he continues: "What shocks the virtuous philosop[h]er, delights the camelion [*sic*] Poet. ... A Poet is the most unpoetical of any thing in existence; because he has no Identity – he is continually ... filling some other Body – The Sun, the Moon, the Sea."

another succeeds, and that also will presently out of sight." According to Leonardo's *Notebooks*, "in rivers, the water that you touch is the last of what has passed and the first of that which comes: so with time present." Machiavelli stressed the element of fluvial unruliness over its constant unidirectionality, likening the flow of fortune to "one of those violent rivers which, when they are enraged, flood the plains, tear down trees and buildings, wash soil from one place to deposit it in another." Hydraulic engineering is as vital for channelling the river of fortune as for controlling watery nature, because fortune "shows her potency where there is no well-regulated power to resist her, and her impetus is felt where she knows there are no embankments and dykes built to restrain her." Italy, felt Machiavelli, was lacking in just such metaphorical dykes and embankments, whence its political instability. Fortune is a woman, he added, and "if she is to be submissive it is necessary to beat and coerce her."[343] Remote from the world of courtly machinations, for the 19th-century US essayist Henry David Thoreau time was but the stream he went "a-fishing" in: "I drink at it; but while I drink I see the sandy bottom and detect how shallow it is. Its thin current slides away, but eternity remains."[344]

Everyday metaphor reinforces the association. In English "water under the bridge" refers to events that are over and done with, while other languages draw on other parts of the hydrological cycle: the Spanish say that it has rained a lot since "then" (i.e. whenever "it" occurred), while the Germans speak of "yesterday's snow" or the water that has flowed down the Rhine.[345] While time's inexorable unidirectionality – and the resulting impossibility of undoing what has been done – is expressed in English by spilt milk and the futility of tears, the Spanish use the proverb that "water that has passed won't turn a mill" (*agua pasada no mueve molino*). The German *passiert ist passiert* turns it into a matter of dry, tautological necessity. Though the punning ambiguity of "passing water" in English underscores the undeniable point that what has passed has passed,

---

343. Marcus Aurelius, *Meditations*, 38 (IV. 35); Leonardo da Vinci, 274; Machiavelli, *The Prince*, 79-81.

344. Thoreau, *Walden*, 142: this eternity is perhaps best understood as an eternal present. God, writes Thoreau, "himself culminates in the present moment" (141).

345. The Spanish expression is: *Ya ha llovido mucho desde entonces*. The German term for yesterday's snow is *Schnee von gestern*, which has the advantage of being considerably shorter than: *Seitdem ist viel Wasser dem Rhein hinabge-flossen*.

Ayurvedic urine-therapy suggests a more cyclical image of time.[346]

The deep association of water and time also incorporates the flow of seas as opposed to rivers. There is a close etymological link between time and tide, both of which – as the proverb has it – wait for no man, and this connection is equally manifest in the German lexical twins *Zeit* (time) and *Gezeiten* (tide). The rhythmic ebb and flow of the ocean's waters has been an archetypal emblem of the passing of time, of birth and death, while the watery moon has symbolized the measured periodicity of the rhythms of nature and life.[347] The word "rhythm" – with its connotations of regular recurrence over time – itself stems from the Greek *rheos*, which means a stream or current and gives us not only "rheology," the branch of physics concerned with flow, but also the name of the River Rhine, as well as "diarrhoea."[348]

Some of the earliest timekeepers were water-based,[349] the regular flow of water into an empty vessel measuring the passage of time much as the flow of sand does in an hourglass. The *klepsydra* or water clock (literally a water-thief) was in fact first used by Empedocles to demonstrate that atmospheric air is a distinct physical substance, to be distinguished both from empty space or void on the one hand and rarefied mist or vapour on the other: nor, conversely, was water the same as liquid air.[350] The device was refined in the 3rd century BCE by Ctesibius, a precursor of the great engineering tradition of ancient Alexandria, and used by the Romans to measure the duration of an orator's speech. Accurate though it was, the flow of water eventually came to be replaced by the descent of a weight under the pull of gravity – the pendulum – in time-measuring devices. Water had served its time.

346. Indeed, the idea of the hydrological cycle also implies a cyclical notion of time, to the extent that water *may after all* pass through the same river twice, if not thrice or who knows how many times. It may well also pass through the same person twice, with or without urine-therapy being involved.
347. On the moon as the "universal measuring gauge," see Eliade, *Patterns*, 154-56.
348. The etymological link between the Rhine and diarrhoea became sadly appropriate in the 19th and early 20th century in the context not only of industrial, agricultural and domestic pollution, but also the speeding up of the river-flow following Tulla's "rectification."
349. The sundial is believed to date back to 3500 BCE, but the water clock and hourglass were not long in following.
350. Burnet, 263-64. Burnet describes this as "one of the most important discoveries in the early history of science."

Whereas Western philosophy has tended to see flowing water as a symbol of impermanence and the passing of time, however, Eastern traditions have stressed the timelessness embodied in rivers, the constancy of change. One of the secrets Siddhartha learns from the river in Hermann Hesse's novel is that its water "continually flowed and flowed and yet it was always there; it was always the same and yet every moment it was new."[351] While traditional Occidental thought has tended to disdain "newness" and change in its pursuit of the transcendentally timeless (or more recently to disdain "sameness" in its pursuit of progress and evolution), more mystical perspectives have recognized the timelessness *immanent within* change. Siddhartha thus learns that "there is no such thing as time." As he explains to Vasudeva, "the river is everywhere at the same time."[352] It is present at the source as much as at the estuary or in the ocean, and it is present everywhere in between. Distinctions between past, present and future become secondary. The flow of the current may embody the now, but for mystics the now may be where the eternal inheres.

The timelessness of flow may also lend it a special value not apparent on first sight, namely as a symbol of patience and subtle force. Ovid's celebrated dictum *gutta cavat lapidem* – "dripping water hollows out a stone"[353] – affirms the value of persistence and constancy as opposed to brute strength or sheer quantity. Further, the flexibility inherent in water's formlessness makes it a potent metaphor for strength in weakness. We have already come across the peculiar near-invulnerability of watery shape-shifters such as Proteus, Nereus and Thetis. The power associated with the yielding or passive quality of fluid water is central to Taoist thought in particular. In the Taoist treatise *Tao Te Ching*, the scholar Lao Tzu elevates water to the highest good, for it bestows life, flows into places rejected by man, and in so doing comes close to the *Tao* itself. Rivers and seas excel in adopting the lower position. "In the world," he writes, "there is nothing more submissive and weak than water. Yet for attacking that which is hard and strong nothing can surpass it."[354]

In Chuang-tzu too, the sage is one who, like water, is sensitive to and adjusts to the pressures imposed from outside. Just as water – irrespective of its source – adapts to the shape of the surrounding topography that

351. Hesse, 81-82.
352. Ibid., 86.
353. Ovid, *Epistulae Ex Ponto*, IV. x. 5. Quoted in the *Oxford Dictionary of Quotations*, 366.
354. Lao Tzu, *Tao Te Ching*, 140. See also 64, 128.

contains it, so the sage is at peace with himself as he follows the Way.[355] In one of the anecdotes related in the *Outer Chapters*, Confucius comes across a man swimming happily in tumultuously cascading rapids where no other animal ventures to go. Asking how he manages to stay afloat, the man replies: "I began in what is native to me, grew up in what is natural to me, matured in what is destined for me. I enter with the inflow, and emerge with the outflow, follow the Way of the water and do not impose my selfishness upon it."[356]

Fluidity is vital to the deeper symbolism of water. It is as a flow that water makes the world go round: for all the magical or mysterious qualities of pools and wells (still waters run deep), stagnant water and ice lack the charisma of rivers, currents or streams. Such notions find expression not only in the folk wisdom that warns against drinking stagnant water, but also, for example, in the poetry of John Donne:

> Waters stincke soone, if in one place they bide,
> And in the vast sea are more putrifi'd:
> But when they kisse one banke, and leaving this
> Never look backe, but the next banke doe kisse,
> Then are they purest; Change'is the nursery
> Of musicke, joy, life, and eternity.[357]

For water-mystics such as Theodor Schwenk and Viktor Schauberger too, it is as a flow that water takes on its life-giving properties. For Schwenk, flow is linked to vitality just as stasis and stagnation is to death. These associations hold both on a physical and on an intellectual or conceptual level, a reflection of water's own deeply protean nature:

> If we ... try to take hold of water, it slips through our hands and flows away unless we put it in some sort of container. If the container is solid we can "catch" water in it; then it quietens down immediately. But this means that it is already well on the way to being dead, to losing the quality that originally made it living water. And the concepts we form of it suffer the same fate: the moment one tries to catch the real nature of water in a hard and fast definition, the reality of it is no longer there.[358]

355. Chuang-tzu, *The Seven Inner Chapters and other writings from the book Chuang-tzu*, 81.
356. Ibid., 136.
357. Donne, "Change," in *A Selection of his Poetry*, 72-73.
358. Schwenk and Schwenk, 3.

Water's elusiveness extends to our conception of it, whence its tendency to reflect the ideas we project onto it. In Schwenk, this indeterminacy comes to light in the very question of whether water is a living entity, to which his answer would seem to be that it is and it isn't.[359] In these terms, he is justified in sometimes referring to living water and sometimes to dead water. Water, as he puts it in one essay, is a mediator between life and death.[360]

Of course, water's protean vigour, its reluctance to stand still, is not restricted to any one pace: there is slow flow and fast flow and a great deal in between. On average, the water in the atmosphere – which amounts to some 13,000 cubic kilometres at any one time – completely renews itself within just over a week; for the 2,000 cubic kilometres of water in the world's rivers and streams, the average "residence time" is 18 days; water may spend as much as 400 years in the depths of Lake Baikal in Russia, while ancient aquifers or ice sheets may hang on to their water for hundreds of thousands of years. The steam spewed out by erupting volcanoes is water that has long since been cut off from the planet's surface, hidden within slowly moving subterranean rocks. When you drink a glass of wine, writes Robert Kandel, some of the water you take in "has cycled through the atmosphere thousands of times since you were born. But you are also absorbing some water molecules that have only been out in the open air for a few days or weeks, after tens or hundreds of millions of years beneath the Earth's crust."[361]

Despite their aura of stasis, even glaciers embody flow, albeit in the form of "slow flow." In descriptions of them, mountaineers have accordingly tended to evoke a combination of stasis and movement. In their presence, writes Robert Macfarlane, one is aware of "motion in the midst of stillness." Glaciers he portrays as an amalgam of "great force and

---

359. Schwenk asks why water, which does not exhibit any of the character-istic features of living organisms such as digestive and excretory processes, can nonetheless be said to form the very basis for all life's manifestations. His answer: "Because water embraces everything, is in and all through everything; because it rises above the distinctions between plants and animals and human beings; because it is a universal element shared by all; itself undetermined, yet determining; because, like the primal mother it is, it supplies the stuff of life to everything living" (ibid., 5).
360. Ibid., 23.
361. See Kandel, 37-38, 96-97, 155-56; quotation, 38.

great time."[362] Whence the special enchantment they exert. The Scottish glaciologist James Forbes described glaciers as "an endless scroll, a stream of time upon whose stainless ground is engraven the succession of events, whose dates far transcend the memory of living man."[363] To descend a glacier was to take a journey back in time and encounter ice compacted hundreds of years ago. Macfarlane invokes the ancient world's most venerable philosopher of flux: "you can never step into the same river twice, said Heraclitus. Had he travelled a few latitudes further north, he would have said the same for glaciers."[364]

Glaciation has played a major role in the architecture of landscapes, carving out great valleys as it advances and leaving a trail of moraine in its wake as it retreats. The rock and stone that has traditionally been a symbol of permanence and resistance to time is thus itself vulnerable to change. The irony is that it is above all weak and submissive water – with its shape-shifting flexibility and its stone-hollowing patience – that acts as the agent of transformation. Through the "spectacles of geology," writes Macfarlane, "*terra firma* becomes *terra mobilis*, and we are forced to reconsider our beliefs of what is solid and what is not."[365] From the perspective of what geologists and others have called "deep time,"[366] the mountains themselves prove as fleeting as the most fugitive manifestations of water's formlessness. "The hills are shadows," wrote Alfred Lord Tennyson, "and they flow / From form to form, and nothing stands; / They melt like mist, the solid lands, / Like clouds they shape themselves and go."[367]

Leonardo noted how "in the end the mountains will be levelled by the waters, seeing that they wash away the earth which covers them and

362. Macfarlane, 129, 132. Macfarlane cites Gerard Manley Hopkins, who spoke of "an air of interrupted activity," and Horace-Bénédict de Saussure, who likened the glacier to "a sea which has become suddenly frozen" (ibid., 129, 116).
363. Quoted in ibid., 132.
364. Ibid., 108-9.
365. Ibid., 43.
366. The term was coined by the geologist John McPhee to distinguish the huge intervals of geological time, spanning millions of years, from the scale of time – days, weeks and years – governing our everyday lives. For an account, see Gee, *Deep Time*. Sitting in his house in Ealing, Gee speculates on what deep time has in store for his "corner of the world": "In a few million years, Ealing could be a tropical beach; a range of jagged mountains; buried under a glacier a mile thick; or submerged under the sea. Given enough time, Ealing might be all of these things" (*Deep Time*, 226).
367. Quoted in Macfarlane, 57.

uncover their rocks, which begin to crumble and subdued alike by heat and frost are being continually changed into soil. The waters wear away their bases and the mountains fall bit by bit in ruin into the rivers."[368] In fact, rivers convey billion of tons of sediment from one place to another: silt, sand and stones are ceaselessly being brought to the sea from landscapes that are in turn being implacably re-designed and re-shaped. The peaks of the Himalayas – constantly forced upwards by the thrust of plate tectonics – are at the same time being unremittingly taken apart by the action of rain, wind and snow, the sediments then being transported to the Indian Ocean by the Brahmaputra, the Ganges or the Indus. Once these sediments reach the sea, turbidity currents in turn proceed to spread them far and wide over vast distances to form huge fan-shaped deposits that may be several miles thick.[369] Far away in the USA, the Mississippi dumps some 15 tons of sediment into the Gulf of Mexico every second. According to William Bryant Logan's calculations, "to equal the silt output of the Mississippi River alone, you would have to run almost 25,000 railroad cars full of silt to the Gulf of Mexico. Daily."[370]

Water's capacity to defy the seeming permanence of rock is heightened by its protean powers of impregnation. Water, writes Logan, "gets into things. It soaks them, drenches them, permeates them. ... There is no legal definition of the word 'waterproof,' because there is no such thing. Nothing resists water indefinitely."[371] Water can thus insinuate itself into the narrowest of cracks or cavities in rock or stone, prising whole fragments away when it starts to freeze and expand. But just as relentless as the *physical* weathering to which rock is subject is the ongoing *chemical* onslaught by rainwater (i.e. water with carbon dioxide dissolved in it, in other words weak carbonic acid), which has the capacity to turn apparently unyielding igneous rocks such as granite – a paradigm of permanence and endurance – into various sorts of clay. Even more spectacular are the effects when rainwater attacks sedimentary rocks such as limestone, on occasion carving out whole networks of subterranean caves and gorges. The only

368. Leonardo da Vinci, 19.
369. Kunzig, *Mapping the Deep*, 58-59: "The Indus Fan covers all the floor of the Arabian Sea as far south as the tip of India. The Bengal Fan extends even farther, past Sri Lanka and out onto the Ceylon Abyssal Plain – a distance of nearly 2,000 miles. The Bengal Fan is about 600 miles wide, and in some places the sediments are more than 12 miles thick."
370. Logan, *Dirt*, 117; see also 96.
371. Ibid., 119.

common stone that is largely resistant to such chemical weathering is quartz, a form of silicon dioxide or silica. The landscape of the Earth, says Logan, is "little more than a monument to the different weathering rates of its constituent minerals."[372]

The "rock cycle," however essential the role of water in it, is clearly a case of "slow flow." Perhaps a third of an inch of a granite tombstone rots away in the course of a millennium, rather more in the case of marble. Yet from the perspective of deep time at least, flow it unquestionably is. Around 5,000 years ago (just a short interval in deep time), the world's largest desert, the Sahara, was a crocodile-infested wetland. Ten millennia earlier it was as dry as bones. In even earlier millennia, it had countless other wet periods, as attested by the vast Nubian Aquifer that lies deep below it, which is thought to contain water that has been there for almost a million years. Even further back, during the Mesozoic era, some 200 million years ago, what is now the planet's highest mountain range, the Himalayas, formed the seabed of the ancient Tethys Ocean. Today the sediments from its peaks are being conveyed back to their watery origins. The deeper truth in Heraclitus, the truth of deep time, is that the world itself – even its most apparently solid, rocky manifestations – is a river into which we can and cannot step twice.

372. Ibid., 121.

4

Passages Beyond

Like water in general, rivers are deeply ambivalent. Embodying time and timelessness, they can be associated equally with life and death, creation and destruction. According to Theodor Schwenk, "in every area water assumes the role of mediator. Encompassing both life and death, it constantly wrests the former from the latter."[373]

From a human perspective, there is no reason to assume any particular life-affirming bias. Water can give life, but it can also take it. It depends whose life we are talking about. Algae may flourish in water at the expense of other life forms. In the process called eutrophication ("good nutrition"), lakes and rivers rich in nitrates and phosphates foster algal blooms that deprive the water of oxygen, wipe out fish and other animals, and generate highly toxic substances. Water may provide a home for bacteria or viruses that are decidedly non-conducive to human life. As Maggie Black writes, "water acts as a conduit for health, providing our means of washing, cleaning, bathing and laundry. But if it becomes polluted, water acts as a conduit for disease in food and beverages. Thus water's role in health is double-edged."[374] Water is responsible for spreading acute intestinal infections such as cholera or typhoid, skin or eye diseases such as trachoma, and parasites such as hookworm, guinea worm or bilharzia; it also provides the breeding ground for the mosquitoes that cause diseases such as malaria or dengue fever. Water may be good for life without the life in question being human.

The Yellow River in China, which the Chinese traditionally refer to as their "joy and sorrow,"[375] is one of the best-renowned manifestations of water's ambiguity: on the one hand, the irrigation it has provided has supported more people over a longer period of time than any other river on earth; on the other hand, its regular, catastrophic floods have probably

373. Schwenk and Schwenk, 24.
374. Black, *No-Nonsense Guide to Water*, 34.
375. Pearce, 130.

caused more deaths than any other natural phenomenon on the planet.[376] According to ancient Chinese mythology, its presiding god was He Bo, the Count of the River, a mortal by birth, who had hurled himself into the flowing current with stones tied to his back and in so doing acquired immortality and magical powers. During much of the Zhou Dynasty (up to the 3rd century BCE), each year a young woman – the count's ritual bride – would be tied to a marriage bed and sent to a watery grave by way of sacrifice.[377] Death and deathlessness, time and timelessness oppose – or complement – one another like the two banks of a single river.

As timeless symbols of the boundary or transition between life and the afterlife or beyond (*viz.* between self and other), rivers partake of the radical ambiguity of any mediator, which by definition both separates but also links or joins what is separated. In Norse mythology it was the River Gjöll that formed the boundary between the realm of the living and of the dead; in ancient Greece it was the Styx that had to be crossed. In some cultures the deceased had to be ferried across the waters (for example, by the ferryman Charon); in others a bridge has symbolized the passage from this world to the next. Islam visualizes a bridge leading to heaven that is as narrow as the blade of a sword; ancient Chinese lore stipulates that those who *fail* to negotiate the bridge plunge into a vile stream of pus and blood.[378] In Christianity, the son of God came to be seen as the bridge connecting earth and heaven, and the building of bridges in general became a holy task. Chapels were commonly constructed on or next to bridges, and niches or improvised dens served as places of refuge for solitaries known as "bridge hermits," who begged alms there.[379]

Not surprisingly, those who have styled themselves as spiritual guides have on occasion seen themselves as bridge-builders, whence the Latin term *pontifex* for priest (from *pons*, "bridge"), which goes back to Roman paganism and was employed in the cult of the divine Roman emperor, the *pontifex maximus*. Though disavowed for this reason

376. Ibid.
377. Scott Littleton, 399.
378. See Biedermann on "bridge" symbolism, 49-50.
379. See Ackroyd, 129-33, on the Thames: "It seems likely that no bridge was without its chapel, except for the smallest and most remote of them. They were pulled down in more sceptical and revolutionary ages, and plundered for their stone. The Reformation no doubt played a large part in their downfall. And they were never rebuilt. The connection of bridges with sacredness had long since been forgotten."

by the Christian emperors of the 4th century, it was soon taken up by Christian bishops and archbishops and its use eventually restricted to the Pope (cf. the English term "Pontiff"). In its original sense, therefore, to pontificate is to construct a bridge, presumably from the secular world to the spiritual, or from unbelief to faith, or perhaps from ignorance to knowledge.[380] In a similar spirit, though perhaps less pontifical, are the ford-makers of Indian religions, in which the *Tirtha* ("ford" or "crossing place" in Sanskrit) represents a sacred spot where one can cross over to the far shore of liberation or release from the cycle of death and rebirth (*moksa*). As thresholds between heaven and earth, such *Tirthas* are places of devotion and pilgrimage throughout the subcontinent, and in Jainism the title *Tirthankara* or "ford-builder" is given to the 24 great spiritual teachers who have shown the way of salvation.[381]

It is not only rivers or streams that have traditionally been understood to separate us from the beyond. Early Etruscan burial art shows dolphins and sea-horses accompanying the souls of the dead *across the oceans* to the felicity awaiting them on the Isles of the Blessed. Sirens too were on occasion depicted on funerary monuments bearing mortals to the Blessed Isles,[382] and it was only subsequently that darker conceptions of the afterlife came to prevail in Greek thought. Fabulous lands of promise were also portrayed in the Celtic mythology of Ireland,[383] and were happily

380. The concept of bridge-building may also have a different set of connotations, suggesting a search for common ground or affinity between apparently diverse belief systems (see Pelikan, 67). Whereas dogmatism burns bridges and excludes the heterodox, mystical and non-dogmatic thought constructs bridges and aspires to be inclusive.

381. On Jainism in general see Sharma, *A Critical Survey of Indian Philosophy*, 48-68. On the *Tirtha*, see also Bowker, 982. While Jain teaching stresses that the *Tirthankara* were mortals who attained omniscience and thus liberation through personal effort, the Jain laity have often tended to deify them.

382. Warner, 400-1.

383. According to Irish myth, the Otherworld was an enchanted realm located beyond the seas. Created as a kingdom for the divine race of the Tuatha De Danann, it was accessible through caves, lakes and fairy mounds, although Manannán, god of the sea, was reputed to have put up invisible barriers to keep out pesky mortals. Occasionally, mortals did enter inadvertently. Falling in love at the sight of the otherworldly princess Niamh as she rode out from the mists of Lough Leane, Oisin the warrior jumped straight on the horse behind her and accompanied her back into the lough, through which they entered the Otherworld. Here they married, had children and enjoyed every conceivable pleasure

taken on board by Christian ideology, for which the Church itself was a ship leading to paradise (the architectural "nave" – *Schiff* in German – betraying this association with navigation and the nautical). The *imrama*, or travel tales, of the seafaring abbot St Brendan record his maritime adventures in pursuit of an earthly paradise or promised land which he judged to be located somewhere in the Atlantic, and many other Celtic saints were moved by the same urge to go on seafaring pilgrimages.[384] Chinese versions of the Islands of the Blessed – the most famous of which was Penglai, said to be located off the east coast of China in the Pacific – also proved a spur to historical exploratory expeditions. Here the Eight Immortals of Taoist legend were said to pass their days in beatitude. To reach their island dwelling-place from the mainland, they flew on clouds or sailed on their own specific objects: a crutch, a feather fan, a magical sword, a paper mule, a lotus leaf, a flower-basket, an official court admission tablet and a pair of castanets.[385]

The ancient and medieval idea of a river or sea girdling the world incorporates a notion of circularity or cyclicality that is central to traditional imagery of life and death. This may take symbolic form. Concentric circles discovered on the walls of megalithic graves have been interpreted as suggesting "ripples in the surface of a lake when an object is dropped in the water," and thus representing "the descent of the soul into the waters of death."[386] Yet there is also a very real sense in which water powers an ongoing cycle of fertility, procreation and growth, followed by decline, death and decay, in turn succeeded by renewal and a fresh start. In ancient Egypt, fertility deities such as Osiris and Hathor, intimately bound up with the annual flooding of the Nile and the renewal of vitality that this produced, were also associated with death and the underworld. The waters they brought were part of a yearly cycle of death and new life. This cyclical motion was echoed each day in the journey made by the sun-god Re, who by day sailed across the sky in the day-barque and at

---

for 300 years. When mortals ventured there on purpose, by contrast, they tended to encounter less idyllic conditions. After all, the Otherworld was also the Land of the Dead, under the rule of a divinity called Donn, the "Dark One." See Scott Littleton, 260-63.

384. Bowen, 106-23. See also Brown, 98.
385. Scott Littleton, 440-45.
386. Biedermann, 91.

night travelled through the underworld, or *Duat*, in the "boat of millions." Among the passengers on this nocturnal barque were the countless human beings who had died and risen to become the blessed, which included Re's own descendants, the pharaoh's ancestors. This perilous night-time boat journey always included an encounter between Re and the god of resurrection Osiris, the two of whom would embrace and emerge with renewed vigour. Re would be given the power to rise anew from the waters of Nun.

The water-powered cycle of death and renewal is further reflected in the circular motion of the hydrological cycle itself (a concept first formulated by Girolamo Cardano in 1550). In the context of such ceaseless circularity, the flow of water comes to resemble the snake-like *ouroboros* perpetually chasing – or swallowing – its own tail. Its beginning and its end merge into indistinctness, and the very flow of time becomes cyclical. What is passed is passed (or past is past), but this does not mean it cannot pass (or be passed) again: water may indeed course down the same river twice. This constant roundelay of evaporation, precipitation and ground flow endlessly renews the water as it goes: some 40,000 cubic kilometres, or 30 trillion gallons, of fresh water are now known to be recycled from sea to land each year.[387] On top of evaporation, moreover, water has a spectacular capacity for *biological* self-purification. Provided there is an adequate level of dissolved oxygen, organic waste such as faeces or even crude oil is swiftly decomposed or biodegraded by the bacteria it contains.[388] The fact that this cleansing may now be given a helping hand by water treatment works (the inhabitants of London drink tap-water that has already been imbibed, excreted and purified several times on its way through Swindon and Reading) is – in the words of Fred Pearce – "just another loop in the water cycle."[389] In fact, the global water cycle consists of an infinity of mini-cycles within cycles. Travellers from Swindon to London may thus end up drinking water they have *themselves* passed just a few hours previously. Truly protean as it is, water is the supreme embodiment of self-renewal.

387. Ball, *H_2O*, 313-14.
388. Levels of dissolved oxygen are in turn determined by factors such as turbulence and temperature. See Kinnersley, *Troubled Water: Rivers, Politics and Pollution*, 17-20.
389. Pearce, 273.

Water's cyclical nature finds perhaps its most famous – and most impenetrably dense – expression in James Joyce's *Finnegans Wake*, where the cyclical course of Dublin's River Liffey – personified as Anna Livia Plurabelle – comes together, among other things, with myths of resurrection (fatal falls followed by wakes that are just as much reawakenings) as well as the theories propounded by the Italian philosopher Giovanni Battista Vico (1668-1744), for whom history took the form not of a straight line, but of a cyclical process of reiterations. In cyclical worldviews such as Joyce's, death tends to go hand in hand with fecundation, or perhaps tail in mouth, *ouroboros*-like.[390] As a dissolution of boundaries, the act of coition is itself inherently transgressive, whence its traditional association not only with death but with *moral* trespass, i.e. with sin and evil. Such erasure or dissolution of limits in turn implies parallels between sexual abandonment and watery immersion. The water of the sea is the natural element of "oceanic" rapture or engulfment, where the self loses (or perhaps transcends) itself in its other. It is also the womb of new life and regeneration.

Predictably enough, this association between flowing water and sexuality is pervaded by ambiguity, tending on the one hand towards erotic sensuality and on the other towards more lustful or vicious carnality. The threat of death or the unknown is always present, even if only latently. There is ambivalence even in such a figure as the much-loved Greek sea-goddess Aphrodite. Here the threat posed by her promiscuity is defused by transferring it to the realm of comedy or playfulness: it is the fact that Aphrodite is "laughter-loving" that helps ensure her popularity.

Yet other such watery figures have lent themselves to demonisation. Having started out as psychopomps with beautiful voices and a wealth of wisdom, the sirens came to be associated not only with death, but increasingly with vicious lust and moral perdition. "Under the influence of the rich Northern mythology about undines and selkies, mermaids and sea-nymphs," writes Marina Warner, "they shed their relation to wisdom

---

390. The link between sex and death may take many forms. The "loss of self" entailed by sex (or "love") has lent itself to metaphor as a sort of "mini-death," while the kinship of death and resurrection with sexual renewal or repetition is a timeless literary – and especially comic – motif: the image of sex as a "resurrection of the flesh" is common to Boccaccio and Rabelais as well as more recent poets and thinkers. In Joyce himself, sexual rises and falls, ups and downs, are inextricably wedded: "Phall if you but will, rise you must" (*Finnegans Wake*, 4).

and retained only their oneness with sex and death – though knowledge of these is a form of wisdom."[391] In the same tradition is the siren-like Maiden of the Lorelei, who entices men to shipwreck and death on the rocks of the River Rhine. In Heinrich Heine's celebrated poem at least, there is no indication that she is intentionally seductive, yet as she combs her golden hair with her golden comb and sings her strange, beautiful melody, no helmsman can keep control of his tiller. In von Eichendorff's poem on the same theme, she is *die Hexe Lorelei*, the Lorelei witch.

Not all female water spirits and nymphs have proved so detrimental to male well-being. In ancient Greece, the Oceanids (or sea-nymphs), the Nereids (who dwelled both in salt and fresh water) and the Naiads (who inhabited springs, rivers, lakes or fountains) were generally benevolent and kindly disposed towards humankind, symbolizing the natural vitality associated with watery places. In ancient Hindu mythology, the *apsaras* were the dancing handmaidens of the rain-god Indra, who resided near lakes or lotus ponds and took pleasure in distracting ascetics with their charms. As so frequently the case with water-spirits, they were said to be able to change their shape at will. The Hindu tradition also features the famous tale of the ill-fated union between King Pururavas and the *apsara* Urvasi, who made her earthly consort promise never to let her see him naked. But accidents happen, and see him she did. Among the hymns of the *Rig Veda* is the discussion the two of them have when Pururavas tries – and fails – to persuade her to return to him.[392] The later, 5th-century play on the same theme by the Sanskrit dramatist and poet Kalidasa, by contrast, ends in reunion and reconciliation.

In the European tradition, marriages between human beings and water spirits such as undines[393] or mermaids have seldom proved happy: in many legends wedlock with a man was a way for the mermaid to acquire the soul she otherwise lacked. Reticence and modesty combine with involuntary powers of seduction – beautiful long hair, a melodious voice – to lend the water-spirits an aura of radical otherness that may transcend or threaten the norms of social decorum. If offended, they are

---

391. Warner, 402.
392. *The Rig Veda*, 252-56.
393. These water spirits were given their name by Paracelsus (on the basis of the Latin word for wave, *viz.* undulation), for whom they were the elementary creatures of water, corresponding to the salamander (fire), the sylph (air) and the gnome (earth). See Ball, *The Devil's Doctor*, 318.

liable to induce floods or other misfortunes. Yet they may also display vulnerability. The little mermaid of Hans Christian Andersen's tale, who falls for a handsome prince, not only loses her tail (which is bloodily split into a pair of legs) and forfeits her beautiful voice in her desire to join him, but ends up dying of a broken heart, dissolving into foam on the waves of the sea.

The motif of exquisite flowing hair is also present in "The Little Mermaid." When she first ventures onto land, the water spirit makes a point of hiding her hair and breasts with sea foam. Later, she covers her naked body with her long, thick hair. In their efforts to save her, her sisters sacrifice their hair to the sea witch. The Maiden of the Lorelei also has long, golden tresses (which she combs as she sings), as does Aphrodite, who is traditionally depicted as stroking, caressing or wringing out her hair as she emerges from the brine. There is an evident parallelism between the flow of hair, the flow of song, and the flow of sea water, each with their gentle waves and harmonious undulations, their meanderings and whirls.[394] The morphological affinities between the flow of hair and the flow of water were most famously brought to light by Leonardo da Vinci. The background to his most celebrated masterpiece, the Mona Lisa, consists of a complex cycle of flowing waters, which – as Leonardo himself was proud to point out[395] – echo the flowing cascades of *La Gioconda*'s hair. Commenting in his notebooks on a sketch of his that presents water in the form of hair, he writes:

> Observe the motion of the surface of the water, how it resembles that of hair, which has two movements – one depends on the weight of the hair, the other on the direction of the curls; thus the water forms whirling

394. Clouds too are often seen to be hair-like, as is reflected in a number of the Latinate terms for the categories of cloud. The *cumulonimbus capillatus* takes its name from the Latin word for hair (*capillus*) and can look, according to Pretor-Pinney (*The Cloudspotter's Guide*, 58), like "the disorderly locks of a child who's just been in a playground scrap." The word *cirrus* is also of Latin derivation, denoting a wisp, tuft or lock of hair. Likewise from the realm of coiffure, *pileus* cloud harks back to the Latin word for a felt cap or hat. The *pileus*, says Pretor-Pinney, is "rather like a cloud haircut. It is a supercooled-droplet bouffant, worn exclusively by the fashionable Cumulus family." It may often take on a "wonderful blow-dried appearance" (ibid., 240-41).
395. See Gould, "The Upwardly Mobile Fossils of Leonardo's Living Earth," in *Leonardo's Mountain of Clams and the Diet of Worms*, 31-33.

eddies, one part following the impetus of the chief current, and the other following the incidental motion and return flow.[396]

Nor need the hair in question be attached to a female head. The same association is present in the image of the great Hindu god Shiva using his long, matted locks to check the power of the River Ganges, which he allows to flow along and through his hair as it tumbles down from heaven.

Hair itself shares the ambiguity of the waters with which it is so often associated. There has existed a straightforward – and at times crudely overgeneralized – "dichotomy" in the symbolism of women's hair, a contrast between hair that is long, loose and free-flowing and hair that is closely cropped and severe. Whereas the latter has been associated with discipline, order and control, suggests zoologist Desmond Morris, free-flowing locks have been seen to symbolize "lack of restraint, sexuality, freedom of spirit, peaceful rebellion and creativity."[397] Yet further ambivalence resides within the symbolism of *long* hair, for rebellion need not be peaceful, and sexuality can represent a threat: freedom from constraint may be evaluated either positively (as natural and spontaneous) or negatively (as viciously carnal or lustful).[398]

Such negative imagery emerges emblematically in the Grimms' fairy tale "The Nixie of the Mill-Pond," in which a miller, having hit upon hard times, inadvertently forfeits his son to the cunning of a malevolent nixie. This nixie is a beautiful woman with a "sweet voice," yet her long hair, which she holds off her shoulders with soft hands and which cascades down over her white body, betrays a sexuality that is rapacious and all-engulfing, presaging ensnarement or captivity.[399] One day, when the son – now a grown man with a wife – strays too close to the mill pond, she swiftly emerges to drag him down into the depths, where … the reader is left in the dark. It is up to the wife, helped by the advice of a wise woman, to free her husband from the nixie's liquid clutch. To do this, she is told,

---

396. Leonardo da Vinci, 25.
397. Morris, *The Naked Woman*, 17.
398. Itself an anatomical outgrowth, hair is *inherently* ambiguous. My hair is both me and not-me: it is a margin or boundary of the human self and as such – like toe-nails or other bodily extremities, or indeed water itself (i.e. blood) – has tended to assume magical or ritualistic significance. The ancient Greeks, for example, sacrificed locks of hair to river gods such as Achelous and Scamander.
399. Grimm and Grimm, *Complete Fairy Tales*, 652-57.

she must perform three tasks, each time tarrying "until the full moon comes again" before performing the next. First, she must go to the mill-pond, comb her long black hair and then leave the comb on the shore; the second time she must play a golden flute and then leave it on the sand; the third time she must spin a distaff and then leave that on the bank. On this third occasion, her grateful husband manages to catch her by the hand and break free from the pond, the vicious nixie flooding the whole area in her angry pursuit. The imagery – in particular the waxing and waning of the moon and the spinning of the distaff[400] – is of death and rebirth: playing music and combing hair likewise serve as symbols of the overcoming of death and disorder by harmony and life.[401]

A more grotesque manifestation of aquatic carnality comes to light in "The Little Mermaid," where the innocent sensuality of the fish-tailed mermaid contrasts with the mature physicality of the sea witch, whose realm is a wriggling, writhing mass of slimy polyps and sinuous serpents. It is this ancient hag, with her big spongy breasts, who offers the little mermaid the double-edged sword of womanhood, painfully splitting her tail to produce legs that part and causing her blood to flow. In the film version of the tale, she is portrayed, in the words of Marina Warner, as "an undulating, obese octopus, with a raddled bar-queen face out of Toulouse-Lautrec and torso and tentacles sheathed in black velvet, (...) a cartoon Queen of the Night, avid and unrestrained."[402]

The association between the fluid, fleshy world of marine invertebrates and the female genitalia is a commonplace. Warner cites a passage of prose-poetry written by the poet Paul Valéry in the 1930s, inspired by watching a film of jellyfish:

> No human dancer, no woman overheated and drunken with motion, with the toxic charge of her overextended energies, with the burning proximity of looks loaded with desire, ever conveyed so imperiously the offering of her sex, that beckoning pantomime of compulsive prostitution, as this great jellyfish who, by undulating shakes of her train

400. See Eliade, *Patterns*, 180-81, on the relationship between lunar divinities and the symbolism of the weaving or spinning of fate.
401. In another tale, "The Water Nixie," a little boy and his sister, playing by a well, likewise fall into the clutches of a cruel water-nixie, who carries them off to make them work for her. But they escape, throwing a hair-brush, a comb and finally a looking-glass behind them as they go. See ibid., 317.
402. Warner, 403.

of ruffled skirts, which she tosses up and tosses up again with strange and shameless insistence, transforms herself into a dream of Eros and suddenly, throwing aside all her vibrating petticoats, her dress of cut-out lips, turns herself upside down and exposes herself, terribly open.[403]

Nor is this simile merely the product of an overheated poetic imagination. "Sober" scientists too have proved unable to resist its seductive charms. The 1771 treatise on molluscs by the founding father of taxonomy, Carolus Linnaeus, describes a fairly remarkable set of parallels between certain bivalves and the sexual anatomy of women. One species of clam is shown – with an accompanying labelled diagram – to consist of *nates* (buttocks), a *hymen, vulva, labia, pubes,* an *anus* and a *mons veneris.*[404]

The likeness between the vulva and the clam or oyster (depending) has been further reflected down the years in everyday, colloquial and bawdy language. The entertainingly exhaustive *Cassell Dictionary of Slang* contains both "bearded clam" and "bearded oyster" as terms for the vagina, as well as "periwinkle" and the rather plain old "shell."[405] The general Latin term for a bivalve or shellfish, *concha,* also meant "vulva," a

403. Quoted in ibid., 403-4. A similar spirit of aquatic-erotic fantasy informs the works of 18th and 19th-century Japanese artists such as Utamaro and Hoku-sai. Inspired by the venerable tradition of Ama sea-women who free-dived for shellfish and pearls, they portrayed diving girls being ravished by octopuses and other such sea-beasts. Shocked and excited by Hokusai's famous *shunga* design *Diving Girl and Octopuses,* J-K. Huysmans described the picture as both beauti-ful and frightening: "it is of a Japanese woman mounted by an octopus; with its tentacles, the horrible beast sucks the tips of her breasts and rummages in her mouth, while its head drinks from her lower parts" (see Sprawson, 286).

404. See Gould, "The Clam Stripped Bare by Her Naturalists, Even," in *Leon-ardo's Mountain of Clams and the Diet of Worms,* 78-80. It need not concern us here whether this is the old-fashioned schoolboy joke of a saucy Latinist, the warped vision of a sex-obsessed scientist, or an accurate and enlightening anal-ogy that only incidentally casts any light upon the workings of the human mind. One outraged contemporary fumed: "Science should be chaste and delicate. Ribaldry at times has been passed for wit; but Linnaeus alone passes it for terms of science" (quoted in Gould, 81). Gould's essay contains the diagram of the clam species in question, which Linnaeus named *Venus dione.*

405. It also contains the surreal, gastronomically challenging "seafood blanc-mange." Mind you, there are quite a few other marine references too, including lobster-pots, haddock pasties, cod trenches and snapping turtles. These clearly have a different set of metaphorical connections.

link that persists to this day, particularly in Argentinean Spanish. In France the word for a mussel, *moule*, is used to denote the same. The Spanish word for clam, *almeja*, is considered somewhat vulgar, while in Germany the clam is a *Venusmuschel* (or Venus mussel),[406] harking back to the painterly convention portraying the goddess of love, Venus or Aphrodite, as standing on or in the vicinity of a scallop shell.[407] Through its association with water and Aphrodite, the mollusc thus brings together sexual symbolism with the promise of fertility, and sea food has traditionally been regarded as an aphrodisiac throughout the Mediterranean.[408] The Hindu god Vishnu is usually depicted as holding a conch, the source of all elements and everything that exists, while the Aztec god Ehecatl, god of wind and bringer of rains (an incarnation of the greatly revered Quetzalcoatl, god of water and fertility), also wore a shell as part of his attire. Some Christian symbolism, by contrast, turned the bivalve into a symbol of the grave, or deathly enclosure.[409] At the same time, the beautifully spherical pearls encased within bivalves have been taken to represent hidden knowledge, esoteric wisdom or the teachings of Jesus, inaccessible to non-believers.[410] The scallop shell has even come to symbolize pilgrims such as Saint James, or Santiago, as well as the pilgrimage to his shrine in Compostela in Spain.

Of course, the metaphorical associations of marine fauna are not exclusively with female sexuality. The ugly, fat water snakes that tumble and sport on the pendulous breasts of the sea witch in "The Little Mermaid" are equally phallic in their connotations, while the Spanish word *pulpo* or octopus denotes a *man* who gropes women, i.e. cannot keep control of his tentacles.[411] Other cultures have male water-spirits that are openly

406. The fairly coarse term *Muschi* presumably has its roots in mussels (*Muscheln*), though it also happens to be a children's word for a feline pussy-cat.
407. See Titian's *Venus Anadyomene* ("Venus Rising from the Sea") and Botticelli's *The Birth of Venus*.
408. Graves, I.50.
409. Biedermann, 40-41.
410. Ibid., 259.
411. The same imagery of slimy invasiveness – of a physical and moral trespass or transgression – was behind the popular nickname *el Pulpo* used to denote the US banana monopoly United Fruit Company (the ancestor of the modern-day banana-growing cephalopod Chiquita Brands), whose tentacles have intruded into so much of Guatemalan and Central American life and society over the last century. A similar perception informs the "octopus maps" of 19th-century

transgressive in nature. Cuban slang, for example, has its mysterious *Güijes* and *Jigües*. The former take the form of black-skinned dwarves with a habit of emerging naked from rivers and ponds to fondle unsuspecting women as they bathe; the latter are dwarf-sized, brown-skinned *indigenous* water spirits with long hair and equally lascivious tendencies.[412] The lecherous *kappa* of Japanese folklore, said to resemble a monkey with fish scales and webbed digits, is an equally impish trouble-maker, who takes pleasure in passing wind and peeping up women's kimonos. On top of his head is a hollow depression filled with water, which if spilt reduces his supernatural powers. *Kappas* are said to have a weakness for cucumbers, which can thus be used for placating or befriending them.

The association of water and sexuality always has its shadow side, connoting transgression, self-loss or death. Nowhere has the association between water, fertility and death taken more concrete form than in the meteorological deities of ancient religion. The ancient Vedic deity Indra was both a storm god responsible for dispensing rain and a warrior god. Adored and venerated by a people dependent upon the monsoon rains to save them from drought, Indra was the supreme deity of the Vedic age, whose most celebrated feat was to dispatch the demon Vritra, who had rounded up all the rainclouds and held back the waters of the monsoon.[413] Yet storms themselves are thoroughly ambivalent, combining their fructifying energies with destructive power and hostility. In the *Rig Veda*, Indra's thunderbolts are "weapons" in both a martial and a phallic sense:

---

graphic artists and cartographers such as Fred W. Rose, whose famous cartoon map *Serio-Comic War Map for the Year 1877* represents the rapidly growing military might of Russia in the menacing form of a huge octopus with tentacles throttling Poland and Finland and threatening Persia, central Asia, Armenia, the Holy Land and the Turkish Empire. Just over a quarter of a century later, the image was still being used, now by Japanese propagandists during the Russo-Japanese conflict. See Barber, *The Map Book*, 284-85.

412. García and Alonso, *Diccionario Ilustrado de Voces Eróticas Cubanas*, 96, 102.

413. The mythology of the Huron Indians of America has a similar tale describing how their saviour god, Ioskeha, dispatched a huge frog that had swallowed all the world's freshwater (Eliot, 225). In the frog myth told by the Aboriginal Kurnai tribe of Australia, the drought was resolved by inducing the frog in question (called Dak) to burst out laughing, thus releasing the pent-up waters she had swallowed (Eliade, *Patterns*, 160-61).

when Indra shoots his bolt, he both does away with his mortal enemy and provides a much-needed source of water and of seed.[414]

Moreover, in an act of divine patricide – with all the symbolic baggage that this may entail – Vedic mythology shows Indra turning against, and killing, his own father Dyaus, often associated with Varuna. Like Indra, Varuna had at one time been the supreme deity. Like Indra, he was a provider of water. As with Ea's overcoming of Apsu in ancient Akkadian mythology or Baal's defeat of Leviathan or Yamm in the Canaanite tradition, therefore, an older, possibly senile water deity is vanquished and replaced by a younger, more vital one. The circularity inherent in the never-ending flow of the water cycle (water replacing water replacing water...) finds an echo in such narratives of death and new life.[415] Certainly, Varuna's authority waned, and Indra assumed many of his attributes. Whereas in pre-Vedic times, Varuna had been the chief of the gods, the keeper of order, and the deity of rain, he later became the god of rivers and oceans. He was also a god of the dead, who looked after the souls of the drowned.

Similar ambiguity also structured the ancient Mesoamerican gods of rain and water. The rain god Chac was one of the most consistently venerated deities in the Mayan pantheon, particularly in the state of Yucatán in Mexico. Endowed with a blatantly phallic nose, Chac was clearly associated with fertility and reproduction, yet his worship also became bound up with human sacrifice, particularly in post-classic times. In the arid region of Yucatán, the only source of fresh water came from the *cenotes*, natural wells formed by the collapse of karst underground caves in limestone formations. The ancient Mayan city of Chichén Itzá was constructed around, and depended for its livelihood upon, a cluster of such *cenotes*, and it was here that sacrificial ritual was centred. Its occurrence has now been corroborated by the discovery of numerous skeletons of men, women and children, along with ceremonial offerings of gold, silver and jade ornamentation.

The Aztecs, who came to prominence in the centuries prior to the arrival of the Spanish conquistadors, inherited the Mayan belief in a constant cycle of destruction and regeneration and the need for human sacrifice. The rain-god Tlaloc, who took on many of the attributes of Chac,

---

414. See *The Rig Veda*, 148-51.
415. At the same time, such conflicts among deities may also be interpreted as reflecting inter-tribal hostilities.

was the most highly revered and greatly feared deity within the Aztec pantheon. Children were regularly sacrificed as part of his cult, often being immured in subterranean caverns where it was believed they would lead a life of eternal bliss in Tlalocán, Tlaloc's earthly paradise. While he could provide rain and generate fertility, moreover, Tlaloc also had the capacity to unleash hurricanes, storms and lightning – he was often portrayed with a jug of water and a jade tomahawk – as well as to withhold his waters, provoking drought and famine, and spread illnesses such as dropsy and leprosy.

While Tlaloc presided over water as it fell from the sky, it was his consort Chalchiuhtlicue ("of the jade skirt") who was responsible for the waters below, the rivers, oceans, lakes and springs that repose or run on the surface of the earth. Associated in particular with fertility, babies and childbirth, Chalchiuhtlicue had her dark side too. Sometimes referred to as the "Agitated" or "Foaming" One, she could conjure up whirlpools and torrents, and images show her sitting on a throne from which there emerges a flood of water washing away struggling human figures.[416] As ever, water – or the water deities – could bring both life and death. In the light of the awe and veneration they inspired, it is hardly surprising that almost half of the regular festivals held in honour of the Aztec gods were dedicated to the deities of water.[417]

416. Scott Littleton, 565-67.
417. Ibid., 567-68.

Chapter Three
Water as Death and the Depths

1

Deluges

Indra was a god of water and a warrior god. He was associated with life-giving rain, but also with storms, thunder and lightning. While cloudbursts can quicken and fructify, they can also take the form of hurricanes, cyclones or typhoons, producing hail stones, torrential downpours, storm surges and flash flooding and causing damage to property and huge loss of life. With the rise of Hinduism, Indra's importance waned. One tale has it that when Krishna, the eighth avatar of Vishnu, persuaded the cowherds among whom he lived to stop worshipping Indra, the warrior god dispatched torrents of rain in his anger. Krishna's response was to lift up the local mountain on the tip of his fingers and use it as an umbrella to protect the population until Indra relented and paid him due homage. Yet in spite of the decline in Indra's powers, the thunderstorms he has traditionally embodied have continued to batter the planet unrelentingly.[418]

418. Worldwide, some 40,000 storms are calculated to take place a day, 2,000 at any one time, unloading as much as 20 billion tons of water onto the Earth below. In terms of energy, a hurricane is considered the meteorological equivalent of a thousand 20-megaton bombs going off at once (see Rupp, 168-69, 205-12). Lightning still claims over 1,000 lives a year. The coastal flooding caused by the storm surges that hurricanes can whip up – with surge waves over 10 metres in height – is devastating in its effect. Central America, the Caribbean and the south-east coast of the USA are especially vulnerable in this respect, as Hurricane Katrina showed in 2005, while Bangladesh is regularly exposed to the tropical cyclones that come raging in from the Indian Ocean. In 1737 a storm surge provoked by a cyclone drowned a million people along the coast of the Bay of Bengal; another in April 1991 claimed over 140,000 lives. Since 1797 the Bangladesh coastline has suffered 66 major cyclones and many more, smaller ones.

Hurricanes take their name from the Mayan creator god who, as the *Popol Vuh* recounts, produced a mighty deluge – as well as fire, brimstone and an orgy of the goriest pandemonium – to wipe out the wooden people produced in an early, unsuccessful attempt to populate the world.[419] In the Aztec universe too, water represented the perpetual threat of a return to the primordial chaos. The world inhabited by human beings was believed to be surrounded by an ocean that curved up seamlessly to merge into the waters of the sky, which could at any time come crashing down to wipe out the world below. This was indeed said to have happened on four occasions. Accordingly, the past comprised four past eras or "Suns," while the present was the Fifth Sun, which would also be the last. The first age was ruled over by Tezcatlipoca and inhabited by a race of vegetarian giants. The second was created and presided over by the water and fertility deity Quetzalcoatl in his guise as the wind god Ehecatl, and came to an appropriate end with an enormous hurricane. The Third Sun, the Sun of Rain, was governed by Tlaloc, before its destruction in a torrent of fiery cinders. Tlaloc's wife Chalchiuhtlicue created and reigned over the Fourth Sun, the Sun of Water, which was destroyed when she caused the underground waters to surge to the surface and inundate the world, drowning all life and bringing down the sky.[420]

Not all flood stories are quite so remorseless in their destruction. South American flood mythology generally allows for a handful of survivors. In the great deluge recounted by the pre-Incan Cañari people of Andean Ecuador, for example, two brothers saved their skin by taking refuge on a magical mountain that grew higher as the waters rose. When the waters eventually receded, the lucky survivors were cared for by two beautiful macaw-women, and their offspring were the ancestors of the Cañari tribe. The Chimu people of coastal Peru and northern Chile also escaped their deluge by clambering high into the mountains. Subsequently visited by a plague of poisonous serpents that further reduced their numbers, only a few particularly hardy survivors were left to set about the business of repopulation. For the Andean Indians of what is now Peru, the only survivor was a single shepherd together with the six llamas that had forewarned him of the cataclysm. As this left unanswered certain nagging

---

419. See *Popol Vuh*, 71-72: "There came a rain of resin [turpentine] from the sky. There came the one named Gouger of Faces: he gouged out their eyeballs." And so on.
420. On the Aztec eras, see Scott Littleton, 544-49.

doubts about the subsequent repopulation of the world, a variation on the myth tells that the shepherd took his six sons and daughters with him to the safety of the mountain peak.[421]

Hindu myth includes one of the most renowned deluges, the survivor in this case being Manu, the father of the human race. Manu was rescued by Matsya the fish-man, who had first appeared to him as a tiny fish during his morning devotions. Manu looked after Matsya, who grew and grew and eventually – when the time had come – warned him of the imminent inundation and told him to build a boat and put seeds and animals into it. When the rains arrived, Matsya – in fact the first avatar of Vishnu the preserver – towed the boat to safety and anchored it to one of the highest peaks of the Himalayas. The tale of Vishnu's third avatar, Varaha the boar, also involved rescue from watery dissolution, in this case after the demon Hiranyaksha had inconsiderately dumped the world at the bottom of the primordial ocean. The fact that in its earliest forms this story was a creation myth[422] betrays once again that the threat of water is the threat of a return to the state of non-differentiation and chaos from which the world has not long since emerged.

The flood myth is perhaps the most universal of all mythological tales. Noah's flood is familiar throughout the Christian world, but this in turn has its origins in the various deluges of ancient Mesopotamia. Oldest is the Sumerian myth of Ziusudra (later called Xisuthros by the Babylonian priest Berossus), believed to be based on a real-life priest-king and a real-life river flood that may have occurred around 2900 BCE.[423] In a version written in Akkadian (the language of ancient Babylon), it is Atrahasis ("Extremely Wise") who dons Ziusudra's mantle as the saviour of his people. According to this tale, human beings had originally been created to spare the deities the hard work of digging the rivers and irrigation ditches. But it was not long before they became a pest and a nuisance, spoiling the peace and quiet that was so precious to the gods. Ellil, the deity who presided over Earth, sent first a plague, then a drought, then a food shortage, but when each of these attempts to extirpate humankind was foiled by the freshwater god Enki, he decided to send a huge inundation

---

421. Ibid., 590-98.
422. See Bowker, 1015.
423. See Johnson, *A History of the Jews*, 8-9. Others have attributed the original, historical flood to sudden oscillations in sea-level following the end of the last ice age (see Kandel, 195, 278).

lasting seven days to finish them off for good. Once again he was foiled: this time, Enki appeared in a dream to Atrahasis, telling him to build a boat, roof it over, seal it with pitch, and save his family and representatives of each species. Which is precisely what he did.[424]

The venerable figures of Ziusudra and Atrahasis assume the name Ut-napishtim in the *Epic of Gilgamesh*, the final version of which is considered to be the work of a Babylonian scribe writing some 3,000 years ago. In this tale, the hero Gilgamesh voyages to the faraway "mouth of the rivers"[425] to find the distant ancestor who many years earlier rescued humankind from a watery grave and now quietly enjoys postdiluvial immortality with his wife. The account Ut-napishtim gives to Gilgamesh is similar to the earlier ones: he was saved by the water-god Ea, who instructed him to build a special vessel to hold all his family and exemplars of each species from the animal kingdom; in this instance the torrential rains lasted for six days and seven nights; and when the waters subsided, their boat was grounded on the highest mountain peak, where Ut-napishtim duly offered a sacrifice.

Noah's flood throws up a number of interesting parallels and discrepancies in relation to the Mesopotamian ones. One contrast frequently commented upon is that whereas the tales of Ziusudra and Atrahasis present the deluge as a product of divine whimsy (the gods seem simply to be sick and tired of the noise), the story of Noah is structured around a dominant framework of ethical values: Noah is a righteous man, and it is his righteousness that is regarded as differentiating him from the sinful masses and exempting him from the ensuing moral castigation. Yet caution is due. Atrahasis in particular is no ordinary mortal. Not only is his name ("Extremely Wise") the very epithet used to describe Adapa or Uan, the sage created by Ea / Enki to teach humankind the secrets of civilization,[426] but it is the special relationship he obviously enjoys with the god of wisdom and water that permits him to thwart the destructive designs of Ellil: "He would speak with his god," the text insists three times, "And his god would speak with him."[427] It is as a model of sagacious devotion that Atrahasis too thus earns his privileged status as the survivor of the deluge.

---

424. See "Atrahasis," in Dalley (trans.), 9-38.
425. See "The Epic of Gilgamesh," in ibid., 50-135; 116.
426. See "Adapa," in ibid., 182-88; 184.
427. "Atrahasis," in ibid., 18, 23-24, 26.

In the case of Atrahasis no less than Noah, the distinction between divine whimsy and moral order is deeply problematic: concepts of "extreme wisdom" or "righteousness" beg the question in that the criteria by which they are judged are themselves purely god-given. To be righteous and wise, says an authoritarian god, is to listen to *me*, to walk with *me*. Vindictive gods have traditionally sent floods to punish their people for failing to acknowledge them, i.e. for being "godless."[428] Yet the concept of "godlessness" – for all its traditional connotations of wickedness – may simply imply worship of a different god or (in today's terms, perhaps) indifference, atheism or agnosticism. If a vengeful deity sends a deluge to punish a society mistakenly worshipping the "wrong" god or (in today's terms) a community of ethical atheists, this is neither more moral nor less capricious than castigating people for "making a din." The problem has particularly serious repercussions because the function of deity as the foundation of "morality" is conflated with his function as a dispenser of punishment. There is no independent court of appeal where miscreant humans can cast doubt on the principles underlying divine justice or question the legitimacy of their imminent immersion.

A second divergence is that unlike the myths of Atrahasis and Ut-napishtim, where the plot incorporates disparate voices among the gods (Ellil or Enlil versus Enki or Ea), the orthodox Christian tale of Noah involves only one God, and its resolution is internalized, as it were, within a single voice from on high. Perhaps to compensate for this autocratic remoteness, the rainbow – a traditional symbolic link between the heavens and the earth – is taken as a token of divine benevolence, representing God's covenant with Noah that he would never again send a flood to destroy the Earth.[429] Heterodox Christianity included a more polyphonic understanding of the truth. The heretical Gnostic texts, which attempted to reincorporate a feminine element into the exclusively masculine conception of Judaeo-Christian divinity, told a different story, in which humankind is saved by the female figure of Sophia, or Wisdom. According to the Gnostic tale, when the creator was angered by the human race

---

428. Witness the punishment of the people of Sheba for their "ingratitude" in the Qur'an (34:15-17). Pariacaca, chief god of the Huarochirí Indians, once flooded a village because its inhabitants did not offer him a drink when he passed through during the local festivals. A water and mountain deity, Pariacaca seems to have launched deluges on quite a regular basis. See Scott Littleton, 596-99.
429. Genesis 9:11-17.

because they did not worship or honour him as Father and God, he sent forth a flood upon them, that he might destroy them all. But Wisdom opposed him ... and Noah and his family were saved in the ark by means of the sprinkling of the light that proceeded from her, and through it the world was again filled with humankind.[430]

Nor is it necessarily the feminine element that saves the day. According to some versions of the flood myth told by the Chibcha people of what is now Colombia, it was the disorderly and self-indulgent female figure of Chia who provoked the floods, and her husband Bochica – the sun deity and patron of civilization – who appeared astride a rainbow and brought the sun to evaporate away the flood waters.[431] In such a case, the flood is a reflection not only of divine disunity, but also – on a more down-to-earth level – of connubial conflict.

A third notable point of contrast between Noah and his precursors is his association with wine. Noah's status as not only the first vintner but also the father of drinkers, as well as the subsequent humiliation he suffers when his son Ham catches him asleep in a drunken stupor with his private parts exposed, has caused a certain amount of perplexity among commentators. Typological Christian interpreters saw the episode as prefiguring the stripping of Christ prior to the Crucifixion.[432] At the same time, wine has itself played an important part within Christian spirituality: in John's Gospel, Christ's first miracle was to turn water into wine at a marriage ceremony in Cana (John 2:1-11). Others have been less indulgent: in the eyes of the 1st-century Jewish philosopher Philo of Alexandria, Noah was the proto-toper, whose tale served as a warning of the perils of inebriation.[433] What is certain is that even though the Biblical Noah did not take up viniculture until *after* the deluge, the legend of his bibulous nature has gathered a momentum of its own. As G. K. Chesterton expressed it in "Wine and Water" (1914):

> And Noah he often said to his wife when he sat down to dine,
> "I don't care where the water goes if it doesn't get into the wine."[434]

430. Quoted in Pagels, *The Gnostic Gospels*, 76.
431. Scott Littleton, 586-89.
432. Biedermann, 239.
433. Philo, "On Drunkenness."
434. The poem first appeared in his novel *The Flying Inn* (1914). Quoted in *The Oxford Dictionary of Humorous Quotations*, 8.

In fact, the tale of Noah is not the only example of this association between inundation and inebriation.[435] According to the ancient Greek flood myth, Zeus's anger with the primordial race of Pelasgians who inhabited pre-Hellenic Greece prompted him to send a flood that wiped out everyone except Deucalion and his wife Pyrrha (this time no animals were saved). Here the link with wine lies in the survivors' names, Deucalion meaning "new-wine sailor" and Pyrrha "fiery red," the colour applied to wine.[436] Deucalion's sister Ariadne, moreover, was the mother, by Dionysus, of various tribes associated with the vine cult. Landing on Mount Parnassus, the two survivors pleaded with Zeus for mankind to be renewed, and their wish was granted. As the two of them cast stones over their shoulders in accordance with oracular instructions, these turned into men or women depending on whether they had been thrown by Deucalion or Pyrrha. Their eldest son was Hellen, father of Greeks; another was Orestheus, said to be the first mortal to cultivate the vine; a third was Amphictyon, the first to mix wine with water.

The connection is further developed in the short story *Los advertidos* ("The Forewarned") by the Cuban novelist Alejo Carpentier (1904-1980). Here the universality of flood mythology is reflected in a diluvial encounter between Amalivaca, the great saviour of a pre-Columbian people, and the prophet from the Chinese Kingdom of Xing, subsequently joined by Noah, Deucalion and Ut-napishtim. No sooner has the storm abated than Amalivaca wets his whistle with a tankard of the strong Peruvian maize liquor *chicha*;[437] the Chinese saviour brings rice wine; the initially presumptuous Noah eventually adds his own contribution of red wine; and as they each discover that they are not the only saviour of mankind, they collectively proceed to get half seas over. With each of them equally mistaken in the assumption of his own uniqueness, the implication is that there are more prophets, saviours and angry gods out there. The myth, like the flood itself, is as universal and all-embracing as the shared drink that the bibulous saviours so heartily enjoy, and the harmonious conviviality among the saviour-soaks represents a moment of utopian peace before the

435. The link is also present in the *Epic of Gilgamesh*, although here it is not the flood-survivor Ut-napishtim who encounters Siduri the goddess of ale and wisdom, but Gilgamesh himself, who asks her for directions on how to reach Ut-napishtim. See Dalley (trans.), 99-102, 149-51.
436. See Graves, I.138-43, esp. 141 on the etymologies.
437. Carpentier, *Narrativa Completa*, I.968.

human race gets back to its bickering. Which is not long.[438]

Noah's flood in particular has caused no end of puzzlement as regards its technical and logistical details, in particular the construction of the vessel and the small matter of how so many animals survived cooped up in such a limited space for such a long time (imagine the smell). Scholars have been intrigued by the question of whether the deluge was local or global in extent. Jewish and early Christian thinkers were unanimous in regarding it as a universal event. With time, however, the hydrological implications of the complete submersion of a whole world in water became more and more of a headache.

The idea had received conventional corroboration from the much-commented presence of marine fossils and ancient sea-shells on mountain tops: how else could they have reached such altitudes if not transported there by the tumultuous waters of Noah's flood? But not everyone agreed that such a proposal stood up to rigorous scrutiny. Leonardo da Vinci, with his special interest in water and its movements, begged to differ. His main argument was that "neither by rain which makes the rivers swell, nor by the overflow of the sea could the shells, being heavy objects, be driven by the sea up the mountains or be carried there by the rivers contrary to the course of their waters."[439] Way ahead of his time as ever, Leonardo believed instead that the presence of marine fossils on high hills was best explained in terms of the emergence of the mountains from the seas. This in turn formed part of his broader worldview, according to which the Earth, as a living "organism" on the macrocosmic scale, corresponded to

---

438. The theme of diluvial drinking is naturally bound up with the realm of bodily humour and bawdry. Like the passing of the flood waters or the passing of any other waters, it is a matter of (possibly comic) relief. This is the effect, for example, when the mighty warrior Thor, one of the best-loved figures from the Norse pantheon, almost drowns in a river of water passed by Gjalp, daughter of the giant Geirrod. Stories of giants and tall tales in general lend themselves to pisspot humour. The most famous, perhaps, involves Rabelais's giant-hero Gargantua, whose annoyance at the tiresome curiosity of the Parisians prompts him to undo his gargantuan codpiece, fetch out his john thomas, and unleash such a cataclysmic torrent that 260,418 of the local inhabitants (not counting women and children) are drowned by the deluge. Being Rabelais, moreover, it is a purely comic prank, perpetrated *par rys* ("for a laugh"). And this, we are told, is where the city's name comes from. See Rabelais, *Oeuvres complètes*, 88-89 (*Gargantua*, chap. 17).

439. Leonardo da Vinci, 27.

the human body on the microcosmic scale, with its four elements – water, earth, fire and air – in a perpetual, self-renewing process of cyclical flux.

Leonardo also doubted the universality of Noah's flood and queried where all the water from such a global inundation could have gone.[440] In Talmudic tradition, it was through the *omphalos* (Greek for "navel"), a rock located in the temple of Jerusalem and regarded as the site of the creation and centrepoint of the world, that the diluvial waters were drained off to the subterranean depths. If the *omphalos* were removed, so it was believed, the waters of the *Tehom* would come gushing forth again.[441] However, this notion of a cosmic bath-plug did not satisfactorily explain *why* or *how* enough water could suddenly spout forth to cover the highest mountain top.

One cosmogony that resolved this question was proposed by René Descartes in the first half of the 17th century. In his *Principles of Philosophy*, Descartes suggested that the Earth had originally formed as a fiery sphere and that when this cooled a crust formed over the watery abyss: the flood was simply the collapse of this crust. These speculations were taken up and set in a more Biblical context by the Englishman Thomas Burnet, whose *Sacred Theory of the Earth* was published in Latin in 1681, appeared in English in 1684, and became one of the most widely read geology books of the late 17th century. Considering the 40 days and 40 nights of precipitation woefully inadequate for a deluge of the required order, Burnet suggested that the Earth had initially been flawlessly ovoid in shape. At its centre, this "mundane egg" had a yolk of fire, around which the albumen took the form of a watery abyss, in turn covered by the crust of the Earth on top. Gradually desiccated by the sun and weakened by the pressure from below, it was only natural that the Earth's shell should eventually yield, with cataclysmic consequences: vast sections of the crust plunged into the abyssal *Tehom* and were swirled about in the chaotic mêlée that ensued. This explanation, Burnet felt, had the twin virtues of providing enough water for a universal deluge that would cover the tallest mountain top and also removing this water when the time had come for the subsequent repopulation of the globe: once the initial agitation

440. The idea of a spherical layer of water universally enveloping the globe contradicted his conception of the Earth as a dynamic self-moving organism. See ibid., 30-31.

441. Biedermann, 246. In Hebrew, *Tehom* or "the depths" refers to the primal waters of creation as well as to the place from which Noah's flood emerged. It is cognate with the Babylonian Tiamat.

and commotion of the deluge had subsided and the waters had gradually settled, the oceans would be those parts of the abyss into which the crust had sunk without trace, while the land – with its hills and dales – would be those parts of the debris that ended up poking out from the depths.[442]

Prior to 1600, the consensus in the Christian world was that ancient history consisted of the Biblical account given in Genesis, the world was rather less than 6,000 years old, and the Noachic flood was a genuine historical event.[443] Burnet's popular speculations did not challenge this view, yet such attempts to provide a naturalistic explanation for the deluge were nonetheless a worry to churchmen, who felt that they marginalized the role of God by explaining away the supernatural. Particularly vexatious to orthodoxy were scientific speculations on the role of *comets* in bringing about the flood (as well as the creation and the final conflagration). Such notions went back to Newton, who – as we have seen – maintained that comets swept through the solar system in accordance with the laws of universal gravitation, conveying vital supplies of aqueous vapour in their tails and thus restoring the waters required by planets for vegetation and life. Newton's ideas on the part played by comets in the Biblical deluge were reported only in private conversations,[444] but similar ideas were taken up and made known to a wider public by Edmond Halley (1656-1742), who likewise held that God acted through natural laws rather than direct or miraculous intervention. For Halley, the most feasible cause of the deluge was the "casual *Choc* of a *Comet*, or other transient Body," which would have sent gigantic waves pounding over the shattered land, returning it to an original state of chaos.[445] Evidence for such global pandemonium, he

---

442. Burnet, *The Sacred Theory of the Earth*, bk. I, chap. 6. See also Macdougall, 19-21; Macfarlane, 25-31. For Burnet, the Earth's rugged topography was a manifestation of postlapsarian ruin and imperfection, whereas the early Earth in its state of paradise was as smooth as an egg. Of course, Burnet was perfectly right to stress the need for a rugged surface to poke through the planet's covering of water. If it were not for the wrinkles and furrows now known to be caused by plate tectonics, the surface of the Earth would be uniformly submerged to a depth of almost three kilometres.
443. According to a 2004 Gallup poll, 45% of the modern-day US population continues to hold this literalistic view of Biblical history.
444. On Newton's understanding of comets, see Schechner Genuth, 133-55.
445. Halley, "Some Considerations about the Cause of the universal Deluge, laid before the Royal Society, on the 12th of December 1694," *Philosophical Transactions* 33 (1724-1725): 121; quoted in Schechner Genuth, 163-64; on Halley, see 156-77.

argued, included not only the marine fossils found high on hilltops and deep below the Earth's surface but also the Caspian Sea, whose crater-like form suggested it was the most likely site of impact. Halley remained uncertain how Noah, his family and the ark-load of animals could have survived such a cataclysm.[446]

For those who deemed it foolish, arrogant and dangerous for modern scientists to venture onto Biblical ground, Halley was a freethinker guilty of the most flagrant intellectual hubris. Conservative wits such as Swift and Pope of the Scriblerus Club satirized him by attributing "all the new *Theories* of the *Deluge*" to their archetypal comic pedant, Martinus Scriblerus.[447] Henry Fielding parodied his theory of the deluge by putting it almost word for word into the mouth of an ant-philosopher addressing the Royal Society of Ants, who of course completely fails to grasp that the deluge in question was in fact caused by a "very large Cow" discharging "a vast Shower on an Ant-hill," which "destroyed a great Number of the Inhabitants." Fielding's rather fatuous conclusion was that "there are some Subjects on which a Wit and a Blockhead, a Man and an Ant, will exert themselves with the like Success."[448]

Whether Halley was a wit or a freethinking blockhead, the influence of his (and Newton's) ideas on comets was to last until well into the 19th century. Attributing the flood to water vapours from the tail and coma of a closely passing comet, the mathematician and theologian William Whiston in 1696 calculated the very day (27 November, 2348 BCE) on which this global drenching had taken place. In 18th-century America, John Winthrop expressed his agreement with the "ingenious and learned Mr. Whiston" that a comet could well have been responsible for the Biblical deluge, creating huge tidal fluxes near coastal areas or dousing the planet with the watery vapours in its tail. Kant's *Cosmogony* speculated that the Earth might have itself once had an aqueous cometary ring (as Kant believed Saturn had), which occasioned the flood when it fell as rain after being disrupted by a passing comet. Laplace too envisioned the dramatic consequences of a cometary impact upon the Earth: "the greater part of men and animals drowned in a universal deluge, or destroyed by

446. He later suggested, possibly on Newton's advice, that the impact was more likely to have taken place *prior* to the creation, reducing a former world to a state of chaos from which the present world subsequently emerged (see ibid., 164).
447. See ibid., 174.
448. Fielding, *Covent-Garden Journal*, no. 70, 11 November 1752, quoted in ibid., 174-77.

the violence of the shock given to the terrestrial globe; whole species destroyed; all the monuments of human industry reversed."[449]

For theologians such as Burnet and Whiston, there existed an essential synchronicity between human history and moral conduct on the one hand and natural history (geophysics or astrophysics) on the other: though its causes were natural, the timing of the deluge necessarily coincided with a level of human sinfulness that called for divine castigation. The chronological framework of events was unquestionable, concertinaed as it was into the few thousand years that had passed since Adam walked the planet. Yet with the rise of modern geology from the mid-18th century onwards, estimates of the Earth's age started to telescope out to incorporate considerably wider spans of time. In a dialogue published posthumously and pseudonymously by the Frenchman Benoît de Maillet (1656-1738), the Earth was calculated to be rather more than two billion years old: de Maillet based his reasoning on the assumption that the Earth had once been globally inundated and the observation that the sea-level was slowly sinking. The French natural historian Georges Buffon (1707-1788) put the age of the Earth at 75,000 years, although he himself seems to have suspected that this was a substantial underestimate of the real figure. Posthumously discovered manuscript notes propose an age of several billion years.

The geological evidence – which intimated the occurrence of such phenomena as erosion by ice, water and wind, and the large-scale transformation of the Earth's crust – was starting to make it clear that the planet had a long history. Commonly regarded as the founding father of the science of geology, the Scotsman James Hutton (1726-1797) followed Leonardo in rejecting the notion that the marine fossils frequently found embedded in the rocks high up mountains had been deposited there during floods. Hutton argued instead that the ancient sea-shells had shifted upwards over millions of years along with the layers of rock of which they formed a part. He also ruled out the possibility that floods might have been responsible for moving huge boulders hundreds of metres up mountainsides and was one of the first to champion the role of large-scale glaciation in landscape formation. The conclusion of his three-volume magnum opus *Theory of the Earth* is "that we find no vestige of a beginning, – no prospect of an end."[450] The major changes that had taken place in the planet's topography over the years were clearly incompatible

449. On Whiston, see ibid., 190; Winthrop, 196; Kant, 203-5; Laplace, 210-12.
450. Quoted in Macfarlane, 34.

with either a 6,000-year time scale or a Noachian inundation.

By the first half of the 19th century, therefore, one of the major scientific controversies of the day was between catastrophism and uniformitarianism. Whereas the former held that the Earth had been shaped by sudden, abrupt, cataclysmic events on a possibly worldwide scale, the latter – espoused first by Hutton and subsequently, with greater rhetorical skill, by Charles Lyell – maintained that the major factors in the shaping of the Earth were gradual processes that had taken place over the course of immense tracts of time. While catastrophism thus permitted its adherents to incorporate such episodes as the Biblical flood – along with earthquakes, volcanoes or comets – into their accounts of geophysical history, a uniformitarian such as Lyell sought to "read" the processes of the present as a way of inferring the events of the past, regarding catastrophism as a lazy and unscientific way of explaining away the unknown.[451] From the 1850s through to the 1980s, indeed, it was uniformitarianism that became the prevailing paradigm, and geologists generally played down the role of cataclysmic occurrences in the history of the Earth's surface. In recent years, however, a scientifically grounded catastrophism has returned to the fray, with many geologists combining a gradualist approach with an openness to catastrophist scenarios.[452]

In 1980, for example, a paper by Walter and Luis Álvarez put forward the idea that the extinction of the dinosaurs – indeed of 70 per cent of the species then in existence – could have been caused by the impact of an asteroid or comet at the end of the Cretaceous period, some 65 million years ago. Observation of the collision between the Comet Shoemaker-Levy 9 and Jupiter in 1994 confirmed the devastation wreaked by such impacts (with individual fragments releasing energy equivalent to millions of megatons of TNT, or hundreds of times all the nuclear weaponry in

---

451. Catastrophism was rather more plausible when it came to accounting for the phenomenon of extinction that was gradually coming to light (with the discovery that certain species of fossils vanished from one rock stratum to the next). The comparative anatomist Georges Cuvier (1769-1832), a prominent catastrophist, held that fossil sequences were a consequence and a reflection of a succession of natural disasters, of which the Biblical flood was just the most recent. Yet the fact that catastrophism was often invoked for religious purposes raised embarrassing questions about how God could be either so cavalier or so cruel as to wipe out certain species and not others, and why He had taken the trouble to create such species in the first place.
452. See Schechner Genuth, 222-24.

existence on Earth). A candidate for the crater produced by the terrestrial collision, measuring over 190 kilometres in width and 48 in depth, has been identified at Chicxulub on the Yucatán Peninsula of Mexico.[453] In fact, the Earth is believed to have undergone five major extinction events (each of which wiped out more than 70 per cent of the species then in existence), as well as a number of smaller ones. It has been estimated that the Permian extinction, which occurred some 245 million years ago, expunged as many as 95 per cent of all species from the planet, taking life itself to the verge of complete obliteration. Possible causes for such events include not only global temperature changes, but also, among other things, epidemics, volcano eruptions, solar flares, as well as asteroid or cometary impacts. The consensus among biologists is that the animal kingdom is now being subjected to an anthropogenic or man-made mass extinction, a phenomenon known as the Holocene extinction event.[454]

* * * * *

Despite the universal significance of flood mythology, therefore, water is far from having a monopoly when it comes to global catastrophes. However, major meteor impacts occur on a scale of millions rather than thousands of years: meteorites over a kilometre in diameter are thought to hit the Earth roughly once every million years.[455] The most recent supervolcanic explosion, the "humongous" eruption of Toba in north-

453. For an account of the global desolation produced by a comet or asteroid impact, see Bryson, 252-56; on extinction events, 416-24.
454. Kandel (*Water from Heaven*, 64-65) points out that the extinction rate is as high now as it probably was at the end of the Cretaceous; see also Ponting, 170: "The extinction rate for mammals in the twentieth century was forty times the 'background' rate and for birds it was about 1,000 times higher. It is clear that this rate will rise even further in the twenty-first century. The best estimates (as published in *Nature* in January 2004) are that as the world's climate changes rapidly and the remaining tropical forests are cleared, about half of all the world's existing species will be extinct by 2100."
455. Kandel, 63.

eastern Sumatra,[456] which is believed to have reduced the global human population to just a few thousand individuals, occurred roughly 74,000 years ago. Within *human* as opposed to geological history, by contrast, it is water that has been the most destructive protagonist[457] – apart from humankind, of course, on occasion acting *in conjunction with* water.

Many of the world's most ancient myths are believed to be based on real-life cataclysms. Just as the Biblical tale of Noah is presumed to have its origins in a great flood that visited Mesopotamia during the time of Ziusudra about 2900 BCE, so the inundation of Sheba cited in the Qur'an (34:15-17) was caused not only by Allah's displeasure at the impiety of its inhabitants, but – in more mundane terms – by the collapse of the great Marib Dam, a sign of the decline of a once flourishing hydraulic culture based on a sophisticated system of agricultural irrigation. It has been speculated that serious and sustained flooding along the Indus river valley was largely responsible for the demise of the ancient Indus civilization and the downfall of the city of Mohenjo-Daro. But it is the river floods of China that have caused the greatest havoc. Seven million people are thought to have perished following the flooding of the Yellow River in 1332, and the inundations of 1887 accounted for six million. Not surprisingly, myths involving flood-control play a special part in Chinese legend.

One such set of diluvial tales revolves around the archetypal flood-tamer Ta Yü, whose subjugation of the river gods was a feat of supreme importance in the mythological history of China. Credited with the construction of canals that allowed the water to flow to the sea, the figure of Yü is bound up with the development of massive hydraulic engineering projects, and as the first emperor of China's earliest dynasty he

456. Toba rates an eight on the official Volcanic Explosivity Index, which runs from none to eight. The eruption of Mount St Helens in 1980 was a five; Mount Vesuvius (79 CE) and Krakatoa (1883) were sixes; the "super-colossal" Tambora (1815) a seven. Yellowstone in the United States is an active supervolcano, whose past eruptions have been on a scale similar to Toba and occurred at average intervals of 600,000 years. The last one was about 620,000 years ago. See Rupp, 268-75.

457. Both river flooding and coastal flooding caused by tsunamis or hurricanes have left a constant trail of devastation since the dawn of civilization. In December 2004, the tsunami generated by seismic activity in the Indian Ocean laid waste to the coastal area of Indonesia, India, Sri Lanka and eastern Africa, claiming well over 200,000 lives. The tsunami that followed the eruption of Krakatoa in 1883 drowned over 36,000 people.

embodies the conjunction of centralized political power and hydrological administration that would come to characterize China over the centuries. Controlling the floods, says Fred Pearce, is widely believed to have been "the single most important reason for the creation and survival over the millennia of the vast Chinese state with its draconian powers," and Yü the Great symbolizes the fact that – here as elsewhere – control of water amounts to control of life. It is no coincidence that the Mandarin Chinese word for "to rule" (*zhi*) also means "to regulate water."[458]

Yet power, truistically, lends itself to both abuse and mis-management. Most shocking, perhaps, was the attempt of Chinese generals to use floodwaters to check the relentless advance of invading Japanese troops during the Sino-Japanese War early in June 1938. The consequence of the Chinese army blowing up the 400-year-old dyke that held back the Yellow River at Huayuankou near the city of Zhengzhou (formerly Chengchow) was not only to delay the Japanese advance (which it did for about a month), but also to flood vast swathes of the wide North China plain, leaving millions homeless and destitute and causing the deaths of roughly 890,000 people, mainly Chinese. It remains "the single most devastating act of war ever."[459] Today the threat of "hydrological terrorism" hangs over such megalomanic dam projects as the Three Gorges project on the River Yangtze. If this – currently the world's largest hydroelectric dam – were to suffer an attack, the 40 cubic kilometres of water that could be unleashed would dwarf even the Huayuankou wartime inundation.[460]

458. Pearce, 130. Another set of such myths involves the mother deity Nü Wa, who saved the world from the consequences of a ferocious quarrel between the gods Gong Gong, the spirit of water, and Jurong, the spirit of fire. In the midst of this cosmic argy-bargy, the mountain that held up the sky was reduced to rub-ble, the sky fell in, and the land was flooded with waters. Nü Wa responded by repairing the damage, damming up the floodwaters, mending the sky, and using the legs of a giant tortoise to prop up its four corners. In a Chinese version of the universal deluge, Nü Wa and her brother Fu Xi are peasant children who survive the flood in a calabash or gourd, subsequently marrying and repopulating the earth (see Scott Littleton, 404).
459. Pearce, 129.
460. See ibid., 207. The military and strategic vulnerability of dams has provid-ed perennial cause for consternation, heightened in the last century by the threat of air power. As Blackbourn reports (*The Conquest of Nature*, 237), Franco at-tempted to blow up the Ordunte Dam near Bilbao in the Spanish Civil War; in

Peacetime incompetence is an equal threat. China was the scene of one of the world's worst dam disasters when the area around the Ru River in central China was visited by a typhoon in 1975. First to burst was an upstream dam, which sent some 120 million cubic metres of water raging down towards the Banqiao dam. This in turn yielded under the impact, releasing half a billion cubic metres of water and debris downstream. The death toll is believed to have totalled between 80,000 and 200,000 people, yet the tight-lipped Chinese authorities for a long time kept the whole episode hushed over and shrouded in the utmost secrecy.[461] There have been more than 2,000 dam failures in human history.[462] The 19th century saw spectacular disasters such as the collapse of the de Puentes Dam in the Spanish province of Murcia in 1802, which claimed over 600 lives, while the Great Sheffield Flood, caused by the rupture of the Dale Dyke Dam on the River Loxley, killed over 250 people in 1864. Dams continued to collapse right though the 20th century. At least 200 failures were recorded, 33 of which took place in the USA between 1918 and 1953.[463] The history of dams has been described as the history of dam failures.[464]

It is now clear that dams themselves are a mixed blessing. Particularly popular with autocratic and militaristic administrations, they can have devastating demographic, social and ecological ramifications without ever producing the efficiency hoped for or expected. Successful management involves a tightrope walk between keeping them empty (in order to be able to catch floods) and keeping them full (in order to generate hydroelectricity). The construction of the Three Gorges dam on the River Yangtze has submerged some of China's best-loved landscapes, led to the forced resettlement of well over a million people, and will represent a constant threat to those who live in its shadow. High-profile dissidence has not been able to avert its construction.[465] Not surprisingly, new variations

---

the Second World War there were German proposals to attack the Aswan Dam in North Africa; and in 1943 the Allies carried out attacks on both the Eder and the Möhne Dams in Germany, the latter wreaking particular havoc in the narrow Ruhr valley, where the floodwaters took more than a thousand human lives (many of them Russian slave labourers).

461. Pearce, 169.
462. See Blackbourn, 232.
463. Ibid., 236.
464. Ibid., 232, citing Richard Hennig.
465. See Pearce, 176-79.

on flood mythology thus incorporate the baneful influence of unwanted dams and clumsily or forcibly imposed technological intervention. In the 1950s, when the Tonga people of Zambia were made to leave their ancestral territory and resettle on higher, poorer land during the construction of the Kariba Dam on the Zambesi River, the river god Nyaminyami was said to be so irate about the forced departure of his people that he sent two catastrophic floods to hamper progress. Even though work on the dam was eventually completed, the Tonga people believe that Nyaminyami is simply biding his time. In due course he will send another deluge to destroy the dam, and they will have their valley back again.[466]

The failure of human technology to tame rivers has come to light particularly drastically in mainland Europe, where the recent flooding of the Danube, Rhine, Elbe and other rivers has caused billions of euros' worth of damage and forced hundreds of thousands to flee their homes. The recognition that much of the flooding was in fact exacerbated by measures taken explicitly to tame the rivers and banish the floods has drawn attention to the need for a major rethinking of the way we deal with our rivers.[467] While rectification had sought to contain the water behind high levees and rush it on its way to the sea, maximizing speed and efficiency and turning the river into a "high-performance drain," the effect it actually had was to make the waters wilder than ever. As Fred Pearce explains, engineers now are "tearing down the banks and dykes and levees to give rivers back their flood plains. They are putting back the meanders and marshes to slow down the flow. They are even plugging up the drains on farms and in cities, encouraging the floodwaters to percolate underground. Rivers need room to flood, they say. And cities need to become more porous."[468] There

---

466. Black, *Water: Life Force*, 111. See in particular Leslie, 107-222, on the continuing plight of the displaced Tonga people and the disintegration of their culture.
467. Of course, the recent spate of river floods is not solely attributable to our obsession with concrete and tarmac. Another critical factor is the increase in the frequency of monsoon-like downpours, clearly an aspect of the more general anthropogenic destabilization of the weather. As the planet heats up, more water evaporates from the oceans (leading to greater precipitation), more energy finds its way into the climate, and the fact that the land warms up more quickly than the sea leads to stronger winds and increased instability. Equally worrying is the submersion of coastal and low-lying areas as a consequence of the increase in sea-level produced by deglaciation.
468. Pearce, 323; see 321-31.

is a new awareness of the value of "soft engineering" that "goes with the flow" instead of pandering to concrete fetishism and an unhealthy fixation on control and mastery. The tendency is for rivers to be allowed back onto their flood plains, wetlands to be restored, and areas to be set aside for "soggy nature"[469] to run its course as a way of protecting the remaining countryside.

The traditional view of flooding as destructive, dangerous and profoundly antithetical to "civilization," order and control has ignored or suppressed the regenerative and restorative properties of water and the benefits of (some forms of) natural flooding. Yet these properties provide the deeper symbolism of flood mythology itself. Almost all the traditions of deluges, writes Eliade, "are bound up with the idea of humanity returning to the water whence it had come, and the establishment of a new era and a new humanity. ... Water is in existence before every creation, and periodically water absorbs it all again to dissolve it in itself, purify it, enrich it with new possibilities and regenerate it."[470] Just as mythological floodwaters reinvigorate humanity by cleansing it of its collective sinfulness, in many parts of the world regular inundations also serve a regenerative function that is vital to agricultural balance and wellbeing. Farmers rely upon such floods, which renew the natural ecosystem, provide free irrigation, and bring the silt that helps fertilize their pastures. In such cases, the construction of dams can reduce fertile flood-plains to arid wasteland, destroying the livelihoods of those who depend upon them.

A spectacular case of flooding viewed as a boon and not as a bane is found on the mighty and mysterious Mekong River, which meanders some 4,500 kilometres through south-east Asia, from eastern Tibet and southern China through to Laos, Cambodia and Vietnam. As one of the most dam-free of the world's major rivers, during the monsoon the Mekong turns into such a torrential flow that in Cambodia it completely overwhelms its tributary the Tonle Sap; in turn, for a few months each year the Tonle Sap becomes one of the few rivers in the world to reverse its flow and run backwards,[471] flooding a large area of rainforest and creating

---

469. Ibid., 328.
470. Eliade, *Patterns*, 210-11.
471. The image of the river flowing backwards (or uphill) is not without interest. In Cambodia, the reversal of the Tonle Sap is a pretext for festival and cel-ebration. In 16th-century Europe, the idea of a river flowing back to its source

one of the world's most bountiful freshwater fisheries. The flooded forest around the Tonle Sap is "one of the most productive natural ecosystems in the world."[472]

In ancient Egypt too, the yearly inundation of the Nile brought the silty soils and free irrigation that allowed the delta to flourish. Indeed, Egyptian civilization is one of very few to have dispensed with mythology of a Great Flood – presumably, suggests Philip Ball, "because the Nile is so vast that it was always able to act as a buffer against intense meteorological events."[473] Instead, the Egyptians provided themselves with the benevolent deity Hapy who presided over the annual flooding. With his big belly and pendulous breasts (as well as a beard), Hapy was associated with fecundity and abundance, as well as with the creator god Khnum, who was believed to control the gates that held back the fertile waters and give the order when the waters were to be unleashed. In later years, Hapy came to be identified with Nun, the divine embodiment of the primal waters.

According to a legend told by the Ibibio people of south-east Nigeria, the flood is a friendly figure, albeit with a tendency to take up rather a lot of space. In the days when the sun and his wife the moon dwelled on Earth, they would often visit this friendly flood, in turn inviting him to come and stay with them. The bashful flood reluctantly declined their kind offer, explaining that he would not fit in their house, but the sun and moon built a new, much bigger house especially for the purpose, and their friend could no longer refuse. At last the friendly flood came to visit them, slowly but surely filling the house and bringing his many friends and relations such as the fish and marine animals. Before long he had filled the house up to its roof, forcing the sun and the moon to perch on top, before submerging it completely. The sun and the moon had no option but to head off for the sky, where they made a new home for themselves beyond the reach of the friendly flood.[474]

---

formed part of the imagery of the "topsy-turvy world" or the "world upside-down," which had both its celebratory and its satirical / apocalyptic sides. An influential poem by the French baroque poet Théophile de Viau (1590-1626) interpreted such topsy-turviness as presaging the end of the world. In the American West, water is said to flow uphill to money.

472. Pearce, 118. On the Mekong and the Tonle Sap, see 115-25. As Pearce puts it, "one of the world's poorest countries is one of its best fed" (117).
473. Ball, H_2O, 50.
474. Eliot, 47-48.

2

The Unfathomable

The threat of the flood is the threat of a return to the watery abyss and the formless chaos from which we emerged. It is a reminder of our insignificance and transience: beside the destructive might of the floodwaters (or of the deity who sent them), we are fragile and fleeting. Arrogance, self-deception and vanity are what make us believe otherwise.

While mythological inundations tend to be episodic in nature, the all-encompassing vastness they embody is more permanently present in the guise of the oceans.[475] The force of the great deluge is reflected in the might of the main, the sheer immensity of which engulfs and overwhelms us. Such is the nature of the "oceanic feeling," the feeling as of "something limitless, unbounded" that underlies much mystical energy, where the loss of the individual self may come to coincide with the finding of an origin that is trans-individual or in some sense transcendental.

In certain of the ancient Chinese writings of the Taoist *Chuang-tzu*,[476] the sea is taken as the image of the greatest thing there is – yet still no more than a drop of water within the bigger picture. When the Lord of the Yellow River, puffed up and swollen with pride during his autumnal flood season, finally arrives at the great ocean, he feels humiliated by the immensity he encounters and the sudden awareness of his own unimportance. "You can't talk to a frog in a well about the sea," he is told by the sea-god Jo, "because it is cramped inside its hole. ... You can't talk to hole-in-the-corner scholars about the Way, because they are constricted by their doctrines. Now that you have come out from your banks and have a view of the great sea, you have the good sense to be ashamed of yourself; it will be possible to talk to you about the grand pattern." Yet the sea-god Jo in turn recognises his own unimportance: "No waters in the world are

---

475. Though see Melville, 270: "Yea, foolish mortals, Noah's flood is not yet subsided; two thirds of the fair world it yet covers."
476. See *Chuang-tzu*, 144-50, for the "Autumn Floods" dialogue.

greater than the sea. ... How far it surpasses the streams of the Yellow River and the Yangtse is beyond measuring or counting; and, if in spite of this I have never made much of myself, it is because I recognise that ... within the compass of heaven and earth I am no more than a pebble or a bush on a great mountain."[477] In the face of such unspeakable immensity, measurements, words and dogmas are best recognised as futile.

More recently, the aesthetic and philosophical concept of the "sublime" has attempted to express such inexpressibility. In the context of natural phenomena, the notion goes back to the turn of the 18th century, when blue-blooded English travellers encountered the awesome splendour of the Alps during the grand tour that was de rigueur for any self-respecting aristocrat. Whereas previously aesthetic value had been sought in tamed and ordered landscapes, a new taste in scenery that was wild, chaotic and intense came to prevalence, finding expression in the writings of such essayists and philosophers as Joseph Addison (1672-1719), David Hartley (1705-57) and, most famously, Edmund Burke (1729-97). In *A Philosophical Enquiry into the Origin of our Ideas of the Sublime and the Beautiful*, published in 1757, the young Irishman Burke drew a highly influential distinction between beauty, attributable to phenomena considered pleasurable to behold, and the sublimity of sights that strike us as frightening, awesome, intimidating or in some sense overwhelming. Terror always lies at the heart of the sublime. A level plain, he writes, is "certainly no mean idea; the prospect of such a plain may be as extensive as a prospect of the ocean; but can it ever fill the mind with any thing so great as the ocean itself?" The reason it cannot, he suggests, is that the ocean is "an object of no small terror."[478] Of course, it must always be terror *at a distance*, enjoyed in safety and with no actual threat or danger. The sublime is produced when "the pain and terror are so modified as not to be actually noxious." The result is oxymoronic in character, a sort of "delightful horror" or "tranquillity tinged with terror."[479]

In his *Critique of Judgment* (1790) the great German philosopher Immanuel Kant took up what by then was a well-established distinction

---

477. Ibid., 145.
478. Burke, *A Philosophical Enquiry*, 53-54.
479. Ibid., 123. See also 36-37: "When danger or pain press too nearly, they are incapable of giving any delight, and are simply terrible; but at certain distances, and with certain modifications, they may be, and they are delightful."

between beauty and sublimity,[480] twice citing the stormy sea or raging ocean – "an abyss that threatens to engulf everything" – as the archetypally sublime.[481] According to Kant, the sublime differs from the beautiful in a number of important respects: firstly, whereas the latter is associated with form and thus with limitation, the sublime is connected with what is unlimited, boundless and in this sense formless; secondly, whereas beauty may be charming and apparently life-enhancing, the sublime has no such charms, and the pleasure it gives results from an alternation of repulsion and attraction; thirdly, the sublime has no purposive or teleological aspect and comes over as too immense to be comprehended or grasped by our limited cognitive faculties, too wild and chaotic to be subject to law.[482]

Kant also distinguished what he called the mathematically sublime from the dynamically sublime: the former relates to what is characterized by absolute greatness or infinite size, whereas the appreciation of the dynamically sublime involves viewing something as fearsome without actually being afraid of it. In both cases, the sublime transcends the world of mere phenomena (as present to the senses). The infinite brings to light the inadequacy of our imagination for grasping it, but also alerts us to the superiority of our higher, rational cognitive faculties and the supersensible side of our being.[483] The dynamically sublime emerges through our capacity

480. So influential were Burke's ideas that by the time Jane Austen wrote her unfinished *Sanditon* fragment in 1817 they had come to be considered "rather commonplace perhaps," lending themselves to parody in the mouth of Sir Edward, a "Man of Feeling" who was "very much addicted to all the newest-fashioned hard words" (323): "He began, in a tone of great Taste and Feeling, to talk of the Sea and the Sea-shore – and ran with Energy through all the usual Phrases employed in praise of their Sublimity, and descriptive of the *undescribable* Emotions they excite in the Mind of Sensibility. – The terrific Grandeur of the Ocean in a Storm, its glassy surface in a calm ... and the deep fathoms of its Abysses, its quick vicissitudes, its direful Deceptions..." (321).
481. Immanuel Kant, *Kritik der Urteilskraft*, 136, 175 (§§ 23, 29). Strictly speaking, he writes, the ocean itself is not sublime; it is *gräßlich* or horrific. The sublimity resides in the mind of the observer and depends upon the presence of certain ideas of reason, such as infinitude, morality or God.
482. Ibid., 175-76 (§ 29).
483. Ibid., 154-55 (§ 27). Given the relativity of scale, even a glass of water may be considered sublime in terms of the number of molecules it contains. As Lewis Wolpert explains, "if one took a glass of water, each of whose molecules were tagged in some way, went down to the sea, completely emptied the glass, allowed the water to disperse through all the oceans, and then filled the glass

to overcome our fear of death at the hands of nature, as it were placing ourselves *above* nature even while we confront our inevitable subjection to it. In both respects, the sublime depends upon our duality as beings both *within* the natural world (as apprehended by the senses) and *above* it.

Another German philosopher, Arthur Schopenhauer (1788-1860), perpetuated and further modified the distinction between the beautiful and the sublime. Schopenhauer listed varying grades in the transition from beauty to sublimity. Raging waters represent the full feeling of the sublime, as when a torrential current drowns out our voices with its commotion or a sea storm bellows and roars, hurling enormous waves (as high as houses) against precipitous cliffs.[484] As in Kant, the dual nature of the observer is invoked: for Schopenhauer too, we embody a duality as a phenomenon or object *within* the world and as the subject who contemplates it, "the bearer of the world."[485] Schopenhauer further follows Kant in distinguishing dynamical from mathematical sublimity. The fullest feeling of the sublime, he argues, comes with an awareness of the immensity of the universe in terms of extent or duration. Schopenhauer here returns to his favoured sea imagery, for confronted with such vastness we realise that *we* are nothing more than a drop in the ocean.[486] At the same time, however, this ocean only exists within us (as a representation or idea within our mind), and the unfathomability of the ocean does not destroy us because there is a sense in which it is we who are infinite. The human being, once more, comprises a duality of impotence (as a tiny and finite being) and omnipotence (as the observing subject): on the one hand, we are nothing; on the other, we coincide with everything. We contain the infinite ocean, just as the infinite ocean contains us.[487]

---

from the sea, then almost certainly some of the original water molecules would be found in the glass. What this means is that there are many more molecules in a glass of water than there are glasses of water in the sea" (Wolpert, 5). Burke refers to the sublime effect of the "wonders of minuteness." The "extreme of littleness" is indistinguishable from "the vast itself" (Burke, 66).

484. Schopenhauer, *Die Welt als Wille und Vorstellung*, I.291 (§ 39).
485. Ibid.
486. Ibid., I.292.
487. Ibid. Thoreau describes a similar tension. In this case, it is *introspection* and *imagination* that allow us to "contain" the watery infinite. While acknowledging our emotional dependence upon the unfathomable in nature ("we need to witness our own limits transgressed," *Walden*, 366), Thoreau himself advocates solitude and inner exploration rather than vacuous exploration of the world out

One of the key aspects of water's many-shaped immensity is its three-dimensionality. It is not just a matter of a two-dimensional expanse, an ocean stretching away into the distance. Essential to the great waters is their depth. This is what lends them their power to embrace and engulf us. There may seem to be a certain paradoxicality in the use of the word "sublime," which (like *erhaben* in German) implies elevation and height, to describe not only lofty mountains but also the deep. In fact, both Kant and Schopenhauer stress that the term refers not to the object or scenery being observed but to a state of mind in the observer (i.e. something akin to mental "elevation" or exaltation). In Schopenhauer's words, it is "elevation over one's own individuality."[488]

Not surprisingly, perhaps, there emerged a tendency to view the lofty human mind or brain itself as sublime. Such an idea finds poetic expression, for example, in Emily Dickinson's striking poem "The Brain is wider than the Sky":

> The Brain is deeper than the sea –
> For – hold them – Blue to Blue –
> The one the other will absorb –
> As Sponges – Buckets – do – [489]

By extension, there has been a natural tendency towards hubris and self-exaltation on the part of humankind, which finds practical expression in the 20th-century concept of the "American Technological Sublime,"[490] reflecting the awe produced by such structures as the enormous Hoover Dam – the world's first superdam – with its capacity of some 35 cubic

---

there. It is easier to sail the seven seas, he says, than "to explore the private sea, the Atlantic and Pacific Ocean of one's being alone" (370). Exploring the oceans within is the *real* challenge.

488. Schopenhauer, I.292: *Es ist Erhebung über das eigene Individuum, Gefühl des Erhabenen.*

489. Dickinson, *Complete Poems*, 312. Noteworthy is the frank materialism of such imagery. It is the brain – not the mind – that contains, and is contained by, the watery depths. It is the brain – not the mind – that thus coincides more or less seamlessly with divinity, "the weight of God," from which it differs, if at all, as "Syllable from Sound."

490. The phrase is the title of a book by the historian David Nye.

kilometres. Far from being an exclusively US-American phenomenon,[491] of course, the idea is the age-old one that the human mastery of (watery) nature is itself a source of wonder. Impressive it may sometimes be, but it coexists uneasily and in tension with the notion of sublimity, which designates precisely what lies *beyond* human attempts at conceptual or technological domination. As Kant and Schopenhauer knew, moreover, any sense of mastery over nature can only ever be ambiguous or provisional. The people of Sheba learnt this the hard way. The sublimity of a dam is inseparable from its inherent precariousness and the threat it poses to those who live downstream.[492]

* * * * *

The unfathomability and dark mystery of water's depths is evident not only in the wide oceans, but in other watery phenomena such as aquifers and the wells that provide access to them. Indeed, the vast majority of the world's fresh water is believed to lie hidden in underground reserves, though precise measurement is notoriously difficult. Experts put the figure at more than eight million cubic kilometres, 60 times more than all the water contained in the planet's freshwater lakes and rivers.[493] The invisibility of such waters has allowed for an unsustainable assault on these hidden reserves, which are commonly dismissed as "occult" or "secret" and therefore *beyond* administration.[494]

In fairy tales and folklore, wells frequently function as passages that penetrate to the unknown realm of the unconscious, to hidden and normally inaccessible worlds that lie below. Traditionally venerated (for

491. See Blackbourn, 185.
492. Hubristic self-exaltation is known to come before a fall, just as human "sublimity" is just a step or a stumble away from the ridiculous.
493. See Rupp, 74; Pearce, 33. The Nubian aquifer system of North Africa contains some 100,000 cubic kilometres of groundwater, while the Guarani in South America is estimated to hold around 50,000 cubic kilometres, equivalent to what flows down the Amazon in the course of seven years. Another aquifer, the Ogallala in the United States, has been pumped virtually dry by the country's profligacy.
494. See *Water: The Power, Promise, and Turmoil of North America's Fresh Water* (National Geographic Special Edition, vol. 184, no. 5A, 1993), 30-33.

providing life-giving sustenance), wells also have their dark side, for they can all too easily swallow the unsuspecting in their gloomy depths. Parents the world over warn their children not to play too near them. In England it is mysterious Jenny Greenteeth who will drag straying innocents down into the murk, never to be seen again. For the ancient Mayas of the Yucatán region, by contrast, the natural wells known as *cenotes*, as well as the karstic labyrinths of interlocking streams and gorges to which they led, were sacred places where children and adults alike were deliberately sacrificed to appease their exacting deities.

Ancient Norse mythology attaches special importance to three wells, the Wells of Urd, Mimir and Hvergelmir. Each is located in the shade of the great ash tree Yggdrasill, the World Tree, together with which they form the cosmic axis linking the worlds of the gods, humankind and the giants, and the dead. Hvergelmir ("Roaring Kettle") lies in grim Niflheim, the world of the dead, and contains a monster that gnaws at the tree's roots. The waters of Mimir – on the level of men and giants – are a source of wisdom. The Well of Urd, situated in the abode of the gods, is where the deities hold council each day.[495] Next to the Well of Urd are the three Norns, the personifications of fate. These three old women tend the branches of the World Tree with holy water from the well and spin out the thread of every mortal being's destiny.

The notable association between wells and weaving or spinning (in other words, the mysterious unravelling of the fate of mortals) is perpetuated in the Grimm canon of fairy tales. "Mother Holle" is the story of a poor, pretty Cinderella figure, who sits by a well and spins and spins till her fingers bleed. Accidentally dropping her spinning-shuttle down the well one day, she is made to fetch it by her cruel stepmother, and jumps in to discover a magical realm of delightful meadows and beautiful flowers. Here she enters the service of old Mother Holle, who treats her kindly and eventually returns her to the surface covered in gold. When the lazy, ugly stepsister hears of her good fortune, she immediately tries her luck too, throwing her shuttle into the well and jumping in after it. But she is soon sent packing covered in pitch. The magical power of the subterranean waters takes us (i.e. the hard-working girl and all the "good" people who

---

495. Scott Littleton, 276-81.

identify with her) to a world of wishful thinking and just deserts.[496]

Rivers too, as we have seen, may embody nostalgic day-dreams of freedom and escape. They may also contain hidden depths and the threat of death: witness Guy de Maupassant's short story "On the Water" (*Sur l'Eau*), in which the narrator's companion spends a night of terror trapped alone in his boat on a ghostly river shrouded in mist. An explicit comparison is drawn between the brutal, blustering but loyal sea and the noiselessly treacherous river; the roar of the ocean waves and the whispering of riverbank rushes; the unknown kingdoms beneath the sea swell and the dreamless putrefaction of the muddy riverbed. The river is "the most sinister of cemeteries," its murky depths concealing a graveyard of dark secrets – in this case, as it happens, an elderly woman with a stone around her neck, whose corpse has become tangled up with the boat's anchor. For Dickens too, the river was a place of mystery and morbid gloom. In an essay from 1853, "Down with the Tide," the Thames is portrayed as "hiding strange things in its mud, running away with suicides and accidentally drowned bodies faster than midnight funeral should … this river looks so broad and vast, so murky and silent, seems such an image of death in the midst of the great city's life."[497] The opening scenes of *Our Mutual Friend* (1865) depict a Thames waterman and his daughter at work retrieving corpses from the river, pocketing what spoils they can before handing the bodies over to the authorities.

With their hidden tides and deceptive currents, rivers have been the undoing of many an unwilling victim. They have offered themselves to criminals as the perfect repository for the disposal of corpses. Yet the lure of their subtle embrace may even make death seem enticing. Linked as it is with transience and tears, water is the "melancholy element." "There is always the sense in which the flowing water induces repose and forgetfulness," writes Peter Ackroyd, "but what if that repose and

---

496. Grimm, 108-12. In "The Goose-Girl at the Well," a wise woman – armed with the obligatory spinning wheel – takes into her care a Cordelia-like figure, discarded from her family for telling the truth, whom she keeps as an "ugly goose-girl." The tears the goose-girl sheds in her sorrow are "precious pearls, finer than those that are found in the sea." Eventually, when the time comes, a magical well transforms the girl back into a beautiful maiden with golden hair "like sunbeams." And they all live, or so it is to be supposed, more or less happily ever after. See ibid., 641-50. See also "The Water-Nixie," in ibid., 317. Here the cruel nixie also lives inside a well.
497. Quoted in Ackroyd, 326.

forgetfulness were to be indefinite?"[498] The flow of water, it seems, not only washes away sorrow and care, but purges us – for good – of the anxieties of individuality and personhood. The Thames has been a favourite haunt for suicides. Around the middle of the 19th century, an average of 30 a year jumped from Waterloo Bridge, which came to be known as "Lover's Leap," "Arch of Suicide" or the "Bridge of Sighs."[499] More than 1,300 people have leaped to their death from the Golden Gate Bridge since it opened in 1937, making it the world's number one suicide spot.

The death wish provoked by and associated with water need not be a matter of world-weariness alone.[500] While the death-drive of poets such as Shelley and Swinburne may have incorporated elements of melancholy (such as languor, estrangement or worldly disillusionment), it was born as much as anything of a passionate romance with the watery element. Shelley's profound attraction to water was matched only by his disinclination to make any attempt to stay afloat in it. His eventual drowning off Viareggio was "the culmination of a love affair with water that influenced him to sink rather than swim."[501] Equally intoxicated with water's sensuality, Swinburne too courted danger and sought erotic or ecstatic union with the breakers. In his *Autobiography*, John Cowper Powys describes swimming out of his depth as something akin to a religious rite with which he defied the world: "It was certainly towards the non-human condition of floatingness and flowingness that I struggled, when, by swimming out beyond my depth, I felt as if I resolved myself into air and sky and sea!"[502]

Water was described by a contemporary as Shelley's "fatal" element. Throughout his life, notes Sprawson, "he tempted fate on the water":

---

498. Ibid., 376.

499. Ibid., 380. As a result of the river pollution, until fairly recently the unfortunates who threw themselves in were in fact more likely to be poisoned than drowned.

500. Another possibility used to be the condition known as calenture, the bane of feverish mariners who had spent too long at sea. According to the OED, calenture was "a disease incident to sailors within the tropics, characterized by delirium in which the patient ... fancies the sea to be green fields, and desires to leap into it." See also Farber, 79-80, on water and suicide.

501. Sprawson, 76. Shelley's first wife Harriet Westbrook drowned herself in the Serpentine in Hyde Park, and his mother-in-law Mary Wollstonecraft almost did likewise in the Thames. Sprawson speaks of "an appetite for death by water" (32).

502. Quoted in ibid., 171.

In England he rowed down a river in a washtub until the bottom fell out, and he once descended the Rhine on a leaky raft. When caught in a storm on Lake Geneva with Byron, their boat full of water, he protested with great coolness that he had no notion of being saved, and begged the great swimmer not to trouble him. In a boat off Spezzia he suddenly proposed to his companions that they should "solve the great riddle" by allowing the skiff they occupied to sink beneath them.[503]

The idea that by descending to the watery depths one might solve "the great riddle" is given expression in one of Schiller's most celebrated ballads, *Der Taucher* ("The Diver"), written in 1797 and published in 1798. The deep here becomes a place of hidden truth, the diver or underwater swimmer gaining access to mysteries beyond the reach of the normal, terrestrial citizen. The ballad recounts a squire's dive into the whirlpool of Charybdis to retrieve a golden goblet thrown in – as a challenge – by his king, who craves knowledge of what is otherwise undisclosed to man. The squire emerges and describes fearsome scenes of dragons and salamanders, rays and hammerheads, but this is not enough. The king wants knowledge of the bottommost recesses of the sea, offering his daughter's hand if the young man returns and goes even deeper. The diver accepts the renewed challenge, plunges into the waters and is never seen again. So what is this deeper truth, so coveted by the king? Perhaps it is defined by its very inaccessibility, embracing whatever is beyond our reach or grasp. Or perhaps it is the inadequacy of the metaphor of "depths" when it comes to grasping "truth": one can plunge to the watery depths – or as a king get one's subjects to do so – but the deeper truth is that there *is* no deeper truth; there are no hidden gems of wisdom in the ocean's belly. Or the deeper truth may simply be death, it being in this sense alone that the depths throw up an answer for the hubristic king.

Death, perhaps, or madness. For this is the fate of Pip, the young black ship-keeper in *Moby Dick*, who comes as close as possible to drowning and is left "an idiot" – at least in the eyes of his shipmates. The sea, it seemed, had "jeeringly kept his finite body up, but drowned the infinite of his soul." But it is not as straightforward as this. In fact, Pip had been "carried down alive to wondrous depths, where strange shapes of the unwarped primal world glided to and fro before his passive eyes; and the miser-merman, Wisdom, revealed his hoarded heaps." Pip's madness is in this sense a form of higher wisdom:

503. Ibid., 80-81.

He saw God's foot upon the treadle of the loom, and spoke it; and therefore his shipmates called him mad. So man's insanity is heaven's sense; and wandering from all mortal reason, man comes at last to that celestial thought, which, to reason, is absurd and frantic; and weal or woe, feels then uncompromised, indifferent as his God.[504]

Such associations of the watery depths with hidden secrets, ecstasy, death and madness bring us back to the depths of our *own* psyche. It is a link that is given explicit poetic formulation by Charles Baudelaire in *Les fleurs du mal* (1857). "L'Homme et la Mer" is a spectacular expression of the relationship of man and sea, mirror images of one another in their lawlessness, violence and unfathomability. Locked in eternal and implacable sibling rivalry, both of them are equally enamoured of carnage and death, both of them equally unknowable in their abyssal intimacy.[505] The parallels that come to light in Baudelaire evoke not transparency or limpid rationality, but something murkier, more primal and profound, something more closely akin to the Freudian unconscious.[506]

Reflecting the inaccessible and unknowable reaches of the human mind, the ocean thus emerges once again as a sort of collective or planetary unconscious. The analogy is commonplace enough to have taken a number of forms. For a start, there is the one drawn in *Moby Dick*, where the relationship between the known and the unknown self is likened to that between "green, gentle, and most docile" terra firma and the dangerous and violent seas with their "universal cannibalism" and "eternal war":

> consider them both, the sea and the land; and do you not find a strange analogy to something in yourself? For as this appalling ocean surrounds

---

504. Melville, 396-97.
505. Baudelaire, *Les fleurs du mal*, 46-47. See, for example, the third of the four stanzas:
> *Vous êtes tous les deux ténébreux et discrets:*
> *Homme, nul n'a sondé le fond de tes abîmes;*
> *O mer, nul ne connaît tes richesses intimes,*
> *Tant vous êtes jaloux de garder vos secrets!*

506. Influenced by Freud, psychoanalysis has traditionally associated itself with archaeology (in its uncovering of the hidden layers of the psyche). Plate tectonics notwithstanding, the ground is rather a static image for the psychic flows of the hidden self. Perhaps oceanography would be a more appropriate analogy. Or spelaeology, for that matter.

the verdant land, so in the soul of man there lies one insular Tahiti, full of peace and joy, but encompassed by all the horrors of the half known life. God keep thee! Push not off from that isle, thou canst never return![507]

As ever, of course, the green and pleasant reader should be careful not to take Melville's narrator too seriously. Elsewhere in *Moby Dick*, the boundless immensity of the oceans is associated with unbounded freedom of thought (just as the human unconscious may be considered a wellspring of creativity as much as a realm of death and destruction). The "mortally intolerable truth," we learn, is that "all deep, earnest thinking is but the intrepid effort of the soul to keep the open independence of her sea; while the wildest winds of heaven and earth conspire to cast her on the treacherous, slavish shore." Recognizing that "in landlessness alone resides the highest truth, shoreless, indefinite as God,"[508] the truth in *Moby Dick* itself refuses to be tied down by the shackles of terrestrial gravity.

The analogy has not been limited, however, to a straightforward contrast between sea and land. In his discussion of the unconscious, Arthur Koestler cites not only Leibniz's view that "our clear concepts are like islands which arise above the ocean of obscure ones," but also the metaphor developed by the German experimental psychologist Gustav Fechner, for whom the mind was an iceberg of which only a fraction was above the surface (of consciousness), the rest remaining concealed by underwater currents.[509] Koestler's own analogy features a boat as the conscious mind, by contrast with the watery depths of the unconscious:

> Thinking is never a sharp, neat, linear process; it could rather be compared to the progress of a boat on a lake. When you day-dream you drift before the wind; when you read or listen to a narrative you travel like a barge towed by a tug. But in each case the progress of the boat causes ripples on the lake, spreading in all directions – memories, images, associations; some of these move quicker than the boat itself and create anticipations; others penetrate into the deep. The boat symbolizes the focal awareness, the ripples on the surface are the fringes of consciousness, and you can furnish the deeps, according to taste, with the nasty eddies of repressed complexes, the deep-water currents of the collective unconscious, or with archetypal coral-reefs.[510]

---

507. Melville, 270-71.
508. Ibid., 116.
509. Koestler, 150, 153.
510. Ibid., 159.

The deepness and darkness of the watery abyss is central to its association with the unconscious or with less than fully human consciousness. Traditionally, everything noble about the human mind strives upwards; progress is conceived as an ascent; the heights are associated with the heavens, divinity, contemplation, and all that is good. Descent, by contrast, tends to be diabolical or deathly, associated with sinful falls or the shortcomings of the human condition. Whereas light signals not only the illumination of deity, but also the enlightenment of knowledge, enquiry and wisdom, the darkness and obscurity of the depths evoke what is blindly instinctive, animalistic, primitive or bereft of the full luminosity of reason. In this respect, "depth" may even suggest a movement "down" the Great Chain of Being or evolutionary ladder to a more primal state of being. At the same time, however, such regression can be experienced as liberation rather than loss. John Cowper Powys thus described the "ichthyosaurus ego" released in him by the activity of swimming, a feeling of being "as primaeval as an ichthyosaurus."[511] A retreat to water – to our timeless, ancestral waters – may represent an escape from the vulgarities of modern life or from the cosseting of civilization. It is a return to origins. For there is a sense in which we all "contain" our past, and this past is not just an individual past (our memories and forgetfulness), but an evolutionary past involving our human and non-human ancestors and the entire evolutionary lineage from which we have developed. Inherited from our aquatic ancestry, our collective unconscious is deeply water-bound.

The nature of the deep – the deep seas – as a metaphor for a collective or planetary unconscious is revealed most obviously in our monumental ignorance of it and the indifference with which we are wont to treat it. While even amateur astronomers can identify the objects of their curiosity simply by venturing into the garden or onto the balcony at night and looking upwards, perhaps with a telescope and a glass of wine to hand, the deep is by nature inaccessible, remaining shrouded in a seemingly impenetrable mantle of water. A general indifference is reflected in government disinterest and the virtual non-existence of funding. "We live at a time when the outside chance of finding a fossil bacterium on Mars is enough to generate tremendous enthusiasm – justifiable, to be sure – for billion-dollar missions of exploration to that planet," muses Robert Kunzig. "And yet we are content to pass over in complacency and almost total ignorance the largest and strangest habitat on Earth. It is odd. It is

511. Sprawson, 171-72.

silly even."[512]

The world we live in is deeply divided. It is only the terrestrial part that we dwell upon (literally and figuratively), and the rest, veiled in water, we generally ignore. In terms of surface area, this terrestrial part amounts to under a third of the world. Yet this is a two-dimensional perspective. In three-dimensional terms, land in fact constitutes as little as half a per cent of the planet's biosphere, shallow seas another 21 per cent, with deep seas accounting for 78.5 per cent. And even this is a highly conservative estimate, depending on where the deep is judged to begin.[513] Whether it starts at a depth of 200 metres or a kilometre, however, the deep clearly represents by far the greatest part of the biosphere. And despite their ugly faces and the demonisation to which they have often been subject, it is the residents of the depths – not the bipedal hominids who strut around on the dry parts of the planet – who are the most typical life-forms on Earth.

This schizoid division clearly reflects the schizoid nature of human self-knowledge. Like the human unconscious, the deep has served as a fount of imaginative creativity that wells up from within. What is unknown is inherently protean or malleable; it can take whatever shape you care to project onto it. Engendered in this way were the myriad monsters formerly believed to populate the watery depths, which bodied forth the fears and anxieties of the cultures and individuals from whose imagination they sprang. Mirror-like as ever, the deep and – as we shall see in the following section – its inhabitants have provided a constant reflection of the turbulent depths of the human mind. At the same time, fear of the unknown coupled with brazen indifference towards non-human forms of life has made it possible for mankind to engage in the systematic brutalisation of the creatures it harbours, decimating stocks of cod, haddock, herring and salmon, industrialising the mass-slaughter of whales,[514] and employing indiscriminate harvesting techniques that

512. Kunzig, 198.
513. See Broad, 45-46. These figures assume that the deep sea starts at a depth of one kilometre. According to other estimates, the deep sea amounts to as much as 97 per cent of the biosphere.
514. The 20th century saw the extermination of several million whales, as the human race hunted blue whales, grey whales, humpbacks, sperm whales, fin whales, sei whales and minkes to the brink of extinction. As wholesale carnage, it is virtually without parallel in the history of wildlife destruction (see Roman, *Whale*, 139-51; Ponting, 162-68). Even when humans were taking time off to kill *one another* in the Second World War, tens of thousands of whales are

destroy entire habitats.[515] It is as though what we don't know does not properly exist. It was in the same spirit of "out of sight, out of mind" that the world's superpowers – a dozen of the richest nations – spent 45 years of the 20th century cheerfully dumping radioactive waste in the ocean depths before a permanent ban was finally introduced in 1993.[516]

The deadly and deathly traces left by human activity may take many forms. The watery depths are a secret storehouse not only for the leaky "containment"[517] of mass destruction; there is also more attractive booty down below in the form of innumerable shipwrecks, on occasion carrying several tons of gold. The end of the Cold War has fostered a boom in undersea treasure-hunting and commercial salvage work using military technology and expertise developed for purposes of deep espionage. The most famous such recovery is the *Titanic*, but Spanish galleons and Japanese submarines have proved equally enticing. In the words of William J. Broad, "the seabed is a vast repository of failed ambition that contains not only crash debris but millions of ships and treasures, arms and artifacts that have been lost over the ages – everything from jeweled tiaras to nuclear warheads. It is in some respects the greatest, and deadliest, of all museums."[518] Many of the lost secrets from man's shadowy past have their home in the depths of the watery abyss.

---

believed to have been killed by depth charges and bombs. The USA was using whales as submarine target practice through to the late 1950s (Roman, 134).
515. The deployment by fisheries of huge drift nets, tens of kilometres in length and dubbed "walls of death," has been much criticised by environmentalists. Drift nets lead to the entanglement not only of the target species, but a by-catch that includes any other marine species that happen to be in the way. Sea turtles and marine mammals such as dolphins are typical victims (see Pernetta, 215). Bottom-trawling, or benthic trawling, described as the "slash and burn" of the fishing industry, has long since been condemned for the environmental havoc it wreaks.
516. Broad, 295-306.
517. As well as being subject to the natural processes of decay, some of the drums containing nuclear waste refused to sink and were duly riddled with bullets by the supremely pragmatic US Navy. See Broad, 296.
518. Ibid., 328.

*   *   *   *   *

If the unconscious represents the unknown within, the uncharted recesses of the human psyche, it is the oceans that constitute the great unknown of the planet we inhabit. For much of human history, the "unfathomable" – in the sense of what lay beyond knowledge – extended horizontally as much as into the depths. While land was finite and delimited by its shores, the seas stretched out to infinity. Homer's conception of the Earth as a plane disc encircled by the ocean-river "Oceanus" was taken on board by the influential Greek geographer Strabo in the 1st century BCE. According to Strabo's *Geographica*, the habitable world was known by experience to be "washed on all sides by the sea and like an island." Strabo considered it irrelevant whether there was uninhabited land to be found beyond the limits of the habitable world or merely the endless ocean, because "the geographer undertakes to describe the known parts of the inhabited world, but he leaves out of consideration the unknown parts of it."[519] Nearly all medieval cartographers seem to have followed this venerable Greek conception of an inhabitable world girdled by a circular ocean, although there was some disagreement as to whether these outlying waters took the form of a narrow strip surrounding a relatively large Earth or extended indefinitely.[520] Either way, their circularity served as a fitting symbol of the infinite nature of the surrounding seas and the sheer immeasurability of the unknown.[521] In the Christian world at least, the consensus was that this watery beyond was *out of bounds*: the mysteries of the ocean pertained to the Almighty alone. Only fools, sinners or pagans were interested in probing the secrets of the universe.

519. Quoted in Brown, 55; on Strabo and his influence, see 12-57.
520. Ibid., 95.
521. This circularity is manifest in the popular T-O maps of the medieval world, where the circular ocean circumscribing the inhabited world forms the O, the cross-stroke of the T corresponds to the Don (Tanais) and the Nile, and the down-stroke represents the Mediterranean. East was the upper part of the map (in accordance with the concept of "orientation"): Asia was above the cross-stroke; Europe to the left of the down-stroke, and Africa to the right. For examples, see Barber, 32, 44, 72.

Part of the reason for this prohibition was the supposed existence of Paradise somewhere beyond the inhabited world. The Irish monk St Brendan famously undertook a voyage in search of it, assuming it to be an island located somewhere in the Atlantic. Such was the faith placed in his travel tales – with their stirring adventures and self-moving isles accessible only to the saintly – that his reputed discoveries found their way onto sea charts for nearly 1200 years, right through to 1759. Brendan's "Promised Land of the Saints," subsequently known as "St Brendan's Island," as well as the "Lost Island" or "Non Trubada" on account of its ability to submerge and re-emerge from the depths, was given a number of locations: Madeira, the Canaries, a hundred miles west of Ireland, eventually even the West Indies. Between 1526 and 1721 the Portuguese sent out several expeditions to try to ascertain its whereabouts once and for all.[522]

Another very good reason for not venturing too far from familiar shores was the danger this entailed. In medieval cartography, the perils of the unknown were embodied in the weird and fantastical creatures that populated uncharted regions such as mountains, deserts and oceans. As late as the 16th century – by which time the contours of world maps had come to bear a considerable resemblance to those of today and the face of the earth had ostensibly become "entirely knowable"[523] – the oceans were still depicted as teeming with fearsome sea monsters and mythological water beings. Particularly spectacular was Olaus Magnus's *Carta Marina* of Scandinavia (1539).[524] This portrayed an array of ferocious sea-beasts that included the terrifying Spouter, said to be able to drown sailors and sink whole ships with the water it spouted. On one ship depicted just off Iceland, the mariners are shown throwing empty casks overboard and sounding a trumpet in an attempt to stave off attack from two marauding Spouters.

To be sure, these embodiments of the watery unknown were on the wane by the late 16th century, as the pioneers of global exploration discovered new continents and mapped the planet with ever greater

---

522. See Brown, 98; Bowen, 127.
523. Barber, 108. For examples of such world maps, see Giacomo Gastaldi and others, *Cosmographia universalis* (1561), in ibid., 110-11; Jodocus Hondius's "Christian Knight" world map (1597), in ibid., 135; Petrus Plancius's world map (1599), in ibid., 139. Other maps with monster-infested waters include Saxton's map of Cornwall (1576) and Woutneel's map of the British Isles (1603): see ibid., 117, 143.
524. Ibid., 96-97.

precision, aided by the constant technological progress that first facilitated the calculation of latitude and later resolved the even more vexed problem of longitude. It was in particular the measurement of longitude – how far east or west one had travelled – that proved essential to "knowing" the globe and countering the deadliness of its waters. For while latitude could be gauged relatively easily in terms of the length of the day or the height of the sun or certain stars above the horizon, longitude was much more complicated, requiring knowledge of the difference in *time* between one's current whereabouts and a given base (now Greenwich).[525] Prior to the development of accurate marine chronometers, miscalculations of longitude – as sea captains relied on what was inauspiciously known as "dead reckoning" – led to hundreds of instances of shipwreck and disaster,[526] as well as the more protracted misery of scurvy that afflicted mariners when their ships failed to find their home port.

The thrust to push back the frontiers of the unknown – to chart previously uncharted regions – might seem to have been a merely horizontal or two-dimensional enterprise, limited to the surface of the planet. But it was not as simple as this: two further dimensions were called upon. For since the seas, logically enough, lack "landmarks" of their own, one of the ways of resolving the longitude problem was to refer to astronomical events – the phenomena of the firmament – as seafaring guides. As Dava Sobel puts it, "the founding philosophy of the Royal Observatory, like that of the Paris Observatory before it, viewed astronomy as a means to an end. All the far-flung stars must be catalogued, so as to chart a course for sailors over the oceans of the Earth."[527] Given the practical difficulties associated with astronomical observation, however, the alternative to

525. It takes 24 hours for the Earth to complete a revolution of 360°, which works out at four minutes for every degree of longitude. In terms of distance, however, one degree varies from next to nothing at the Poles to as much as 68 miles at the Equator. See Sobel, *Longitude*, 5.

526. Dava Sobel cites the sea disaster that sunk four out of five returning warships under Sir Cloudesley Shovell off the Scilly Isles in October 1707, claiming the lives of some 2,000 troops. It was this disaster that led to the Longitude Act of 1714, which offered a substantial financial reward to whoever discovered an accurate method of determining longitude at sea.

527. Ibid., 32. See also Broad, 324. Galileo successfully worked out a solution to the longitude problem involving the eclipses of the moon of Jupiter, which occurred a thousand times a year and with great predictability. By 1650, Galileo's method was generally accepted, but only for land, because the necessary observations could only be made at night and in clear conditions.

this was to resort to the fourth dimension, time, as providing a means of accurately establishing one's whereabouts within the four-dimensional sea of space-time. The idea was that efficient timekeeping would permit sailors to "carry the home-port time aboard ship with them, like a barrel of water or a side of beef."[528]

Here, too, there were many practical obstacles to be overcome. In the 16th century, when the idea was first broached, timekeepers were simply too imprecise, often losing or gaining fifteen minutes a day. This discrepancy, it was calculated, had to be reduced to a mere three seconds. As the problem gained in urgency and notoriety, the notion of "discovering the longitude" came to be equated with "attempting the impossible"[529] and was considered a pastime fit for fools and fodder for satire. The archetypal comic pedant Martinus Scriblerus thus had the bright idea of building "*Two Poles* to the *Meridian*, with immense Light-houses on the top of them; to supply the defect of Nature, and to make the Longitude as easy to be calculated as the Latitude."[530] In the eighth engraving of *The Rake's Progress* (1735), William Hogarth portrayed a "longitude lunatic" working obsessively on the problem in a madhouse.[531]

Yet a solution did eventually come, in the form of the marine chronometers developed by John Harrison in the mid-18th century. Harrison's timekeepers were not only sufficiently accurate on land but could also cope with the rolling and lurching of the high seas, which had meant finding an alternative to the pendulum of traditional land clocks.[532] Hogarth himself was completely won over by the perfection of Harrison's solution, describing the working of his first sea-clock (known as H-1) as "one of the most exquisite movements ever made."[533] In the wake of Harrison's chronometric masterpieces, the rapidly growing craft of marine timekeeping became an essential part of Britain's success as a maritime nation. It was "by dint of the chronometer," suggests Sobel, that "Britannia ruled the waves."[534]

528. Ibid., 35.
529. Ibid., 56.
530. See the Scriblerus Club, 334-35, 343. Imagining the pleasures of immortality, Swift's Gulliver includes "the Discovery of the *Longitude*, the *perpetual Motion*, the *universal Medicine*, and many other great Inventions brought to the utmost Perfection" (*Gulliver's Travels*, 210-11).
531. See Sobel, 87.
532. Ibid., 69-73.
533. Ibid., 87.
534. Ibid., 153.

* * * * *

The urge to map the world – and chart the skies – has often coincided with man's urge to expand his territory, to cover and control more of the globe. In symbolic terms at least, a return to the depths, by contrast, implies a move downwards or inwards. On a planetary scale, perhaps, it is a call to introspection or self-knowledge, based on the holistic awareness that an understanding of what is going on deep down is vital to the well-being of the planet in its entirety and that ignorance of the depths is ignorance of the very foundations of the life-supporting orb on which we are perched.[535] Yet even today, many of our maps in effect "stop" at coastlines, and 70 per cent of the globe's surface remains shrouded in a great swathe of blue that fails to betray the subaquatic presence of mountain ranges that stretch further than the Andes, ocean trenches that descend more than ten kilometres, and a whole physiognomy of fissures, pock-marks and seamounts.

There are three particular features of the ocean depths that contribute to their continued unfathomability: opacity, heaviness, and what might be called "placelessness" – the absence of a two-dimensional surface.[536] Clearly, this unfathomability is species-based. If we were among

535. In practice, modern-day deep-sea exploration too may simply be a matter of national aspirations to political and military-strategic "security." Certainly, the two-and-a-half-mile descent of the deep-diving Russian submersibles *Mir I* and *Mir II* to the ocean floor beneath the North Pole in 2007 seems to have been motivated more by territorial expansionism, resource exploitation and nationalistic self-assertion than any spirit of scientific enquiry. Moreover, much of the recent progress in deep-sea research has been a consequence of cold-war technology developed, above all by the United States, for purposes of undersea espionage, targeting the ships, planes, weapons and rockets that the Soviet Union lost to the deep. According to Broad, the more general availability of such technology in the aftermath of the Cold War "shook the foundations of civil oceanography." Civilians found themselves newly equipped with state-of-the-art exploratory gear, which they proceeded to use for such purposes as rescuing shipwrecks and salvaging the hoards of treasure they contain (Broad, 85).
536. For a description of the ocean as a place without fixed places, see Kunzig, 191, discussing the work of the marine biologist G. Richard Harbison.

the gelatinous cephalopods or siphonophores that prevail over the millions of cubic miles of midwaters, the deep would represent the very epitome of what *can* be fathomed. It is only because our amphibian ancestors some 400 million years ago made the bold decision to leave the shark-infested waters and slither, crawl or lollop onto a terrestrial environment – an environment to which we have since adapted our weight-bearing internal architecture and our means of oxygen-intake – that we find ourselves restricted to a mere half per cent of the Earth's biosphere, effectively ruling out the remaining, aquatic 99.5 per cent as a viable habitat. And it is because our more recent ancestors chose not to follow the marine mammals back into the waters some 50 million years ago that we lack the diving capacities or echolocation skills, say, of sperm whales or other cetaceans. In the absence of such faculties, the possibility of fathoming the depths (for humans at least) must depend either on counterfactual imagination or technological progress.[537] Before turning to technological attempts to get to the bottom of matters, the following paragraphs briefly look at the three obstacles to fathomability and indulge in a few *what ifs*: above all, what would it mean for us if our ancestors *had* stayed with the jellies or the whales?[538]

The opacity of the sea is so great that less than one per cent of the sunlight penetrates to a depth greater than 200 metres. This upper region, known as the epipelagic zone,[539] is the habitat of the phytoplankton, the single-celled algae that through the process of photosynthesis utilise the energy of the sun to convert carbon dioxide and water into carbohydrates and

537. The diving skills of some human beings have been interpreted as evidence in support of the "Aquatic Ape Theory," suggesting that our ancestors *did* in fact return to a watery habitat for a while. Thoroughly admirable though these skills may be, diving to a depth of 100 metres for a few seconds hardly amounts to fathoming the deep when the *average* depth of the ocean is four kilometres.
538. Of course, such a question gets us no further than the question: what if I had been born to different parents? Or: what if I were not me? If our ancestors had stayed with the jellies, they wouldn't be our ancestors. But anyone who has ever started a sentence with "if I were you" – i.e. anyone who has ever empathized with, or put themselves in the place of, a human or non-human fellow creature – implicitly recognises that counterfactuals are not *completely* useless. And unlike technology they do not require funding.
539. The mesopelagic zone lies between the depths of 200 and 2,000 metres, while the bathypelagic zone stretches from 2,000 to 6,000 metres in depth. The abyssopelagic zone refers to ocean trenches greater than 6,000 metres in depth. See Pernetta, 132-33.

oxygen. The importance of these floating sea-plants cannot be overstated: not only was it the phytoplankton that originally provided the Earth with its oxygen atmosphere, but marine life virtually in its entirety depends – directly or indirectly – on their photosynthetic activity.[540] Except for isolated deep-sea communities based on chemosynthesis, all ecosystems below the epipelagic zone – in the absence of sunlight, photosynthesis and plants – rely on the constant rain of faecal materials and dead organisms that sink down from the higher-level ecosystems above. If our ancestors had chosen to inhabit the deep, in other words, our gastronomic sensibilities would have had to adapt to a food-chain based on phytodetritus and other deep-sea gunk known flatteringly as "marine snow."

At depths below 1,000 metres there is virtually no light at all. The most glaring searchlights make little headway in such obscurity. As oceanographers take pleasure in pointing out, this opacity means that we are today better acquainted with the topography of the moon than the seabed of our own planet.[541] The predominantly *visual* nature of human cognition means that in the total darkness of the deep we are quickly disoriented, and gathering information is a laborious task. In fact, it is not true that there is no light at all in the abyssal depths. The phenomenon of bioluminescence – the light signals produced by predator fish such as deep-sea anglers to lure prey within reach or by jellies as a defensive mechanism for warding off, dazzling or distracting predators – can light up the dark with quite staggering pyrotechnics. Between 80 and 90 per cent of deep-sea creatures are believed to produce their own light.[542] If our ancestors had chosen to dwell in the depths, we too would in all likelihood have a bioluminescent fishing rod dangling in front of our heads, making the deep that little bit less unfathomable. And we would either be as ugly as the notoriously unprepossessing anglerfish or as filmy and gelatinous as the sinuous siphonophores.[543]

540. On phytoplankton see Kunzig, 200-34, esp. 200-2.
541. Kunzig, 64.
542. See ibid., 188-91 on possible explanations for bioluminescence and descriptions of its effects; also Broad, 211-12; Nouvian, *The Deep: The Extraordinary Creatures of the Abyss*, 85-86, 94-95.
543. Fortunately, our criteria of piscine or cnidarian beauty would be different too, possibly incorporating an enormous mouth, dagger-like teeth, and a huge flashing rod in the case of anglers; or thousands of tentacles, scores of stomachs and a flawlessly transparent complexion in the case of siphonophores. The transparency of certain deep-sea organisms is one of the riddles of the deep. One

As an alternative to bioluminescence, if our ancestors had been among the terrestrial creatures that followed the early cetaceans back into the waters, perhaps we might have evolved an ability to emit sound waves that enabled us to identify shapes, gauge distances, and generally navigate the seas. The use of echolocation by sperm whales and other odontocetes (toothed whales) is vital to their success in finding prey and mates. Experts remain uncertain whether baleen whales such as humpbacks and blue whales also possess this capacity, although their use of squeals and moans for social contact is much documented and much celebrated. Capable of communicating over distances of 3,000 kilometres, the blue whale produces abyssally deep rumbles and gurgles that are believed by some scientists to facilitate echolocation for navigational purposes as well.[544] If our ancestors had evolved into a species of echolocating basso profundos, perhaps again the depths would not be quite so unfathomable. Perhaps they would resonate with the sound of deep-sea Johnny Cashes.

In fact, it would have to be a species of echolocating basso profundos with collapsible lungs, for the most pressing hindrance in any human relationship with the depths is the sheer density of the medium, which is over a thousand times greater than that of air. The practical limit for most scuba diving is a depth of little more than 70 metres: even at these levels there is a danger of contracting the extremely painful and on occasion fatal condition known as the bends. At a depth of four kilometres, which is roughly the average for the world's oceans, the pressures are equivalent to being squashed underneath "a tower of solid lead overhead that rises to the height of the Empire State Building."[545] The creatures of the deep are almost all water themselves, and as this is virtually incompressible, they are able to go about their daily business blissfully unaware that they have what amounts to a solid lead skyscraper on top of them. Humans too are largely aqueous and to this extent immune to the compression. The problem resides in our bodily cavities and hollows, especially the lungs, which would immediately collapse or implode under the pressure.

---

explanation currently favoured is that in the absence of sunlight no pigmentation is even necessary. While our own skins provide much-needed protection from harmful ultraviolet rays, the jellies of the deep – shrouded in obscurity – have never required such protection. See Broad, 239.

544. See Roman, 157-61.

545. Broad, 19. This was the depth of the resting place of the *Titanic*.

Again, it is the sperm whale that serves as a role model when it comes to fathoming the depths. Thanks to their ability to store oxygen in muscle tissue, as well as a flexible ribcage that allows lung collapse, the giant odontocetes are able to dive to depths of more than two kilometres, further than any other mammal.[546] Yet even a sperm whale can get the bends if forced to dive unprepared or to resurface in a hurry.

The third notable aspect of the unfathomability of the deep is its placelessness. As Kunzig points out, the fact that human beings are natural surface-dwellers means we have an innate propensity to fix our attention on surfaces:

> when we dive below the surface of the sea, we usually head straight for the next one, the seafloor. But between the top and the bottom of the ocean lies 320 million cubic miles of water, around four-fifths of it deep ocean, far from shore: blue water. All that water is inhabited, and only a tiny fraction of it has been explored with anything but nets, which generally kill the inhabitants.[547]

Opening up a whole new dimension of ignorance, this shifting, placeless three-dimensionality compounds the scale of the ocean's unfathomability, its immensity and immeasurability. An estimate made by a team of leading oceanographers in 1991 put the proportion of the total seabed explored to date at somewhere between one thousandth and one ten-thousandth.[548] When it comes to the volume, it may be a millionth or a billionth. We haven't got a clue.

The gelatinous creatures of the midwaters do not – as far as we know – indulge in soul-searching calculations about the scale of their ignorance. They do not need to. They are ideally suited to the placeless place they inhabit, a boundless environment where gravity is of no account and there are no fixed surfaces.[549] Rooted as we are in our terrestrial environment, with gravity keeping us closely pegged to the two-dimensional surface of the planet, human beings depend largely upon skeletal muscle for maintaining posture and position. For the jellies of the deep, by contrast,

546. Roman, 110.
547. Kunzig, 169-70.
548. Broad, 46.
549. See Kunzig, 191. The marine biologist Harbison regards the jellies as the perfect expression of life in the three-dimensional midwater environment.

floating is the most sensible thing to do in a truly three-dimensional world, and being 95 percent water and gelatinous is the best way to float. It is also the best way to take advantage of the absence of light, of gravity, and of other mechanical stresses; in the slow-moving water beneath the waves, you do not need a backbone or even a shell to retain your integrity.[550]

Being a jellyfish can sound suspiciously like the life of Riley. Naturalist Ann Zwinger describes a life "supported and fed, adrift in an infinite womb, bathed in a life-support medium full of needed nutrients, ... suspended easily in this friendly bath without having to battle the incessant pull of gravity."[551] Perfectly adapted to a place without boundaries or surfaces, gelatinous deep-sea philosophers would doubtless be ultra-Heraclitans, teaching that everything really is flow. The very idea of stepping twice into the same river would be unfathomable to them. But then again, jellies are so at one with their environment that they wouldn't need philosophers to "fathom" it for them anyway.

* * * * *

One of the technological attempts to reduce our non-knowledge of the depths, albeit one that betrays our two-dimensional bias, has been the science of bathymetry, i.e. the study of the physical form of the seabed. Legend has it that in 1521 the Portuguese navigator Ferdinand Magellan lowered a cannonball more than 400 fathoms (or 2,400 feet) into the Pacific and, failing to touch bottom, concluded that the ocean was unfathomably deep.[552] Even by the mid-19th century, when interest in mapping the deep was increasing, pioneering bathymetrists were still using the line and sinker to prepare their maps. Matthew Fontaine Maury published the first map of the North Atlantic Ocean floor in 1854, on the basis of 200 soundings made from his ship the *Dolphin*. A huge step forward was taken in the 1870s by H.M.S. *Challenger*, the "mother ship of oceanography,"[553] a converted British navy corvette that undertook what was the first global

550. Ibid., 192-93.
551. Quoted in Farber, 6.
552. Broad, 22.
553. Kunzig, 34.

oceanographic expedition, a scientific marathon lasting some three and a half years. Still working with line and sinker, the *Challenger* discovered the first oceanic trench, the Mariana Trench, which was found to be more than five miles deep, and the submarine mountain range now known as the Mid-Atlantic Ridge. In 1904, the International Hydrographic Bureau published the first standardised bathymetric map of the world's oceans, using all the 18,400 soundings previously made, yet even then it was still fumbling in the dark.[554]

Further progress was made in the following years. It had long been known that water is a much better transmitter of sound than of light. Despite initial technical difficulties, therefore, the US Navy's invention of the deep-ocean echo sounder – which involved transmitting a sound downward and timing the interval until the echo was heard – speeded up measurement drastically: whereas a line-and-sinker sounding had taken several hours, the new sonic depth finder took a minute. In the years after the Second World War, the "fathometer" made continuous seafloor profiles possible. Nowadays, highly sophisticated multibeam sonar measurements, as well as satellite radar measurements of the Earth's gravity field, have provided a much more exact picture of the seabed's topography.[555] For all its many qualities, however, radar does not penetrate water itself. In 1992, when the US spacecraft *Magellan* used radar to map Venus through its thick clouds of sulphuric acid, it succeeded in attaining a degree of resolution notably in excess of what is achieved by oceanographers.[556] Thanks to water, there seems to be an insuperable limit to the planet's self-knowledge.

Given such opacity, the other approach to overcoming our ignorance is not merely to *measure* the depths (from above) but to *penetrate* those very depths. The first problem to resolve is respiration, for since (like marine mammals, but unlike fish) we lack gills, we cannot drink oxygen directly from the aqueous environment. A number of options are open, which we shall look at in turn. The first is to cheat by *bringing the depths up*. This is the relatively easy solution offered by the marine aquarium, which became

---

554. For a detailed account of the history of soundings, see ibid., 28-42.
555. On gravity field measurements see ibid., 64-69; on multibeam sonar, see ibid., 70-76.
556. Ibid., 68: "the physical limit is a resolution of about two or three miles – which not coincidentally is also the average depth of the ocean." "You can't beat that limitation," says David Sandwell of the Scripps Institution of Oceanography, "unless you drain the oceans."

a defining craze of the 1850s, as typified by P. H. Gosse's instruction manual of 1856, *The Aquarium: An Unveiling of the Wonders of the Deep Sea.*[557] The enormous impact of this mid-Victorian fad on the common conception and visualization of aquatic organisms – at a time when diving equipment was still rudimentary and few people in the Western world could even swim – can hardly be overstated. In artistic representations and illustrations prior to the mid-19th century, writes Stephen Jay Gould, "marine organisms were almost always drawn either on top of the waters (for swimming forms, mostly fishes) or thrown up on shore and desiccating on land (for bottom dwellers, mostly invertebrates)."[558] It was only with the aquarium craze that this highly stylized viewpoint yielded to the more "natural" or "eye-to-eye" perspective taken for granted today, with aquatic creatures portrayed *within* their three-dimensional environment. The aquarium, writes Gould, had "converted the formerly inconceivable (because unseen) into a commonplace."[559]

The second way of dealing with the respiration problem is to hold one's breath, i.e. not breathe. The spectacular feats of competitive free-diving may hint at our natural affinity with the dolphins and whales, but not even the best divers can last more than a few minutes below the surface without breathing apparatus. Even so, adepts are constantly setting new marks in underwater endurance. In the Victorian era, subaquatic performances in water tanks known as "crystal aquaria" were popular spectacles. The celebrated "artiste" Lurline remained below water for nearly three minutes at Oxford Music Hall in 1881, while in 1898 the diminutive show-woman Elise Wallenda, whose underwater act included undressing, writing, sewing, eating and drinking, lasted just over four minutes 45 seconds. Most spectacular, perhaps, was the music-hall figure of Annette Kellermann, who would perform elaborate ballets in glass tanks on stage, remaining beneath the surface for three and a half minutes. For Kellermann, the attraction of swimming was "love of the unknown."[560]

Today's competitive free divers have developed a variety of disciplines to test their tolerance, including "static apnoea" (holding one's breath underwater for as long as possible), "dynamic apnoea" (swimming a

557. For an account of the influence exerted by the marine aquarium on popular thought, see Stephen Jay Gould's piece "Seeing Eye to Eye, through a Glass Clearly," in *Leonardo's Mountain of Clams and the Diet of Worms*, 57-73.
558. Ibid., 67.
559. Ibid., 69.
560. On Lurline, Wallenda and Kellermann, see Sprawson, 33-35.

horizontal distance underwater), "constant ballast diving" (diving down as far as possible with no aids except a mask and a weight belt), and "no-limits free-diving," where the diver can use, for example, a weighted sled of his own choice to descend and a gas-filled balloon to return to the surface. It is in this last discipline that the greatest distances have been achieved.[561] At the time of writing, the record for static apnoea lies at over nine minutes, while even greater lengths of time – over 15 minutes – can be achieved by inhaling pure oxygen beforehand. As regards depth, the modern-day diving legend Umberto Pelizzari was the first person to achieve a "no-limits" dive of 150 metres, a record that has now been pushed to over 200 metres by Herbert Nitsch.

A third approach to the respiration problem is to provide an air supply from the surface. The idea is an old one. Aristotle reports attempts to supply sponge divers with air in the 4th century BCE: divers were provided with bells or "urns" of air from which they could periodically take a gulp and then continue their underwater work.[562] Roger Bacon too referred to bell-like devices that allowed divers to spend considerable periods working underwater without resurfacing, and by the late 16th century diving bells were in use across much of Europe. Further improvements were made in 1691, when Edmond Halley designed a diving bell that was fed with air by a leather pipe from a weighted barrel,[563] and the later stages of the 18th century saw the development of diving suits supplied with air pumped from the surface. By 1837 the German Augustus Siebe had adapted the "smoke helmet" used in firefighting to underwater use, fitting his new diving helmet to a full-length enclosed diving suit made of canvas.

Variations on this design were used for salvage work for the next hundred years, and this was the image of the deep-sea diver – a cumbersomely moving figure in an unwieldy helmet with an air hose connected to a pumping wheel at the surface – that came to epitomize the Victorian underwater adventurer battling the forces of the deep. "Before astronauts made space the final frontier," writes Ecott, "the deep-sea diver was the archetypal hero."[564] Dramatic underwater duels between diving heroes and villains made theatre-goers gasp, while films such as the Williamson brothers' 1916 version of Jules Verne's *20,000 Leagues under the Sea* captured the popular imagination with their subaquatic scenes. The slapstick and the surreal potential of the deep-sea diver were exploited

561. Ecott, 309-11.
562. Ibid., 7.
563. On Halley's design, see ibid., 18-22.
564. Ibid., 25.

by Buster Keaton in *The Navigator* (1924), which also features Buster's celebrated underwater swordfish-fight. In general, dramatic tension was a constant. With the air still coming from the surface, things could – and did – go horribly wrong if the pumps failed.

Towards the end of the 19th century, the pioneering diving engineer Henry Albert Fleuss designed the first self-contained breathing apparatus, which was refined in the course of the 20th century to produce what is now more or less universally known as scuba equipment. Scuba divers carry with them their own supply of air – or some other breathing gas such as a mixture of oxygen and helium – in a high-pressure diving cylinder, thus dispensing with the clumsy diving suits and hosepipes and making underwater exploration a much more versatile activity, available nowadays to millions of participants. Scuba divers can descend to a depth of 15 metres for as long as 70 or 80 minutes; at 40 metres the maximum time is generally limited to five minutes. Yet the diver remains unprotected from the pressure of the water. The bends – or decompression illness – still poses a painful and potentially deadly threat,[565] while nitrogen narcosis and oxygen poisoning can lead divers swiftly and lethally from light-headedness to oblivion.

These three afflictions are all caused by *breathing* in the context of pressure changes, and so one way to avoid them is not to breathe (i.e. free diving). The other strategy – a fourth response to the difficulties of penetrating the deep – involves cocooning divers in an environment that somehow maintains an internal pressure of one atmosphere. Such is the case with the atmospheric diving suit, which eliminates most of the physiological dangers of diving (such as the bends) by keeping the diver at a constant pressure within a man-shaped, highly articulated, submersible "robot" made from carbon fibre, reinforced plastic and aluminium alloy. The JIM suit of the 1970s, perhaps the best-known model, is capable of descending to depths of more than 400 metres. Another such submersible, known as *Wasp* and originally developed for oil-rig maintenance work, could go down to more than 600 metres while still maintaining an internal pressure of one atmosphere. But it had no legs, was a "cross between a tethered diving suit and a personal submarine," and being inside it,

---

565. On the bends, see ibid., 83-96. According to Ecott, the reputation of the bends as an affliction is "as alarming and sinister as the man-eating shark" (84). When the modern diving helmet first became commercially viable in the 1850s, hundreds of Mediterranean sponge divers were killed and thousands crippled as a result of the bends.

according to one venturesome marine biologist, was "like being a Michelin man in a garbage can."[566]

Other underwater vessels use the same principle – an internal pressure kept at roughly one atmosphere – to hold more than just one person. Early submersibles were used in the American Revolution and Civil War, and by the First World War many navies were developing submarines. Above all in the 1960s, scientists engaged in a succession of sub-sea habitation programmes, which involved keeping "aquanauts" living in underwater structures – at depths of up to 600 feet – for extended periods of time.[567] Yet even the most cutting-edge military submarines are unable to go down to depths greater than a few hundred metres, and it is with the development of the *bathysphere* by William Beebe and Otis Barton in the 1930s that modern-day exploration of the deep ocean begins. The device was basically a robust cast-iron sphere big enough for two men to fit in, and with two small portholes for them to peer out. Lowered into the deep on a cable from a surface support ship, the first dive in 1930 descended to 183 metres; by 1934, the record was over 900 metres; in 1948 Barton went down 1,370 metres. Records were further shattered by a later submersible, the bathyscaphe *Trieste* developed by Auguste Piccard, which – without the support of surface cables – descended over 3,000 metres into the Mediterranean in 1953. In 1960, manned by Piccard's son Jacques and Lieutenant Don Walsh of the US Navy, the *Trieste* took a nine-hour round trip to the bottom of the Challenger Deep in the Mariana Trench, at 10,918 metres the deepest of the deep. Schiller's king would have surely settled for this. Human beings have not descended to such depths since. At present, all the great ocean trenches are out of bounds to humankind.[568]

Yet submersibles have continued to evolve. One of the most successful has been *Alvin*, designed by the US Navy in 1963-64 and now run by the Woods Hole Oceanographic Institution. With its original aluminium structural frame now replaced by the superstrong but lightweight metal titanium, *Alvin* can transport a crew of three to depths of 4.5 kilometres,

---

566. Kunzig, 188.

567. On sub-sea habitats, see Ecott, 237-78. Sub-sea habitation exercises eventually fell victim to the much higher-profile space race. In the words of one former aquanaut, "men found the moon's behind much more interesting than the ocean's bottom" (quoted in ibid., 254).

568. On Beebe and his bathysphere, see Broad, 38-42; on the Piccards and their bathyscaphe, see ibid., 49-56. See also Nouvian, 24.

and attracted particular attention in the 1970s with its investigation of the unimaginable world of three-metre tube worms living on and around the deep-sea hydrothermal vents off the Galápagos Islands. More recent models include the French *Nautile*, instrumental in salvage work on the *Titanic*, the Russian *Mir I* and *Mir II*, and the Japanese *Shinkai 6500*, currently the world's deepest piloted craft, capable of reaching depths of 6.5 kilometres.[569] Such submersibles are nowhere near reaching the depths of the Challenger Deep or other ocean trenches. Yet they do descend to the "abyssal plain," the deep ocean floor that covers much of the planet's surface, and provide previously unthinkable insights into the world below.

In the light of current technological trends, the fifth approach to penetrating the depths provides an option that may prove more feasible than the use of manned submersibles. This is to allow technology to *mediate* our presence underwater, in effect extending the range of our sensory apparatus while remaining comfortably seated in front of a computer screen on dry land (i.e. getting machines to do the dirty work). Manoeuvred from support vessels to which they are attached by cables, today's ROVs (remotely operated vehicles) are endowed with cameras that provide real-time footage and mechanical arms that can gather samples from the seabed. They can dive for days at a time and are considerably cheaper to run than submersibles. The deepest-diving ROV reached depths of over 10,000 metres before being lost at sea in 2003. Even more remarkable, perhaps, are the untethered robots which can freely negotiate the seabed, in some cases keeping contact with surface controllers through pulses of sound, in others dispensing with even this acoustical link and using their own computer intelligence to guide themselves on their various missions.[570]

* * * * *

Writing in the 1st century CE, Pliny the Elder waxed effusive at the extent of human knowledge of the seas. "By Hercules!" he enthused, "in the sea and in the Ocean, vast as it is, there exists nothing that is unknown to us, and, a truly marvelous fact, it is with those things that Nature has concealed in the deep that we are best acquainted."[571] On Pliny's reckoning, the total

569. On the *Nautile* and *Mir* submersibles, see Broad, 176-84; on the *Shinkai 6500*, see 272-73.
570. For a description of one such untethered robot, *Odyssey*, see ibid., 319-23.
571. Kunzig, 86, citing the Challenger Report.

number of marine species was 176. The fanciful and fantastic speculations of subsequent centuries were fuelled by half-sightings, misinformation and sheer, knock-kneed fear. When superstition and myth started to yield to scientific enquiry in the early 19th century, one of the prominent theories was that nothing at all could live in the abyss. According to this view, known as azoic theory, the deep was cold, dark, dense and stagnant. As such, it was felt, it could only be barren, sterile and utterly hostile to life.[572] Nor was this the most eccentric theory of the time. Ignoring that water is as good as incompressible, one popular myth had it that the density of the abyssal deep would be so great that there would come a point when nothing would sink any more, and objects would merely float in a never-ending state of eerie suspension. Forgetting that ice floats, the Frenchman François Peron propounded the theory that a thick layer of ice covered the bottom of the ocean.[573]

The azoic misconception, which conveniently dismissed the unknown as uninteresting, was persistent enough to require a century of refutation. A series of oceanographic expeditions undertaken in the 1860s and 1870s and culminating in the voyage of the *Challenger* discovered new deep-sea species by the bucketful. Even then, the predominant view was that the ocean depths were a "faunally depauperate desert," a homogeneous and stable fauna that was all in all pretty boring. Yet the deployment of deep-sea submersibles, improved dredging and trawling techniques, and the use of ROVs and robots have transformed our vision of the depths. The deep is now known to be anything other than faunally depauperate: though its population is relatively sparse, it is a haven of diversity on a par, it is believed, with the rain forest. "We're brought up to believe that the abyss and the hadal zone are really hostile environments to all life, because they're hostile to us," says marine biologist J. Frederick Grassle. "But in fact, for a lot of life they're not hostile. It may in general be a more 'benign' environment ... than most parts of the planet."[574] The

572. According to the 19th-century naturalist Edward Forbes, the inhabitants of the deep "become fewer and fewer, indicating our approach to an abyss where life is either extinguished, or exhibits but a few sparks to mark its lingering presence" (quoted in Broad, 28).
573. Kunzig, 89.
574. Quoted in Kunzig, 127. The word "hadal" alludes to the Greek underworld Hades, deriving from the Greek word "unseen." Unlike the later Christian Hell, as we have seen, Hades did not necessarily imply fire and brimstone. In this context, the hadal zone refers to the deepest parts of the abyssopelagic, i.e. the ocean trenches.

unfathomable is not dead, but is alive and kicking. Pliny notwithstanding, there are millions of species still waiting to be discovered.

3

Monsters of the Deep

The human mind has reacted to the limitations of its reach by populating the unknown deep with beasts of myth and fantasy of its own creation. These symbolize the immeasurability and unfathomability of the depths themselves, incarnating our fear of being engulfed or swallowed whole by a monstrous maw. Such a beast was Jormungand, the gargantuan sea-serpent of Norse mythology, who encircled the whole world like an ouroboros biting its own tail. Jormungand was to be a major player in Ragnarok, the inevitable fate or destruction of the world, sending the ocean surging over the land and spewing venom into sea and sky in his fury. He would finally be vanquished by his arch-enemy Thor, but would mortally wound him in the process.

No less awesome is Leviathan, the Biblical sea monster of the Book of Job in the Old Testament, an image of immeasurability and the incomprehensible. "Can you draw out Leviathan with a fishhook? or press down his tongue with a cord?" God asks Job from a convenient whirlwind. "Who can open the doors of his face? Round about his teeth is terror. His back is made of rows of shields, shut up closely as with a seal. ... Out of his mouth go flaming torches; sparks of fire leap forth. Out of his nostrils comes forth smoke, as from a boiling pot .... When he raises himself up the mighty are afraid" (Job 41:1-33). Yet worldly foes that have mortal men quaking in their boots are easily dispatched by God: according to Isaiah (27:1), the day will come when "the Lord with his hard and great and strong sword will punish Leviathan the fleeing serpent, Leviathan the twisting serpent, and he will slay the dragon that is in the sea." In Psalms (74:13-14), this is reported as having occurred in the past: "Thou didst divide the sea by thy might; thou didst break the heads of the dragons on the waters. Thou didst crush the heads of Leviathan, thou didst give him as food for the creatures of the wilderness." The Book of Enoch draws a distinction between the female, ocean-dwelling Leviathan and the male, land-lubbing Behemoth (1 Enoch 60:7-8).

Leviathan may be understood as an expression of Satanic or diabolical opposition to God's will, of the dangers of the sea (or sea-faring invaders), or merely as puffed-up worldly pride and presumption.[575] Yet he is commonly supposed to have his origins in the sea-deity Yam or Yamm of ancient Canaanite myth. In the form of the hydra-like dragon or serpent Lotan, Yam was slain and replaced as king of the gods by the Lord of Rain and Dew, the fertility deity Baal – just as the Babylonian goddess of the primal waters, Tiamat, had been vanquished by Marduk. Like Tiamat and Yam, Leviathan to this extent represents the primordial watery chaos prior to the intervention of the creator-god, an obsolescent water-divinity replaced by the shaping force of civilization.

Despite the serpentine features in most descriptions of him, Leviathan has in fact – perhaps on account of his size – come to be synonymous with the whale.[576] In *Moby Dick*, for example, the term is commonly used to denote the sperm whale, highlighting the mythical dimensions and the sheer immeasurability of the novel's true protagonist. After an examination of some of the common misrepresentations of the sperm whale, the narrator thus concludes that "any way you may look at it, you must needs conclude that the great Leviathan is that one creature in the world which must remain unpainted to the last. True, one portrait may hit the mark much nearer than another, but none can hit it with any very considerable degree of exactness." The only way to gain an idea of his figure and proportions is to go whaling oneself – running the risk of "being eternally stove and sunk by him."[577]

Until fairly recently, little distinction was drawn between sea monsters, giant fish and cetaceans. Difficult to categorize and freakishly large, whales thus made exemplary sea monsters. Aristotle recognized the strangeness of whales as aquatic creatures that nonetheless breathed air and gave birth to live offspring, and the Romans too noticed that whales,

---

575. According to the *midrash*, in fact, Leviathan – a "marvellous beast" – was "the plaything of God, in whom He takes His pastime." His real purpose, however, was "to be served up as a dainty to the pious in the world to come" (Ginzberg, I.27).
576. Also on the basis of size, the term was famously used by the 17th-century English political philosopher Thomas Hobbes to denote a commonwealth of people united for the common good – "that great Leviathan, or rather (to speake more reverently) … that *Mortall God*, to which wee owe under the *Immortall God*, our peace and defence" (Hobbes, *Leviathan*, 227). As a mortal god, Leviathan again comes over as rather a second-division divinity compared with the Supreme Being.
577. Melville, *Moby Dick*, 262 (chapter 55).

dolphins and seals resembled mammals rather than fish in suckling their young.[578] But it was not until the great taxonomist Linnaeus that the distinction between whales and fish was formalized. The Biblical story of Jonah – the reluctant prophet who was swallowed and then spewed out by a sea creature – refers in Hebrew to a "big fish," while in the Greek version it was a *ketos* that swallowed him, a term associated with whales, sharks or even cephalopods.[579] Yet the Latin word *cetus* that was used in the New Testament (Matthew 12:40) has gradually become synonymous with – and given its name to – cetaceans (i.e. whales, porpoises and dolphins),[580] and this is the standard Christian interpretation today.[581] Anatomical feasibility is little help in identifying the creature in question: the biggest whale of all, the enormous blue whale, feeds on plankton and would not be able to ingest a sailor's arm without divine assistance; the largest shark, the gentle whale shark, is also a filter-feeder and equally incapable of getting such an object down its gullet; the sperm whale or cachalot is perhaps the most likely candidate, but Jonah would have still had to negotiate its sizeable teeth and the gastric juices.

Yet tall tales and legends suggest otherwise. Most famously, when harpooner Bully Sprague was swallowed by Timor Tim, a grizzled old cachalot, he was able to make out graffiti on the whale's stomach wall that said "Jonah. BC. 1683." The fearless harpooner then went on to extract himself from his confinement, resourcefully using his tobacco leaves to churn the sperm whale's stomach into regurgitating him.[582] According to one popular account from 1891, the 35-year-old English sailor James Bartley was said to have been swallowed by a sperm whale while whaling with the *Star of the East* off the Falkland Islands. When the whale was subsequently – within a couple of hours – killed and brought to the mother ship for butchering, the crew were flabbergasted to find their lost shipmate,

578. See Roman, 99.
579. Ibid., 12.
580. The order of Cetacea is divided into two suborders, the Mysticeti or whalebone / baleen whales (which include right whales and rorquals such as the enormous blue whale) and the Odontoceti or toothed whales (which include dolphins, porpoises and sperm whales as well as the narwhal and beluga).
581. The Islamic version in the Qur'an sticks to the "big fish": "Jonah too was one of the messengers. He fled to the overloaded ship. They cast lots, he suffered defeat, and a great fish swallowed him, for he had committed blameworthy acts. If he had not been one of those who glorified God, he would have stayed in its belly until the Day when all are raised up" (37:139-44).
582. Roman, 13-14.

"unconscious, bleached to a deathly white by the gastric acids, but still living."[583] After two weeks of delirium, he made a full recovery.

In religious as in humorous anecdote, of course, to talk of veracity is to miss the point: preposterous tales are the order of the day. Here it is perhaps the illustrious preposterous-tale-teller Baron von Münchhausen who takes the biscuit. In G. A. Bürger's version of the tales, the Baron has two encounters with the innards of sea creatures. In the first case, he convulses the "big fish" by wriggling and hopping and dancing a Scottish jig until his tormented captor is harpooned by a passing Italian merchant vessel. In the second – even more preposterous – case, his entire ship ends up inside the monster. Here they come across around 10,000 sailors of all nationalities – many of them long-term inhabitants – and a whole fleet of some 35 previously swallowed vessels, likewise rising and falling with the tide as and when the animal imbibes or lets water. (According to rough calculations, the creature generally drinks a volume somewhat greater than that of Lake Geneva). Again, the Baron's enterprise saves the day, as the various crews join forces and use their masts to prevent the monster from closing its great maw.[584] Interestingly, and perhaps not coincidentally, the Baron and his crew had been sailing in a sea of the "most excellent" red wine just a few hours previously.

In such cases, the whale resembles the ocean itself in its capacity to engulf insignificant homunculus, and subsequent regurgitation – be it god or tobacco-induced – is akin to resurrection or rebirth. The tale of Jonah has commonly been interpreted as anticipating Christ's own resurrection.[585] The "monstrosity" of the whale is largely a question of size and reflects the "monstrosity" of its medium: whale, ocean and death alike engulf man within their watery maw. Yet if the whale's cavernous belly has been the most common metaphor for the all-consuming hunger of the sea, its enormous back has also provided the stuff of legend. The *imrama* of the 6th-century navigator St Brendan recount how the seafaring monks' quest for the Land of Promise took them to what appeared to be a barren island, where they landed to celebrate mass. Lighting a fire for breakfast, however, they felt the earth stir beneath them and beat a hasty retreat to their boat – only to see the island swim away. The whale in question,

583. Paxman, 409-10.
584. Bürger, *Münchhausen*, 84-86, 179-82.
585. In Matthew 12:40, Christ is understood to be drawing such a parallel: "For as Jonas was three days and three nights in the belly of the whale, so will the Son of man be three days and three nights in the heart of the earth."

Jasconius, turned out to be a good-natured but enormous cetacean with frustrated aspirations to put his tail in his mouth, ouroboros-like. The monks would subsequently use his back for mass again, though not for cooking breakfast on.

The motif of the whale as an island also turns up during the first of Sindbad's seven voyages in *The Thousand and One Nights*. On this occasion the whale – likewise aroused by the heat of a man-made fire – plunges into the depths, sending the mariners scattering and leaving Sindbad himself drifting with the tide and resigned to certain death.[586] The tale is still in healthy circulation in the 19th century, albeit in a more sceptical or ironic guise. In Jules Verne's *Twenty Thousand Leagues under the Sea*, it signals the gullibility of the harpooner Ned Land, who describes gigantic sperm whales – up to 300 feet long and weighing 100,000 tons – which are said to "dress up with weeds and fucus. They are taken for small islands and fishermen set up camps on them, settle down, build fires."[587] Common to Islamic and European culture, the motif of the island-sized whale is believed to have originated in Indo-Persian folklore and has been traced to a similar tale from the Talmud: "we thought it was an island, descended, baked, and cooked upon it. When the back of the fish grew hot, it turned over, and had not the ship been so near we would have been drowned."[588]

Given the immensity of Leviathan and its all-engulfing mouth, it is hardly surprising that whales and sea monsters have traditionally been associated with the diabolical or satanic. In Anglo-Saxon bestiaries, the whale stood for the Devil, who enticed the damned into his yawning maw with strangely pleasant-smelling halitosis.[589] Unprepossessing, odd-looking or fearsome sea-dwellers have often been given names that betray this association. The poor old anglerfish – admittedly no beauty with his dagger-like teeth, gaping mouth and warty complexion – has been endowed with epithets like blackdevil or triplewart seadevil.[590] One of the

586. *Arabian Nights: Tales from the Thousand and One Nights* (trans. N. J. Dawood), 116-17.
587. Verne, *Twenty Thousand Leagues under the Sea*, 289. Ned Land is here interrupted by the more astute but implacably dull taxonomist Conseil, who jokes "And build houses on them also, don't they?"
588. Quoted in Roman, 19.
589. See Roman, 19-21.
590. See Broad, 24, 342.

unofficial mascots of the deep[591] is the "much-maligned" *Vampyroteuthis infernalis*, the "vampire squid from hell," a weird hybrid of squid and octopus that may be the common ancestor of both. The manta ray, the largest of the rays, with its "wings" spanning almost eight metres and its distinctive horns, is also known as the devil ray or devilfish, a name it used to share with octopuses and grey whales. The genus name for the killer whale *Orcinus* means "from hell," Orcus being another name for Pluto, the god of the underworld. Indeed, the term "orca"[592] is now preferred to "killer whale," for it is known to be a member of the dolphin family *Delphinidae* rather than a whale, and though an apex predator that feeds on juvenile whales and sharks as well as seals, turtles and fish, it does not kill humans.

Greek mythology did not need a devil-figure. There was no Manichean separation of good and evil, and every god had an ambiguous character, capable of both righteousness and vicious vindictiveness.[593] When it came to sea monsters the emphasis was on brute fearsomeness. This is exemplified by the tale of Perseus and Ceto, in which Gorgon-slaying Perseus rescues beautiful Andromeda – tied naked to a rock – from the clutches of a horrific sea monster (Ceto) sent by Poseidon.[594] In *Moby Dick* Perseus is duly championed as the prince of all whalemen for his overcoming of "Leviathan."[595] Remarkably similar features structure Heracles's rescue of Hesione: the wrath of Poseidon, a terrifying sea beast, a naked maiden chained to a rock, the threat of sacrifice, a passing hero. On this occasion, brave Heracles leaped fully-armed down the monster's

---

591. See Nouvian, 134-35, also 50.
592. As it happens, the species name *Orca* is not thought to have the same ety-mological root as the genus name *Orcinus*.
593. Even Hades denoted not only death and the underworld but – as Plutus (Pluto) – wealth and abundance. The god that most inspired the iconography of the Christian Devil was lusty Pan, god of forests and fields and unbridled, joyful sexual desire.
594. Graves, I.240. Andromeda's mother had rubbed Poseidon up the wrong way by boasting that she and her daughter were as beautiful as the Nereids.
595. Melville, 348-50. The figure of St George is judged to be another, equally illustrious whalemen: "Akin to the adventure of Perseus and Andromeda – indeed, by some supposed to be indirectly derived from it – is that famous story of St. George and the Dragon; which dragon I maintain to have been a whale; for in many old chronicles whales and dragons are strangely jumbled together, and often stand for each other" (ibid.).

throat and spent three days in its belly, hewing at its intestines from the inside before emerging victorious (though the struggle "had cost him every hair on his head").[596]

When these episodes are parodied in Ludovico Ariosto's *Orlando Furioso* (1532), the sea monster – this time sent by vengeful Proteus – has become an *orca* or orc, "a great coiling, twisting mass, quite unlike an animal in shape, except for its head, with protruding eyes and teeth like a boar's."[597] Exaggeration, farce and misidentification here colour the account. First Ruggiero on his hippogryph rescues the lovely Angelica and carries her off to safety, though he fails to dispatch the orc and is impeded by his shining armour when he tries to have his way with the girl. Then comes Orlando, also hoping to rescue the lovely Angelica, though in fact it is the lovely Olympia he ends up saving. Following venerable literary tradition, Orlando sails into the beast's gaping maw, wedges its jaws open, and proceeds to slash it to pieces from within. The very sight sends Proteus fleeing for the ocean depths, and even Neptune is prompted to beat a hasty retreat for Ethiopia.[598]

Notwithstanding the fearsomeness of the monsters sent by Poseidon or Neptune, there is an underlying ambiguity in attitudes to the unknown monsters of the deep. Brendan encountered both friendly and extremely unfriendly sea creatures in the course of his travels. Jasconius was certainly affable enough, and it was a whale that saved Brendan's men from the clutches of a formidable sea cat with bulging eyes and horrific tusks. Poseidon was associated not only with havoc-wreaking Ceto, but with the human-friendly dolphin. One of a "school of music-loving dolphins" is said to have rescued the Greek bard Arion when he threw himself overboard to escape from piracy[599]; Apollo, god of light, poetry, music, healing and prophecy, assumed the form of a dolphin to ferry the Cretan Icadius to Delphi (where he was revered as Apollo Delphinios, Lord of the Dolphins); and early Etruscan burial art often portrays dolphins and sea-horses bearing the souls of the dead to the Islands of the Blessed. According to the ancient wisdom of the *midrash*, dolphins are "half man and half fish; they even have sexual intercourse with human beings; therefore they are called also 'sons of the sea,' for in a sense they

---

596. Graves, II.168-69.
597. Ariosto, *Orlando Furioso*, 104 (canto 10).
598. Ibid., 109-11 (canto 11).
599. Graves, I.290-92.

represent the human kind in the waters."[600]

By the time of *Moby Dick* the whale itself, embodying the sublimity of the unbounded oceans, had come to hover between the divine and the diabolical. The narrator Ishmael is keen to draw the reader's attention to the tendency for exaggeration and hyperbolic fantasy in the realm of seafaring in general and whaling in particular:

> ... in maritime life, far more than in that of terra firma, wild rumors abound, wherever there is any adequate reality for them to cling to. And as the sea surpasses the land in this matter, so the whale fishery surpasses every other sort of maritime life, in the wonderfulness and fearfulness of the rumors which sometimes circulate there. ... No wonder, then, that ever gathering volume from the mere transit over the widest watery spaces, the outblown rumors of the White Whale [Moby Dick] did in the end incorporate with themselves all manner of morbid hints, and half-formed foetal suggestions of supernatural agencies, which eventually invested Moby Dick with new terrors unborrowed from anything that visibly appears.[601]

Quite apart from his "unwonted magnitude" and his "unexampled, intelligent malignity," therefore, he also came to be regarded by the "superstitiously inclined" as ubiquitous as well as immortal ("for immortality is but ubiquity in time"[602]). The narrator, by contrast, muses on the "profundity", "dignity" and "sublimity" evidenced by the sperm whale's spouting:

> I account him no common, shallow being ... He is both ponderous and profound. And I am convinced that from the heads of all ponderous profound beings, such as Plato, Pyrrho, the Devil, Jupiter, Dante, and so on, there always goes up a certain semi-visible steam, while in the act of thinking deep thoughts. While composing a little treatise on Eternity, I had the curiosity to place a mirror before me; and ere long saw reflected there, a curious involved worming and undulation in the atmosphere over my head. ... And how nobly it raises our conceit of the mighty, misty monster, to behold him solemnly sailing through a calm tropical sea; his vast, mild head overhung by a canopy of vapor, engendered by his incommunicable contemplations ... [603]

600. Ginzberg, I.35.
601. Melville, *Moby Dick*. 181-82 (chap. 41).
602. Ibid., 183-84.
603. Ibid., 359 (chap. 85).

Ishmael is only half-joking. The sperm whale's "incommunicable contemplations" are just one aspect of a radical unfathomability that – in the narrator at least – provokes veneration and awe rather than naked fear. Waxing lyrical about the cetacean fluke, he concludes: "The more I consider this mighty tail, the more do I deplore my inability to express it. … Dissect him how I may, then, I but go skin deep; I know him not, and never will. But if I know not even the tail of this whale, how understand his head?"[604] By the end it is the language of deity that is used to describe the novel's hidden protagonist: "not Jove, not that great majesty Supreme! did surpass the glorified White Whale as he so divinely swam"; "the grand god revealed himself, sounded, and went out of sight."[605]

Much had certainly changed in the relationship of human beings with cetaceans, though not for the better. The shift from subsistence to commercial whaling, i.e. to the profit-oriented mass slaughter pursued first by the Basques, then by northern Europeans and US Americans, did lead to a greater emphasis on empirical observation and scientific measurement and a certain demythologization of the giant sea mammals; many of the old legends were found to have their roots in exaggerated portrayals or simple misidentifications of animals such as sharks, whales or squid. The killing of cetaceans thus became simply another aspect of man's domination over mute, brute, watery nature, and the element of fantasy – or divinity – was relegated to whalers' folklore, to be viewed with ironic detachment or amusement in the face of what was still a dangerous occupation.

The ferocity of this subjugation of nature was justified both by the traditional Judaeo-Christian opposition to paganism[606] and by a deeply

604. Ibid., 363 (chap. 86).
605. Ibid., 511, 512 (chap. 133).
606. As Mary Midgley explains (in *Beast and Man: The Roots of Human Nature*, 35), any hint of veneration shown towards animals (or nature) was fiercely resisted by Jewish and Christian monotheism. Though there may co-exist a relatively hospitable side to monotheism (which sees animals as manifestations of the glory of God), predominant has been a "sharply exclusive and destructive side, in which the Lord tolerates no rival for our regard. In this mood, the church often and explicitly insisted that all plants and animals must be viewed merely as objects given to man as his instruments, that to have any sort of regard for them in themselves was sinful and superstitious folly." Such was the view propounded by Augustine (see ibid., 219). It provided the theological foundation for the long-prevalent idea of *conquering* nature, which is, says Midgley, "about as sensible as for a caddis worm to talk of conquering the pond that supports it, or a drunk to start fighting the bed he is lying on" (ibid., 196).

schizoid metaphysics – formalized by Descartes in the 17th century[607] – that posited a radical separation of mind (i.e. the mind of "rational" man) from body (i.e. objectified nature). Compared with the greatness of God or the reified mind of man, nature was generally considered contemptible and vile. Though opposed to killing baleen whales "just for the sake of killing," therefore, even Verne's Captain Nemo did not extend his clemency to sperm whales, which he viewed as "dreadful creatures," which "one is perfectly justified in exterminating."[608] For the obsessive captain Ahab of *Moby Dick*, the sperm whale represented "the monomaniac incarnation of all those malicious agencies which some deep men feel eating in them, till they are left living on with half a heart and half a lung." To Ahab, all evil "was visibly personified, and made practically assailable in Moby Dick. He piled upon the whale's white hump the sum of all the general rage and hate felt by his whole race from Adam down."[609] In the schizoid mind of man, the whale could thus embody nature viewed not only as base and worthless (except in economic terms) – but as evil and diabolical. To vanquish it was a duty.

Things were to get worse for cachalots and all other whales before they got better. Melville's book was written in the 1850s, Verne's in the 1860s, a decade regarded as a watershed in the history of whale slaughtering with the invention of the explosive harpoon.[610] Factory ships and the industrialization of whaling in the early 20th century represented the ultimate suppression of awe and wonder and the reduction of living

607. In his mechanistic world, Descartes could only avoid the unpalatable view that human beings too are merely machines by introducing the notion of the rational soul or mind, wholly distinct from the body. Of all material beings, Descartes believed, humans are alone in having such a soul, which he identified with consciousness as well as intelligence. Animals, by contrast, are just machines or automata, governed by the same underlying principles as a clock. They might squeal or writhe in agony if someone cut them with a knife – as Descartes did – but this would not indicate the presence of mind or intelligence: clocks too make a noise if you take them apart. See Descartes, *Discourse on Method*, 79-82. For a discussion of Descartes' attitude to animals, see Singer, *Animal Liberation*, 200-2; Midgley, *Beast*, 209-12.
608. Verne, *Twenty Thousand Leagues under the Sea*, 291. The narrator notably agreed that if not curbed "the barbarous slaughter and lack of forethought shown by whalers would one day wipe out the last whale from the ocean." Yet he did not contest the damning verdict on sperm whales.
609. Melville, 185, 186 (chap. 41).
610. Roman, 127.

beings to lifeless blubber, sperm oil and the possibility of profit. In post-Cartesian society, the psychotic dualism that split off a hypertrophic rationality from an inferior, watery nature led to the wholesale decimation of almost all species of whales, in many cases leaving just a few hundred individuals. While some 37,000 sperm whales are estimated to have been killed in a hundred years of Yankee whaling, 337,604 individuals were massacred in the North Pacific alone between 1950 and 1970.[611] It was only once human beings developed scuba technology, underwater cameras and hydrophones – as well as the television to broadcast such images – that a cetocentric perspective could start to emerge and the fear-based hatred of Leviathan be challenged. The underwater photographer James Hudnall described the 30-ton rorquals he had photographed as "gentle, clever, passive and rational beings."[612] Man started to ask: so who is the real monster?

*   *   *   *   *

Jeremy Paxman writes: "The monster is the ultimate expression of our fascination with the unfathomableness of water. ... We are obsessed by monsters. Not just the great prehistoric leviathans said to lurk in the depths of so many inland seas, but perfectly normal fish grown to abnormal size."[613] Given this fixation with size, it is perhaps no coincidence that psychoanalytical theory sees the fish as a symbol for the penis, an association reinforced by bawdy slang.[614]

Sheer immensity is perhaps the prime characteristic of traditional monsters of the deep, both imaginary and real. In his 16th-century survey of Scandinavian zoology, Olaus Magnus, the exiled archbishop of Uppsala, referred to sea serpents "of vast magnitude, namely 200 feet

611. Ibid., 168.
612. Quoted in ibid., 153.
613. Paxman, 78, 291.
614. The *Cassell Dictionary of Slang* includes the one-eyed zipper fish, the trouser trout, the eel and of course moby dick. It also includes the 18th-century cod, although "cods" originally referred to the testicles (as in medieval codpieces). The worried male of our species is as a rule keen to have a leviathan or a moby dick lurking in his pants, not a sprat, an anchovy or a trifling goby.

long, and moreover 20 feet thick,"[615] which could devour more or less whatever they came across, including unfortunate sailors. In reality, when it comes to size, it is the benign plankton-eating blue whale who rules the waves. Possibly the largest animals ever to have inhabited the planet, these 30-metre-long baleen whales weigh as much as 2,000 men.[616] They are the fastest-growing of all organisms, plant or animal. They emit sounds that can be heard by other blue whales some 3,000 kilometres away. Sperm whales are the animals with the biggest brains on the planet, six times the size of human brains;[617] bowhead whales have the biggest mouths; right whales have one-ton testicles the size of washing machines;[618] killer whales can attain speeds of more than 60 kilometres an hour and are the fastest marine animal. Even the sober, empirical reality of whales is the stuff of tall stories and preposterous tales.

The immensity of whales – by contrast with most fish – has to do with certain features of their mammalian metabolism resulting from the return of their ancestors from a terrestrial to an aquatic life some 47 million years ago. No longer bound by the restrictions of gravity, their limbs were freed from the onus of weight-bearing, and the buoyant proto-cetaceans of the Tertiary Period could develop to prodigious proportions. As Joe Roman explains:

> Such body size is a critical adaptation for a warm-blooded animal in a cold sea. In the ocean, heat is dissipated much more rapidly than it is on land. A bigger animal has a smaller proportion of its body exposed to the environment. Even the smallest marine mammals are quite a bit larger than their terrestrial relatives. There are no sea mice or marine shrews; only the otter, with its thick fur, has managed to colonize the sea successfully. Most sea mammals are hairless, large and full of fat.[619]

615. Quoted in Coleman and Huyghe, *Lake Monsters, Sea Serpents, and Other Mystery Denizens of the Deep*, 50-51.
616. The first episode of the BBC series *The Blue Planet*, narrated by David Attenborough, begins with a memorable description of the blue whale: "its tongue weighs as much as an elephant, its heart is the size of a car, and some of its blood vessels are so wide that you could swim down them."
617. Moreover, "cetacean brains are highly convoluted, like our own, but, unlike humans, whales have had a long time to get accustomed to their super-size grey matter. Cetaceans first evolved one-to-two-kilogram brains about 30 million years ago. We have had our 1.3 kilograms of neurons for a mere 100,000 years or so" (Roman, 156).
618. Ibid., 116.
619. Ibid., 108.

This also helps explain the hugeness of certain other species that reverted to a watery existence after having adapted to terrestrial conditions. For just as mammals such as the cetaceans (whales, dolphins and porpoises), sirenians (manatees and dugongs) and pinnipeds (seals, sea lions and walruses) have returned to the seas since the demise of the dinosaurs, the Mesozoic Era (roughly 250 to 65 million years ago) saw the return of three major groups of *reptiles* to the waters, the ichthyosaurs, the plesiosaurs and pliosaurs, and the mosasaurs, each of which could attain an enormous size. These long-extinct marine groups spent their whole life in water, surfacing to breathe air (like marine mammals, but unlike fish) and in some cases evolving viviparity. Copious insulation – layers of blubber – would have countered the hostile conditions of a cold aquatic existence, helping to balloon the pre-historic sea monsters into the shape of the 50-foot ichthyosaur *Shonisaurus*, the 40-foot pliosaur *Kronosaurus*, or the formidable 60-foot mosasaur *Mosasaurus*, bone-crunching apex predators of the ancient oceans that would have dwarfed and presumably devoured their modern-day counterparts.

Of course, the marine reptiles of yore and today's marine mammals are not the only monstrously big sea animals. The world's biggest – or at least the heaviest – bony fish is generally considered to be the beautiful ocean sunfish (so called because of its habit of sunbathing on the waves), a strange oval-shaped creature that can grow up to eleven feet in length and weigh as much as two tons. The enormous, anadromous beluga sturgeon,[620] whose roe is plundered by humans for caviar, can reach similar weights and even greater lengths – provided it does not fall victim to petrochemical or miscellaneous man-produced pollution or the implacable fishing industry. Among the biggest purely freshwater fish are the giant catfish of the Mekong and the arapaima of the Amazon, which can grow up to nine feet long and weigh over 200 kilos. The longest bony fish, the freakishly elongated oarfish, can reach as much as 35 feet in length, and its occasional beachings have proved an invitation to legends of sea serpents. The longest invertebrate is the stunning *Praya dubia* or giant siphonophore, a relative of the jellyfish that is known to reach lengths of

---

620. Like the salmon, it lives in saltwater but migrates upstream to fresh water in order to spawn. On caviar and the beluga sturgeon, see Kurlansky, *Salt: A World History*, 409-15.

150 feet.[621]

Most fearsome, however, in reputation at least, is the group of fish with a cartilaginous instead of a bony skeleton, in particular the elasmobranch subclass, which includes rays, dogfish, skates and sharks. Modern myth portrays the shark in general as a man-eating monster, yet in fact there are eight orders and hundreds of species ranging from the diminutive pygmy shark to the enormous whale shark, of which only a few present any sort of danger to humankind. Just a handful of unprovoked attacks occur in any one year, whereas conservative estimates are that 10,000 sharks are slaughtered (unprovoked) by humans across the globe each day. The whale shark is the largest shark and the biggest of all fish, believed to grow to up to 60 feet in length. Yet like the slightly smaller basking shark, it is a gentle giant, posing a threat only to the plankton it filters from the surrounding waters.

The world's biggest predatory fish – and the chief target of humankind's fear and loathing – is the great white shark, *Carcharodon carcharias*, which can reach 20 feet and is commonly viewed as a superbly efficient biting or killing machine, as living nature at its most destructively mechanistic.[622] Apparently not over-keen on human flesh, great whites prey on seals, sea lions and dolphins. Yet diver Tim Ecott, who is sympathetic to their plight, believes their lack of appeal is due not primarily to their voracity but rather their failure to show emotion:

621. With as many as 300 stomachs, the gelatinous siphonophore is modular in structure, comprising a colony of jellies living in a very long line. On the siphonophore, see Nouvian, 26, 84, 102, also 116: "Though they do not have powerful jaws, sharp teeth, or threatening fins, siphonophores are still veritable killing machines that number among the most voracious predators of the oceans."
622. This is exemplified by their "mindless" feeding frenzies. See the description by Paxman: "no one can have any doubts about the terrifying savagery of these beasts. Some reports even speak of bodies in armour or an entire horse being found inside sharks. In the grip of bloodlust a shark will snap at anything: fishermen who have tried to gaff one from a boat have discovered it so enraged by the smell of blood that it will tear at its own entrails" (*Fish, Fishing and the Meaning of Life*, 394). Even more fearsome was *Carcharodon megalodon*, which – at 60 feet – is estimated to have been three times as big as the great white, with teeth three times as long (whence *megalodon*, which means "big-toothed"). Thought to have been the biggest predatory fish ever, it has nonetheless been extinct for some 100,000 years, perhaps due to competition from the more intelligent cetaceans on which it preyed. See Ellis, *Sea Dragons: Predators of the Prehistoric Oceans*, 259-60.

"Much as we might wish to, we cannot establish a relationship with an individual shark. Its eyes do not allow us to make contact with whatever lies within, and we believe that their brains are too small to allow much in the way of reason. ... And so we envy them for their grace, despise them for their stupidity, and fear them for their power."[623] Fear and contempt, in conjunction with resentment towards what is more powerful, have thus conspired to produce a scapegoating of the species unparalleled in its mercilessness.

Clearly, it would be uncharitable to call a peaceful colossus such as the blue whale or the whale shark a monster and not the much smaller terrestrial species whose warped understanding of self and other (i.e. of mind and body, man and nature) has almost wiped them out, and may well yet do so. Size, it is evident, is not the only criterion for "monstrosity." Even from a human viewpoint, the question of *danger* – to the individual or the species – seems more relevant. The sperm whale represented a danger because it thoughtlessly and unhelpfully thrashed around in its agony when whalers were trying to butcher it; the great white shark constitutes a danger because it is responsible for four human fatalities a year (although what does that make hominoid car-drivers?). By the same token, conger eels – which have themselves been reported to reach more than ten feet in length – can get distinctly shirty when forced to share a boat with anglers;[624] barracuda are known to use their ferociously sharp teeth to rip sizeable chunks out of human beings; and many are the anglers who have lost bits of their body to the voracious pike, which also happens to be one of the many forms assumed by the shape-shifting evil water spirit or *vodyanoy* of Slavic mythology (whose hobbies include drowning human beings). Perhaps the most unthinkable example of piscine brutality is the much-feared *candiru* or toothpick fish of the River Amazon described by Jeremy Paxman:

> This little chap is attracted to the taste of uric acid and will cheerfully swim up the stream of urine from anyone peeing into the Amazon and thence into the urethra. Once there, it raises its gill-cover and sticks out a set of spines. It is then a race to get to hospital before your bladder explodes. Once there, having a surgeon wield a knife is blessed relief.[625]

623. Ecott, *Neutral Buoyancy*, 179.
624. See the amusing account of a losing battle with a conger eel – "about 20ft long with a head like a bull terrier at each end" – in Paxman, 119-20.
625. Paxman, 392.

A disconcerting immediacy is created by Paxman's shift to the second-person (*whose* bladder explodes?) in his account of the phenomenon. It sounds like the language of tall tales and myth-making.

Sharp teeth, nasty spikes and a predisposition to ply them on human flesh form important criteria in our notions of monstrosity, yet just as often the threat is a matter of sheer force or violence. Figures such as Poseidon or Aegir, the awe-inspiring sea-deity from Norse mythology, personify the brute power of the ocean. For the Greeks Poseidon was also the bringer of earthquakes, pounding the sea-floor with his trident when he got in a huff (which was not infrequently). One such huff gave rise to the *Odyssey*, in which Poseidon pursued "the heroic Odysseus with relentless malice"[626] for 20 years because the latter had killed his son, the ferocious one-eyed Polyphemus. Likewise armed with a spear, Aegir was equally irascible, whipping up tempests and shattering ships at the drop of a hat, though he also enjoyed a reputation for throwing the most thundering of parties for the gods. His consort, the sea goddess Ran, used a net to catch people who had died drowning, hauling them off to her realm of shades. Their daughters, the billow maidens, represented the different sorts of waves.

If Aegir and Poseidon thus symbolize the perils of the waters in a generalized form, lesser monsters may represent more specific challenges thrown up by the seas. Such were the sea monsters sent by Poseidon or his consort Amphitrite to torment those who had antagonized them.[627] Among the most frightening beasts Odysseus and his crew had to face in the course of their wanderings were Scylla and Charybdis, who inhabited the narrow straits between two cliffs. The daughter of Gaia (Mother Earth) and Poseidon, Charybdis took the form of a voracious mouth that sucked in and then belched forth huge quantities of water three times a day; Scylla, the daughter of Phorcys (one of the "Old Men of the Sea") and hideous Ceto, was a dog-like monster with twelve feet and six serpentine necks each ending in a grisly head, who would snatch passing mariners, crack their bones and slowly swallow them. In his efforts to avoid Charybdis, Odysseus sailed too close to Scylla, who plucked six of his companions

---

626. Homer, 21.
627. Storm-tossed and shipwrecked, Odysseus reasons: "some monster might be inspired to attack me from the depths. Amphitrite has a name for mothering plenty of such creatures in her seas; and I am well aware how the great Earthshaker [Poseidon] detests me" (*The Odyssey*, 99). In other contexts such monsters included the havoc-wreaking beasts slain by Perseus and Heracles.

from their boat to be devoured at her leisure.[628] Beasts such as these were poetic embodiments of the constant threat of death hanging over sailors as they ventured onto uncharted waters, creative projections of mariners' fears in the face of all-consuming whirlpools, sinuous squid and treacherous rocks and currents.

One of the most unnerving features of dog-like Scylla is that her bark is "no louder than a new-born pup's."[629] Death may indeed be much less noisy than the figure of tumultuous Poseidon might suggest: the waves may rage and roar, but there is something silent and ghostly about a death by drowning, a presence followed by mute absence. Many of the most frightening representations of watery death are whispering spirits rather than booming monsters. For sailors from the 18th century onwards, Davy Jones's Locker became a euphemism for a watery grave, and Davy Jones a nickname for the devil of the oceans. In Tobias Smollett's *The Adventures of Peregrine Pickle* (1751), Davy Jones is referred to as "the fiend that presides over all the evil spirits of the deep, and is often seen in various shapes, perching among the rigging, on the eve of hurricanes, ship-wrecks, and other disasters to which sea-faring life is exposed, warning the devoted wretch of death and woe."[630] Another ghostly apparition from European maritime lore was the Flying Dutchman, the phantom ship doomed to sail forever, the sight of which was believed to presage imminent misfortune. The sight of a mermaid during a ship voyage could also be an omen of shipwreck. Though generally benign, mermaids could bring floods or other watery tribulations if displeased.

Fresh water too has its silent or unearthly monsters, figures such as Creeping Jenny or Jenny Green-teeth of English nursery folklore, who haunts ponds or wells in the guise of a duckweed lawn, sucking children under if they venture too close, then closing quietly over them again as though nothing had happened. In Mesoamerican lore, the disquieting figure of the wailing woman, *la Llorona*, lures those who hear her to a watery end in river, lake or well. The bunyip of Australian swamps and billabongs, the cucumber-loving kappa of Japanese ponds and rivers, the malevolent *vodyanoy* of Slavic waters, all thrive on human prey, in particular women and unsuspecting children. In John von Düffel's novel *Vom Wasser* (*On Water*, 2000), the slime-covered river spirit known as the

---

628. Homer, 194-201; see also Graves, II.361-62.
629. Homer, 196; see also Graves, II.362.
630. Smollett, *The Adventures of Peregrine Pickle*, 61.

Harkemann surreptitiously rakes the narrator's great-great-grandfather into the murky depths when he stops to pass water (into the river) on his way home after a night-time tipple.[631] Fanciful projections of our fear of engulfment, these hidden monsters represent death as an *ambush*, and warn the anxious landlubber to steer clear.

* * * * *

Like water itself, such death is thought to constitute a silent, unknown realm[632]; indeed, the notion of *unknowability* is a recurrent feature of aquatic monstrosity. An intrinsically vague term, the attribute "unknowable" has already been seen to apply to Moby Dick both in his sheer physical immeasurability and in his inscrutability. These days, of course, most marine mammals are as subject to physical measurement and empirical observation, to anatomical analysis and taxonomic classification, as any other creature. Quite apart from their generally benign disposition, therefore, they can in this respect no longer be said to be monsters (we are too familiar with them), and for the most part at least, cetaceans are no true descendants of Ceto. Nonetheless, other facets of unknowability remain fundamental in considering the nature of "monstrosity" in fiction, reality and the fuzzy area in between.

Even today, certain cetaceans are notoriously shy and elusive. The less a sea animal needs to surface for air, the more difficult it is to make its acquaintance. The ziphiids or beaked whales, some species of which

631. See von Düffel, *Vom Wasser*, 22, 25, 35, on the *Harkemann*. This was in fact the river spirit's revenge on the founding father of the family concern, who had sought to tame and subdue him with a paper factory that turned "the water into paper and the paper into money" (20). Many thanks go to Bertram Gerber for alerting me to this.

632. Jacques Cousteau famously called the underwater realm "the silent world" in his book by the same title. In fact, as Tim Ecott points out (*Neutral Buoyancy*, 104), the aquatic world is not entirely silent. As well as the sound of one's own breathing, "coral reefs crackle, like ageing bones. Many fish and crustaceans make pops and grunts, slight sounds, muffled to the human ear, but they add to the noise none the less. The silence that divers seek is more internal."

can reach 40 feet in length and a weight of 15 tons, are still virtually unknown to human investigation, for they rarely enter shallow waters and are able to dive to prodigious depths for extended periods of time. Half of their species are known from a single specimen, and there are many species yet to be identified.[633] The transparent or gelatinous nature of many other forms of deep-sea life further compounds this evasiveness.[634] An evolutionary strategy of trying to pass unnoticed has resulted in the almost complete transparency of the bathyscaphoid squid (named after the pioneering submersible), the googly-eyed glass squid and the glass octopus.[635] The same goes for the fantastic bioluminescent camouflage of the bent-tooth bristlemouth, *Cyclothone acclinidens*, which uses belly lights called photophores for counter-illumination to match the colour and intensity of the background sunlight from the surface: thought to be the most abundant vertebrate on the planet, few people have ever seen or heard of it.[636] Almost as secretive are the legendary giant squid or *Architeuthis* and the even bigger – but lesser known – colossal squid, the world's largest invertebrates, which grow to up to 50 feet in length yet have never been scientifically observed in their native habitat. The tireless attempts of zoologists to see one alive have so far always ended in frustration,[637] and encounters with them have been restricted to dead ones washed up on beaches or their indigestible remains found inside sperm whales.

Equipped with complex brains, vicious beaks, possibly the biggest eyes in the animal kingdom (a foot in diameter), and tentacles with suckers (in giant squid) and rotating hooks (in colossal squid), they make seemingly ferocious predators, and the scarred skin of the sperm whales that prey on them bears testimony to many a titanic struggle. Moreover, their elusiveness seems to function as an invitation to imaginative speculation, spawning such monsters as the enormous tentacled kraken of Norwegian legend or the sea monks and Polish bishops cited in 16th-century natural history books. In fact, it is now known that the giant squid

633. See Coleman and Huyghe, 12-13, 124-27. By the same token, over half of the known species of sharks are slow-living deep-sea creatures that as a result remain "highly enigmatic" (Nouvian, 190-91).
634. Jellies in particular are not only hard to see but especially difficult to gather intact for research purposes. The use of nets, for example, reduces them to a mush.
635. See Nouvian, 34, 54-55, 62.
636. Ibid., 86.
637. Kunzig, 2.

feeds on small animals, is benign and generally shuns contact.[638] Yet such is the temptation to exaggerate and demonize that the narrator of *Twenty Thousand Leagues under the Sea* – ever keen to maintain his posture of detached scientific rationality – cannot resist spotlighting the creature's mythological antecedents before launching into his own description:

> When it is a question of monsters, there is no limit to the flight of the imagination. Not only has it been alleged that these squids could drag ships down beneath the waves, but a certain Olaüs Magnus mentions a cephalopod one mile long that looked more like an island than an animal. Another tale relates that the Bishop of Nidros one day set up an altar on a large rock; once the Mass was over, the rock began to move and returned to the sea. That rock was a giant squid. … Another bishop, Pontoppidan of Berghem, also speaks of a squid on which it was possible to maneuver a regiment of cavalry![639]

Placing his own account in the context of tall tales and maritime folklore is a double-edged sword: on the one hand, it validates the veracity of the report to come (implying that the narrator is aware of the tendency to embroider, but is himself above such fabrication); on the other hand, it may foster a more generalized sceptical or ironical distance towards the subject as a whole, which thus ends up hovering between science and speculation, fact and fiction. In Verne's novel, the ambivalence is compounded by the strange mixture of scientific sobriety and rhetorical extravagance in the description of the beast and their struggle with it:

> Before my eyes there wriggled a terrible monster, worthy to figure among all the legends of these creatures. It was a squid of colossal dimensions, about twenty-five feet long. … Its eight arms, or rather, its eight tentacles … were twice as long as its body, and swirled about like the hair of the Furies. … We hurled ourselves pell-mell into that mass of truncated tentacles that squirmed like serpents all over the platform, in the midst of a deluge of blood and black ink. Like Hydra's head, those slimy arms seemed to grow back almost instantly.[640]

A similar compound of scientific objectivity and imaginative licence is characteristic of the discipline known as cryptozoology,

---

638. On the giant squid and the colossal squid, see Nouvian, 120-25.
639. Verne, *Twenty Thousand Leagues under the Sea*, 344-45.
640. Ibid., 346, 349.

the study of "hidden animals," of animals "unrecognized by Western science,"[641] otherwise known as cryptids. In these terms, a monster is what is *cryptic* or hidden, both literally (by water) and figuratively (by a shroud of ignorance). It emerges from its epistemological hiding only to scare or surprise us, instead of obligingly offering itself for scientific observation or taxonomic categorization. Though frequently derided by mainstream science, the discipline has a bright medium-term future. Efforts to quantify human ignorance suggest that between one and ten million deep-sea species remain to be discovered[642]; these are currently being found at a rate of just above a hundred species a year. Admittedly, only a few of these will be "big" (longer than six feet): in 1758 Linnaeus identified 23 marine species longer than six feet, whereas by 1995 the figure had risen to 217. Statistical extrapolations from the past rate of discovery – which each year is slowing – have led the aquatic ecologist Charles Paxton to the conclusion that some 47 species still await discovery, most likely cetaceans or sharks.[643]

Understood thus, monstrosity is what has not *yet* been discovered or officially classified as a species: it is what has so far eluded categorization or what precedes conceptual schematization. The implication is that this can be remedied and that the beasts are not *intrinsically* unclassifiable (in the way the medieval devil was). Cryptozoologists point to recent successes such as the megamouth shark and the giant squid to illustrate a natural progression from a cryptozoological unknown – a sea monster – to a known zoological species.[644] But does the same fate await Nessie, the fabled Lock Ness Monster said to inhabit the most voluminous freshwater body in Scotland?

The legend is a venerable one, possibly dating back 1,500 years to the encounter of the great Irish monk St Colomba with a "dragon" in the nearby River Ness. Ancient highland tradition tells of the *Each-Usige* or water-kelpie, a "merhorse" or water-horse which had an equine head and flowing mane and would entice its victims to ride on its back before

641. Coleman and Huyghe, 271, 5.
642. Kunzig, 124.
643. See Coleman and Huyghe, 3-5. The title of Paxton's paper was "A Cumulative Species Description Curve for Large Open Water Marine Animals," published in the *Journal of the Marine Biological Association of the United Kingdom*, 1998, 78, pp. 1389-91. Three years later, Paxton revised his estimate of big species still to be discovered upwards to 51.
644. Coleman and Huyghe, 5-15.

plunging into the depths to drown them.[645] Just 70 miles to the south-west of Loch Ness, Loch Morar – the deepest lake in Britain, descending over a thousand feet – is said to harbour another popular Gaelic merhorse, Morag,[646] while the Welsh tarns are the traditional home of the *afanc*, though myth has it that this monster was banished by Hu Gadarn, Hu the Mighty, inventor of the plough and leader of the ancient Welsh.

Since Nessie entered popular culture in the 1930s, moreover, there has been a proliferation of Nessies around the world. Quite apart from traditional lake monsters such as the Ogopogo from British Columbia, Slimy Slim from Idaho, the ancient Icelandic Skrimsl or the Lindorm of Scandinavia, recent decades have spawned a whole fleet of cousins such as Tessie from Lake Tahoe in Nevada, Mussie from Muskrat Lake, Ontario, Chessie from Chesapeake Bay, off Virginia, as well as Japan's Issie and Kussie, Wales's Teggie and Norway's Mjossie.[647] In an age of hard-boiled empiricism, the lake monster has entered the realm of humour and light-hearted fabrication. Even before Nessie hit the big time, sightings of sea serpents were a pretext for hoaxing and leg-pulling.[648]

To the rational mind, there is a whole host of explanations for such beasts (in addition to the hoax factor). Sightings have been attributed to the *misidentification* of inanimate phenomena such as seaweed, driftwood, waves or tricks of the light. Animate candidates for misidentification have included animal communities such as the long, snake-like colonies of tiny salps (a type of tunicate), as well as crocodiles, porpoises, manatees, long-necked pinnipeds, sturgeon, oarfish, sunfish or eels, possibly mating or swimming in line (to account for the volume or – where necessary – the humps).[649] By the same token, sirenians such as the dugong have on occasion been invoked to account for sightings of mermaids.

However, more speculative accounts have ventured to suggest that such cryptids might be relics of a distant past. From the 1850s through to the

645. On the water-horse see ibid., 72-123. The water-horse or "merhorse" is one of the two traditional fundamental categories of water monster, the sea serpent being the other.
646. Ibid., 109-110.
647. Ibid., 22-25, 251-67.
648. In the mid-19th century, sightings of the "Silver Lake Sea Serpent" in the resort town of Perry, New York, turned the place into a veritable Mecca for curious tourists. The enthusiasm lasted even after the discovery of a 60-foot artificial sea serpent in the ashes of a burned-down hotel in 1857. Nowadays, the town celebrates the hoax in an annual Sea Serpent Festival. See ibid., 22, 296.
649. Ibid., 26-31.

1970s, one of the most popular candidates for Nessie was the implausibly long-necked sea beast known as the plesiosaur, famously described as looking like a snake threaded through the body of a turtle.[650] The fact that plesiosaurs were Mesozoic marine reptiles that evolved during the Triassic, flourished in the Jurassic, and became extinct some 65 million years ago has only added to their mystique. The idea of a lost animal that somehow neglected to die out with all his friends and colleagues reinforces our notion that deep waters are in a sense "timeless" or "forgotten by time"[651] – indeed, that they offer a route to our own evolutionary past, to the oceanic womb, the amniotic origin from which we came.

In today's cryptozoology, the emphasis is less on the plesiosaur than on a creature known as zeuglodon, a serpentine cetacean dating from the Eocene between 40 and 37 million years ago.[652] Bear-size beavers, giant chelonians (turtles) and enormous sea-centipedes – relict populations from an era when animals were bigger – are likewise cited as possible candidates. In the same spirit is the proposal that *Mokele-mbembe*, the strange Nessie-like beast said to dwell in the swamps of the Congo basin, is some species of sauropod dinosaur. Clearly, the implication is that the supposedly "unmapped" Congo rainforest is as "timeless" as the seas. Error and imposture aside, the ageless waters of the deep past seem to provide a sort of sanctuary or refuge where cryptic creatures that remain unknown or unknowable in the present can be nurtured and imaginatively fleshed out.

650. See Ellis, 119. One of the weirder species of plesiosaur, *Elasmosaurus*, is known to have reached a length of 47 feet, at least half of which was neck, with a rather small head on the end.
651. This explains the excitement produced by the discovery in 1938 of a recently dead coelacanth off South Africa (and others since). An ancient lobe-finned fish dating back to the Devonian (410 to 355 million years ago), coelacanth was for a long time believed to have died out with the dinosaurs. The revelation that it was still going strong turned it into a sort of "living fossil" and raised the question of whether the deep sea might be home to other such denizens of deep time. Of course, sharks too – which also go back to the Devonian – are just as much living fossils. The venerable sturgeon is another such prehistoric creature, thought not to have evolved for the last 180 million years. If anatomically modern human beings are taken to have been around for roughly 100,000 years, one human second corresponds to half a sturgeon hour.
652. Measuring some 50 feet in length, *Zeuglodon* was originally misidentified as a plesiosaur and given the name *Basilosaurus*, "king of the lizards." In fact, it was not a reptile but a mammal. However, the original name – though misleading – cannot now be changed. See Ellis, 124.

Marine reptiles such as the plesiosaur came to prominence prior to the land-dwelling dinosaurs and fired the Victorian imagination much as the terrestrial reptiles do today. They were the first prehistoric fossils to be discovered,[653] and their remains were more complete and therefore more striking than those of their rather fragmentary dinosaur contemporaries. In 1839 the geologist Henry De la Beche published a "realistic" illustration of a prehistoric marine scene featuring ichthyosaurs, plesiosaurs, sharks, squid, ammonites and pterodactyls, while in 1840 Thomas Hawkins's *Book of Great Sea-Dragons* drew further public attention to these long-extinct "monsters." In Jules Verne's highly popular *Journey to the Centre of the Earth* (1864), his heroes come across a vast underground sea where they witness a combat of "indescribable fury" between two terrifying marine monsters, each of which is initially mistaken for a whole herd of diverse sea beasts, cetaceans, lizards and crocodiles. The first has "the snout of a porpoise, the head of a lizard and the teeth of a crocodile" and is the "most formidable of the antediluvian reptiles, the ichthyosaurus." Its opponent is "a serpent with a turtle's shell, the mortal enemy of the first – the plesiosaurus." Verne's depiction of their battle again hovers between scientific realism and a surreal extravagance more usually associated with the realm of dreams or exceedingly tall tales.[654]

* * * * *

The term "ichthyosaurus ego" coined by the poet John Cowper Powys[655] captures the idea of a regression to primordial origins, of archaic memories from a collective deep past or unconscious. In this respect, our ambivalent fascination with monsters may be an expression of an ambiguous relationship to the "monsters" from which we have ourselves evolved; the ancient reptiles are long-suppressed memories surging up from the planetary unconscious. Yet the titanic struggle depicted by Verne also brings to light a further criterion essential to the "unknowability" of what

653. The ball was set rolling in 1812 by the remarkable fossil collector Mary Anning of Lyme Regis, who found the fossilized remains of a 17-foot ichthyo-saur embedded in the cliffs of Dorset and subsequently discovered the first plesiosaurs and an early pterosaur.
654. Verne, *Journey to the Centre of the Earth*, 186-87.
655. See Sprawson, 170-72.

is monstrous: the failure of the creatures to fit into existing categories. As a result, the descriptions of Mesozoic sea beasts by marine palaeontologists have often amounted to highly imaginative exercises in anatomical bricolage, presenting us with a hotchpotch of strangely fitting parts. In 1837, the fossilist Gideon Mantell described the plesiosaur as combining "the head of a lizard with teeth like those of a crocodile, a neck resembling the body of a serpent, a trunk and tail resembling the proportions of a quadruped, with paddles like those of turtles."[656] Of the frankly horrific 40-foot pliosaur *Kronosaurus*, which had a skull twice the length of *T. Rex*'s and terrorized the waters of the early Cretaceous, it has been said that rather than looking like "a killer whale with big flippers … [it] was more of a sea lion with the skull of a croc."[657]

There is a venerable tradition of such "mix-n-match" monsters. The sea-god Triton, son of Poseidon and Amphitrite, had the upper parts of a man in conjunction with the tail of a fish (as well as a conch-shell trumpet he blew to raise the waves). The hippocampus had the forelegs of a horse and the tail of a fish, while the ichthyocentaur combined a fish-tail with the forepart of a horse and a human body. In the course of his seven voyages, Sindbad came across not only gigantic serpents and whales as massive as mountains, but one sea monster with the head of an owl, another with a head like a donkey's, and yet another which looked like a cow. The traditional Australian bunyip has been said to combine a horse's head with the body of a giant pinniped,[658] incorporating flippers and the tusks of a walrus.

Eluding conventional attempts at classification, such grotesqueries have at times had diabolical connotations suggesting dissolution and transgression. In late-medieval and Reformation visual art, the Devil was frequently made up of grotesque juxtapositions of incongruous animal parts, a "non-thing" suspended somewhere between form and disconcerting formlessness. Yet even without roping in the Devil, Jules Verne's depiction of the giant squid (in *Twenty Thousand Leagues*) insinuates that nature itself can be distinctly freakish: "The mouth of that monster – a horny beak, shaped like that of a parrot – opened and closed with a vertical motion. Its tongue, also horny in texture and armed with several rows of sharp teeth, vibrated in and out between the blades of those

656. Quoted in Ellis, 119.
657. Quoted in ibid., 177.
658. Coleman and Huyghe, 265-67.

shears. What a fantastic creature of nature! A bird's beak in a mollusk!"[659] That its truncated tentacles seemed to grow back "like Hydra's head,"[660] moreover, recalls the protean shapelessness of another legendary sea-monster. The Hydra slain by Heracles as the second of his twelve labours was a venomous many-headed water serpent, whose heads – when cut off – would come back twofold.[661]

When the element of threat is reduced, however, grotesque play with animal forms and anatomical categories may equally well have a comic or surreal effect. The same principle underlay 19th-century pantomime beasts such as the "Nondescript," which was composed of a motley jumble of diverse animals' bodily parts, or the "Cameleopard," part camel, part leopard, with a hint of the chameleon thrown in to boot. It comes to light, for example, in the weird creatures now believed to have inhabited the ancient seas of the Cambrian period, some 500 million years ago, the (relatively) early days of multicellular life prior to the colonization of land by animals or plants. As evidenced by the fossils of the Burgess Shale, the Cambrian displayed what Stephen Jay Gould controversially described as a "range of disparity in anatomical design never again equaled, and not matched today by all the creatures in all the world's oceans."[662] Evolution itself seemed to have gone into pantomime. One creature inhabiting the Cambrian seas was *Anomalocaris*, described as "a metre-long predator that looked like a stream-lined lobster with a circular mouth like a kitchen-garbage-disposal unit." *Opabinia* had "five stalked eyes, a prawn-like body and a long, hosepipe-like snout tipped with a pair of barbed jaws – less like a real animal than a design for a vacuum cleaner by Salvador Dali."[663]

---

659. Verne, *Twenty Thousand Leagues under the Sea*, 346.
660. Ibid., 349.
661. Hydra was one of the offspring of Typhon and Echidne, another of the many children of Phorcys and Ceto. According to a euhemeristic interpretation of the episode, the figure of Hydra had its origins in a system of underground rivers that used to rise and flood the land: if one of the channels were closed off, the water would simply surge up elsewhere (see Graves, II.107-10). In this respect, the Hydra clearly reflects the protean nature of water itself.
662. See Gould, *Wonderful Life: The Burgess Shale and the Nature of History*, 208.
663. Gee, 77. In fact, whereas Gould believed that many of the Burgess Shale creatures did not belong to any recognized phylum, recent research has now assigned a good number of the specimens to extant phyla. Both *Opabinia* and *Anomalocaris* are now thought to belong to a group of very primitive arthropods, a phylum that includes insects, spiders, crustaceans and the now-extinct trilobites.

Also present was little *Pikaia gracilens*, initially assigned to the worms, but now recognized – on the basis of its primitive spinal column – as a chordate, a member of our own phylum and precursor of all vertebrates.

Even today, the so-called "hadal" fauna inhabiting the deep sea is known to exhibit an extraordinary diversity of species. The abyssal depths have been described as the kingdom of holothurians, or sea-cucumbers.[664] Slow-moving cylinders that can range from an inch to six feet in size, holothurians belong to the phylum of echinoderms, which also include starfish, brittle stars and sea urchins. They are characterized by a complex water vascular system – a hydraulic network of reservoirs and channels that conduct water to the animal's tube feet whenever there is seabed crawling to be done – and pentaradial or five-rayed symmetry of the sort shown by starfish. Some species bury themselves mouth-first in the mud, with just their anus – through which they breathe – protruding into the water. When startled they are capable of ejecting their own innards, in effect turning themselves inside out.[665] Even weirder, perhaps, are the tube worms recently found to exist around volcanic hydrothermal vents, which grow to lengths of nine or ten feet but dispense with a mouth, anus or digestive tract, depending instead on a symbiosis with chemosynthetic[666] bacteria living inside them. Indeed, whole ecosystems have been found to be powered not by light (and photosynthesis), but by chemicals that would prove utterly noxious to most terrestrial creatures. Not only can life develop, but it positively flourishes in conditions that – from a terrestrial perspective – are alien and inhospitable.

The holothurian stance of burying one's head in the mud and mooning at passers-by may seem a thoroughly human one; even dispensing entirely with mouth, anus and gut could on occasion be viewed as commendable from a human perspective; but few would deny that the deep-sea fishes – with their oversize jaws and huge heads capable of swallowing prey that in some cases exceed them in size – are hideously ugly. The monstrous features of anglers, viperfish, rat-tails, gulper eels and the ominously named black swallower, *Chiasmodon niger*, may be extraordinarily effective adaptations to

664. While invertebrates such as holothurians, polychaete worms and corals dominate in terms of numbers, small scavenging crustaceans such as amphipods also vie for scraps with fish such as hagfish and rat-tails.
665. Kunzig, 103-4.
666. Whereas in photosynthesis carbohydrates are synthesized using the energy from sunlight, in chemosynthesis the energy comes from the hydrogen sulphide abundantly present around such hot vents.

the constraints of the deep-sea environment, but they tend not to appeal to the fastidious human sensibility.[667] Or how about the Picasso-esque weirdness of the flatfish – an order of fish that includes sole, turbot, plaice, halibut and brill – which exhibit "the Quasimodo grotesqueness of having a mouth well to the left of your left eye"?[668]

Obviously, we are misapplying human aesthetic categories in a non-human context where they have no business. Oversize mouths, ferocious teeth, warty complexions and an abundance of slimy mucus may well be the last word in deep-sea aesthetics, and Quasimodo a role model for adolescent turbot anxious about being too symmetrical. The same applies to the human aversion to octopuses and squid with their writhing tentacles and groping fleshiness, which has its roots in a deeper fear of all-engulfing formlessness, just as the gelatinous fragility of the weird ctenophore is disconcerting for a species that sets such store by keeping its shape and maintaining the boundary between self and other, me and everything else. Yet as Broad writes, "the deep is the Earth's largest habitat. And its residents are undoubtedly the most typical forms of life on the planet, despite what seem to be their odd looks and unfamiliar ways, despite their often being denigrated as devils and demons, as freaks and monstrosities of nature."[669]

There is presumably not much we can do about our aesthetic sensibility and the criteria by which we judge "monstrosity" defined in terms of ugliness. It is perhaps natural to assume a species-centric perspective and to feel in some sense "closer" to the species with which we are most familiar, starting of course with the human and extending to those species with which we have most "in common" or in which we recognize most "human" traits. Given what is now known of our genealogy or evolutionary history, this would suggest

667. The rat-tail, for example, is described by Broad as being "like some kind of mythological beast made of dissimilar parts" with "a bulbous head and huge eyes, while the rear part of its body narrows down to become curiously thin" (*The Universe Below*, 287). Terminological cosmetics is required to induce humans to serve such deep-sea cuties for consumption, the rat-tail being more commonly referred to as a grenadier for marketing purposes, just as the unappetizing slimehead magically becomes orange roughy when it is time to eat it.
668. See John Murray's comic novel, *John Dory*, 57. The turbot and the brill, moreover, are protean in their capacity for camouflage. As the aquarium-gazing narrator himself finds out, "the turbot, like the brill, has no fixed morphology, no stable identity in the visual sense. It changes its spots to suit its background, to confuse ocean predators as well as oddballs like me…" (ibid., 101).
669. Broad, 46.

that human beings might tend to form a closer emotional bond with cetaceans, sirenians and pinnipeds (as mammals) than with bony fish or sharks, and with bony fish and sharks (as vertebrates) than with invertebrates such as cnidarians (including jellyfish), marine polychaetes (worms), crustaceans, molluscs (including squid) or echinoderms. Yet such a hierarchy should not be taken to imply either "improvement" or increased complexity or intelligence. Squids are known to be exceedingly intelligent, exhibiting great mobility and highly complex behaviour.[670] Indeed, for most of history there was no clear distinction between whales, fish and other sea creatures anyway. Right through to the modern period, a lack of empirical observation kept Cetus firmly ensconced in the realm of misinformation and grotesque fancy.

Rather than "intelligence," the main issue today is emotional contact and the possibility of communication, which brings us back to the fascinating and frustrating matter of unknowability. The expressionlessness of fish is well documented. Jeremy Paxman has written:

> there is something utterly enthralling about these cold-blooded creatures. It may have something to do with the fact that they cannot survive in our element nor we in theirs. It certainly has something to do with the lustre of their squamous beauty. Most of all, it has to do with the fact that, for all their dull-witted remoteness, they remain unknowable.[671]

Paxman also cites D. H. Lawrence's poem "Fish": "They are beyond me are fishes," admits the poet. "I am not the measure of creation. / This is beyond me, this fish. / His God stands outside my God."[672] Of the shark, diver Tim Ecott writes that "we cannot establish a relationship with an individual shark. Its eyes do not allow us to make contact with whatever lies within."[673] But what is it that lies within? And how much can the eyes tell us? As a window to the soul, the shark's "small impenetrable specks" doubtless compare unfavourably with the gargantuan optical apparatus of a blue whale, but what about the huge orbs

670. It is at least possible that human beings have more "in common" with certain species of squid or octopus than with a tunicate such as a sea squirt, though the tunicate is classified as a chordate and thus belongs to the same phylum as vertebrates such as *Homo sapiens*.
671. Paxman, 77.
672. Lawrence, "Fish," in *Complete Poems*, 268-74; 272, 273, italics deleted. The narrator in John Murray's novel *John Dory* refers to the "magnificently ugly, indescribably inscrutable and charismatic species known as John Dory" (102).
673. Ecott, 179.

of the goggled-eyed ichthyosaur *Ophthalmosaurus* or a hungry giant squid?[674] Do or did these creatures lead a rich inner life? Like the type-writing monkey, is the ink-squirting cephalopod hoping one day to give expression to a literary masterpiece? Surely gigantic eyes are just as susceptible to misinterpretation as a tearful crocodile's.

For would-be aquatic Dr Dolittles, the gaze of a rat-tail or anglerfish may be stony or vacant, but the question is how we could even start to distinguish the vacuous gaze (if such it is) of a fish from the incommunicable wisdom (if such it is) of a whale or dolphin. The narrator of *Moby Dick*, as we have seen, recognized that the inscrutability of the sperm whale was partly a consequence of *his own* limitations, and here – once again – he hit the nail on the head. Yet in a fundamental and possibly banal sense, this applies to the possibility of knowing what is going on not only inside other intelligent mammals, but in our own species as well. A question such as "how can I know what it feels like to be you?" ultimately points up my own limitations as a non-infinite being stuck within my own subjectivity, unable to transcend my own mind. In this respect, "you" – like everyone else – are unknowable to "me," tautologically so, simply by virtue of not being me: for the chronic mind-body dualist, "you" are something radically alien or monstrous to "me."[675]

Yet in saying that we understand or can communicate with another living creature, whether human or non-human, we are not in practice claiming some form of privileged, pure, private access to that subject's thoughts and feelings, but using essentially public, external criteria to classify its behaviour and put it into a more general context of pattern and predictability. In distinguishing a friendly approach from a threatening one, we are using what we have learned from the past behaviour of that individual or species to predict – as far as possible – what it will do in the immediate future. This goes for both human and non-human animals. Seen

---

674. See Ellis, 109-10. The eyes of the 15-foot-long *Ophthalmosaurus* were eight inches in diameter, roughly the same size as those of the 100-foot-long blue whale, and slightly smaller than those of the giant squid. In fact, of course, eyes as big as this say less about the animals' inner life than about their need to detect prey at depths where there is little light.

675. In his *Meditations*, Descartes writes: "if I chance to look out of the window upon the passers-by in the street below, I have no hesitation in saying that I see men, although their hats and cloaks may be no more than a disguise for clock-work figures" (*Discourse on Method, and other writings*, 115). The fact that other people have a *body* offers no guarantee that they have a *mind* as well.

in such a light, the unknowability formerly attributed to whales was not so much a matter of intrinsic inscrutability as a lack of experience of their habits. And this can be remedied. As Mary Midgley shows, "whether, and how far, interspecies communication works for feelings and motives is an empirical question. On the whole, it does. *That* it does is not surprising given our evolutionary relationship, and the fact that it could often be quite dangerous to misconstrue the behaviour of creatures outside one's species, and quite convenient to read it. Threats had to be understood, and useful warnings developed."[676]

Knowing what it is like to be a seal, dugong, whale or dolphin thus requires contact, observation and analysis. The human faculty of language – the ability to subsume individual instances within more general concepts – is an important tool, allowing us not only to associate (for example) anger, well-being or playfulness with a specific range of behaviours but to formalize such associations. Equally important is empathy, the ability to put ourselves in their place and *imagine* (counterfactually) what it would be like to be a particular creature. This is not to deny the element of mystery and the limitations of understanding. Midgley poses the question what it would be like to be an incubating gull or an emperor penguin[677]: "They

676. Midgley, *Beast*, 350.
677. In a paper first published in *The Philosophical Review*, the philosopher Thomas Nagel famously asks the question "What is it like to be a bat?" Nagel expressly chose an animal not "too far down the phylogenetic tree" but with sensory apparatus different enough from the human (i.e. echolocation) to make his thought experiment vivid. A sperm whale would have been an interesting alternative. It will not do, Nagel might have said, to imagine myself wrapped up in tons of blubber, perceiving the surrounding world by a system of reflected sound signals, diving down two kilometres and having a strenuous workout with a gigantic squid: "Insofar as I can imagine this (which is not very far), it tells me only what it would be like for *me* to behave as a [sperm whale] behaves. But that is not the question. I want to know what it is like for a [*sperm whale*] to be a [sperm whale]. Yet if I try to imagine this, I am restricted to the resources of my own mind, and those resources are inadequate to the task" (Nagel, "What Is It Like to Be a Bat?," 394). Nagel claims he is not concerned with the "alleged privacy of experience to its possessor" (ibid., 396), yet in fact the questions are deeply related: even when it comes to other human beings, indeed the closest of friends, I can only ever imagine what it is like for me to be you, not for you to be you. I can never clamber all the way inside your mind (and it's probably a good job too). "The distance between oneself and other persons and other species can fall anywhere on a continuum," Nagel admits. "Even for other

spend the Antarctic night standing without food on ice at almost lethal temperatures, nursing an egg. Of course this baffles our imagination. But not in the way that we are baffled when we try to imagine what it is like to be a star or a sewing-machine. It is simply a much further-out version of the kind of bafflement we encounter if we try to think what it is like to be Mozart or a newborn baby. The imagination is *meant* for that kind of job."[678] Given the lack of a shared language (a barrier that also exists with respect to humans from other cultures), it is clear that care, respect and empathy – i.e. an awareness of our limitations and a will to overcome them – are indispensable in our dealings with the monsters of the deep. As our experience of them grows, and as we learn how to encounter them without massacring them, they can only become "less" unknowable.

* * * * *

It is partly thanks to our species-centric viewpoint and the criterion of unknowability that humankind has generally tended *not* to see itself as a monster. Humans are too familiar with the sight of other humans. Yet if this essay were being written by a shark, a whale or a one-in-a-billion squid capable of squirting out English sentences, it can well be imagined that the perspective would be reversed. "Monster" would be a term applied to the bipedal primates who prowl the seas on huge factory ships and have decimated fish populations, butchered many species of whale to

---

persons the understanding of what it is like to be them is only partial, and when one moves to a species very different from oneself, a lesser degree of partial understanding may still be available" (ibid., 397). For the radical sceptic or the radical dualist, by contrast, it is all or nothing: if I cannot know you completely, I cannot *really* know you at all (not the way I know myself). It is in this sense that you – like every other human or non-human creature – are "unknowable" to me. In practice, it is language and the imagination (similes and counterfactuals, including that most fundamental of counterfactuals, "if I were you") that enable us to bridge the epistemological gap. It is the constraints of continued functional existence that make it necessary to do so.
678. Midgley, *Beast*, 351n.

near extinction,[679] killed tens of millions of shark each year, exterminated millions upon millions of seals, walruses and sea-otters, and wiped out, among other species, the flightless sea-bird the great auk and Steller's sea cow, a gentle sirenian incapable of saying boo to a goose.[680] Perhaps the ships themselves would be the monsters, the floating factories with their vicious exploding harpoons, reaching an average weight of 19,000 tons (in the 1960s) and effortlessly out-cetoing Ceto in their powers of industrialized murder. Perhaps it would be the gargantuan drift nets – each big enough to catch several jumbo jets – which enmesh and drown turtles, marine mammals and millions of tons of unwanted fish each year, or the trawl nets employed in benthic trawling, which casually annihilate entire seabed habitats. Perhaps the individual primates might be the monsters, the duck farmers whose factory-farmed animals lead short, brutish lives of abject squalor, never experiencing their natural aquatic existence[681]; the fishermen who slice the fins off sharks, then dump them back in the water to die; or multi-millionaire entrepreneurs like the shipping magnate Aristotle Onassis, who blatantly flouted international whaling regulations (once these were introduced) and ostentatiously used the skin of sperm whale penises to cover the bar stools on his yacht and whale teeth as footrests.[682]

Perhaps in cetacean or sirenian lore, the monster would assume the guise of the human species as a whole, whose use of the ocean as a universal dust-bin has already produced over 200 "dead zones" (fishless regions of oxygen-depleted water) including an area almost the size of Wales in the Gulf of Mexico; a species that is bringing the marine environment to its knees with its highly toxic organic pollutants (such as pesticides), its industrial waste, its untreated sewage, the non-degradable plastics that kill more than a million seabirds and 100,000 marine mammals per year, its oil spillages, as well as the military dumping and electronic and radioactive

679. It is believed that 1,500,000 great whales were exterminated in 200 years of human history. See also Ponting, 162-68. According to Lucien Laubier, the biomass of these creatures would be equivalent to 1.5 billion human beings (see Nouvian, 246).
680. On the slaughter of seals and walruses, see Ponting, 159-62; in the early years of the 21st century Canada still authorizes the annual slaughter of 330,000 seals. On the extermination of the great auk see ibid., 138.
681. See www.viva.org.uk
682. See Roman, 146.

waste we collectively excrete.[683] Or perhaps the chief cetacean concern would be with what has been termed "the rise of slime,"[684] the "red tides" or harmful algal blooms that are flourishing as human activity overdoses the oceans with nutrient pollutants such as nitrogen and phosphorus. Such micro-monsters include *Lyngbya majuscula* or fireweed, a strain of primitive cyanobacteria that spreads over the seafloor at alarming rates and produces blisters, weals and irritation of the human skin, and *Pfiesteria piscicida*, known as the "cell from hell," a virulent fish-killing dinoflagellate which eats not only bacteria and plankton but also fish 10,000 times its size.[685]

It has been suggested that harmful human activity is causing the oceans to regress to the state of the primeval seas of hundreds of millions of years ago. Complex forms of sea life are battling extinction, while the most primitive are prospering; fish and marine mammals are struggling to survive, while algae, bacteria and jellyfish are having a ball.[686] It is probably no exaggeration to describe *Homo sapiens* as the greatest global disaster since the asteroid that did for the dinosaurs and half the world's species 65 million years ago.[687] Yet who is to say how long it will be before *Homo sapiens* and his kamikaze "civilization" follow the great auk and Steller's sea cow into collective watery oblivion? In terms of deep time, we are in deep water. Given the bigger picture, it is the ocean itself that perhaps emerges as the real monster, whether in its immeasurability, the brute violence it embodies, its powers of death and engulfment, the grotesqueness of its creatures, its timelessness, protean shapelessness or sheer unknowability. Monstrous individuals and species – whether Ceto or sea cucumber, fireweed or flatfish, man or manta ray – may strut and swagger for a while, but the endless uterine waters embody both the possibility of their life and the inevitability of their eventual death.

683. On the harm being done to the world's oceans by human activity, see, for example, the issue of *New Internationalist* no. 397 "State of the World's Ocean" (Jan / Feb 2007).
684. Jeremy B. C. Jackson, quoted in Kenneth R. Weiss, "The Rise of Slime," in ibid., 6.
685. See Kunzig, 230-32, for an account of its devastating effects on fish; also Goodall, 91. In the course of six weeks in 1991, it is believed to have killed roughly one billion fish in the Neuse River in North Carolina.
686. Weiss, "The Rise of Slime," 6.
687. See Richard Leakey, quoted in Nouvian, 22.

4

Salt and Ice

The ocean may be the womb of life, the deepest uterine origin of humankind and all our fellow creatures on the planet. Our life-blood may be iron-tainted seawater; our cellular fluid may recall the salty oceans in which our single-celled forebears once dwelled. Yet the waters of the briny deep fail spectacularly when it comes to the small matter of slaking human thirst. Slowly dehydrating on a becalmed ship, Coleridge's Ancient Mariner famously lamented "Water, water, everywhere, / Nor any drop to drink," which also happens to be a fair assessment of the predicament facing the modern world. Of all the planet's water, less than three per cent is fresh water; most of this is locked up either in ice caps and glaciers or in the pores of rocks or aquifers; and the "drop to drink" amounts to just one hundredth of a per cent of the global total.[688]

The rest – roughly 1.37 billion cubic kilometres – is salt water. Such is the quantity of salt contained in this immensity of brine that, if the world's water were to evaporate in its entirety, the salts left behind would bury the whole planet to a depth of some 150 metres.[689] This is not simply a matter of the common salt, sodium chloride, with which we season our food: as the French chemist Guillaume-François Rouelle surmised as early as 1744, a salt is any substance formed when an acid reacts with a base. Other common salts include the magnesium chloride that gives the Dead Sea its bitter nauseous taste, the magnesium sulphate of Epsom salt, sodium hydrogen carbonate (bicarbonate of soda) and potassium chloride (potash). With their remarkable resemblance to sea water, both our blood and the cytoplasm of our cells contain sodium, magnesium,

688. See Kandel, 86. According to Pearce, the planet contains some 1.4 billion cubic kilometres of water, of which roughly 200,000 cubic kilometres constitute the "drop to drink" (*When the Rivers Run Dry*, 33). See also Ball, *H2O*, 313.
689. My source here is Bryson, 342, quoting Jerry Dennis. Such calculations occupied the 19th-century mind too. In *Twenty Thousand Leagues under the Sea*, Captain Nemo's more conservative estimate was that the salts left behind would amount to "four and a half million cubic leagues, which, spread out over the globe, would form a layer more than thirty feet high" (Verne, *Twenty Thousand*, 128).

potassium, bicarbonate and chloride ions: chloride is vital for respiration and digestion; sodium plays a key role in the transport of nutrients and oxygen and the transmission of nerve impulses; magnesium too is essential to cellular metabolism. Adult humans contain roughly 250 grams of salt, which we constantly lose in the form of sweat, tears and urine, and which thus require constant replacement.

Although the analogy between sweat and seawater goes back to Empedocles and Aristotle, imbibing the latter will not do to replenish the former. Indeed, not only will seawater never quench our thirst, but it will actually dehydrate us further. The ingestion of too much salt into an organism is quick to send the metabolism spinning. If the fluids around the cells in our body become too salty, osmosis rapidly depletes those cells of the water they need for normal functioning. Freshwater fish suffer in like manner, while the same phenomenon of osmosis – albeit working in the other direction[690] – means that seawater fish cannot cope in fresh water. Relatively few and far between are the so-called diadromous fishes, such as eels, salmon or the beluga sturgeon, which can migrate between marine and freshwater habitats by regulating the salinity of their bodily fluids.

In fact, salt and salinization has been a bane not just to the thirsty individual but to human civilizations as a whole. Increased salinity caused by over-irrigation and poor drainage is thought to have led to the downfall of ancient Sumerian culture, as the small quantities of dissolved salts brought by the rivers Tigris and Euphrates gradually accumulated in the fields (for even freshwater is not salt-free), eventually poisoning the soil and choking the plants. At first the farmers changed from wheat to barley, a more salt-resistant crop; then they practised fallowing in an attempt to allow the water table to drop; but harvests dwindled inexorably and the fields turned to dust. Crop yields declined by two thirds between 2400 and 1700 BCE, by which time Sumerian civilization was bereft of its agricultural base and in chronic decline. Mesopotamian society shifted permanently northwards, leaving Sumer in a state of dereliction and destitution. Between 1300 and 900 BCE, central Mesopotamia would go on to suffer its own agricultural collapse brought on by excessive irrigation and the subsequent waterlogging and salinization.[691]

The problem has continued through to the present day, as salts from excessive irrigation continue to poison fields and turn fertile land

690. As their cellular fluid is more salty than fresh water, the cells *absorb* fresh water until they rupture. See Ball, *H₂O*, 225.
691. Ponting, 69-72; Pearce, 212-13.

to desert. Current estimates are that two million hectares of agricultural land are lost to salinization each year and that a quarter of all irrigated land is afflicted.[692] The problems are particularly acute in the Indus valley of Pakistan, which is blighted by waterlogged fields, salt-poisoned crops and some of the lowest productivity in the world. According to one set of calculations,[693] each year the Indus delivers some 22 million tons of salt onto its plain, only half of which is carried on into the Arabian Sea: the other half remains behind to form a toxic white crust on the soil, almost a ton of the stuff for each irrigated hectare. As in ancient Sumer, barren fields are being abandoned to their fate at a rate of thousands of hectares a year. In the United States, megalomanic irrigation schemes and blatant water profligacy are choking up the River Colorado, which shrivels and dies waterless before its reaches its delta. As a result, virtually none of the nine million tons of salt that enters the system each year ever reaches the ocean. Instead, it is gradually clogging up the Colorado Basin, and will eventually render it sterile. The River Murray in Australia is likewise on its last legs: scarcely any of its water now reaches the sea, while 25 million hectares of the river basin are given over to irrigating land that is drowning in salt.[694]

Perhaps the most arrant hydraulic folly of all has taken place in the Central Asian countries that formerly belonged to the Soviet Union, where the once beautiful Aral Sea – fed by two major rivers, the Syr and the legendary Amu, known in ancient times as the Oxus – has been reduced to a salty desert in order to irrigate notoriously water-thirsty cotton crops. Once the fourth largest inland sea on earth, covering an area equal to Belgium and Holland combined, the Aral has shrivelled to three hypersaline pools with a tenth as much water as before. Meanwhile, the ex-Soviet countries around the Aral Sea – Uzbekistan, Kazakhstan, Turkmenistan, Tajikistan and Kyrgyzstan – are five of the seven highest per-capita water users in the world, squandering what would have flown into the Aral not on drinking or sanitation but on inefficient cotton production. The UN has described what has happened to the Aral Sea as the greatest environmental disaster of the 20th century. As it receded, the sea left vast plains covered with salt and a toxic mantle of pesticides and fertilisers; what remains of its water no longer supports fish; its once bustling coastal towns and resorts

692. Ball, *H₂O*, 319.
693. Pearce, 43. For a more detailed account of the problems facing Pakistan, see ibid., 40-45.
694. See ibid., 218-25, on the River Colorado; 248-55, on the River Murray.

are bleached, desiccated and abandoned. The 1.5 million people of the autonomous republic of Karakalpakstan in Uzbekistan are the human victims of this man-made devastation, exposed as they are to poisonous dust storms that blow 50 days a year and the all-pervasive presence of salt. The incidence of cancer and lung disease has risen 30-fold, and chronic allergies such as asthma are rampant. The collective salt-poisoning of the area around the Aral is yet another testimony to the human obsession with the massive-scale subjugation and enslavement of watery nature.[695]

There is clearly a deep association between salt and death. The French Mediterranean port of Aigues-Mortes, founded in the 13th century, takes its name from the "dead waters" beyond the famed city walls, a great expanse of salt evaporation ponds which Louis IX hoped to use to raise valuable salt revenue. One of the saltiest bodies of water in the world, given the name Yam ha-Melah (the Salt Sea) in Hebrew, is commonly known as the Dead Sea.[696] Already so dead that virtually no living creature can survive in it,[697] the Dead Sea is in fact getting progressively deader, evaporating away at a rate of up to a metre a year and becoming more and more salty. It has now reached the density at which sodium chloride precipitates, and crystals of common salt are forming round the shore and on the bed. Writing in the 1st century CE, Pliny claimed it measured 100 miles by 75; now it is 45 by 11 and shrinking fast.[698] The River Jordan once delivered a billion cubic metres of water a year to it, but hydropolitically motivated dam-building has reduced the inflow to less than a tenth of what it was, and most of that is sewage. The place where John is said to have baptized Jesus is now "a sewage seep behind the barbed wire of a military fence."[699]

In rabbinical literature the Dead Sea is known as the "Sea of Sodom" in reference to the Old Testament tale of Sodom and Gomorrah,

695. Ponting, 263-64; Caldecott, 104-8; Pearce, 226-43; Black, *The No-Non-sense Guide to Water*, 20.
696. On the Dead Sea, see Kurlansky, 355-68. The mineral concentration of the Dead Sea is 26 per cent (almost all of which is salt) as opposed to the typical ocean level of three per cent.
697. The exception is a class of extremophiles called the halophiles, which require and thrive on highly salty environments. Extreme halophiles such as the *Halobacteria* (or *Haloarchaea*) flourish at salinity levels of between 20 and 30 per cent, as are found in the Dead Sea, and would perish if exposed to anything less salty.
698. Ibid., 365.
699. Pearce, 197.

the two Canaanite towns destroyed by fire and brimstone as punishment for their moral turpitude. The towns' inhabitants are believed to have been salt workers.[700] When God destroyed Sodom, he spared Abraham's nephew Lot, but Lot's wife – who turned to look back at the destruction – was transformed into a pillar of salt. Sodom and Gomorrah are generally assumed to lie beneath the southern part of the Dead Sea, and to this day, its southwest shore features a mountain of rock salt known as *Jabal Usdum* or Mount Sodom, which has a natural tendency to form columns and pillars bearing an uncanny resemblance to whatever Lot's wife is presumed to have looked like. Another Biblical reference throws further light upon this link between salt and devastation. In Deuteronomy Moses describes the consequences of a breach of the covenant with God, a covenant symbolized (paradoxically) by salt as a token of both purity and preservation[701]: the whole land would become "brimstone and salt, and a burnt-out waste, unsown, and growing nothing, where no grass can sprout, an overthrow like that of Sodom and Gomorrah, ... which the Lord overthrew in his anger and wrath" (29.23).

The idea of salt as divine retribution goes back to the ancient Mesopotamian tale of Atrahasis, in which – prior to the flood – Ellil sent a drought to punish the human race for making such an unholy din: "The dark pastureland was bleached, / The broad countryside filled up with alkali... The dark fields became white."[702] It also recalls the ancient practice known as "salting the earth," which referred to the punitive measure of covering one's enemies' territory with salt in order to leave it barren. The Romans are said to have done this after the destruction of Carthage,[703] and according to the Old Testament Book of Judges Abimelech did the same thing to his own capital, Schechem, after quelling a revolt there: "Abimelech fought against the city all that day; he took the city, and killed the people that were in it; and he razed the city and sowed it with salt" (Judges, 9.45). As a symbol of God's covenant with his people, however, salt also assumed a positive role, signifying both permanence and purification. It was in this capacity that it was required to accompany all sacrifices (Leviticus, 2.13)

---

700. Kurlansky, 357-58.
701. See ibid., 7: "Salt was to the ancient Hebrews, and still is to modern Jews, the symbol of the eternal nature of God's covenant with Israel."
702. Dalley (trans.), 22-25.
703. Biedermann, 294.

and was used by Elisha to purify a spring (II Kings, 2.19-22).[704]

The downfall of Sodom thus highlights a rather complex set of associations between salt, death, dissolution and purification. Indeed, salt displays an ambivalence that echoes the water with which it is so intimately associated. In the Pahlavi (Middle Persian) texts of Zoroastrianism, the dualistic conflict of good and evil (embodied in the incessant battle between Ahura Mazda and the wholly malign Angra Mainyu) is reflected in an opposition between fresh water and salt water: hardly had the world been created when it was attacked by the evil spirit Angra Mainyu, who succeeded in turning some of its waters salty. In Scandinavian legend too, the seas were originally freshwater bodies: the saltiness came later, produced by a misplaced salt mill, which grinds away incessantly in the increasingly briny deep.[705] More often, however, the primordial waters are salty. In Babylonian mythology, the infinite and all-encompassing primal saltwater embodied in Tiamat had to be overcome by Marduk, who imposed shape, structure and order upon the chaos.

Yet as in most modern-day narratives of the evolution of life, the primordial brine still represents the source or origin of every living thing. By the same token, salt is linked not only with death and blight, but also with fertility, productivity and life. In 1912 the psychoanalyst Ernest Jones published an essay investigating what he regarded as the timeless and universal human fixation with salt, which he considered subconsciously sexual in nature. Jones laid particular emphasis on its connection with fertility. This connection, he suggested, may have had its roots in the observation that fish reproduce in greater number than terrestrial animals or in the long-held belief that mice could procreate simply by being in salt (as they seemed to do on salt-bearing ships). Jones argued that salt even has the same etymological root as salacity, going back to the Roman *salax* (in a salted state), and cited numerous examples

---

704. In Mark 9.49-50, Jesus seems to bring these diverse associations together with his cryptic words: "For every one will be salted with fire. Salt is good; but if the salt has lost its saltness, how will you season it? Have salt in yourselves, and be at peace with one another." The believer's purification, it appears, must be an *inner* one. The salt reference in Matthew (5.13) seems unconcerned with imagery of purification or preservation: "You are the salt of the earth," says Jesus, "but if salt has lost its taste, how shall its saltness be restored? It is no longer good for anything except to be thrown out and trodden under foot by men."

705. See Rupp, 102-3.

from around the world of associations between salt and sexual desire or fecundity: at marriage ceremonies in France and Germany (where it warded off impotence), among celibate Egyptian priests (who renounced it as an excitant), or among sacred prostitutes in certain parts of India (who periodically abstained from both salt and prostitution).[706] His conclusion: "There is every reason to think that the primitive mind equated the idea of salt, not only with that of semen, but also with the essential constituent of urine."[707] The sin of the salt-working Sodomites would have been that they were too salty and thus too salacious for their own good.[708]

Like water, moreover, salt is uncommonly protean in its functions and uses: the modern-day salt industry claims that there are 14,000 of them. These include applications in pharmaceuticals and medicine, agricultural fertilizer, soap-making, water-softening, the dying of textiles, not to mention its uses in food seasoning and preservation, the de-icing of roads and the removal of red wine stains. Medieval uses of salt included curing leather, soldering pipes and glazing pottery, as well as medical treatments for toothache, stomach disorders and "heaviness of mind." Most fundamental of all has been salt's ability to preserve what is otherwise susceptible to decomposition. The ancient Egyptians used a salt called natron, a mixture of sodium bicarbonate, sodium carbonate and sodium chloride, in their process of mummification, and for thousands of years prior to modern times salt provided the principal means of preserving food. "This ability to preserve, to protect against decay, as well as to sustain life," writes Mark Kurlansky in his history of the substance, "has given salt a broad metaphorical importance – what Freud might have considered an irrational attachment to salt, a seemingly trivial object, because, in our unconscious, we associate it with longevity and permanence, which are of boundless significance."[709] The capacity to resist the ravages of time lent salt its symbolic association not only with covenants – such as God's with Israel – but also with loyalty and friendship, which are sealed with it. The Old Testament Book of Ezekiel (16.4) refers to the custom of rubbing new

706. On Jones's essay on salt, see Kurlansky, 2-5.
707. Quoted in ibid., 4-5.
708. In fact, a more common etymology for salacity and the Roman *salax* links it to *salire*, "to leap." To be salacious is to be fond of leaping or jumping. The inhabitants of Sodom can be assumed to have taken pleasure in both salt and saltation.
709. Ibid., 6-7; on the uses of salt, see 5, 120.

born children with salt as protection against evil, and in Europe the ritual of placing salt on the tongue of infants or immersing them in saltwater is believed to have predated the Christian practice of baptism.[710] While salt's function as a preservative gave rise to connotations of permanence, protection and longevity, moreover, its role in seasoning has also led to a link with wit, repartee and conversational grace.[711]

Despite the Ancient Mariner's lamentation, therefore, saltwater has frequently been attributed medical properties. Though half a gram of salt a day is usually plenty to maintain our body's essential sodium levels, and too much salt can quickly pickle our kidneys to the point of no return, the boom in sea-bathing in 19th-century Britain – as the railway made the seaside a more accessible and inviting alternative to the spas that had flourished before – led to a vogue for seawater taken internally. A few tumblers of the stuff taken on a daily basis became a household panacea. As early as 1750, Dr Richard Russell had written a bestselling *Dissertation on the Use of Seawater in Diseases of the Glands* in which he claimed that a pint taken daily was "commonly sufficient in grown persons to give three or four sharp stools."[712] Epsom salts in particular were traditionally used as a laxative, and the famed "dose of salts" has proved so effective in getting things moving that it now denotes anything quick and efficient. But this is certainly not what Coleridge's mariner had in mind.

Rather than imbibing it, bathing in seawater or saltwater – sometimes known as thalassotherapy – is also considered highly beneficial to human wellbeing. A spell of time spent gently marinating, whether on

---

710. Ibid., 8.
711. In his epistle to the Colossians (4.6), Paul thus says: "Let your speech always be gracious, seasoned with salt, so that you may know how you ought to answer every one." The Latin word *sal* also means wit, as does the Italian *sale*. Although the link still exists in modern-day English, where saltiness implies a wit that is dry, laconic, pungent or perhaps even caustic, it is stronger in Spanish, where *salado* is a common term meaning not only salty, but also witty, amusing, lively and perhaps even a little saucy (and where *salido*, by contrast, means "fond of leaping").
712. Described by the French historian Jules Michelet as "the inventor of the sea," Russell was an early advocate of sea-bathing at Brighton, which became a flourishing resort thanks to his influence. See Ashenburg, *Clean: An Unsanitised History of Washing*, 133; also Staveacre, 144. See also Sprawon, 26-27: "Salt water was a novel alternative to spa waters, as a cure for almost anything. One drank several tumblers of it, or dipped in it before breakfast."

the Dead Sea or in the Brine Baths at Droitwich,[713] is acknowledged to produce a host of salutary physiological effects, relieving skin conditions and arthritis, relaxing the joints and the spine, lowering the blood pressure, providing welcome weightlessness, and generally making us feel good. As the fashion of seaside bathing gained momentum in the 19th century, salt water – as well as encouraging a snappy production of stools – came to be seen as something invigorating, indeed vital for physical and mental health. In the words of the seaside speculator in Jane Austen's last, unfinished novel *Sanditon*, the sea cures colds, stimulates the appetite, builds up strength and boosts the spirits. No-one could be truly and lastingly healthy "without spending at least six weeks by the Sea every year."[714] Jane Austen herself loved bathing in the sea.

Coleridge's mariner was presumably no more interested in relaxing his joints than his bowels. For him the endless brine was a bane, and it was the salt that prevented the water from quenching his thirst. Without salt, however, his fate would have been even less enviable, for like all seafarers he is certain to have relied on food provisions that required salt as a preservative. For centuries, the British navy fed its sailors on salt cod and Irish salted beef, which came to be known as corned beef on account of its "corns" or salt crystals. Crews under the 18th-century English navigator and explorer Captain James Cook – believed to be the inspiration for Coleridge's poem – were served sauerkraut or salted cabbage with every meal.[715] By a cruel irony, such salty fare would have only exacerbated the mariner's need to drink.

The ability of salt to prevent decomposition was one of the foundations of civilization, reducing a community's reliance on the seasonal availability of food, facilitating travel and adding a new dimension to warfare. Unsurprisingly, salt thus acquired exceptional strategic importance. As Kurlansky recounts, "by the fourteenth century, for most of northern Europe the standard procedure to prepare for war was to obtain a large quantity of salt and start salting fish and meat." On land campaigns, each British soldier would be given his own ration for salting fresh meat as he went along. Gunpowder, invented by the Chinese, was also made of a salt,

713. See Roger Deakin's account of his trip to Droitwich in *Waterlog*, 104-6.
714. Austen, *Sanditon*, 302.
715. See Kurlansky, 124-25, 149-51.

potassium nitrate or saltpetre.[716] In ancient Rome soldiers were on occasion even paid in salt, which has given rise to the word "salary" (salt-money), the expression "worth one's salt," and also, it has been conjectured, to the French word *solde*, from which the word "soldier" derives.[717]

As one of the foundations of civilization, the history of salt is thus as old as the history of water. Salt played a vital role in the domestication of animals in the millennia following the end of the last Ice Age. Cows, for example, require up to ten times as much salt as human beings, and whereas the wild aurochs would have found their own salt licks or brine springs, domesticated cattle needed their salt to be provided for them. It has been conjectured that by 6000 BCE the Chinese were gathering the salt crystals from Lake Yuncheng when its waters evaporated in the summer months; written records from 800 BCE tell of salt production and trade during the ancient Xia dynasty; and in 252 BCE Li Bing – perhaps China's greatest hydrological genius[718] – supervised the drilling of the first wells to tap the vast underground reservoirs of natural brine in the province today known as Szechwan. By this time, Chinese governments had long since recognized that the universal human need for salt would make it an invaluable source of tax revenue: though opposed by Confucius, a controversial salt tax was used to finance the army, build the Great Wall, and generally keep at bay the Huns and other undesirables from the north.[719]

While the Chinese were obtaining their salt primarily from brine wells, the ancient Egyptians developed one of the other main sources of salt,[720] using the heat of the sun to evaporate seawater in the delta of the Nile. Like the Chinese, the Egyptians acquired a taste for pickling vegetables in brine, and they are thought to have been the first to cure

716. Ibid., 127. See also 258: "As generals from George Washington to Napoleon discovered, war without salt is a desperate situation. In Napoleon's retreat from Russia, thousands died from minor wounds because the army lacked salt for disinfectants. Salt was needed not only for medicine and for the daily ration of a soldier's diet but also to maintain the horses of a cavalry, and the workhorses that hauled supplies and artillery, and herds of livestock to feed the men."
717. Ibid., 63.
718. On Li Bing see ibid., 23-26; on the history of salt in ancient China, 17-35.
719. The Chinese custom of fixing an artificially high price for salt and using the profits to finance its military objectives would subsequently be adopted by the empire-building Romans. In France, the much-hated *gabelle* provoked dissent and division from the 14th-century until it was finally abolished in 1946. In his book *Das Salz*, the 19th-century German botanist Matthias Schleiden posited the existence of a direct correlation between salt tax and despotism. See Kurlansky, 61-79, 225-37.
720. The third main source is rock salt.

meat and fish with salt, some time prior to 2000 BCE. They were certainly, writes Kurlansky, "the first civilization to preserve food on a large scale,"[721] starting a ball rolling that would lead to the salt cod and pickled herring that became staples of the medieval diet, as well as cured hams and salamis, salted anchovies, pickled vegetables, salt-based sauces such as soy sauce, garum and anchovy sauce (the original ketchup), and cheese, which was developed as a way of preserving milk in salt.

In the last 200 years, the use of salt to preserve food has been steadily on the wane. Canning developed as an alternative in the early 19th century, and in the British navy, for example, tinned food was part of general provisions by the 1830s. Around the same time, the idea of using ice or cold to preserve food – "salting in snow"[722] – was gradually incubating, and in 1925 Clarence Birdseye founded a frozen seafood company that would open up the availability of unsalted fish to the inland market. The consumption of salt is now declining worldwide; the average European has halved his or her intake over the last century. The largest salt producer, the United States, still turns out some 40 million tons a year, extracted largely from rock salt mines and from the Great Salt Lake in Utah. Yet it is salt's ability to lower the freezing temperature of water that is now its most important quality, and much more salt is used to deice roads than to preserve or season food. The upshot of this decline in fortune is that we now tend to forget or ignore the crucial part salt has played in human history, relegating it to a function – deicing – that may itself decline in importance if the manmade global deicing kicks in as feared. Instead of evaporating seawater, the emphasis today is on its desalination.[723] Like Coleridge's mariner, we want the *water* from the waters, not the salt.

721. Ibid., 38.
722. Ibid., 305-6; see 303-8.
723. Most desalination is still done by distillation, which – like sea-salt production – involves the evaporation of seawater, but in this case followed by condensation of the resulting vapour. Reverse osmosis, which works by passing water repeatedly through a semi-permeable membrane that separates the water molecules from the salt ions, is gaining in popularity, but both technologies are extremely heavy on energy (which means burning more fossil fuels) and a worry to ecologists. The worldwide desalination capacity now covers between 0.1 and 0.2 per cent of total water use, and is not currently regarded as providing more than a limited and highly localized solution to the global water problem. Another issue, as Fred Pearce points out, "is what to do with the salt extracted from the sea water during desalination. It emerges as a vast stream of concentrated brine. Most plants, naturally enough, dump it back in the sea" (*When the Rivers Run Dry*, 291-93).

*　*　*　*　*

Salt was described by D. H. Lawrence as "scorched water." It is water "that the sun has scorched / into substance and flaky whiteness / in the eternal opposition / between the two great ones, Fire, and the Wet."[724] The ambivalence of this scorched water in its associations with death and preservation is paralleled by similar ambivalence and similar associations in ice and frost, which is water scorched into flaky whiteness *by cold*. The old notion of "salting in snow" to keep food fresh is a telling one. In a modern, global context, the ambivalence of ice is exemplified by the vast ice-sheets of Greenland and Antarctica, which – for all their uninhabitability – we are loath to see melt. Indeed, the planet's frozen and its salty waters are closely interdependent: while the oceans, seas and lakes contain some 1.37 billion cubic kilometres of salty water, and most of the rest is locked up in ice sheets and glaciers, the proportions can and do change. Since the most recent "glacial maximum" roughly 18,000 years ago, global sea-levels have risen by 120 metres as about 50 million cubic kilometres of land-bound ice have returned to the oceans in liquid form.[725] If the remaining land-bound ice on the planet were to follow suit, it is estimated that sea-levels would rise by another 70 to 80 metres.[726]

On the ice caps of Greenland and the Antarctic, human settlement is limited to research stations. Further afield, though certain of the moons of Jupiter and Saturn are entirely encased in thick shells of ice, only one of them, Europa, is believed to harbour even the remotest possibility of life, and this depends on the presence of a briny ocean deep beneath the surface. Ice itself is generally considered non-conducive to life, which requires flow. It is vital for living organisms to prevent their aqueous body fluids – blood, lymph or cytoplasm – from freezing solid, and failure to do so will lead to death. Yet this does not mean that there is no life below zero. For a start, the salt dissolved in the ocean lowers the water's freezing point, and

724. In the poem "Salt," Lawrence, 592; in another poem, salt is "the boundary mark between Fire that burns, and the Wet" (ibid., 593). The Spanish word for hoarfrost (*escarcha*) betrays that cold too can scorch.
725. Floating sea-ice, by contrast, does not produce a rise in the global sea-level when it melts because it is already displacing its own volume of water as it floats.
726. See Kandel, 76ff., 85ff.

the temperature of the salty surface water of the Antarctic, for example, generally remains somewhere between –1.5°C and –1.9°C. Blood likewise freezes below zero, albeit at a slightly higher temperature of about –0.5°C. In order to avoid freezing, therefore, the cold-water fish of the Antarctic further manufacture antifreeze proteins to suppress ice formation and keep their blood in a supercooled state, while certain high-latitude amphibians fill their body fluids with solutes called cryoprotectants, which are usually sugars.[727] As we have seen, moreover, the bizarre fact that ice floats rather than sinks – in other words that water freezes from the top down – means that when temperatures fall a surface layer of ice or snow can function as a form of insulating blanket, retaining the residual heat and protecting the flora and fauna in the waters beneath.[728]

Despite this protective function, ice is deeply bound up with death and with the *slowing down* of life to a point of irrevocable stasis. "Amongst ice," writes Philip Ball, "life is not consumed; it just stops."[729] Admittedly, the annual coming and going of the mini-ice-age known as winter has traditionally provided it with a reassuringly cyclical context. While winter has served as an archetypal symbol of old age, decay and death, therefore, spring is a metaphor for rebirth and the return of youth and joy. Some literary critics and theorists have seen the ritual overcoming of winter and death as a mythic principle underlying art and drama in general. For a critic such as Northrop Frye, for example, comedy and tragedy alike are structured around the sacrificial "ritual of the struggle, death and rebirth of

---

727. See Ball, *H_2O*, 194-99. The tardigrades or water bears are a phylum of tiny aquatic invertebrates that can survive extremely low temperatures (little above *absolute* zero) by replacing virtually all their bodily water with the sugar trehalose, which does not crystallize.

728. Deep under the ice at the Russian Antarctic research station at Vostok is a body of liquid water that has been severed from contact with the atmosphere for over 400,000 years. Insulated by more than three and a half kilometres of ice, Lake Vostok has remained unfrozen all this time and is thought to contain bacteria or other life forms long since isolated from the rest of the biosphere. For the present, researchers have halted ice core extraction until the risk of contaminating the lake has been overcome. Meanwhile, British scientists have developed sophisticated ice-drilling technology specially designed to maintain sterility, with which they plan to break through a 3.4-kilometre-thick ice-sheet to a smaller lake called Ellsworth in West Antarctica in the Antarctic summer of 2012-13. Lake Ellsworth is thought to be about as big as Lake Windermere.

729. Ball, *H_2O*, 170.

a God-Man, which is linked to the yearly triumph of spring over winter."[730] Even the Christian drama of struggle, death and resurrection lends itself to interpretation in such comedic terms, as a magical triumph over winter and evil. In C. S. Lewis's *The Lion, the Witch and the Wardrobe*, commonly considered a Christian allegory, the reign of the White Witch is one of perpetual winter – yet never Christmas! Flowing water is frozen solid, and those who disobey the cruel Queen of Winter are glaciated in mid-gesture and kept as garden ornaments. When her magic starts to wear off, the waters begin to flow again and a great thaw ensues.[731] The happy ending is just round the corner.

Yet the onset of ice may be more apocalyptic in character. According to ancient Norse legend, the end of the world will be preceded by Fimbulwinter, a ferociously severe winter continuing unabated for three years, in the course of which the sun will finally be swallowed by the wolf believed to be chasing it[732] – though this is just the prelude to the monumental free-for-all still to come. Among non-canonical Christian writings, the Second Book of Enoch envisions hell as an icy as well as a fiery location (2 Enoch 12), while the apocryphal book of Sirach, also known as Ecclesiasticus or the Wisdom of Ben Sira, incorporates a chilling account of the effects of God's wrath: "The hoarfrost also as salt he poureth on the earth, and being congealed, it lieth on the top of sharp stakes. When the cold north wind bloweth, and the water is congealed into ice, it abideth upon every gathering together of water, and clotheth the water as with a breastplate. It devoureth the mountains, and burneth

---

730. Frye, "The Argument of Comedy" (1949), in Palmer (ed.), *Comedy: Developments in Criticism*, 78. This special emphasis on the role of ancient myth and ritual in the development of European drama was rooted in late 19th-century work in anthropology, comparative religion and classics. Both the anthropology of J. G. Frazer and Jungian psychoanalysis exerted a major influence on such archetypal criticism. In *The Origin of Attic Comedy*, the Cambridge classicist F. M. Cornford had also traced the origins of the Old Comedy of Ancient Greece back to prehistoric ceremonies such as the ritual of death and resurrection and the defeat of winter by summer.
731. Edmund hears "a strange, sweet, rustling, chattering noise – and yet not so strange, for he'd heard it before – if only he could remember where! Then all at once he did remember. It was the noise of running water. All round them though out of sight, there were streams, chattering, murmuring, bubbling, splashing and even (in the distance) roaring" (Lewis, *The Lion, the Witch and the Wardrobe*, 108).
732. On Ragnarok, see Scott Littleton, 320-25.

the wilderness, and consumeth the grass as fire" (Sirach 43.19-21). Robert Frost's poem "Fire and Ice," published in *Harper's Magazine* in 1920, gives a more humorous take on the apocalypse:

> Some say the world will end in fire,
> Some say in ice.
> From what I've tasted of desire
> I hold with those who favor fire.
> But if it had to perish twice,
> I think I know enough of hate
> To say that for destruction ice
> Is also great
> And would suffice.[733]

Winter, however harsh, has traditionally been something to be endured and overcome, while hell and the end of the world – whether fiery or frosty – have been an admonition to right living and virtue. Yet for most of history the greater part of the planet's population has been cheerfully oblivious to the vast ice sheets of Greenland and Antarctica, which remained in large measure unexplored until the end of the 19th century. Of course, a glimpse of icy immensity has been provided at lower latitudes by mountain glaciers, whether Alpine, Himalayan or even the equatorial glaciation of the Andes or Mt Kilimanjaro in Tanzania. Like tumultuous seas or giddy precipices, glaciers and icebound mountains came to captivate the imagination of the 18th-century traveller with their harsh sublimity. The Alpine glaciers of Savoy filled the brooding fancy of the poet Shelley with thoughts of an icy end to the world, evoking the "sublime but gloomy theory – that this globe which we inhabit will at some future period be changed into a mass of frost by the encroachments of the polar ice, and of that produced on the most elevated parts of the earth."[734] They exerted a similar effect on Shelley's friend Byron, whose poem "Darkness" recounted a dream "which was not all a dream" in which "the bright sun was extinguish'd" and the "icy earth / swung blind and blackening in the moonless air."[735]

Byron and Shelley were writing in 1816, the year that came to be known as the year without summer. The previous year had witnessed the

733. Frost, *Robert Frost's Poems*, 237.
734. This quotation is from a letter to his friend Thomas Love Peacock, quoted in Macfarlane, 122.
735. Ibid., 123.

spectacular eruption of the Indonesian volcano Tambora, which had not only claimed 100,000 lives with its blast and the ensuing tsunamis, but also spewed millions of tons of dust and ash into the atmosphere, blocking the sun's rays, causing a worldwide drop in temperature, and killing thousands more as a consequence of crop failure, famine and disease.[736] With the planet shrouded in a deathly pall, it is no wonder that apocalyptic fantasies were spawned in sensitive souls. Yet it was not long before these visions of an icebound planet were corroborated as a reality of the past by geological science. Within two decades, the charismatic Swiss naturalist and glaciologist Louis Agassiz was starting to propound his notion that Europe – and possibly the whole world – had once been covered by a thick sheet of ice, a phenomenon that explained certain apparent geological anomalies (such as erratic boulders[737]) which had perplexed the experts for decades. In his *Études sur les glaciers* (published in English as *Studies on Glaciers*), Agassiz paints an almost Biblical portrait of ice-age devastation:

> The development of these huge ice sheets must have led to the destruction of all organic life at the Earth's surface. The land of Europe, previously covered with tropical vegetation and inhabited by herds of great elephants, enormous hippopotami, and gigantic carnivora, was suddenly buried under a vast expanse of ice, covering plains, lakes, seas, and plateaus alike. The movement of a powerful creation was supplanted by the silence of death. Springs dried up, streams ceased to flow, and the rays of the sun, rising over this frozen shore ... were greeted only by the whistling of the northern wind and the rumbling of crevasses opening up across the surface of the huge ocean of ice.[738]

736. The even more cataclysmic explosion of Toba some 74,000 years ago is thought to have led to a volcanic winter that lasted six years and preceded a thousand-year glaciation which almost did for the human race.
737. Erratic boulders, often known simply as erratics, are huge stones – on occasion weighing thousands of tons – that bear no resemblance to the rock types around them. Prior to ice age theory, the consensus had been that the erratics had been deposited across the land by great inundations, which were also thought to account for the rocky debris now known as glacial drift. In the late 18th century this position was known as Neptunism, by contrast with the Plutonism that attributed a greater role to volcanoes and earthquakes. On Louis Agassiz see Macdougall, 25-44; on erratics and glacial drift, see ibid., 46-49.
738. Quoted in ibid., 38.

Agassiz's bleak vision initially met with resistance and ridicule. This was due above all to the limited imagination of his fellow geologists, many of whom were simply unable to conceive of ice sheets several kilometres thick covering thousands of square miles, or of the pulverizing force exerted by a such a mass, which would grind its way through landscapes, gouge out valleys and basins and scatter the debris far and wide. To many, the idea of frozen water causing such ravages was a patent absurdity.

By the time he died in 1873, however, Agassiz's ice-age theory was more or less universally accepted by the scientific community. The consensus today is that but for the effects of human activity the ice would be almost certain to advance again within the next few thousand years. This may still happen. As Doug Macdougall explains:

> We are already about ten thousand years into the current warm episode. If history is any guide, and if human activities don't warm the Earth too severely, the ice will return, and quite soon on a geological timescale. The sites of cities such as Montreal and Edinburgh and Stockholm, and perhaps even New York and Chicago, will be buried deep in glacial ice, as they were in the past.[739]

In fact, it is not just a matter of burial. The pressures exerted beneath several kilometres of ice recall the solid lead skyscrapers in the depths of the ocean. "Should a glacial interval recur in the future," continues Macdougall, "the ice would not just bury northern cities, it would simply scrape them off the surface of the Earth and, eventually and quite unceremoniously, dump the twisted and mangled remains far to the south."[740]

Leaving aside the very real possibility that human interference may instead catapult us into a global sauna, today's climate is in fact an interglacial interlude, a geologically brief warm spell in an ongoing ice age known as the Pleistocene. The evidence suggests that since the last time worldwide hothouse conditions and a completely ice-free Earth prevailed, which was during the Eocene some 55 million years ago, the planet has been subject to a more or less steady decrease in temperature, with particularly sharp drops occurring roughly 35 million years ago (when glaciation began in the Antarctic) and three million years ago (when permanent glaciers began to form in the Northern Hemisphere).

739. Ibid., 8.
740. Ibid., 14.

Interglacial interludes such as the present one – which have been recurring with a periodicity of the order of 100,000 years – have tended to last for 10-20,000 years, and for the remaining time ice sheets have covered up to three times as much of the planet's surface as today. The last time the Earth enjoyed such a benign climate was some 120,000 years ago.[741]

By comparison with most of the last three million years of Pleistocene iciness, therefore, the present interglacial interlude, which began about 10,000 years ago, has been the exception rather than the rule, an oasis of mildness within a desert of ice. Within an even longer-term context, by contrast, the planet has been significantly colder during the few million years of the Pleistocene Ice Age than for the greater part of its existence as a whole. There are currently thought to have been four major periods of severe glaciation prior to the Pleistocene: the Archaean 2.9 billion years ago, the Early Proterozoic 2.4 to 2.2 billion years ago, the Late Proterozoic 850 to 630 million years ago, and the Permo-Carboniferous between 340 and 260 million years ago.[742] Yet there is no sign of an ice age at any point in the 1.4 billion years between the Early and Late Proterozoic ice events, the almost inconceivably vast stretch of time during which early life evolved to incorporate the highly sophisticated, though still unicellular, eukaryotic organisms endowed with cellular nuclei and a complex internal structure.

The Earth's ice ages prior to the Pleistocene may have been few and far between, but when they did come they are thought to have been big ones. The Late Proterozoic Ice Age – also known as the Cryogenian Period as well as the "Snowball Earth" – has been a particular focus of scientific debate in recent years. Possibly the most pervasively cold period of them all (with average surface temperatures falling as low as –50°C), the Cryogenian world is believed by some to have frozen over in its entirety, which means a thick layer of ice covering not only the continental landmasses but the whole ocean too. Others speak of a Slushball Earth, which allows for the persistence of ice-free waters in the vicinity of the Equator. Any theoretical model for the Cryogenian glaciation(s) is restricted by two vital factors: there must be a way out of the scenario (i.e. the ice age must come to an

741. For an overview of the planet's climate history, see ibid., 1-14.
742. See ibid., 141-63.

end),[743] and life itself – still limited to unicellular marine organisms – must not be completely wiped out either. Proponents of the Snowball Earth have proposed various possible "refugia," including hydrothermal vents, small temporary pools warmed by volcanic heat, and areas where the ice is thin enough to admit the light necessary for photosynthesis. Yet however it came about, the end of the deep freeze seems to have heralded a period of remarkable evolutionary diversification, as multicellular organisms came on the scene and increased in size and complexity, first the mysterious soft-bodied *Ediacarans* and then – possibly after another glacial event – the "Cambrian explosion" of creatures by now proudly sporting shells, skeletons and carapaces. Possible links between ice ages and evolutionary surges have been posited, but remain a matter of surmise and speculation. Might such periods of glaciation in some sense have given evolution just the kick up the backside it needed to end up producing da Vinci, Newton and Einstein?

Norse mythology knew that life started with melting ice. According to the myth of creation, life began when the grim cold of Niflheim (later the land of the dead) met the flaming warmth of Muspell. The opposing forces of ice and fire combined to generate the earliest animated beings, first the primeval giant Ymir (who engendered the race of frost-giants) and then Audhumla the Cow, who licked the first man out of salty blocks of ice.[744] Perhaps modern humans emerged from the cold of the Pleistocene in the same way?

Beyond question is that hominid evolution has coincided in extraordinary measure with the three million years of the Pleistocene Ice Age, which has witnessed a threefold increase in brain size. It has been speculated that the global cooling – and above all the accompanying increase in aridity – led to decisive changes in vegetation in tropical Africa, with shrinking forests and expanding grasslands compelling hominids to descend from the trees and become fully bipedal ground-dwellers in order

743. The difficulty is that in a period of global glaciation the low temperatures would be maintained by the high albedo or reflectivity of the snow and ice, which would throw back much of the solar energy required to warm the planet back up. The most likely escape mechanism is the accumulation of the greenhouse gas carbon dioxide as a result of volcanic activity (in the absence of the photosynthesis and chemical weathering of rocks that normally remove carbon dioxide from the atmosphere). Concentration levels several hundred times greater than at present would have been necessary to thaw the planet out.
744. Scott Littleton, 276-79.

to survive. No longer needed for tree-climbing duties, hominid hands were thus freed for communication, tool-making and the axe-throwing that was essential to hunting activities.[745] More recently, a short sharp cold snap such as the Younger Dryas, which lasted for some 1,200 years starting 12,800 years ago, will not only have caused hunger and suffering, but also been a spur to migration and human resourcefulness, just as the inclement climate of the "Little Ice Age"[746] from 1300 to 1850 is thought by some to have resulted not only in famine and disease, but also by extension social unrest, dissent and possibly innovation. Ice may thus have functioned as a dynamic or driving force in pre-human and human development. It has also had others sorts of repercussions. The spectacularly rich soils produced by the trituration of the landscape under the weight of huge ice sheets are believed to have provided the basis for the agriculture on which modern civilization has depended.[747]

In these terms ice may be regarded as an agent of change and vitality, gouging out the evolutionary channel that has led to good or bad old *Homo sapiens*. Alternatively, perhaps, it might be argued that it is only the *end* of ice – the ensuing thaw – that makes life possible. More typical, and perhaps more fundamental, is the association of ice with stasis and immobility, its ability to arrest time. Like salt, indeed, ice not only kills but preserves, slowing down processes of organic decay and seemingly freezing the flow of time just as the White Witch of Narnia froze disobedient subjects. What in Narnia was clearly intended as a punishment, however, in fact amounts to a form of cryonics, for when magically brought back to life the icy statues are unchanged by time – and have rather conveniently avoided all the nastiness of the witch's reign. The theme of cryopreservation is a staple of science fiction, where it also serves as a mode of time travel (as in Woody Allen's comedy *Sleeper*). The service of freezing[748] a dead person's body – or just the brain – in liquid

745. On the possible links between ice ages and evolution, see Macdougall, 187-211.
746. Not strictly speaking an ice age, the "Little Ice Age" was in fact a cooler interlude within the current interglacial thaw. Some climatologists restrict its duration to the period between 1600 and 1800.
747. Without the productive soils composed of glacier-ground dust, suggests William Bryant Logan, "we would still be hunting and gathering in small bands" (*Dirt*, 36).
748. The word "freezing" is misleading: in fact, the idea is to use cryoprotect-ants to minimize the formation of ice crystals – and the damage this causes – even at extremely low temperatures. This is known as vitrification. Strictly speaking, therefore, it is the cold that preserves, not the act of freezing.

nitrogen in the hope that medical science might one day be able to bring it back to life is currently available in the United States, but the process is at present irreversible, and is likely to remain so in the near future.

A limited and usually involuntary form of cryopreservation has long since been provided by natural glaciers. A 5,300-year-old human body, tattoos still intact, was in 1991 disgorged from the melting ice of a retreating Alpine glacier, and mountain literature abounds with tales of ill-fated climbers found months or years after their death, seemingly in a state of suspended animation. Disconcerting though it is, the deglaciation currently taking place around the globe has provided a field day for archaeologists, throwing up whole animals, hunting tools, bones and "fresh-frozen animal dung" and thus providing a wealth of information about the flora and fauna of the past. Even by Agassiz's time, a number of specimens of the long-extinct woolly mammoth had been found in the melting ice of Siberia and Alaska, well enough preserved for polar bears to feed on them as they emerged from their several-thousand-year deep freeze.[749]

Yet organic material is not the only thing stored and preserved in ice. Hundreds of thousands of years of changing atmospheric conditions

749. See Macdougall, 11, 37. While 19th-century polar bears were benefiting from the capacity of ice to preserve mammoth meat that would have otherwise gone the way of all (unfrozen) flesh, the citizens of 19th-century North America too were enthusiastically using ice as a way of preserving their meat and milk products, as well as icing their drinks and making ice cream. Even prior to the 19th century, Alpine ice had provided refrigeration for Mediterranean towns, and snow from the Andes had been sold in Lima. European and North American ice-houses, however, had tended to be a privilege of the exceptionally well-heeled. Yet as Gavin Weightman recounts in *The Frozen Water Trade*, ice – cut from lakes and rivers in winter and stored in ice-houses insulated with sawdust – came to be big business in 19th-century North America. The harvested ice was "shipped down the eastern seaboard and carried across the continent in insulated railroad cars to satisfy the ever-growing demands of the first nation in history to enjoy refrigeration not as a luxury for the rich but as an everyday necessity for a very wide section of its population" (xv). According to official statistics, some eight million tons were harvested annually by 1879, five million of which were estimated to reach the consumer (see ibid., xix). The biggest market was New York, which right through to 1907 was entirely reliant on natural ice gathered from rivers and ponds. It was only with the increase in river pollution and the rise of "artificial" ice produced by steam-driven industrial refrigerators, and subsequently domestic fridges, that the natural ice industry went into terminal decline. For a description of the ice industry, see also Thoreau, *Walden*, 342-45.

are recorded in the layers of snow that have turned into glacial ice, and at the Vostok research station in Antarctica more than 420,000 years of the planet's meteorological memory have already been deciphered. The chemical properties of the ice crystals – the proportions of the various isotopes of hydrogen and oxygen – provide a record of the fluctuations in local temperature at the time of their formation; particles of dust transported and deposited by long bygone winds remain embedded in the ice, lending themselves to analysis; and tiny bubbles of trapped air allow scientists to study the composition of the prehistoric atmosphere. In this sense ice sheets constitute a form of global deep memory, adding a further dimension to the idea of the world's waters as a planetary unconscious.[750]

Until recently, the consensus among scientists, based on extrapolation from the past, was that the present mild interlude would soon end and a return of the ice sheets was imminent (geologically speaking). Global warming, caused by man-produced emissions of the greenhouse gas carbon dioxide, has changed all that. The current worry is that the global defrosting or thaw that is already clearly underway might rapidly swell to calamitous proportions, producing inundations of an order hitherto unknown in human experience. The melting of the Greenland ice sheet would in itself lead to a rise in sea level of six or seven metres. The Antarctic ice will take longer to disappear, but experts are particularly concerned about the West Antarctic ice sheet, which – if it were to collapse into the sea – could also produce a rapid global rise of four or five metres. Positive feedback could exacerbate matters. The massive loss of ice and snow will reduce the Earth's reflectivity and cause even more solar energy to be absorbed. The methane released by the possible melting of the planet's vast supply of methane hydrate – a solid form of water that contains high concentrations of methane and is plentiful in the permafrost of Siberia and Alaska as well as in the seafloor sediments of the continental shelf – is an even more powerful greenhouse gas than carbon dioxide and would trap even more of the sun's energy in the atmosphere.[751]

750. Macdougall, 164-86.
751. Analyses of the air bubbles trapped in the Antarctic ice of the last few hundred thousand years – the planet's glacial "memory" – have shown both methane and carbon dioxide to have been particularly abundant in warmer periods, even before human activity had had any significant impact (see Kandel, 79). The tangled question of causality – what is cause and what is effect? – is of course more difficult to unravel. Geologists have also proposed a possible causal link between sudden releases of methane from methane hydrate and abrupt temperature increases in the more distant past, including the Eocene greenhouse event

In fact, the most important greenhouse gas of all is water vapour, for increased temperatures will lead to increases in evaporation and humidity (an even thicker blanket of cloud covering the planet like a duvet in summer), trapping even more infrared radiation within the planet's atmosphere. A certain amount of greenhouse insulation is vital for life on Earth: without it, the planet would lose the sun's energy almost as quickly as it acquired it, leaving the world a much colder place, with average temperatures of −18°C.[752] The problem, as Robert Kandel explains, is that what he calls the "anthropogenic intensification" of the carbon dioxide greenhouse effect will ultimately upset the hydrological cycle in ways we can at present hardly conceive:

> Up to now, only relatively weak warming has occurred, but if major warming takes place, it will be because humans will have perturbed the water cycle by way of CO_2 and in particular because the conditions of evaporation and condensation of water will have changed. … Most specialists believe that reinforcement of the greenhouse effect and global warming will be accompanied by acceleration of the hydrological cycle, with both evaporation and precipitation being enhanced.[753]

The water cycle is in danger of careering hopelessly out of control. This is because it is being ridden by a blindfolded maniac.

If all the world's remaining glaciers were to melt, the sea level would rise by at least 70 metres, submerging densely populated coastal areas and lowlands. Glacial thaws in the past have been devastating. Geological evidence of the flooding associated with the thaw of the Pleistocene glaciers, which occurred mainly between 15,000 and 10,000 years ago, suggests some extraordinary scenarios. In his work on the Channeled Scablands of eastern Washington, the geologist J. Harlan Bretz came to

---

some 55 million years ago (see Macdougall, 241-42) and possibly even the devastating Permian extinction event. A surge in global temperatures, it is thought, could have warmed the oceans, thawed out the methane hydrate, and caused the gas to burst forth into the atmosphere in a Gargantuan "ocean burp." Mark Lynas suggests that methane hydrate explosions could more or less wipe out terrestrial life: "Major oceanic methane eruptions could release energy equivalent to 10,000 times the world's stockpile of nuclear weapons." See Lynas, "Six Steps to Hell," in *The Guardian*, 23 April 2007.

752. Macdougall, 234.

753. Kandel, 249-50; also 253.

realize that he was dealing with a landscape that had itself been shaped not by ice but by an unimaginably large flood, a sudden discharge of water now assumed to be from the thawing glacial Lake Missoula. It was "a volume of flowing water so immense that it had eaten its way through hundreds of meters of loess, cut channels in solid basalt, and thrown up gravel bars so large that they made those of even the largest present-day rivers look positively Lilliputian."[754] Estimates are that as much as ten million cubic metres of water per second – more than 30 cubic kilometres an hour – raced across the landscape, a release of water more than ten times greater than what is today discharged into the ocean by all the world's rivers in conjunction. There is evidence for other such melt-water "superfloods" in Sweden, Canada and Siberia, the Siberian inundation possibly rivalling Lake Missoula's in magnitude. Some scholars attribute the near-universal tale of the deluge to the collective memory of cataclysmic inundations that have taken place as a result of the 120-metre rise in sea-level over the few thousand years since the Pleistocene's last glacial maximum. It has been posited that the Biblical flood had its origins some 7,600 years ago in the sudden flooding of what is now the Black Sea following a breakthrough of the rising waters of the Mediterranean.[755] Traditionally associated with spring, hope and new life, the sound of melting ice and thawing snow may itself take on apocalyptic dimensions.

754. Macdougall, 92; on Bretz and the Channeled Scablands, see 89-114.
755. See Kandel, 270, 278.

Chapter Four
Water as Purity and Panacea

1

Cleanness and Sanitation

Reflecting the underlying ambivalence of water, both salt and ice may be associated not only with death and destruction, but also with life and creation. The nature of water as the universal solvent further underlines this ambiguity. The peculiar chemical structure of water molecules endows them with a capacity not only to bring other atoms and molecules together, but also to rip them apart. It is water that transports nutrients into living cell, and water that then removes the waste. It plays a vital part in combining and chemically breaking down proteins and carbohydrates. All the biochemical processes essential to metabolism take place in water.

Water can perform these functions because of what seems like an inner aversion to purity. Even rainwater – water that is newly distilled by the processes of evaporation, condensation and precipitation – may well contain traces of radioactive material, sulphuric acid from industrial pollution or volcanic activity, as well as the carbonic acid produced when it dissolves carbon dioxide from the atmosphere. Surface and groundwater is likely to be a solution comprising not only sulphates, chlorides, and bicarbonates of sodium and potassium, but also the mineral salts and gases that provide it with its characteristic taste. Humans provide a constant supply of pesticides, industrial by-products and often untreated domestic waste. Given half a chance, water has a natural tendency to pick up "stuff" and transport it somewhere else. Just for the hell of it. Though the nutrients it carries may be the foodstuffs of a living organism, they may equally well be toxins or pollutants. Water can vivify and fructify, but also kill and envenom. Protean as ever, water is cheerfully indiscriminate in what it dissolves and the identity it thereby adopts.

Contaminated water – i.e. water harmful to human beings – is responsible for 80 per cent of all diseases and a third of all the deaths in the developing countries.[756] Excessive concentrations of fluoride are slowly poisoning millions of people in India; in Bangladesh traces of naturally occurring arsenic originally from the rocks of the Himalayans are envenoming tens of millions more in what the World Health Organization has called "the largest mass poisoning of a population in history."[757] Water propagates and disseminates parasites such as bilharzia and hookworm, bacterial diseases such as cholera and typhoid, as well as mosquito-transmitted scourges such as malaria and dengue fever. As early as the 17th century, the Dutch lens-grinder Antony van Leeuwenhoek peered at a drop of water through the newly improved microscope he had devised and found it to be pullulating with a whole array of what he called "animalcules," known to modern science as micro-organisms, bacteria or even germs. Van Leeuwenhoek calculated that there were more than eight million such creatures in one drop of pond water. A bead of water may host a microscopic metropolis[758] – not necessarily to the advantage of the thirsty macro-organism who happens to imbibe it.

In addition to mineral salts, organic compounds and bacteria, naturally occurring water also contains a small amount of what is loosely

756. Ball, *H₂O*, 315.
757. Pearce, 74. On the fluoride and arsenic disasters in India and Bangladesh, see 72-78; Caldecott, 161-63.
758. Many of van Leeuwenhoek's contemporaries were unconvinced, but the animalcules did exist. A bizarre parody of van Leeuwenhoek's discovery occurs in Hans Christian Andersen's tale "The Drop of Water," written well over a century later. This begins: "You are familiar, of course, with a magnifying glass, a round spectacle lens that makes everything a hundred times larger than it is. When you hold it up to your eye and look at a drop of water from the pond, you can see more than a thousand strange creatures that are otherwise never seen in the water, but they are there and it is real. It looks almost like a saucer full of shrimps frisking about one another, and they are so gluttonous that they tear arms and legs and bottoms and edges off one another – and yet they are happy and contented in their own fashion" (*Fairy Tales*, 212). When the inquisitive Mr Wiggle-Waggle, disconcerted by all the hacking and biting, shows the drop to a passing troll, the latter suggests it must be Copenhagen or some other big city. The narrator agrees: "It really did look like a whole city, where all the people ran about with no clothes on."

known as "heavy water" or deuterium oxide (D_2O), as well as minute traces of tritium oxide (T_2O).[759] Though chemically very similar, heavy water lacks the life-giving magic of "light" water and fails to sustain biological systems such as plants and animals. While it would take several days of ingesting nothing but pure heavy water for its toxicity to be noticed (which effectively rules it out as a first-choice poison), it has come to be associated with the threat of more wanton mass-destruction on account of its use in certain types of nuclear reactor, where it functions not as a fuel but as a neutron moderator in the fission of uranium. Light water can also perform this function, but heavy water has acquired a special strategic importance in nuclear power generation – with the concomitant threat of nuclear-weapon proliferation – because whereas the use of light water requires *enriched* uranium and calls for specific uranium-enrichment facilities, heavy-water reactors can employ natural or unenriched uranium, considerably simplifying the process. Heavy water is also a source of the deuterium which – in conjunction with tritium – is the essential component of so-called hydrogen bombs, i.e. the much more powerful thermonuclear weapons based on nuclear *fusion* as opposed to fission.[760] Industrial quantities of heavy water – in the "wrong" hands – thus tend to be viewed with suspicion or trepidation.

The easy or intuitive association of purity with nature and goodness thus proves rather problematic. Even the "purest" of water is not quite H_2O, and even water's most "natural" manifestations contain the seeds of death within their atomic structure. At the same time, water's inherent impurity – its compulsive aversion to being unadulterated – has been essential to the development life on Earth, making it the natural medium

759. Deuterium is a heavier isotope of hydrogen. In other words, its atoms comprise not only a proton and an electron (like regular hydrogen), but also a neutron; tritium has two neutrons. In fact, more common in naturally occurring water is "semiheavy water" (HDO), where one of the water atoms is regular hydrogen and the other is deuterium: one molecule in 3,200 takes this form (i.e. one atom in 6,400 is deuterium).
760. The idea of nuclear fusion is that deuterium (and tritium) atoms fuse to form helium, releasing neutrons and nuclear energy in the process. While nuclear fission involving the splitting of uranium also constitutes a major source of power for non-military purposes, attempts to exploit the fusion of deuterium and tritium as a peaceful form of energy-generation have proved more problematic and at present remain unviable. The main drawback is that extreme heat and pressure are required to get the process going.

for all biochemical reactions. Moreover, the fact that water contains not only solids but gases – a litre of water holds as much as 19 millilitres of air at "room temperature" (20°C)[761] – is a precondition for the respiration of aquatic animals such as fish, molluscs and crustaceans, which use the dissolved oxygen to burn carbohydrates and produce the energy that keeps them alive.[762] The waters of the ocean also contain some 50 times more carbon dioxide than the atmosphere, and absorb between 30 and 40 per cent of what is generated by humankind, acting like a gigantic sponge or storehouse that regulates the planet's greenhouse gases.[763]

Indeed, water is often valued for its very impurities, dissolved minerals lending it therapeutic properties and an agreeable taste. The "purest" water is distilled water, which in principle has had more or less all its impurities removed through the process of distillation. Though relatively few people bother to drink the stuff, it does have its advocates and its committed imbibers. Such people argue that distilled water is not only free of all the harmful bacteria, viruses, organic compounds, minerals and heavy metals to which we are otherwise exposed, but itself has an intrinsic propensity to act like a magnet, picking up and removing our own discarded minerals on its way through the body. An even more powerful solvent than in its "impure" form, distilled water is thus more effective in cleansing the body of toxins. Opponents counter that not only does it lack any beneficial minerals in its own right, but its tendency to dissolve whatever crosses its path causes it to "leach" vital minerals from the body. Besides, add the proponents (or perhaps the marketing agents) of mineral water, it tastes bland and insipid. But isn't that like blaming tap water for being colourless?

Distilled water seems to be strangely free from the mythical or symbolic associations of "pure" water. So too, for that matter, does tap water, our common-or-garden piped drinking water. Perhaps it is because the public authorities now establish and enforce rigorous standards to ensure its *potability*: the European Commission lists more than a hundred parameters in its norms on water quality, including "not only turbidity (cloudiness) and microbiological parameters but also acidity (pH), radioactivity, nitrate contents, different metals, minerals, dissolved gases,

761. Kandel, 5.
762. The oxygen is commonly inhaled through gills or gill-like structures; in the case of jellyfish, by contrast, the oxygen simply filters into their body through the skin. Most micro-organisms also need oxygen.
763. See Stow, "Climate Control," in *New Internationalist*, (Jan / Feb 2007), 17-19.

pesticides, etc."[764] Perhaps it is the very fact that it has been "treated" that in some sense sullies it.

Underground water in ancient aquifers, by contrast, may have been isolated from the atmosphere – and thus from the hydrological cycle in general and human contact in particular – for thousands or even millions of years.[765] Sources and wellsprings emerging from such subterranean seclusion are clearly more likely to evoke notions of purity, though here of course there is no guarantee that their own specific concoction of dissolved minerals and metals does not include excessive traces of some toxin such as fluoride or arsenic. In fact, the enormous symbolic import of the (in places) shockingly contaminated waters of the Narmada or the Ganges clearly has little to do with their purity or the lack of it – i.e. their actual chemical composition or the minerals and effluent they may contain – and much more to do with the universal imagery of flow, renewal and revitalization they embody. The concept of "purity" is misleading, therefore, for purity depends upon fixity of identity ($H_2O = H_2O$), whereas the waters of a river are too protean to be limited by the simplistic Manichean dichotomy of pure versus impure; their sacredness transcends any such straitjacket. Or rather, perhaps, the purity of water should be understood not as a state or condition (i.e. as something static), but as a verb, an action or a dynamic process. This would explain the symbolic significance of water not as something clean or pure, but as cleansing or purifying.

This is evident in water's obvious capacity to rinse off or remove dirt and carry it away in its flow. Yet the detritus is not just unceremoniously dumped somewhere else. The bacteria contained by river water, for example, themselves purify the flow, rapidly biodegrading or breaking down organic waste such as faecal matter. Much of what is contained in domestic sewage decomposes within a matter of days or weeks. Paradoxically, it is water's impurities (its bacteria) that keep it clean. Water's constant flux is a process of ongoing self-transformation, and the Ganges in particular is reputed to have extraordinary powers of self-purification. Lake Baiyangdian, the largest lake in northern China, is commonly known as the "Kidney of North China" for its capacity to cleanse the region's waters.[766] In a process of virtuous circularity, water cleans water (cleans water (cleans water))….

764. Kandel, 202.
765. See ibid., 167-68.
766. Caldecott, 97.

Water's renewability is reinforced by the hydrological cycle, the atmospheric part of which acts like a still, returning an annual total of roughly half a million cubic kilometres of water to the planet's surface freshly purged of the dirt and debris it contained before it was evaporated. Or so it would if water did not have an almost neurotic obsession with picking up new particles and gases and in the process performing the invaluable task of cleaning the *atmosphere* of pollutants and contaminants. Without precipitation, writes expert cloud-gazer Gavin Pretor-Pinney, "the atmosphere would be unspeakably hazy, acrid and – certainly in the temperate regions of the world – deadly."[767] The reason water is virtually always soiled is that it simply cannot resist doing the planetary housework. The world's system of flowing water has thus been characterized as its "inbuilt self-cleansing system" and its "inbuilt laundry and washing up system."[768]

The world's waters are not only self-cleansing, therefore, but also Earth-cleansing. Yet this self-regulating laundry arrangement is at present being seriously overloaded by anthropogenic dirt. Humankind is collectively dumping its load more prodigally than ever, annually depositing six billion metric tons of domestic waste and ten billion tons of sewage sludge – quite apart from all its other agricultural and industrial toxins and poisons – into the world's waters. Of course, rivers have always been dumping grounds for human filth, with downstream water-users condemned to imbibe the waste of those lucky enough to dwell upstream. The Thames is a case in point. The river was used as a public sewer even in Roman times, and in the Middle Ages the public privy on London Bridge discharged its contents directly into the waters below. Five men met their Maker when it finally collapsed into the Thames in 1481.[769] Particularly notorious was the River Fleet, a tributary of the Thames that had always attracted refuse and waste and by the late 16th century had turned into an open sewer. The river's stench was immortalized in Ben Jonson's poem "The Voyage Itself" (1610), which described its "merd-urinous load,"[770]

767. Pretor-Pinney, 167. Just over an inch of rainfall, he suggests, is "enough to remove around 99 per cent of airborne particles and almost all soluble gases, such as sulphur dioxide, from the part of the atmosphere below."
768. See Black, *Water, Life Force*, 34, 95. See also Black, *The No-Nonsense Guide to Water*, 89.
769. Ackroyd, 270, 140. London Bridge continued to support houses and shops through to 1760.
770. See Ackroyd, 49-51.

while just over a century later Pope's *Dunciad* (1728) sang of its "mud-nymphs": the "nut-brown maids" Lutetia, Nigrina black and Merdamante brown.[771] In Tobias Smollett's epistolary novel *The Expedition of Humphry Clinker* (1771), the Thames is the butt of one of Matthew Bramble's satirical outbursts: "Human excrement is the least offensive part of the concrete," he complains in a letter to his doctor, "which is composed of all the drugs, minerals, and poisons, used in mechanics and manufacture, enriched with the putrefying carcases of beasts and men."[772]

With a steadily rising population, however, things were to get worse before they got better. The quality of Thames water continued to decline in the 19th century. A famous cartoon dating from 1827, entitled "MONSTER SOUP commonly called THAMES WATER," recalled van Leeuwenhoek's drop of water with its animalcules, only now the animalcules had turned into "hydras and gorgons and chimeras dire."[773] During the "Great Stink" of 1858 the *City Press* declared: "Gentility of speech is at an end – it [the Thames] stinks; and whoso once inhales the stink can never forget it and can count himself lucky if he live to remember it."[774] In the same year a satirical illustration in *Punch* portrayed a hideous Father Thames introducing his three children, Diphtheria, Scrofula and Cholera, to an aloof-looking Fair City of London. In 1851 the magazine had described the Thames as the "Great Tidal Drain," while in a letter to *The Times* Michael Faraday complained that it was "a fermenting sewer."[775]

Of course, the problem was by no means restricted to London. Even in villages or smaller towns, it was common for privies to be built over brooks, streams or rivers in order to carry the waste away.[776] The major cities of 19th-century Europe vied with one another in their toe-curling foetor. In his poem on Cologne, Samuel Taylor Coleridge famously claimed to discern "two and seventy stenches" in the city,

771. Pope, *The Dunciad*, ll. 333-34; in *Collected Poems*, 146. Lutetia was the ancient name for Paris, meaning mudland or quagmire (from Latin *lutus*). In Roman times Paris was a collection of mud-hovels, and the Parisians were known as "frogs."
772. Smollett, *The Expedition of Humphry Clinker*, 120.
773. Ackroyd, 251.
774. Quoted in Carter, *Flushed: How the Plumber Saved Civilization*, 98-99.
775. See Eveleigh, *Bogs, Baths and Basins: The Story of Domestic Sanitation*, 35; Faraday quoted in Ball, *H₂O*, 313.
776. See Eveleigh, 8-9, on the riparian privies in 19th-century Bristol and two Somerset villages.

All well-defined – and several stinks.
Ye nymphs, that reign o'er sewers and sinks,
The river Rhine, it is well-known,
Does wash your city of Cologne.
But tell me, Nymphs, what power divine
Shall henceforth wash the River Rhine?[777]

As late as 1970, the German weekly *Die Welt* declared the Rhine "Germany's largest sewer,"[778] and until the 1960s half the sewage from the Parisian system was dumped untreated into the Seine. Moscow was still discharging almost all of its sewage, untreated, into the Moscow River in the 1980s.[779] Today it is the poorer cities of the developing world that lack the resources to construct sanitation systems. In Manila, untreated sewage accounts for some 70 per cent of the volume of the Pasig River.[780]

If the world's rivers resemble the drains of a swarming megalopolis, it is no wonder that the seas have been described as the "universal sewer." Until recently – where possible – even the rich countries of Europe dumped the sludge from their sewage treatment straight into the waters of the ocean, though a European Commission directive has now made this illegal. Coastal cities in poorer countries continue to release their sewage into the sea untreated, making bathing a health hazard and causing untold damage to nearby aquatic ecosystems. And on top of this there is the agricultural and industrial pollution, the military dumping, the oil spills, radioactive waste, heavy metals, non-degradable plastics and general marine litter.[781] Water's mythological power stems from its capacity for self-regeneration and renewal and the concomitant self-regulatory cleansing of the Earth. But human civilization is doing its level best to clog the whole system up.

777. Coleridge, *The Complete Poems*, 399.
778. *Die Welt*, 6 Nov 1970, quoted in Blackbourn, 324.
779. Ponting, 350.
780. Ibid., 351.
781. It is common to talk of an enormous field of plastic debris "as big as Texas" in the central gyre of the North Pacific. Composed of billions of bags, balls, bottles, dolls, nets, floats and limitless fragments of "plastic confetti," it has been described as a "plastic soup." In fact, the reference to a Texas-sized area is misleading. Disdaining boundaries, it extends throughout the gyre and ends up inside fish, turtles, sea birds and cetaceans much further afield. See Anna Cummins, "Sea of Garbage," in *New Internationalist* (Sept. 2008), 14-16; also Caldecott, 66-67.

*   *   *   *   *

Leonardo da Vinci and others have seen the waters of the world as the planet's lifeblood. Conversely, the human body is itself a moulded river, a channelled flow of water. River-like, our life comprises the maintenance and renewal of form and shape in conjunction with an exchange of matter. For our continued existence, it is vital for us to ensure that a regular supply of water enters the aqueous river-channel or conduit that constitutes our body and that a regular release of water subsequently removes our wastes. The two aspects of this exchange with our environment are closely bound up: waste must flow out, and there must be a "clean" inflow to replace what is expelled. As in all animals and plants that have shifted from aquatic to terrestrial existence, one of our most basic concerns is the threat of desiccation or dehydration. We need water – an average of two and a half litres a day in our food and drink – in order to avoid drying out: without it we are unlikely to survive more than a few days. Though the human skin is waterproof, the body's waters constantly leak and flow through its various orifices,[782] making replenishment essential. A net loss of more than 15 per cent of our body's water is likely to prove fatal.

Such leakage – whether through urine, faeces, sweat, tears or breath[783] – is indispensable to our internal cleansing. This is most obviously the case with the waters that we pass as urine, which is the body's way of

782. According to Robert Gardner (quoted in Marks, *The Holy Order of Water*, 186), our total daily water leakage amounts to some 2.75 litres, comprising about 1.7 litres in urine, 150 millilitres in faeces, 400 millilitres in exhaled breath, and 500 millilitres in sweat. This is replaced by 1.65 litres of water from drink, 750 millilitres taken from food, and 350 millilitres further released by the oxidation of food.
783. On the water in our exhalations, see Pretor-Pinney, 34: "The air we breathe is always packed with water vapour. Our bodies make sure that it is, since our moist bronchial tubes are designed to stop dust and pollution getting into our lungs." Over four per cent of the warm air we exhale is water vapour, which is why a cold window-pane clouds over when we breathe on it. Sneezing, or sternutation, is a more explosive way of getting rid of irritants from inside the nose. See Rupp, 153.

expelling the toxic ammonia (a combination of nitrogen and hydrogen) formed in the metabolism of protein. By converting it into soluble urea and uric acid, the body can flush its unwanted nitrogen out of the system in a solution that is 96 per cent water. In some animals, the urine also contains odoriferous chemicals such as pheromones that announce claims to territory or sexual availability, but the human sense of smell has been so repressed that visual signals tend to figure more than pheromonal whiffs and pongs in our social and sexual decision-making. Human urine is not usually valued for the subtleties and hidden implications of its bouquet.

In fact, it is generally laden with connotations of defilement: there is a time and place for pissing, and it is usually well out of the public eye. Saliva and sweat, especially when they emanate from strangers, also tend to provoke distaste or revulsion. Our bodily waste waters must always go through the official channels. In an emotionally buttoned-up society, even tears – though currently fashionable – generally call for regulation and must be restrained if thought to be inappropriate. Like other forms of gushing water,[784] tears have an immediate cleansing function, rinsing and bathing the eyes and washing away dust or dirt. However, they also enjoy a special association with the "higher" faculties – as opposed to lowly digestion or procreation – which perhaps explains why they are rarely considered a pollutant or contaminant. As a product of laughter or weeping, tears have commonly been seen as a sort of "psychological" overflow, releasing pent-up emotions and leaving us all the healthier in the process. According to the ancient Greek *Tractatus Coislinianus*, a text thought by some to be a summary of Aristotle's lost poetics on comedy, both tragedy and comedy are cathartic in nature, using representations of real events to move us to tears or laughter and purge us of an emotional overload.[785] Outside the theatre too, the shedding of tears can be a release and a relief. This image of tears as a form of emotional waste-removal or sanitation may be more than just a metaphor. According to Desmond Morris, "chemical analysis of tears produced by distress and those produced by irritation to the surface of the eyes has revealed that the two liquids spilling down the face contain different proteins. The suggestion is that emotional weeping

784. In Henry Fielding's 18th-century parody *Tom Thumb*, the King asks his tearful wife, "Whence flow those Tears fast down thy blubber'd Cheeks, / Like a swoln Gutter, gushing through the streets?" (Act One, Scene Two).
785. See Aristotle, *Poetics I* (trans. R. Janko), xxiii.

is primarily a way of ridding the body of excess stress chemicals."[786] The function of tears, no less than urine, is to eliminate waste matter from the human system.

The 19th-century public-health reformer Edwin Chadwick influentially formulated the analogy between the individual organism and the city in terms of the water passing through them. Appalled by the sanitary squalor that was swamping London, Chadwick came to understand urban space as something akin to a body which required water to be constantly flowing through it, washing it of its excrement, filth and waste and leaving it again as sewage. He realized that the city's health and wellbeing depended on establishing the appropriate channels for bringing water in and getting waste out, which meant constant piped water, house drains and an efficient system of mains sewerage. Without the ceaseless flow of water through the city's network of pipes, urban space could only stagnate and fester. Chadwick is said to have "redefined the city by 'discovering' its need to be constantly washed."[787]

Chadwick was by no means the first to have such ideas. In the third millennium BCE the ancient Harappan civilization of the Indus river valley was already constructing water systems that equalled or surpassed any other prior to the Victorian era. Not only was every house within the city walls provided with a bathroom and indoor plumbing, but it was the first known culture to develop a system that permitted its citizens to defecate in the comfort of their own home and have the waste washed away to Somewhere Else. This consisted of a simple hole in the floor that opened into the brick drain that came from the bath. The collected sewage in turn flowed into a cesspit that emptied into a system of sizeable sewer mains, which dumped the wastewater in the river outside the city walls.

The Romans too recognized the vital importance of water that *flowed*, building luxurious baths and a great system of brimming aqueducts

786. Morris, 56. The fact that we are the only primate to weep has also been interpreted as support for the aquatic ape hypothesis; seals and sea otters also shed tears in situations of acute distress. The idea is that the shedding of tears in humans, seals and sea otters could be a "by-product of the improved eye-cleaning function of tears in mammals that have returned to the sea. ... If man went through an aquatic phase several million years ago, stepped up his tear production in response to prolonged exposure to sea water and then returned to dry land as a savannah hunter, he might well retain his tearful eyes, exploiting emotional weeping as a new social signal" (ibid., 55).
787. Illich, 45. On Chadwick see also Eveleigh, xv-xvi.

that by 97 CE was bringing the city 100 gallons a day per capita from the Apennines, ten times more than the inhabitants of London, Paris or Frankfurt were getting in 1936.[788] Essential to the Roman project was the water's constant motion: the proud and mighty empire could bring fresh water from 50 miles away and flush it through the city and into the Tiber with unprecedented prodigality. Yet the hydraulic prowess and ostentation was not without its drawbacks: most of the water was appropriated by the privileged; municipal hygiene in general was poor; indeed, the Romans only needed their magnificent aqueducts because they had already polluted the Tiber. The aqueducts, it has been suggested, "represent not the intelligence but the utter environmental mismanagement of the great Romans."[789]

The most demanding users of the water brought by the aqueducts were the baths, both the functional but well-loved *balneum* of the Republic and the ever more extravagant *thermae* of Imperial times. The decline of the Empire saw the decline of aqueducts and baths alike and a radical shift in attitudes to water that would pervade much of western society right through to the 18th century. Particularly in the early years of Christianity, the public baths of Roman civilization came to be regarded as places of dissolution and lechery. Keen to deny themselves such worldly pleasures, Christians and philosophers bathed only once or twice a month in these "cathedrals of paganism" and cultivated a grubby beard as a sign of their austerity.[790] Of course, the change in attitudes to bathing and water was gradual and far from uniform. In the 2nd century, Tertullian declared that taking a bath was indeed compatible with being a Christian, while Clement of Alexandria decreed that it was permissible provided it was not for pleasure but for health (and cleanliness in the case of women); the 4th-century theologian John Chrysostom regarded it, like eating, as one of life's necessities. St Jerome, by contrast, opposed even the most innocent of dips: women were to cultivate unmitigated bodily squalor.[791] In the years following the fall of the Roman Empire, public baths virtually disappeared from western Europe. The Christian aversion to all water except that of baptism became ever stricter, and hermits and saints piously wallowed in their own extreme dirtiness. In his guidelines for monastic life, written in

---

788. Illich, 36-37.
789. Sunita Narain, "Foreword," in Black, *The No-Nonsense Guide to Water*, 5. See also Illich, ibid.
790. See Veyne, "The Roman Empire," in Veyne (ed.), *A History of Private Life: From Pagan Rome to Byzantium*, 198-99.
791. Ashenburg, 55-58.

the third decade of the 6th century, St Benedict decreed that the healthy should never wash, and saints such as St Agnes, St Olympias and St Francis of Assisi are said to have enhanced their sanctity by achieving a state of complete *alousia* ("unwashedness"). Such mortification of the body allowed the soul to soar.[792]

Naturally enough, the availability of clean water and sheer double standards also played a part in practice. Many monasteries were fortunate enough to be provided with a system of running water, and while the common masses had little alternative to the squalor that was preached, religious leaders enjoyed the blessing of hygiene and cleanliness.[793] From the 11th century on, moreover, the Christian aversion to water became rather less rigorous and all-pervasive: personal hygiene ceased to be incompatible with piety, and smelliness was no longer a prerequisite for saintliness. *Ancrene Wisse*, an early 13th-century book of instructions written in English for anchoresses, told aspiring contemplatives: "Wash yourself whenever there is need as often as you want, and your things, too – filth was never dear to God, though poverty and plainness are pleasing."[794] The Crusaders returned home from their holy wars with joyous tidings of the Turkish bath or *hamam*, inspiring the return of public baths to such cities as London, Paris and Florence.[795]

Yet if medieval Christianity was showing signs of wavering in its view of swimming and bathing – like sexual pleasure – as licentious, sinful and devilish, these moralistic associations were soon to receive decisive support from a different direction, namely medical authority. In the wake of the devastation caused across Europe and Asia by the bubonic plague from the mid-14th century on, bathhouses came to be identified with the transmission of disease and infection, and water – especially the warm water of bathing

792. On *alousia* and its proponents, see Ashenburg, 58-63. Notably, their spectacular filthiness did not stop such saints from washing others (including lepers) as a sign of their charity and humility.
793. Islamic civilization avoided such hypocrisy, developing sophisticated public bathing facilities that combined religious, hygienic and social functions. As Katherine Ashenburg points out, "the cleanest corner of early medieval Europe was Arab Spain" (70). The Christian *Reconquista* thus also meant the re-establishment of a reign of no doubt breathtaking hydrophobia (an odour of unwashed piety known as *olor de santidad*). During the Inquisition, to be "known to bathe" was a damning charge levelled against Jews and Moors. Unencumbered by the conflict between Christian virtue and Roman or Arab debauchery, the Russians and Finns of north-eastern Europe were meanwhile developing the steam baths that have come to be known as saunas.
794. Quoted in Ashenburg, 75.
795. See ibid., 78-80.

houses – was seen as a threat to life and limb. As early as 1348, hot baths were cited by the medical advisors of Philippe VI of France as a possible cause of the Black Death, allowing the plague to invade the body by opening the pores of the skin.[796] Writing in 1513, the French doctor Guillaume Bunel exhorted his readers: "Flee sweating-rooms and baths, I beg you, or you will die."[797] The association between water and deathly dissolution reasserted itself with renewed vigour. "Even when a plague did not threaten," writes Katherine Ashenburg, "the porosity of the body made water a threat to the bather, who might contract syphilis or diseases as yet unknown and unnamed, or even become pregnant from sperm floating in the bathwater."[798] The bathhouses had disappeared again by the mid-16th century, and water-fearing dirtiness renewed its grip on the population.

The core of the problem was this natural *porosity* of the human body – the fact that it was not hermetically sealed off from a hostile, watery environment. When the English philosopher Francis Bacon (1561-1626) gave advice on how to take a bath, it entailed a series of the most convoluted precautions for closing the pores (involving oil, salves and a waxed cloth) and keeping the body as tightly sealed as possible.[799] More common, however, was simply to shun the watery element more or less entirely.[800] In the 17th and 18th centuries, warnings against the use of water continued to be commonplace, alleging (among other things) the harm it did to the skin and the increased risk of catching a cold. Well into the 19th century, dirt was even seen – especially

---

796. Ibid., 93-94.
797. Quoted in Elias, *The Civilizing Process*, 531.
798. Ashenburg, 94-95.
799. Ibid., 101. Not until the 1830s did the idea of the skin's respiratory function gain acceptance. The threat of porosity is given forceful expression by Smollett's Matthew Bramble, who describes his revulsion at the communal bathing that took place at Bath. The idea of sharing the waters with a child "full of scrophulous ulcers" he finds particular worrying: "Suppose the matter of those ulcers, floating on the water, comes in contact with my skin, when the pores are all open, I would ask you what must be the consequence? – Good Heaven, the very thought makes my blood run cold! we know not what sores may be running into the water while we are bathing, and what sort of matter we may thus imbibe; the king's evil [scrofula], the scurvy, the cancer, and the pox; and, no doubt, the heat will render the *virus* the more volatile and penetrating" (Smollett, *Humphry Clinker*, 45-46).
800. Even in hydrophobic times, washing hands before meals remained de rigueur: medieval and later manuals of etiquette insisted on it, also instructing readers to keep their fingernails clean and avoid playing with dogs at mealtimes (see Rupp, 67-68).

by the poor – as providing a form of protection, sealing them off from the threat of bodily invasion. According to French peasant wisdom, "people who take baths die young," while "dirt nourishes the hair."[801] A generalized aversion or indifference to water persisted in Victorian and post-Victorian England. Faced with the prospect of being washed on admittance to a workhouse, one man described it as like being robbed "of a great coat which he had had for some years."[802] Many young women from working-class areas believed that washing one's head was dangerous (as a result of which scalp diseases were rampant), and among older miners in 1930s Wigan George Orwell came across a "lingering belief" that washing the legs could cause lumbago.[803] As a London social worker put it in the 1910s, "the people of the neighbourhood do not clamour for facilities for bathing and washing, but when such are there, the fashion for using them steadily increases."[804]

In the 17th and 18th centuries it was *linen* that stepped in to provide a safe and attractive way of keeping clean. The fabric itself was ascribed cleansing, sweat-absorbing properties, and putting on fresh linen was regarded as making washing unnecessary.[805] The 18th-century "toilette," writes Ivan Illich, was "hydrophobic, in no way connected with running water." It referred to a process of "combing, grooming, powdering, applying makeup and perfumed cosmetics, dressing, and then, as a last stage … receiving visitors in the boudoire."[806] The general mistrust of water was matched by a more

---

801. See Ashenburg, 194.
802. Quoted in ibid., 173.
803. See Eveleigh, 160-61.
804. Quoted in Ashenburg, 232.
805. On the 17th-century passion for linen, see ibid., 106-11.
806. Illich, 65. Reinforcing this link with linen, the *toilette* originally referred to the piece of cloth, *toile*, on which the brush, comb and assorted accessories were laid out for use. The current meaning of "toilet" as a device used to carry away human waste stems from the early 20th century, "water closet" being the most widely accepted term in the second half of the 19th century, when the appliance was being given its modern-day form. The use of the term "lavatory" for the WC is relatively recent too, originally designating the washbasin (from the Latin *lavare*, which also gives us latrine and laundry). The Spanish term *wáter* clearly betrays its link with the water closet, while the etymology of the English *loo* has been traced back to the French words both for water (*l'eau*) and for place (*lieu*), in the sense of a place of relief. Yet the most traditional English words are as water-free as the 18th-century *toilette*: cf. the closet (and the German *Klo*), the close stool, the privy or privy-midden (where "midden" means a pile of dung), the necessary or necessary house, and the good old-fashioned bog or bog house. The traditional word "jakes" – echoed in the modern-day

robust, or less squeamish, attitude to smell. Prior to the 19th century, a strong body odour was often considered attractive and a sign of good health. Medieval seductresses presented their favourites with peeled apples (known as "love apples") which they had kept in their armpits until steeped in their sweat.[807] Napoleon famously wrote to tell Josephine not to bathe until he had returned from the field of battle. According to traditionally hydrophobic French peasant wisdom (again), "the more the ram stinks, the more the ewe loves him."[808] Depending on the context, smelliness can be not only saintly but sexy.

The widespread mistrust and antipathy towards water further extended to what was drunk as well as what was used for washing and bathing. One of the reasons that beer was so popular during the Middle Ages was that the purity of drinking water could not always be counted upon, whereas the water of which beer was mainly composed had been boiled as part of the brewing process.[809] As a major source of nutrition as well as safe water, beer was commonly drunk with every meal in the more northern parts of Europe, and during the early days of the Industrial Revolution it was observed that men working in factories – who supped large quantities of beer to slake their thirst – were much less prone to diarrhoea than women, who drank water that was not yet chlorinated or treated. From the 18th century, tea too provided an effective and convenient

---

"john" and suggesting a man's place – perhaps reflects the fact that "ladies" didn't do dirty things like have a crap. Montaigne knew better: "kings and philosophers shit," he pointed out, "and so do ladies." Bowel movements are one of the great levellers (see Montaigne, *Complete Essays*, 1231).

807. Morris, 120. Morris also cites the story of the beautiful young princess Mary of Cleves, whose sweat-soaked chemise was inadvertently used as a face-towel by the Duc d'Anjou (later King Henri III of France), who promptly fell for her pheromones.

808. Ashenburg, 194.

809. The advantages of drinking beer as opposed to water go back to the origins of civilization and the switch from a hunter-gatherer lifestyle to the cultivation of cereals. As Tom Standage puts it, "beer helped to make up for the decline in food quality as people took up farming, provided a safe form of liquid nourishment, and gave groups of beer-drinking farmers a comparative nutritional advantage over non-beer drinkers" (*A History of the World in Six Glasses*, 22). Wine too was a handy way of making water safe, containing natural antibacterial agents released by fermentation. During military campaigns, a cheap wine called *posca* was issued to Roman soldiers as "a form of portable water-purification technology" (ibid., 80).

form of water purification and was regularly drunk by the working populace. As well as having the considerable advantage of sharpening rather than dulling the wits, tea also had antiseptic properties thanks to its tannin or polyphenol content and is thought to have made a considerable contribution to lowering the incidence of dysentery and other waterborne diseases.[810]

Such wariness towards water was doubtless fostered by the appalling sanitary conditions that have generally prevailed ever since the downfall of the hydraulically enlightened Harappan civilization, which used the flow of water through brick gutters to rid itself of domestic waste (and dump it in the river), and Roman civilization, which flushed at least parts of the city clean with water from the hills. City streets in medieval Europe frequently degenerated into cesspits, for people had little option but to collect their waste in chamber pots or other such receptacles and then toss the contents out of the window at night with a warning shout to those below.[811] Where buildings had separate structures or rooms set aside for the purpose, such privies or bog houses typically had no outflow and amounted to little more than a "storehouse of excrement,"[812] i.e. a seat with a hole in and with a pile of dung, the midden, festering underneath. The leakage and overflow from such bog holes and cesspits posed a major health risk, seeping through porous soil, contaminating local wells, and spreading diarrhoea and disease. According to one account from 1873, it was common for the soil near wells to be sodden with the seepage from nearby bog houses: people lived "in an atmosphere charged with the ... gases given off by the decomposition of their own excrement" and drank "water tainted by the

810. See ibid., 200-1. As an extremely efficient form of water-purification technology, tea is also believed to have been instrumental in Chinese expansion in the 7th and 8th centuries CE, combating water-related afflictions and creating a healthier and longer-living population.
811. The French are said to have shouted *Garde l'eau!* (Look out for the water!), which crossed the Channel as "Gardy loo!" and yields one possible etymology for the word "loo" (although the chronology is dubious). Smollett's *The Expedition of Humphry Clinker* provides a description of the custom in a letter by the semi-literate lady's maid Winifred Jenkins bemoaning the lack of geaks (jakes) in Haddingborrough (Edinburgh): "at ten o'clock at night the whole cargo is flung out of a back windore that looks into some street or lane, and the maid calls *gardy loo* to the passengers, which signifies *Lord have mercy upon you!* and this is done every night in every house in Haddingborrough" (220).
812. See Eveleigh, 10-11, and in general 1-17, for an overview of the privy in Britain prior to the 1850s.

foul liquid which oozes from the excremental mass."[813] A pint of beer or a cup of tea must have seemed like nectar.

Instead of flushing waste away with flowing water in the style of the Harappan civilization, therefore, the task of emptying a city's cesspools was assigned to bands of intrepid workmen known in Tudor times as "gongfermors" or "gong farmers" and subsequently as nightmen or scavengers. These labourers carted the accumulated dung off to nightyards, where enormous piles of nightsoil – which in 19th-century London reached "the size of a tolerably large house"[814] – were left to dry out before being sold as manure to local farmers. Where available, of course, water never stopped being exploited as a convenient dumping ground: medieval castles habitually conveyed their waste into some sort of moat or ditch, and in the riverside dwellings of towns and cities, the privy often overhung the local river, dumping raw sewage that would end up being washed away downstream, though often only at spring tide.

Indeed, the same principle – the use of a flow of water to remove waste – underlay the water closet, which started to become widespread among the middle and upper classes from the 1750s onwards.[815] Yet initially the WC only exacerbated the sanitary problem. As the spread of water closets outpaced developments in sewage disposal, the sophisticated new flushes washed the waste down the pan, out of the house and straight into the local cesspool, from which it would often then overflow into the main sewers or water courses and on into the nearest river. The deeper problem was that human waste thus finished up in the very rivers from which a city's water supply was taken, and drinking water was drawn just yards away from where sewage was discharged. The drawback with the water-carriage system of waste disposal was that – in an almost parodic distortion of water's natural cyclicality – one person's polluted outflow was denied the chance to regenerate or renew itself before

813. George Wilson, author of *A Handbook of Hygiene* (1873), quoted in Eveleigh, 11.
814. Henry Mayhew, author of *London Labour and the London Poor* (1851), quoted in Eveleigh, 13.
815. The first water closet was the "ajax" (a pun on "jakes") designed by Sir John Harrington during the reign of Queen Elizabeth I. The idea seems to have taken a while to catch on, but there is evidence of occasional use in the late 17th century (for example at Chatsworth House in Derbyshire, where ten were installed between 1691 and 1694), and the concept of a closet flushed by water gradually gained in popularity in the first half of the 18th century. Important improvements in design were made in the 1770s first by Alexander Cummings and then Joseph Bramah, who in 1778 patented what proved to be the first commercially successful WC. On the history of the early water closets, see Eveleigh, 18-42.

becoming another person's inflow; the normally virtuous water cycle turned into a vicious circle in which pathogens were passed into and out of human bodies with the passage of water.[816] In a first attempt to solve the problem in London, the brilliant civil engineer Joseph Bazalgette designed and oversaw an entirely new sanitation system consisting of 1,300 miles of sewers and 82 miles of main intercepting sewers that flushed the city out from the 1870s onwards[817]: the sewage was sent much further downstream than previously and was only pumped into the river just after high tide to make sure that it did not return upstream. Yet the inhabitants of Beckton and Crossness, where the untreated sewage was discharged, continued to suffer the consequences. Another 30 years would elapse before sewage *treatment* was introduced.

While the great water-carriage systems of waste-removal built in London and other cities were monumental feats of civil engineering, therefore, they ultimately only shifted the problem elsewhere – generally somewhere further downstream which was out of sight, out of mind, and beyond the olfactory range of those in power. Not surprisingly, there were those who opposed the dumping of untreated sewage into the Thames estuary, especially as this wasted the nightsoil that had traditionally been utilized to manure the land. Henry Mayhew, the author of *London Labour and the London Poor* (1851) as well as a cofounder of the satirical *Punch* magazine, described it as "folly, not to say wickedness," and reflected, "we import guano and drink a solution of our own faeces."[818] In 1861 the trade journal *The Ironmonger*

816. The water closet heightened a perennial problem – the dual functionality of rivers as a means of sewage disposal and a source of drinking water – faced by human settlements ever since the Romans decided the Tiber was too disgusting to imbibe back in 312 BCE. Nor has the problem been confined to the sprawling megalopolis. The small Cambridgeshire village of Foxton had to issue bye-laws on eight separate occasions between 1541 and 1698 in order to outlaw the discharge of cesspools, gutters and "other noysome sinks" into the stream that provided the villagers' drinking water (see Ponting, 341).
817. Bazalgette had originally submitted plans for an urban drainage system in 1853 after an outbreak of cholera to which more than 10,000 had succumbed, but it was the Great Stink of 1858 that effectively stank the newly built Houses of Parliament into submission and finally got things moving. Work on the project was started in 1859 and lasted into the 1870s. See Carter, 98-103.
818. Quoted in Eveleigh, 43. Quite apart from the inadvisability of drinking a solution of one's own faeces, the importation of guano (dried sea-bird excrement) to replace other forms of manure also had serious ramifications of its own, above all the appalling conditions to which the (often immigrant) guano miners were subjected in South America. The subsequent development of artificial fertilisers – superphosphates –

wrote that "there is something radically wrong in the plan ... for it leads to the pollution of our rivers with matter which might be used to fertilise our lands," while Justus von Liebig, professor of chemistry at the University of Giessen, came up with the figures: "the introduction of water closets into most parts of England results in the loss annually of the materials capable of producing food for three and a half million people."[819]

One of the responses to the sanitation predicament caused by the flood of water closets was thus (at least for the poor) to improve the traditional privy-midden or bog, transforming it from a wet into a dry privy and in the process making it safer and a good deal more healthy. In 1860 the Revd Henry Moule, for whom waterborne sewage represented "a great national evil," designed an earth closet that successfully used garden soil (about 1.5lb per stool) to deodorize human excrement.[820] Three years earlier the medical doctor John Lloyd had patented a dry closet in which cinders and ash functioned as the deodorizing material, and in the late 19th century many of the industrial towns of northern England adopted this combination of an ash pit – where householders dumped the refuse from their fireplace – with a dry privy-midden. The eventual decline of dry closets was presumably due in large measure to people's ever more "refined" sensibilities: such direct dealings with one's own doo-doo were viewed as offensive and repulsive when water could simply wash it all away, out of sight and mind. The inexorable rise of the water-carriage system of waste disposal sealed the fate of the earth system. Yet as David J. Eveleigh puts it, the dry-closet movement represented "a serious attempt by progressive Victorian sanitarians to improve closets without expending vast capital sums on sewage projects only to pollute rivers and coasts."[821]

only increased the demand for phosphate rocks and in the 20th century led, among other things, to the systematic despoliation of the Pacific islands of Nauru and Ocean Island for their phosphate deposits. The worldwide annual use of inorganic fertilisers reached a peak of 150 million tons in 1990. Today's fertiliser production generates a radioactive by-product called phosphogypsum, which gets dumped on huge mounds a mile square and 60 feet high. On the rise of fertilisers, see Ponting, 193-96, 239-40.
819. Quoted in Eveleigh, 43-44.
820. Ibid., 45-48. On dry privies and earth closets in general, see 43-60.
821. Ibid., 60. French resistance to the water closet lasted rather longer, although the water-carriage system ultimately won the day in Paris too. See Illich, 67-69. Resistance to the WC, writes Illich, "was motivated neither by anti-British sentiment nor by concern for the river but by calculating the enormous economic value that would be washed down the drain with the excrement of horses and people."

Nor is it by any means a thing of the past.

At a time when the planet's natural self-cleansing system is being put under increasing pressure by the escalating world population and the accompanying pollution, the waterborne system of sewerage has come to be regarded by many as inefficient and profligate. Large quantities of water are required to flush away small quantities of pathogenic waste, along with urine that is perfectly sterile.[822] So while waterborne sewerage may be the best solution where water supplies are reliable or the population density is high (in tenements or multi-storey housing), its water-inefficiency makes it an unsuitable system particularly for impoverished and water-stressed areas.[823] As with traditional nightsoil and the manure derived from more recent earth closets, modern forms of ecological sanitation not only avoid flushing harmful bacteria into drinking water supplies, but reutilize the nutrients in human waste – the organic matter and phosphates – for the benefit of the land. Of course, it is vital for such "humanure" to have been properly composted in order to eliminate the disease-causing microbes in human faeces. In early-20th-century China, where there was a tradition of using human excrement as a fertiliser, about 90 per cent of the population suffered from intestinal worms, and by the middle of the century one in four deaths was caused by faecal-borne infection.[824] By contrast, in India, where the task of "scavenging" or nightsoil-removal was traditionally left to the untouchables, the new ecological latrine designed by the well-known sociologist Dr Bindeshwar Pathak allows its waste one and a half years to decompose into wholesome manure that can safely be handled by anybody.[825]

822. See Black, *The No-Nonsense Guide to Water*, 41.
823. For a more detailed discussion, see the debate between David Satterthwaite and Mayling Simpson-Hébert in *New Internationalist* (Aug. 2008), 12-13.
824. Ponting, 348.
825. See Carter, 204-15; see also *New Internationalist* (Aug. 2008), 10-11, 18-19. Pathak's system of waste disposal has already liberated some 60,000 scavengers from their task, though this still leaves between 676,000 and 1.3 million people (depending on your source) shovelling shit for a living. His system also generates biogas, a mixture mainly of methane and carbon dioxide that can be used for cooking, heating or even generating electricity – in short, almost anything natural gas can be used for. The use of sewage to produce biogas was first tried at a leper colony in India in 1859, and subsequently in Exeter in 1895, where the gas was utilized for street lighting. Modern-day water utilities also generate energy from the biogas produced by sewage sludge treatment.

*   *   *   *   *

The current predominance of waterborne sewage disposal in wealthy countries presents sanitary engineers with the choice "of applying their always limited resources either to the treatment of sewage before its disposal or to the treatment of water supplies."[826] Our bodily waste – and the lowly water with which it comes to be associated – must be flushed away into the depths, and must not re-enter our lives until *treated*. The danger or threat inherent in water calls for an act of repression that hides it from view and thought. The flow of our bodily gunk – an individual and planetary "unconscious" – must be banished to subterranean conduits.

This repression has gone hand in hand with a repression of smell, producing a society that is not only sanitized but also deodorized and – in olfactory terms – homogenized. The new individual, writes Ivan Illich, "feels compelled to live in a space without qualities and expects everyone else to stay within the bounds of his or her own skin. He learns to be ashamed when his aura is noticed. He is embarrassed at the thought that his origins could be smelled out, and he is sickened by others if they smell."[827] Failure to abide by the unwritten rules of smell means shame, embarrassment, and nose-wrinkling ostracism. A social and moral dimension has also been involved: smelliness came to be associated with poverty, and social improvement thus entailed deodorization. For the public health reformers of 19th-century Britain, dirt suggested disorder, moral dissolution and possibly even a public threat. Cleaning and deodorizing the "great unwashed" became the target of educators and reformers. Sanitation and civilization went hand in hand.

The spread of piped water supplies and efficient water-based sewerage systems in the second half of the century made it possible for domestic baths and the constantly improved water closets to become established parts of middle-class life[828]: the ability to flush away one's

---

826. Illich, 74.
827. Ibid., 60. On the repression of smell in general, see ibid., 47-64; also Ashenburg, 243-61.
828. On the rapid developments in the design of the water closet in the 1870s and 1880s, see Eveleigh, 115-37. By the early 1890s the bog-standard modern loo of the 20th century was already in existence.

waste and enjoy a regular scrubbing in one's own tub was an expression of a nexus of middle-class values such as cleanliness, decency and respectability. This was accompanied by a new awareness of the link between dirt – and especially dirty water – and disease. Whereas the traditional theory of "miasma" had held that disease was transmitted by bad air and offensive smells, the work of the German bacteriologist Robert Koch on germ theory underlined the role of harmful microbes present in water, providing further justification for the idea of personal hygiene and domestic cleanliness.[829] Access to "germless" water for washing and drinking became a basic pillar of public health. By the end of the 19th century the consensus in Europe and North America was that the public authorities were required to provide their citizens with safe drinking water and a system of drainage. A house lacking a safe water supply was deemed to be "unfit for human habitation."[830] Cleanliness and hygiene were to be within the grasp of the entire population.

In Europe and North America, it was the wealth generated by industrialization that helped finance the provision of piped water and sanitation. Such is this wealth that 24 per cent of the houses built in the USA in 2005 had three or more bathrooms, the average size of these rooms tripling in just ten years. The bathroom, writes Ashenburg, has turned into an inner sanctum "where hedonism, narcissism, over-the-top luxury and hygienic scrupulosity meet."[831] Yet for the majority of countries, even relatively basic facilities have been limited to just a few privileged city-dwellers. In 1970, more than 70 per cent of the world's population still lacked access to a safe water supply and 75 per cent were without sanitation. Global sanitary reformers declared the 1980s the International Drinking Water Supply and Sanitation Decade, which had the provision of

829. Miasma theory remained influential throughout much of the 19th century and was not in itself inconsistent with the push for sanitary improvement. Edwin Chadwick, a linchpin of the sanitary revolution, had stated that "all smell is disease," and the notion was supported by Florence Nightingale and many others. The reason Chadwick wanted to banish cesspools was their effect on the atmosphere rather than the pollution of groundwater. The shift in thought had its origins in such figures as Dr John Snow, who during the 1854 cholera epidemic attributed its cause to the contamination of drinking water by sewage, and Robert Koch, who in 1883 identified the presence of the cholera bacillus in water polluted by the faeces of those infected.
830. See Black, *The No-Nonsense Guide to Water*, 32.
831. Ashenburg, 265-66.

"water and sanitation for all" as its target.[832] As in late Victorian Britain, the underlying ideology continued to be that access to safe water and sanitation was a basic human right and should be provided by public authorities for the common good.[833]

Yet in the early 1990s even these most basic of principles were undermined. To overcome the inefficiency and incompetence perceived in the public administration of water, advocates of free-market reform developed the idea that private enterprise should be called in to reduce waste and make the industry pay its way. Instead of being a natural commons – a communal asset freely available for the public good – water was turned into an economic commodity, subject to the law of supply and demand and the rigours of profit-making. According to a 2003 report in the *Economist*, the most efficient way of providing drinking water and removing waste water was to treat water "as a business like any other."[834]

In practice, however, this meant not just business but *big* business, involving multinational corporate giants such as the French Véolia (formerly Générale des Eaux) and Suez (formerly Lyonnaise des Eaux), as well as Bechtel, Enron and RWE. Instead of being run by local democratic power, distant corporations stepped in to take control and make a profit. Most famously, in 2000 this led to the so-called *guerra del agua* (water war) in the city of Cochabamba, when the people of Bolivia took to the streets to protest against the doubling of tariffs caused by the privatization of water supplies (which had gone into the hands of a Bechtel subsidiary). There have been other examples of injustice, irresponsibility and free-market failure in Manila, Jakarta and Buenos Aires.[835] In the early 21st century, a sixth of the world's population still lacks access to safe drinking water, and 12 million children die each year as a consequence of drinking water that is unfit for

832. Black, *The No-Nonsense Guide to Water*, 33.
833. In fact, not until the International Convention on the Rights of the Child of 1989 was there any formal, explicit statement of the human right to safe water and sanitation. Though taken to have been implicit within the Universal Declaration of Human Rights of 1948 and the International Covenant on Economic, Social and Cultural Rights of 1966, these texts omitted any explicit articulation of safe water as a universal human right. In 2002 the UN Committee on Economic, Social and Cultural Rights added a reference to the obligation of governments to "extend access to sufficient, affordable, accessible and safe water supplies and to safe sanitation services" (see ibid., 120-22).
834. Quoted in ibid., 70.
835. See, for example, ibid., 72-79.

human consumption. In cities such as Manila, Dhaka and Karachi, more than four fifths of the population is without a connection to a sewerage system.[836]

While public utilities are blamed for being incompetent and corrupt, therefore, the intervention of the private sector – unwilling and unable to eschew the need to satisfy its shareholders – has not only failed to solve the problem, but has led to distress, conflict and heightened inequality, with the poor having to pay proportionally more for the right to stay alive. Given water's scarcity, it clearly makes sense not to treat it across the board as a free resource, yet the universal right to safe drinking water is incontrovertible. It is now realized that in many cases this is best guaranteed by decentralized, community-based water management in conjunction with support from public authorities. While there is no reason for the water used on golf courses and in swimming pools – as well as in agriculture and industry – *not* to be treated as an economic good, the universal right to wholesome water for drinking and sanitation evidently cannot be trusted to market forces.

Flexible solutions are required in order to do justice to water's own infinite flexibility. As Philip Ball and others have pointed out, there is no point in having a single water supply if this means that drinking water is used as an industrial coolant or is squandered washing cars and irrigating lawns. The old Manichean dichotomy of water as either pure or impure, clean or waste – symbolically polarized as either an elixir or "irredeemably corrupt and foul"[837] – is an obstacle both in practical and conceptual terms. Water is protean, has a thousand faces and functions, and lends itself to fluid adhocism rather than dogma and rigidity. The challenge, according to Sandra Postel, is "to take the 'waste' out of wastewater."[838] The "grey water" generated by domestic activities such as laundry or dish-washing requires relatively low levels of treatment in order to be suitable for use in commercial irrigation, just as within a domestic context water from the shower or bathtub can be recycled to flush the toilet.

Drinking water throws up particular complications in that it must not only meet the demands of health and hygiene but also satisfy fickle human taste buds. Attempts to find the solution – the perfect solution – can be traced back to ancient Sanskrit texts and the wisdom of Hippocrates. The earliest record of water purification appears in the *Sus'ruta Samhita*,

836. Ponting, 337, 309.
837. Ball, *H₂O*, 330. See also Kandel, 208.
838. Quoted in Ball, *H₂O*, 330.

a Sanskrit medical treatise dating from 2000 BCE, which proposed filtration through sand and coarse gravel. The ancient Egyptians are also believed to have purified water, while Hippocrates suggested boiling water and straining it through a cloth bag – as well, ideally, as finding the healthiest source in the first place. The philosopher Francis Bacon devoted considerable attention to the purification of water,[839] and by the 18th century water filters using sand or sponge were becoming increasingly viable in technical terms. In 1804, Paisley in Scotland became the first town to use a filter facility in its municipal water supply, and by the end of the century – once the importance of removing pathogenic micro-organisms had been recognized – the traditional sand filters were being supported by the use of chlorine and ozone for disinfection. Modern water treatment incorporates a whole succession of stages, which may include decanting, flocculation, sedimentation, filtration (using sand, activated carbon, and ultra-fine membranes), aeration and finally disinfection (by means of chlorine, ozone or ultraviolet radiation).

Yet modern-day tap water frequently gets a bad press. While chlorination is an effective disinfectant in eliminating most disease-causing microbes, fears have been voiced that it can react with certain organic compounds to form potentially carcinogenic by-products such as trichloromethane, or chloroform. Such concerns have led to the use of ozone, which is highly toxic to most waterborne micro-organisms and is thought to produce fewer harmful by-products, though there have been complaints about the unpleasant taste and smell produced by its reaction with organic material in water.[840] Even more controversial has been the addition of fluoride to water, ostensibly for the purpose of preventing tooth decay in children who eat too much sugar – and certainly not as part of the purification process. Quite apart from the justifiability of such globally imposed mass medication and the fine line acknowledged to exist between medically acceptable and toxic doses, opponents of fluoridation have suspected that it may merely be a strategy devised by certain heavy-

---

839. See Bacon, *Sylva Sylvarum: Or a Natural History in Ten Centuries*, 7-8: "Dig a pit upon the sea-shore," he suggests, "somewhat above the high-water mark, and sink it as deep as the low-water mark; and as the tide cometh in, it will fill with water, fresh and potable. ... The clarifying of water is an experiment tending to health; besides the pleasure of the eye, when water is crystalline. It is effected by casting in and placing pebbles at the head of a current, that the water may strain through them."
840. Ball, *H₂O*, 326.

metal industries – and other fluoride polluters – as a cheap solution to the problem of industrial waste disposal.[841]

Some of the voices raised against chlorination seem to object to the idea of disinfection in itself, suggesting that by eliminating beneficial and harmful bacteria alike it impairs the body's immune system. According to Viktor Schauberger, for example,

> those of us who live in cities and are forced year-in and year-out to drink sterilized water should seriously consider the fate of that "organism" whose naturally-ordained ability to create life has been forcibly removed by chemical compounds. Sterilized and physically-destroyed water not only brings about physical decay, but also gives rise to mental deterioration and hence to the systematic degeneration of humanity and other life-forms.[842]

Drinking such water, he suggests, leads to our "degeneration into cancer-prone, mentally and physically decrepit, physically and morally inferior individuals."[843] While such talk of moral degeneracy can itself leave just as unsavoury a taste as over-chlorinated tap water, it is perhaps a natural product of Schauberger's own schizoid division of water into good and bad, natural and unnatural, pure and sullied, wholesome and degenerate. Manichaeism of this sort is entirely at odds with water's underlying proteanism: the dualisms are simply not watertight. Heedless of life or death, water does not give a dam what is in it, and it is anthropomorphic self-indulgence to imagine it being "sad" or "frustrated" about the chlorine it contains or the poor microbes it no longer harbours.

Similarly romantic yearnings emerge in Ivan Illich's denigration of modern tap water as "recycled toilet flush"[844] as opposed to the mythical nectar of yore. While our recycled toilet flush is certainly not as emotionally or aesthetically appealing as the pristine waters of a babbling brook, even nature-lovers and the most implacable hydraulic Luddites

841. See Bartholomew, 153-55.
842. Quoted in ibid., 153.
843. Ibid., 155.
844. Illich, 3; see also 75-76: "Water throughout history has been perceived as the stuff which radiates purity: H_2O is the new stuff, on whose purification human survival now depends. H_2O and water have become opposites: H_2O is a social creation of modern times, a resource that is scarce and that calls for technical management. It is an observed fluid that has lost the ability to mirror the water of dreams. The city child has no opportunities to come in touch with living water."

would surely prefer it to the *unrecycled* bog seepage commonly drunk by the poor in ages past, and by millions now. Ultimately, all water – apart from what has spent uncounted years isolated from the hydrological cycle in underground aquifers – is either recycled or unrecycled toilet flush. W. C. Fields famously claimed that he never drank water because "fish fuck in it,"[845] but the truth of the matter is that they do all their other bodily business in it too.

Beyond question is that chlorination has made an enormous contribution to public health, greatly reducing the prevalence of water-borne disease. There is widespread consensus among specialists that the wholesale abandonment of the chlorination of drinking water would be disastrous in its consequences. A major factor in the 1990-91 cholera epidemic in Peru and Colombia, which claimed more than 16,000 lives, is believed to have been the decision to halt chlorination of the public water supply.[846] Certainly, the 1.1 billion people in the world who lack access to safe drinking water, or the 600 million who suffer from gastrointestinal infections at any one time, would be unlikely to have many qualms about drinking recycled toilet flush – as long as it *is* recycled.

For many Europeans there is perhaps something unsettling in the fact that our tap water comes to us "treated" in advance in ways we cannot control, as typified by the fluoride controversy and the conspiracy theories to which this lends itself. After all, who knows what "they" are putting into us? But for others, the bottom line is simply that they prefer the taste of water that hasn't been through the process of chemical treatment – a perception bolstered by the marketing of "natural purity" by the multi-billion-dollar bottled-water industry. In the 1970s, moreover, a number of scares over the presence in drinking water of possibly carcinogenic pesticide residues such as DDT and industrial solvents such as carbon tetrachloride led to an increasing mistrust of tap water and a widespread switch to bottled water. In effect, the supply of drinking water in the western world was privatized, plastified and made more than a thousand times more expensive.[847]

845. See *The Oxford Dictionary of Humorous Quotations*, 71.
846. See Kandel, 200-1; see also 278.
847. On the bottled water industry, see, for example, Black, *The No-Nonsense Guide to Water*, 104-6: According to the Natural Resources Defense Council (see below), "people spend from 240 to over *10,000* times more per gallon for bottled water than they typically do for tap water." Half a litre of water that would cost a few hundredths of a penny as tap water is now sold in plastic bottles for a pound or more.

Yet the industry really started to boom in the mid-1980s, when a number of transnational corporations – some of them with a particularly hard-earned reputation in ethical bankruptcy – realized that there was a killing to be made in areas of the world that lacked reliable access to safe water sources. Not surprisingly, these companies have proved to have little respect either for environmental issues or the concerns of local populations. In the state of Michigan in the USA, for example, one citizen group[848] has filed a civil lawsuit to prevent Nestlé – the largest bottled-water company in the country, with annual bottled-water sales of more than $2.2 billion – from pumping some 210 million gallons of water a year from the local aquifer and leaving groundwater levels seriously depleted.[849] The same company is meeting with similar opposition in California, Florida and Maine and is also mired in controversy for its abuse of groundwater supplies in the historic spa town of São Lourenço in the state of Minas Gerais in Brazil. Coca-Cola and PepsiCo, the other major players in the bottled water industry, have faced less criticism than Nestlé because their major brands are processed tap water rather than water extracted from aquifers.

Despite the industry's claims to purity and healthiness, moreover, bottled water has on occasion proved to be less safe than tap water. In a four-year survey of more than a thousand bottles of 103 brands by a US-based environmental lobby group called the Natural Resources Defense Council, a third of the waters tested "contained levels of contamination – including synthetic organic chemicals, bacteria and arsenic – in at least one sample that exceeded allowable limits under either state or bottled water industry standards or guidelines."[850] In 1990, millions of bottles of Perrier

848. See www.savemiwater.org on Michigan Citizens for Water Conservation.
849. For an account of the harmful impact of Nestlé's operations, as well as the local opposition they have provoked, see www.babymilkaction.org, as well as the BBC Radio 4 programme *Face the Facts*, 22 July 2005. Worldwide public opposition to Nestlé's activities has come to light at recent editions of the Edinburgh Fringe Festival, where the best comedy show was for many years rewarded with the prestigious Perrier Comedy Award, sponsored by the Perrier brand of bottled water. Following the acquisition of Perrier by Nestlé in 1995, many critics and dissenters – including former winners such as Emma Thompson and Steve Coogan – called for the awards to be dropped, and the non-corporate Tap Water Award was established as an alternative and a countermeasure to the now devalued traditional prize. In 2006 Perrier finally withdrew its sponsorship from the event.
850. See http://www.nrdc.org/water/drinking/depth.asp; see also Goodall, 253-54.

had to be recalled when it was discovered that the water was contaminated with carcinogenic benzene. An estimated 25 per cent of all bottled water is just tap water anyway, sometimes given further treatment, but often subjected to less rigorous regulations and tests for contaminants – such as faecal coliform bacteria – than the original tap water itself. Headlines were made in 2004 when it came to light that Coca-Cola's Dasani brand, newly launched in the UK, was actually mains water from Sidcup in Kent; just two weeks later, the entire stock had to be withdrawn when the water was found to contain potentially harmful concentrations of carcinogenic bromate, produced by the effect of Coca-Cola's own treatment process on the original tap water's naturally occurring – and completely harmless – bromide.[851]

The health risk posed by the plastic itself is as yet unclear. Certain bottles contain endocrine-disrupting chemicals such as bisphenol A (BPA) or phthalates, which may leach into the water over time. More openly outrageous is the systematic wastage of the planet: the several million barrels of oil per year used to produce the plastic, the several million tons of carbon dioxide generated in the process, the energy used in filling the bottle and transporting it to its market, and the millions of tons of plastic that end up clogging landfill sites or choking marine birds and mammals. And the fact that the manufacture of this plastic itself consumes five litres of water for every one-litre bottle produced. As Julian Caldecott points out, "meeting the UN goal of halving the proportion of people who lack a secure water supply by 2015 would need an extra investment of US$15 billion per year, so spending US$100 billion a year instead on bottled water seems rather perverse."[852]

In spite of the often unsustainable plundering of limited groundwater reserves, the needless production of millions of tons of plastic, and the bogus health claims, bottled water has become the height of fashion. The marketing imagery of glacial purity and alpine springs taps an ancient

---

851. See Felicity Lawrence, "Things get worse with Coke", in *The Guardian*, 24 March 2004. To their considerable amusement, the media were quick to point out the parallels with a feature-length episode from the BBC sitcom *Only Fools and Horses* ("Mother Nature's Son"), in which Del Boy solves his financial problems by selling bottled tap water as "Peckham Spring Water."
852. Caldecott, 149, 175.

mythic yearning for what is unsullied.[853] People have allowed themselves to be persuaded that constant hydration is vital to well-being; sporty, health-minded individuals constantly have their own plastic supply of water to hand. People feel squeamish about public fountains. They are oblivious to the time-honoured folk wisdom that warns against what is stagnant.[854]

2

Purity and the Sacred

Just as water transcends any easy dichotomy of life and death, there is no watertight distinction between cleanliness and dirt, the pure and the impure. While the 8th-century Christian theologian John of Damascus could thus describe water as "the most beautiful element and rich in usefulness," which "purifies from all filth, and not only from the filth of the body but from that of the soul,"[855] others vigorously denied any correlation between bodily and spiritual cleanliness and were keen to do without the dubious services of anything so worldly as water. For early Christians, bathing could represent the dissolution of one's sins or the dissolution of morals.

The concepts of dirt and purity are themselves riven by contradiction. In her classic study *Purity and Danger*, Mary Douglas defines dirt in terms of the transgression of a conceptual structure. As such, she writes, "there is no such thing as dirt; no single item is dirty apart from a particular system of classification in which it does not fit."[856] Dirt does not exist as something absolute, but in relation to a context or form

853. One of the brands tested by the Natural Resources Defense Council in the USA was called "spring water" and depicted a beautiful mountain lake on the label. The water came from the middle of an industrial warehouse facility next to a hazardous waste site. The well is apparently no longer being used for bottled water following public disclosure of the contamination levels.
854. See the Spanish adages, *agua estancada, agua envenenada*, whereas *agua corriente no mata a la gente*: i.e. "Stagnant water, poisoned water," whereas "running water does not kill people." See Fernández, *Diccionario de Refranes*, 21.
855. See Rupp, 71.
856. Douglas, *Purity and Danger,* preface to the 2002 edition, xvii. See also 2-3.

that fails to contain it. Seen thus, it parallels what in aesthetics is known as the grotesque, and an association with the diabolical is common to both. It is also inherently linked with outsiders and foreigners. To any particular culture, its own notions of cleanliness generally seem natural and absolute, while other cultures with different habits of washing or bathing tend to be identified with dirtiness or filth – whether for using still water instead of flowing, hot water instead of cold, not enough water, too much water, the *wrong* water.

However, the very marginality of dirt as a hotchpotch of unnameable or ungraspable "stuff" located on the boundaries of our conceptual universe lends it an intrinsic ambivalence. What is polluted in one context may be sacred in another. Douglas cites a case occurring among the Havik peoples of Karnataka in India, where the arrival in a village of a holy woman or *sadhvi* called for special respect on the part of the villagers. As a mark of this respect, the liquid in which her feet had been bathed "was passed round to those present in a special silver vessel used only for worshipping, and poured into the right hand to be drunk as *tirtha* (sacred liquid), indicating that she was being accorded the status of a god rather than a mortal."[857] Similarly, the saliva of medieval Christian saints or the water they had used for washing was sometimes venerated for its curative properties.[858]

As Freud and others have pointed out, the Latin term *sacer* can mean both "holy" and "accursed."[859] The devil may be a *parody* of the divine, the unspeakability of the one mimicking or caricaturing the unfathomability of the other. At the limits of what can be thought, dirt may signal deity or devilry. Context is decisive: Douglas refers to a "complex algebra"[860] of variables that determine whether a particular thing or phenomenon is viewed as unclean or clean, polluted or sacrosanct. Yet this is not all. In

857. Ibid., 11, citing a paper by E. B. Harper.
858. Ashenburg, 58, cites the saliva of St Lutgard, the washing water of St Lidwina, and the crumbs chewed by St Colette of Corbie.
859. See also Eliade, *Patterns*, 15. Eliade points out that the same ambivalence is found in the Greek word *hagios*, which can express both purity and pollution, as well as in the early Semitic world and among the Egyptians.
860. Ibid., 10. Douglas stresses that this should not be understood as a matter of *confusion*: "this is not to say that the sacred is unclean. Each culture must have its own notions of dirt and defilement which are contrasted with its notions of the positive structure which must not be negated. ... But it still remains true that religions often sacralise the very unclean things which have been rejected with abhorrence" (ibid., 196).

a lived world of change and flux, purity undermines *itself* to the extent that it is defined in terms of static self-identity and categories of non-contradiction.[861] Dirt and impurity, by contrast, may be both destructive of existing patterns and contain the potentiality for creative change.

As Douglas's conception of dirt implies and the conduct of the Havik people of India corroborates, water itself is the epitome of dirt: "everything that is said to explain the revivifying role of water in religious symbolism can also apply to dirt."[862] As we have seen, water embodies the formlessness that can signify danger, death and destruction (as in the flood, a return to the primal origin) and yet also contain the possibility of a new beginning (again like the flood, which repeated the original creation). Water is almost always dirty to someone: it may be muddy, impure, polluted, mineralized, chlorinated, heavy, hard, acidic or salty; it may assume the guise of wine, beer, saliva, urine or blood[863]; it may inundate and dissolve landscapes and civilizations. Yet it is this very capacity for impurity and dirt – for taking things up into itself and rearranging them – that also signifies its creative potential. With a dialectical flourish, water not only transgresses form and structure, but transcends the mere negation of form to offer a new synthesis and new life. Water is thus *also* the archetypal symbol of life-giving purity and a timeless manifestation of the divine.

Accordingly, water has enjoyed a special relationship with paradise, the garden of delights set aside for those who are absolutely free of sin. The Biblical Genesis (2:10-14) mentions a single river within Eden which branches into four streams, the Pishon (which remains unidentified), the Gihon (which has been associated both with the Blue Nile and the Amu Darya or Oxus), the Hiddekel (the Tigris) and the Euphrates. In the paradise described in the legends of the Jewish *midrash*, the four rivers are the Ganges, the Nile, the Tigris and the Euphrates, which flow forth from beneath the tree of life. Elsewhere among the legends, they are said to be rivers of honey, milk, oil and wine.[864] The deep

861. As exemplified by concepts of racial or moral purity. See ibid., 199, 202: "when purity is not a symbol but something lived, it must be poor and barren. It is part of our condition that the purity for which we strive and sacrifice so much turns out to be hard and dead as a stone when we get it. … Whenever a strict pattern of purity is imposed on our lives it is either highly uncomfortable or it leads into contradiction if closely followed; and if not observed, hypocrisy."
862. Ibid., 198.
863. Blood provides an especially graphic illustration of water's inherent ambiguity, ranging from the "accursed" flux which issues from a menstruating woman to the sacred blood of Christ, which brings salvation.
864. Ginzberg, I.70, 132.

symbolic link between the water of life – living water with its powerful qualities of rejuvenation, healing and fertility – and the tree of life is also manifest in the "heavenly Jerusalem" of the Book of Revelation, as well as in the symbolism of Norse mythology and the Upanishads of ancient Hindu philosophy.[865]

Water imagery is also abundant in the Islamic paradise described in the Qur'an, where the pure are rewarded with a garden "graced with flowing streams" (whereas wrongdoers are given "water like molten metal"). As if these cool-flowing waters were not enough, the righteous will also enjoy silken garments, comfortable seating, refreshing shade, nectar made from fragrant herbs, and maidens with large, dark eyes.[866] To attain this heavenly goal in the world to come, the Muslim must strictly comply with a system of precepts that forms the divinely ordained path of conduct for the believer in the here and now: this Islamic law is known as the *shari'a* or "path worn by camels to the watering-place," a term that goes back to a sura (45:18) in the Qur'an: "We gave you [Mohammed] a *shari'a* in religion, so follow it, and do not follow the passions of those who do not know."[867] The religious path – the path to be followed in a proper Muslim life – is a path that leads to water.

In such a context, water is tantamount to a divine favour. For ancient agricultural society in particular, rainwater was quite simply a gift from God. Central to the divine nature of water was its capacity to vivify and fructify, to support and sustain plants, animals and human life. In the Old Testament, precipitation and drought formed a constant economy of divine recompense and chastisement. If you are obedient to the Lord your God, Moses announces in the Book of Deuteronomy, the Lord will "open to you his good treasury the heavens, to give the rain of your land in its season and to bless all the work of your hands." If not, He will "make the rain of your land powder and dust; from heaven it shall come down upon you until you are destroyed."[868] For the semi-nomadic Israelite tribe that

---

865. See the Book of Revelation, 22:1-2: "Then [the angel] showed me the river of the water of life, bright as crystal, flowing from the throne of God and of the Lamb through the middle of the street of the city; also, on either side of the river, the tree of life with its twelve kinds of fruit, yielding its fruit each month." In the *Kaushitaki Upanishad* (I.3), the "ageless river" flows beside the all-sustaining tree. Yggdrasil, the cosmic tree of Nordic mythology, stands next to the magical fountain of Urd. On this association between the water of life and the tree of life, see Eliade, *Patterns*, 193, 276, 282.
866. See, for example, 13:35, 18:29-31, 44:51-54, 76:13-21.
867. I am here citing the translation given in Bowker (ed.), 886.
868. Deuteronomy, 28:12, 28:24. The same message is proclaimed in 11:14 and 11:17.

left Babylon for the land of Canaan and subsequently Egypt, the search for water was a constant preoccupation, and the legends of the *midrash* stress that the tribe's spiritual leaders or Patriarchs – Abraham, Isaac and Jacob – happened to be endowed with a special gift for finding it.[869]

Moses has a particularly intense relationship with water, as suggested both by his name and his origins as a water baby, abandoned floating in a basket on a river (the word for the basket carrying him, *tebah*, being the same as the word used for Noah's ark). Much has been speculated about the precise derivation of his name, which possibly comes from the ancient Egyptian for "drawn out from" or "son of water," but beyond question is that the Hebrew Bible itself propounds a water-based interpretation: the Pharaoh's daughter who finds him in the bulrushes proceeds to give him the name Moses because, she says, she "drew him out of the water" (Exodus, 2:10). Moses's gift with water is to prove invaluable to the travelling Israelites. Perhaps the most spectacular of his feats is the parting of the Red Sea when they are being pursued by the Egyptians ("the horse and his rider he has thrown into the sea," rejoices his sister Miriam (Exodus, 15:21)), but on repeated occasions he is also called upon to provide the grumbling Israelites with fresh water, as when he sweetens the bitter waters of Marah and uses a rod to make water flow from a rock at Meribah.[870] For a long time, indeed, Moses was himself ascribed authorship of the five books of Moses (Genesis, Exodus, Leviticus, Numbers and Deuteronomy), also known as the Pentateuch or the Torah in Jewish tradition. There are now assumed to be four principal authors, yet the watery influence of Moses remains. Jewish thought makes an explicit link between the Torah and water. According to the *midrash*, God tells Abraham that just "as the earth is blessed only when it is moistened

869. When Isaac comes to Gerar during a drought, he is described as finding "the well of water that followed the Patriarchs" (Ginzberg, I.324) and thus provoking the envy of the Philistines. When Jacob journeyed to Haran, he likewise followed "the spring that appeared wherever the Patriarchs went or settled." As a result, even though Haran was likewise in the grip of a drought, "Jacob's sojourn in the city produced a change. By reason of his meritorious deeds the water springs were blessed, and the city had water enough for its needs" (ibid., 349, 353). When he left, the wells suddenly ran dry (ibid., 372).
870. See Exodus, 15:25-27; Numbers, 20:1-13. See also the Qur'an, 2:60: "Remember when Moses prayed for water for his people and We said to him, 'Strike the rock with your staff.' Twelve springs gushed out, and each group knew its drinking place."

with water, so his offspring would be blessed through the Torah, which is likened unto water."[871]

A more modern variant on the holy man with a miraculous knack of providing water is furnished by San Isidro, the patron saint of Madrid, whose fiesta is still celebrated in the third week of May. Born in 1082, Isidro was a well-digger and labourer with an uncanny gift for finding springs of water, a priceless quality in an arid land.[872] He could also perform miracles. He and his wife Maria (venerated in Madrid as María de la Cabeza) were said to be able to cross rivers using no more than "faith and a mantilla" (though this possibly reflects what a dribble the Manzanares had become), and when his son fell into a well, he brought him back to the surface by praying until the waters rose. In the years following his death, miraculous qualities came to be attributed to the wells he had opened on his master's lands, and whenever rain was short his body would be taken from its casket and borne through the streets of Madrid in the hope that God might thus be induced to put an end to the drought. The last time this was done was in 1896, with the king of Spain, Alfonso XIII, among those praying for rain as the saint's body was paraded around the city. It worked more or less immediately, or so they say. Even today there is an annual pilgrimage to a hermitage on the land where Isidro ploughed his master's fields, with long queues of people waiting to gather water from the nearby holy fountain. Tradition has it that they are to recite the words: "Beautiful San Isidro / patron of Madrid / who brought forth water / from the rock."[873]

The association of water with what is sacred is here clearly based upon an awareness of its pivotal role in continued human existence: if the rain is turned to powder and dust, as Yahweh and Moses knew only too well, then we are all doomed to destruction. The sense of water as a manifestation of the sacred – a "hierophany"[874] – is far less prevalent in the modern, secular, industrialized world. For the Hopi native Americans of the Arizona desert,[875] each of the springs (*paahu*) from which they draw their

871. Ginzberg, I.228-29.
872. For an account of San Isidro, see Nash, *Madrid: A Cultural and Literary History*, 95-99.
873. Celebration is rarely a matter of water alone. An account from 1876 describes the occasion as "bacchanalia disguised as pilgrimage," with holy water from the fountain playing second fiddle to other less saintly potions. See ibid., 99.
874. See Eliade, *Patterns*, 1-4.
875. See Ball, H_2O, 335-37; also Caldecott, 165.

water for irrigation and drink is a sacred place and a shrine to the Plumed Water Snake who presides over water in heaven and earth. The world's biggest private coal producer, the Peabody Western Coal Company, by contrast, sees water through different, utilitarian eyes, extracting over a billion gallons of drinking water each year from the aquifers beneath the Hopi lands in order to pump coal slurry along their pipelines to Nevada, where the coal is burnt to generate electricity to power the bright lights of Las Vegas and southern California.

With an inherited awareness of the precariousness and preciousness of their water supply in a parched environment, the Hopi blame the mining activity for the fact that their springs are now drying up (and there have been signs of mining-induced subsidence as well), but the Peabody Company denies all responsibility. For the Hopi, water is a gift to be reverentially shared as part of the environment as a whole: when they pray for water, they pray "for rain so that all the animals, birds, insects and other life-forms will have enough to drink too."[876] What in their eyes is *sacred*, to the industrialist is *useful* or *functional* – a means to a profit. To mix cheap, high-quality and seemingly plentiful water with pulverized coal in order to transport it as slurry makes perfectly sound economic sense, even if only in the very short term and with no regard for sustainability.

Throughout the Occidental world, this sense of the sanctity of water has been largely diluted over the years, tending to be channelled into or contained within the institutionalized Christian ritual of baptism (to which we shall come shortly) or scattered cases of miraculous springs.[877] The ancient Greeks had their sacred rivers and springs. There were cults of river deities such as Scamander, who fought against Achilles and to whom girls were said to yield their virginity before marrying, and Achelous, who was venerated in Athens and many other cities and famously struggled with Heracles. Hera renewed her virginity each year by bathing in a

---

876. Quoted in Ball, *H₂O*, 336.
877. Eliade, by contrast, places less emphasis on the gradual secularization of water in mainstream thought and more on the continuity of cult: "The cult of water – and particularly of springs held to be curative, hot springs, salt springs and so on – displays a striking continuity. No religious revolution has ever put a stop to it; fed by popular devotion, the cult of water came to be tolerated even by Christianity, after the fruitless persecuting of it in the Middle Ages. ... In some cases the cult seems to have lasted from the Neolithic Age until the present day" (*Patterns*, 200). Ancient cult, he writes, was "assimilated" by Christianity.

holy spring at Kanathos.[878] The emphasis was shifting by the time of the Roman Empire. "From the Greeks the Romans inherited their passion for water," writes Sprawson. But "the element that to the Greeks seemed so mysterious and fugitive, the Romans attempted to regulate and control. ... Byron alludes to Roman water 'imprisoned' in marble."[879] Roman functionalism replaced Greek wonder, and the de-mystification of water had begun.

When water power became the major driving force behind the early stages of the industrial revolution, it was thus to ancient Greece that the poets of Romanticism looked back with nostalgic yearning. Lamenting the loss of the Greek sense of oneness with nature and the universe, it was "to the deities of their waters that they turned in despair. It was their absence that they felt most strongly, through them that they expressed their disgust with contemporary life."[880] The new god of technological progress was largely to blame. In his sonnet "To Science," Edgar Allan Poe admonishes Science for having "torn the Naiad from her flood," while J. K. Huysmans's "La Bièvre" ("The River Bievre") portrays the agonies of a water nymph as her river is ravaged by industrial pollution.

Yet the sources of water are still revered. For the Aborigines of Australia the waterholes and billabongs of the outback are sacred sites. In Shinto, waterfalls are held to be holy places, and the sources from which rivers emerge are marked by temples. Ancient holy wells can be found sprinkled across Europe even today. In the course of his swimming journey through Britain, Roger Deakin pays a visit to the holy well at Madron near Penzance in Cornwall, "festooned with all manner of tokens," living relics "of our formerly lively dialogue with the deities":

> There were handkerchiefs, bits of coloured ribbon, a pack of cards, someone's tie, shoelaces, gloves, a skein of a woman's hair, long and brown, skanks of bladderwrack and kelp, a restaurant bill, strands of wool, an improvised mobile of drinking straws, a star of painted lolly sticks on a silk cord, threaded bottletops, a plait of bracken, hairbands, posies of wild flowers, a size-38 clothing label, even the business card of a Welsh "Osteopath, Iridologist, Psychotherapist" with sixteen letters after his name and a Llangollen telephone number ... This damp shrine could have been Lourdes, it could have been almost anywhere on the

878. Graves, I.51-52.
879. Sprawson, 58-59.
880. Ibid., 56-57.

Ganges. The bits of clothing and relics left behind on the tree symbolised the "old" person before their ritual cleansing in the water.[881]

As Deakin's description of the scene recalls, it is on the Indian subcontinent that the sacredness of water – and particularly of rivers – is lived with particular intensity. The Ganges (Ganga) is the focus of supreme veneration. In some Hindu traditions, Shiva himself is known as Gangadhar, the bearer of Ganga in his matted locks; in others, the goddess Ganga is a consort of Shiva. Lore has it that anyone who swims in the Ganges is cleansed of all sin and will reach *Svarga*, the paradise of Indra, and millions of Hindus bathe in the river each year at holy places known as *tirthas*. The Ganges also provides a graphic illustration of the relative or context-bound nature of purity: in 1990 the Ganges basin had a population of roughly 450 million people, of whom some 70 million discharged their mainly untreated waste directly into the river; moreover, funeral rites are commonly held near rivers, and thousands of cremated and partially cremated bodies are cast into the river at the holy city of Varanasi.[882] Yet the river continues to symbolize fecundity, health and life: its purity is dynamic, an ongoing process of self-purification. If possible, the dying are given its waters to drink. Borges makes the observation in his "Poem of the Fourth Element" that given the porosity of the planet, we have all bathed in the Ganges.[883] By the same token, we have all imbibed its holy waters. And having imbibed them, we *are* its holy waters.

Six other rivers also have special status: the Yamuna, Godavari, Sarasvati, Narmada, Sindhu and Kaveri. Countless pilgrimage sites are located on the banks of these rivers, and exceptional significance is ascribed to points of confluence. Allahabad, the confluence of the Ganges with its major tributary the Yamuna (and also, in some traditions, with the legendary Sarasvati), is one of the holiest places in India. Of particular importance and sanctity is the Narmada, said to have been sent by Shiva to clean the world from evil – and to have been formed from the rivulets of perspiration from one of his ascetic trances.[884] Such is this sanctity that according to the Puranic scriptures there are 400 billion sacred spots along

---

881. Deakin, 157.
882. Ponting, 345-46.
883. Borges, *Selected Poems*, 163. Or, to adapt the words of the 17th-century poet Abraham Cowley writing about the Thames, "all the liquid world" is "one extended Ganges." Choose your river.
884. See Mehta, 8. See 143-45 on the river's holiness.

its river-banks. The ambivalence of "purity" again emerges in the character of Narmada as an erotic temptress (the Sanskrit word means "harlot") of whom the "Song of the Narmada" nonetheless sings: "Drop by transparent drop, / Each weighted with our separate sins, / You flow into the ocean's surging tides. / O holy Narmada."[885]

Ambivalence is inherent in the relationship of believers to what is sacred (i.e. in the knowledge or awareness of it), for the absolute, eternal or spiritual otherness of the sacred is in a sense compromised by its *manifestation* as something relative, time-bound and physical.[886] The Ganges, the Narmada and the now non-existent Sarasvati are not only holy in themselves, but also point *beyond* themselves to deities that transcend their merely physical manifestations. Rain-clouds too may be holy in themselves, signifying renewal and fecundity, but they are also *tokens* of the higher presence of Indra, Baal or Yahweh.

Indeed, the cloud exemplifies this duality of revelation and concealment. It may be an apparent obstacle blocking off access to the celestial powers, hiding the sun or covering the mountain peaks where the gods dwell; yet it may equally be interpreted as "mediating" what would otherwise simply be beyond us, out of our reach or grasp, too much for us to cope with. In the Book of Exodus, Yahweh went before the Israelites "in a pillar of cloud to lead them along the way," and His presence on Mount Sinai is announced by thunder and lightning and a cloud that both conceals and reveals Him.[887] In Jewish mythology, "Bar Nifli" or "Son of a Cloud" is a name given to the Messiah, who according to the Book of Daniel (7:13) will appear riding one,[888] while the New Testament says that on the Last Day humanity will see "the Son of man coming in a cloud with power and great glory" (Luke, 21:27). Jupiter – himself a divine cloud-gatherer and god of rain – assumed the form of a cloud to have his way with Io, a priestess of Juno, in a scene depicted with relish by the Renaissance artist

885. From Mehta, 219. The narrator wonders whether the river-pilgrims "brood on the Narmada as the proof of Shiva's great penance or … imagine her as a beautiful woman dancing towards the Arabian Sea, arousing the lust of ascetics like themselves while Shiva laughed at the madness of their infatuation" (132-33).
886. See Eliade, *Patterns*, 29, for whom every hierophany – even the most elementary – reveals a "paradoxical coming-together of sacred and profane, being and non-being, absolute and relative, the eternal and the becoming."
887. Exodus, 13:21; 19:16-19.
888. See Pretor-Pinney, 30-37, on some of the associations between clouds and divinity.

Correggio.[889] In this case Jupiter is clearly doing his best to reveal himself to Io while concealing himself from the sight of his jealous wife Juno.

In mystical and esoteric thought the cloud has been a recurrent symbol of the inscrutability or unknowability of the divine. So while for some people clouds may merely be a barrier to knowledge, a hindrance that comes between human beings (in their imperfection) and the pure light of God, others have recognized that such limitations are necessary (for our senses or faculties would not be able to cope with the blinding force of unmediated perfection anyway). In *The Cloud of Unknowing*, the author, an anonymous 14th-century Christian mystic, develops the image of a cloud to express the impossibility of knowing, describing or rationally understanding God. Rejecting the easy dichotomy that splits light as divine from darkness as diabolical (just as Rabi'a the Sufi mystic had rejected the dualistic symbolism of fire and water), the unknown monk suggests that the believer should yield to the cloud and the darkness and accept the necessary limitations of his understanding: "This darkness and this cloud is, howsoever thou dost, betwixt thee and thy God, and letteth thee that thou mayest neither see Him clearly by light of understanding in thy reason, nor feel Him in sweetness of love in thine affection. And therefore shape thee to bide in this darkness as long as thou mayest, evermore crying after Him that thou lovest. For if ever thou shalt feel Him or see Him, ... it behoveth always to be in this cloud in this darkness."[890]

Perpetuating a venerable tradition of wise folly and knowing by unknowing, the anonymous author is well aware of the traps presented by an image such as the cloud, as indeed by concepts and words in general. He takes pains to warn his readers against spatial notions of height or upwardness: those who take the cloud too literally "will sometime with the curiosity of their imagination pierce the planets, and make an hole in the firmament to look in thereat." Heaven, he continues, is "as nigh down as up, and up as down: behind as before, before as behind, on one side as other."[891] But from here it is just one step (in any direction) to the conclusion that – in worldly terms at least – heaven is nowhere (or Nowhere) and God Himself is nothing (or Nothing). But we are not to worry: "Reck thee never if thy wits cannot reason of this nought; for surely, I love it much the better. It is so worthy a thing in itself, that they cannot reason thereupon.

889. See ibid., 35-37. The painting is "Jupiter and Io."
890. *The Cloud of Unknowing* (ed. E. Underhill), 5-6.
891. Ibid., 99, 106.

This nought may better be felt than seen: for it is full blind and full dark to them that have but little while looked thereupon."[892]

The flip side of this association of clouds with the divine Nothing of negative theology – fomented by the protean insubstantiality of clouds themselves – is an association with the woolly nothings of idle speculation and vacuous theoretical word-mongering. When Aristophanes mocks the intellectual aberrations of ancient Greece in *The Clouds*, the eponymous clouds (who form the Chorus of women) are portrayed as the patron goddesses of chronically useless sophists and pseudo-intellectuals, concerned solely with whether gnats produce their hum by way of the mouth or the bum.[893] Wittgenstein's professed intention in the *Philosophical Investigations* was to condense whole clouds of philosophy into a few droplets of grammar.[894] For a thinker aspiring to analytic clarity rather than speculative nebulosity, precipitation is to be preferred to having one's head in the clouds.

*   *   *   *   *

One of the most universally revered of water's holy attributes is its capacity to cleanse. This not only means removing the grime from our body, but also washing away our sins. Water is equally capable of literal and figurative cleansing, in other words, although the famous case of Lady Macbeth shows both the aptness and the limitations of the trope. After Macbeth has killed Duncan, she tells her husband: "Go, get some water, / And wash this filthy witness from your hand. ... A little water clears us of this deed." Yet Macbeth has his doubts:

> Will all great Neptune's ocean wash this blood
> Clean from my hand? No, this my hand will rather
> The multitudinous seas incarnadine,
> Making the green one red.[895]

---

892. Ibid., 117.
893. Aristophanes, *Lysistrata, The Acharnians, The Clouds*, 125, 127.
894. Wittgenstein, *Werkausgabe*, 1.565.
895. *Macbeth*, 2.2.46, 66, 59-62.

And Lady Macbeth herself ends up spluttering "Out, damned spot, out, I say!"[896] as she tries in vain to wash away the guilt of the crimes she has committed.

The symbolic use of water for inner purification is as ancient as it is widespread. In the third millennium BCE, the pre-Aryan city of Mohenjo-Daro in the Indus Valley had its "Great Bath," which measured 23 by 40 feet and was used for ritual cleansing,[897] just as the Hindus of today immerse themselves in sacred rivers such as the Ganges or Narmada to wash away their sins. The Old Testament too turns to water as a way of "blotting out" one's transgressions, as in Psalms (51:2: "Wash me thoroughly from my iniquity, and cleanse me from my sin"), while according to the *midrash* Adam and Eve try to purge themselves of their sin by immersion in the Jordan and the Tigris respectively.[898] The ashes of women believed to be witches were commonly strewn into rivers as a way of dispersing every last trace of them (and preventing their return). Even today it is common to wash one's hands of blame or responsibility (in the same way that Pontius Pilate absolved himself of blame for the condemnation of Jesus (Matthew, 27:24)), while foul-mouthed children have traditionally been threatened with having their mouths washed out with soap and water.[899]

The nature of this metaphorical connection between the inward and the outward person – and by extension between pollution of body and pollution of soul – is complex. Ivan Illich insists on a sharp distinction between purifying and cleaning: in order to purify, water has to "penetrate body and soul and communicate to them its own freshness, clarity, and purity," whereas in its function as a cleaning agent it has to "detach what sticks to people," which means washing dirt from the surface.[900] If the distinction, as Illich admits, is "obvious yet difficult to clarify," the confusion is only natural: bathing not only cleans the skin and detaches outward gunk, but may also make us feel reinvigorated, renewed, refreshed or relaxed. We feel better *inside* (wherever that is), our spirits lifted. At the same time, the outer manifestations of dirt – most specifically the dirt of

---

896. Ibid., 5.1.28.
897. See Biedermann, 31.
898. Ginzberg, I.87. Adam tells Eve: "Arise, and go to the Tigris, take a stone and stand upon it in the deepest part of the river, where the water will reach as high as thy neck. ... Remain in the water for thirty-seven days." He sentences himself to forty days in the Jordan.
899. See Rupp, 71.
900. Illich, 27.

bodily pollutions – have been intimately bound up with inner sinfulness and transgression.

Others have attempted to reduce inner purification to a matter of outward cleaning, claiming that the origins of ritual cleansing are ultimately hygienic in nature.[901] However, as Mary Douglas explains, the stress on hygiene is largely a modern fixation:

> There are two notable differences between our contemporary European ideas of defilement and those, say, of primitive cultures. One is that dirt avoidance for us is a matter of hygiene or aesthetics and is not related to our religion. ... The second difference is that our idea of dirt is dominated by the knowledge of pathogenic organisms. ... So much has it transformed our lives that it is difficult to think of dirt except in the context of pathogenicity. ...
>
> If we can abstract pathogenicity and hygiene from our notion of dirt, we are left with the old definition of dirt as matter out of place. This ... implies two conditions: a set of ordered relations and a contravention of that order.[902]

This concept of "dirt" as something that transgresses our normal system of classification is neither interior nor exterior (the categories are simply inappropriate). Nor does it involve us in any "clear-cut distinction between sacred and secular."[903] Whether by washing away our bodily grime or cleansing us of sin and transgression, the symbolic function of water is to control the constant threat of disorder (from within or without).

Ritual cleansing, known as ablution, may range from wholesale immersion in water to the washing of specified parts of the body. In Judaism a woman is obliged to purify herself in a ritual bath or *mikveh* after menstruation as well as after contact with the dead, and ritual immersion also forms part of the initiation ceremony for proselytes. For Brahmins a rite of bathing is essential in order to be able to perform daily worship to the gods; even one's own saliva is so polluting that inadvertently touching one's lips calls for washing or bathing. In Islam, the daily prayers of the devout must be preceded by *wudu* or the "minor ablution," which involves

901. This position is dismissed by Mary Douglas as "medical materialism" (*Purity and Danger*, 36-37). It is a pity, she says, to treat a spiritual leader such as Moses as "an enlightened public health administrator." This is not to deny that ritual cleansing may have hygienically beneficial side-effects.
902. Ibid., 44.
903. Ibid., 50.

washing the hands (up to the elbow), face, head and feet[904]; the "major ablution" or *ghusl* is required after sex and recommended prior to the Friday prayer, the two main feasts and before touching the Qur'an. Shinto worship of the *kami*, the sacred powers venerated in the thousands of shrines dotted throughout Japan, must also begin with a ritual act of washing. The Eleusinian mysteries and other ancient Greek cults incorporated baths of purification, and there were ritual baths in ancient Mexico as well.

The timeless symbolism of purifying immersion in water was also adopted and adapted by Christianity. The Christian rite of baptism is believed to have its origins on the one hand in the Jewish immersion of converts, and on the other in the baptisms administered in the flowing waters of the River Jordan by John the Baptist (Mark, 1:4), venerated as a forerunner of Jesus Christ himself. The very name "John" has been taken to betray an association with the ancient Sumerian figure of Uan (equated with the Babylonian Oannes), the first of the seven great water-men or sages said to have been sent by the god of fresh water, Ea, to teach humankind the arts of civilization.[905] The immersions performed by John – which included the baptism of Jesus – did not signify initiation so much as repentance for one's sins in the face of God's wrathful judgement: "I baptize you with water," he proclaimed, "but he who is mightier than I is coming ... ; he will baptize you with the Holy Spirit and with fire" (Luke, 3:16).

The Christian ritual is founded on the command Jesus issued after resurrection that all nations should be baptized "in the name of the Father and of the Son and of the Holy Spirit" (Matthew, 28:19). Initially, most of those baptized were adults converting from Hellenistic paganism, and on occasion it took the form of a special "redemption" rite administered to the dying. However, infant baptism seems to have been common by the 3rd century CE and by the 5th had come to be underpinned as a precept by Augustine's doctrine of original sin (the state of sinful concupiscence passed down from generation to generation ever since Adam's first trespass).[906] Pessimistic post-Augustinian Christianity, which viewed the

904. Instructions are given in the Qur'an, 5:6.
905. The association with John has been entertained by the mythologist Joseph Campbell and others.
906. In medieval Roman Catholic theology, infant baptism was one of the seven sacraments or channels of God's grace to the recipient. Protestant theology has generally interpreted baptism as one of just two sacraments, along with the Eucharist. The image of the cleansing of inherited sinfulness has not been the

human race itself as a *massa damnata*, has not been alone in using water to wash newborn infants of inherited sinfulness. In pre-Columbian Aztec civilization, a rite closely resembling infant baptism was presided over by the divine figure of Chalchiuhtlicue, goddess of rivers, lakes and oceans and consort of the rain-god Tlaloc. Water was sprinkled over the newborn child, and the midwife prayed: "Take this water, for the goddess [of the waters] Chalchiuhtlicue … is thy mother. May this bath cleanse thee of the sins and blemishes thou hast from thy parents. … Receive, child, thy mother, Chalchiuhtlicue, the goddess of the waters."[907]

In the early days of the Christian Church, baptism not only entailed a free choice made by adults, but preferentially involved the "living" waters of rivers and streams, just as John had used the waters of the Jordan. By the 4th century, however, the waters had been brought to a standstill within the baptismal font of the Church and had to be blessed with the sign of the Cross. The healing power of water had been assimilated, contained and appropriated by the institution of the Church, which at the same time claimed a monopoly on what was to count as truth (the four gospels of the New Testament, duly interpreted). Bishop Irenaeus of Lyons, an early adversary of heretics and Gnostics, wrote towards the end of the 2nd century CE that the apostles, "like a rich man (depositing money) in a bank, placed in the church fully everything that belongs to truth: so that everyone, whoever will, can draw from her the water of life."[908] Yet Gnostic Christians could hardly agree with this. In *The Apocalypse of Peter*, the risen Christ tells Peter that those who "name themselves bishop, and also deacon, as if they had received their authority from God," are in fact "waterless canals."[909]

---

only interpretation. For some Reformers, baptism symbolized admission to the Christian community. In an attempt to restore the spirit of the early Church, radical groups such as the Anabaptists of the 16th century sought to reinstate adult baptism as a profession of personal faith, a capital offence under the laws of the time insofar as it was seen to involve *re*baptism (which the Anabaptists themselves denied, dismissing their own infant baptism as vacuous). The tenet of adult baptism is perpetuated today by the Baptists and other denominations.
907. See Scott Littleton (ed.), 565; Eliade, *Patterns*, 192.
908. Quoted in Pagels, 49.
909. Quoted in ibid., 52; also 65, 118.

Not all Gnostics renounced baptism itself.[910] For the only surviving Gnostic sect, the Mandeans,[911] baptism (*maswetta*) in flowing water is the central liturgical act, a cleansing of sin that takes place on a regular basis, generally on Sundays. Believed to have descended from a possibly pre-Christian amalgamation of Gnosticism with a heretical Jewish baptismal sect, the Mandeans were for a long time known as "Christians of St John" or "John-Christians" (though they are not in fact Christians). Christian missionaries of the 17th century considered them to be descendants of the "disciples of John the Baptist," to whom they accord special status, and one of their sacred books is the *Book of John*. The river in which they administer immersion is known as "Jordan," though it can be any flowing water.[912] Other Gnostics, however, considered faith in sacraments such as baptism to be naïve superstition or reliance on merely outward gestures in the hope of salvation, where what was required was *inner* enlightenment. According to the author of the *Testimony of Truth*, physical rituals like baptism are irrelevant because "the baptism of truth is something else; it is renunciation of [the] world that it is found."[913]

Modern-day non-conformism shows similar concerns. The Quakers dispense entirely with sacraments, stressing the importance of "inner light" as opposed to external or institutionalized guidance. Others have preferred flowing waters and the presence of nature. Roger Deakin describes the total immersions that used to take place at Isleham in the waters of the River Lark in the Fens, an area of England that has always been "strongly non-conformist" in outlook and has a considerable Baptist presence. Like the local rivers of Mandeans, the holy waters of the Lark were famed enough to be known as Jordan. Yet as Deakin points out, there is something "wonderfully pagan" about baptism: "It takes nothing away from the symbolic re-enactment of Christ's death, burial and resurrection and the washing away of sin, to say that the ritual is really grafted on to

910. See, for example, Rudolph, *Gnosis: The Nature and History of Gnosticism*, 226ff. and 360ff., on the water rites practised by the Valentinians, disciples of the Gnostic Valentinus, and by the Mandeans.
911. Until recently most Mandeans lived in southern Iraq and parts of Iran, but the Iraqi Mandean population has fallen drastically since 2003. Many have fled to Syria and Jordan.
912. In fact, the "Jordan" is a pool adjacent to their local river, to which it is connected by an inflow and an outflow that provide the necessary "flowing (living) water" (Rudolph, 360-61).
913. Quoted in Pagels, 122.

something much older and pre-Christian. It clearly harks back to a time when the rivers themselves were deities."[914] Since 1972, much to Deakin's regret, no-one has been baptized in the Lark owing to worries about pollution. As though to justify the concerns, in the late 1980s the local sugar factory at Bury St. Edmunds released enough highly toxic effluent to kill off every living thing in the river. Different forms of defilement now have to be washed away by the waters of the Lark.

Baptism is of course not simply a matter of ritual purification or initiation; other dimensions are at play. Although the New Testament does refer to immersion "for the forgiveness of your sins" (Acts, 2:38), baptism is also described as a dying with Christ (Romans, 6:3-4) as well as a rebirth (John, 3:5). Not only are dying and rebirth inextricably connected, of course, but the theme of death and regeneration is itself inseparable from the dissolution of sin that is regarded as taking place in water. As Eliade explains,

> Breaking up all forms, doing away with all the past, water possesses this power of purifying, of regenerating, of giving new birth; for what is immersed in it "dies," and, rising again from the water, is like a child without any sin or any past, able to receive a new revelation and begin a new and *real* life. ... Water purifies and regenerates because it nullifies the past, and restores – even if only for a moment – the integrity of the dawn of things. ... Man dies symbolically with immersion, and is reborn, purified, renewed; just as Christ rose from the tomb.[915]

Immersion in water, in these terms, is a way of partaking in the death, burial and resurrection of Christ. The old self dies, and a new, regenerate one is born. Such was the interpretation of baptism given by the Church Father John Chrysostom: "it represents death and burial, life and resurrection. ... When we plunge our head into water as into a tomb, the old man is immersed, wholly buried; when we come out of the water, the new man appears at that moment."[916]

There is a marked parallelism with the Biblical – but also universal – theme of the flood, which cleanses the world of its sinfulness so that a new start can be made. Operating on a cosmic or collective rather than an individual level, the tradition of the deluge is founded upon the idea of a blemished human race returning to the waters from which it first emerged, to be followed by regeneration, re-emergence and a fresh attempt at humanity. In both cases water performs a purifying function, wiping out all

914. Deakin, 65. See *passim* 64-68.
915. Eliade, *Patterns*, 194-96.
916. Quoted in ibid., 197.

traces of a flawed past, and dissolving the stains of sin. In the Bible these analogies are underscored by the repeated imagery of a dove, in the one case announcing that the flood is over, in the other descending upon Jesus after he has been baptized in the Jordan by John.[917] A similar immersion – likewise understood as prefiguring the death, burial and resurrection of Christ – has traditionally been seen in the episode of Jonah, who spends three days and three nights in the watery depths (inside the whale's belly) before being spewed back out into dryness.

Again, this association of water with life and death is as deeply ambivalent as its association with cleanliness and dirt or with purity and pollution: there is simply no watertight distinction between the terms of the dichotomy. Water symbolizes both creation and destruction, or perhaps destruction as a necessary prelude to creation. On the one hand, there is a sense in which ritual immersion in water is a repetition or re-enactment of the drama of creation, representing a return to and emergence from the state of formlessness or potentiality that preceded creation.[918] On the other, formlessness is not only potential (for what is new), but also a threat (to what is old). The flood wiped out virtually in its entirety a human race judged to be degenerate, which was fine for Noah, Atrahasis, Deucalion and their families and descendants (i.e. everyone since), but not so good for the unlucky degenerates; the mighty oceans – like the grotesque sea-monsters that inhabit them – are undiscriminating in their powers of destruction.

Water may thus represent death, but it may also overcome it. To the extent that death itself is conceived as a form of defilement or transgression, water may be required to cleanse those who have come into contact with it, as is the case with the Jewish ritual *mikveh*. In Sri Lanka, anyone attending a funeral is vulnerable to a form of pollution known as *killa*, which is removed by washing or touching water.[919] Yet the emphasis

---

917. Matthew, 3:16: "And when Jesus was baptized, he went up immediately from the water, and behold, the heavens were opened and he saw the Spirit of God descending like a dove, and alighting on him."
918. Tertullian associated water's redemptive function with the special status it enjoyed in the creation: water was the first "seat of the divine Spirit, who gave it preference over all the other elements. ... Water was the first to produce what has life, so as to prevent our being astonished when one day it came to give birth to life in baptism. ... Therefore all natural water, because of the ancient privilege with which it was honoured from the first, gains the power of sanctifying in the sacrament, as long as God is invoked to that effect" (*De Baptismo*, iii-v, quoted in Eliade, *Patterns*, 197).
919. Black, *Water: Life Force*, 109.

may not only be on dissolving or dispersing the powers of death, but also on regenerating the forces of life. While the ashes of medieval witches were commonly strewn into rivers as a way of ensuring that they did *not* return, in the Quiché Mayan *Popol Vuh* the triturated ashes of the Hero Twins Hunahpu and Xbalanque – undergoing a series of ordeals devised by the evil Lords of Xibalba – were *reconstituted* by the flowing water into which they were tipped. Within five days they had emerged from the river in the form of beautiful fish-men.[920]

Inherent in water's ambivalent association with death and new life is the ambiguous relationship of water to memory. In Greek mythology, the element of forgetfulness was embodied in the River Lethe, one of the symbols of the transition between life and afterlife, whose waters had the quality of rinsing away all memories from whoever crossed it. The dead drank from these waters in order not to remember their previous lives when reincarnated. Yet Hades was also believed by some to possess another river, the Mnemosyne, which harboured all the memories that had been washed away in the Lethe. Its clear waters held the residue from the experiences of the dead, and those who ventured to drink them would recollect hidden mysteries of past, present and future. Under the protection of Mnemosyne, known as the "Mother of the Muses," the wellspring of remembrance thus provided the source of inspiration for musicians, poets and prophets.[921]

Water is understood as destroying traces or forms, breaking up or dissolving the past, much as Lady Macbeth had hoped (in vain) that she could erase her guilt by rinsing away the stains left by the physical act of murder. Yet the concept of dissolution is ambiguous. Water may *dissolve* the past, but in a sense it then *contains* it. This propensity to retain traces (of the past) – more than may meet the eye – is bound up with its life-creating and sustaining properties and underlies the sense of water as a medium of remembrance. Age-old claims relating to water's "memory" are perpetuated even today by practitioners of homeopathic medicine and were ostensibly corroborated by the work of Jacques Benveniste.[922]

---

920. *Popol Vuh*, 131-32. See also 278-80 on the background to this symbolic link between water and rebirth in Mesoamerican lore. The healing powers of water are further illustrated by legends of martyrs whose mutilated body parts are cast into rivers, but miraculously recombine into their original form as they flow downstream with the current.
921. On Lethe and Mnemosyne, see Illich, 30-34.
922. See below, chap. IV.4.

3

Temperance and Inebriation

In the gospel according to John, Jesus describes himself as "living water." In his encounter with a Samaritan woman beside Jacob's well, he contrasts the water of the well with the water he dispenses: "Every one who drinks of this water will thirst again, but whoever drinks of the water that I shall give him will never thirst; the water that I shall give him will become in him a spring of water welling up to eternal life" (John, 4:13-14). This conception of Christ as a wellspring of living waters has commonly been regarded as prefigured in the Book of Jeremiah, where the Lord says "my people have committed two evils: they have forsaken me, the fountain of living waters, and hewed out cisterns for themselves, broken cisterns, that can hold no water" (Jeremiah, 2:13). The Church Father Clement of Alexandria writes that not only is water the natural source of all life, such that "without the element of water, none of the present order of things can subsist," but it is essential to the life of the soul, which cannot exist without it either: this water Clement identifies with Christ.[923]

Intrinsically connected to water's powers of cleansing and purification are its powers of healing, restoring youth and bestowing eternal life: water is the supreme medicine or panacea. The "water of life" (or "living water") and the "fountain of youth" are near-universal metaphors for strength, vitality, longevity or even immortality. Such elixirs need not necessarily take the form of "pure" water, and are not necessarily available to everyone. They may be hidden in inaccessible locations or guarded by monsters or snakes. We have already encountered the profound metonymic link between the water of life and the tree of life, or between what Eliade has termed water hierophanies and plant hierophanies. The ancient Vedic conception of *soma* is manifest on the one hand as a stream or spring, but on the other as a heavenly plant with miraculous powers of intoxication and regeneration. By the same token, Jesus is represented both by water and by wine and the vine from which it is derived. Here we shall look at aspects of this intimate relationship between water and wine, focusing above all on the link with inebriation, sacred or otherwise.

923. See Marks, 114.

Jesus himself made the wine imagery explicit: "I am the vine," he told his disciples, "you are the branches" (John, 15:5).[924] These words were to prove highly influential in medieval art, where the cross and the tree of life were often portrayed as grapevines.[925] Also according to John's gospel, Christ's first miracle was to convert six 20-gallon jars of water into wine at a wedding feast at Cana near the Sea of Galilee (John, 2:1-11).[926] At the Last Supper his offering of bread and wine to his disciples with the words "this is my body" and "this is my blood" was to lead to the central Christian ritual of the Eucharist, as well as to painstakingly elaborated doctrines such as transubstantiation and consubstantiation, as theologians laboured to pin down the exact nature of the relationship between the bread and wine and Christ's body and blood. Apocryphal legends lend further support to the image of Christ as a vine. A Slavonic compilation known as *Questions and Answers*, dating from before the 17th century, relates how Pontius Pilate found his wife naked beside a vine that had sprung forth from Christ's bloodstained clothes and miraculously borne fruit.[927]

The traditional teaching has been that the ritual of drinking Christ's blood and eating his body allows believers to partake of his sacrifice and resurrection: again in the gospel of John, Jesus says: "unless you eat the flesh of the Son of man and drink his blood, you have no life in you; he who eats my flesh and drinks my blood has eternal life … He who eats my flesh and drinks my blood abides in me, and I in him" (John, 6:53-54, 56). There are striking continuities with the cults of the Greek and Roman wine gods, Dionysus and Bacchus, who were likewise associated with the vine

---

924. Likewise: "I am the true vine, and my Father is the vinedresser" (John, 15:1).
925. Biedermann, 384.
926. A German proverb has it that "thirst turns water into wine" (*Durst macht aus Wasser Wein*), though the Galilean wedding guests might have begged to differ. However, reversing the transformation is a miracle in which we can all take pleasure. As Austrian liedermacher Wolfgang Ambros sings (*Wolfgang Ambros Live, BRD-Tournee April 1979*):
> I feel a bit like Jesus
> Though I haven't got his class:
> All I convert is wine
> Into the water that I pass.

Or in German: *Mir geht es wie dem Jesus / … nur hab ich nicht die Klasse, / denn ich verwandle nur den Wein / in Wasser, das ich lasse.* Many thanks to Winni Schindler for drawing my attention to this.
927. Eliade, *Patterns*, 285-86.

and its miraculous powers and with regeneration and resurrection. Yet Christianity was quick to dissociate itself from the excesses of Dionysian intoxication. In Paul's First Letter to the Corinthians, he warns his readers not to take advantage of the Lord's Supper to sate their hunger or get drunk: "Whoever ... eats the bread or drinks the cup of the Lord in an unworthy manner will be guilty of profaning the body and blood of the Lord" (1 Corinthians, 11:27). Today, some Protestant churches replace wine with grape juice, while the Mormons use bread and water to symbolize Christ's body and blood.

Wine has been a notably ambivalent symbol from the outset. Yet the wine/water duality seems fundamental to Christianity. Bearing in mind the identification of blood and wine, one striking passage comes from the First Epistle of John, in which Jesus Christ is referred to as "he who came by water and blood, ... not with the water only but with the water and the blood. ... There are three witnesses, the Spirit, the water, and the blood" (1 John, 5:6-8).[928] A mixture of wine and water – the "fire" of wine with the "passivity" of water – was seen as reflecting the dual nature of the person of Jesus, incorporating both the divine and the human. The Church saw itself in similar terms.[929] In Christian art, the "cardinal virtue" of temperance was represented by two containers for mixing water and wine.[930]

This ambivalence has its roots in the tale of Noah in Genesis. According to the Jewish *midrash*, Noah lost his epithet "the pious" once he began to engage in cultivating the vine, and Satan was his assistant in viniculture. Yet in growing wine and drinking too much of it, Noah was merely following the example of Adam, "whose fall had also been due to wine, for the forbidden fruit had been the grape, with which he had made

---

928. Particularly intriguing is a clause known as the *Comma Johanneum*, which was incorporated in many translations of the Epistle between the 16th and the 19th century, although its authenticity is disputed. This reads: "For there are three that bear record in heaven, the Father, the Word, and the Holy Ghost: and these three are one. And there are three that bear witness in earth, the Spirit, and the water, and the blood: and these three agree in one." The heavenly Trinity of the Father, Son and Holy Spirit is reflected in an earthly trinity of water, wine/blood, and spirit.
929. Biedermann, 44, 373.
930. See ibid., 369: the four cardinal virtues are courage, justice, prudence and temperance. The three theological virtues are faith, hope and charity.

himself drunk."[931] Wine is associated with life and hidden truth on the one hand, but also with what is dangerous and prohibited: knowledge itself is the epitome of danger. Islam denounced wine – along with games of chance – as abominations devised by Satan and called upon Muslims to practise abstention from alcoholic drinks, yet according to the Qur'an wine mixed with water from a refreshing spring will be available in Paradise (83:25-28).[932]

The association of wisdom and insight with wine – or in ancient Mesopotamia with beer, the staple drink before wine became more widely available – goes back to the *Epic of Gilgamesh*, which incorporates Sumerian tales from the third millennium BCE. In the course of Gilgamesh's quest for immortality following the death of his friend Enkidu, he comes across Siduri the alewife, goddess of brewing and of wisdom, who gives him advice on how to reach Ut-napishtim, the survivor of the deluge. Ut-napishtim in turn tells Gilgamesh how to obtain the plant that bestows immortality, and Gilgamesh duly dives into the waters of the Apsu to fetch it – only to be tricked out of it by a snake on his return trip. In another account of the tale, Siduri tells Gilgamesh that immortality is not for humankind: he should stop worrying about death and live the present to the full.[933] It has been suggested that in even more primitive versions of the legend the beer-goddess's role is more important and Gilgamesh asks immortality of her directly.[934]

For the early farmers of Mesopotamia, beer was naturally associated with divine powers. The seemingly supernatural process of fermentation, which could convert an ordinary gruel of grain soaked in water into intoxicating nectar with the power to alter one's state of mind, made the drink seem like a gift from the gods, and it lent itself to religious ceremonies and agricultural fertility rites.[935] When wine subsequently grew in popularity in the first millennium BCE, this in turn became linked with divinity and higher truths: "wine reveals what is hidden," said the Greek

---

931. Ginzberg, I.167-68. This is not the only interpretation of the forbidden fruit: elsewhere it is the fig (see 75, 96-97).
932. This was the complaint underlying the *Ruba'iyat* of Omar Khayyam, who was impatient with promises of wine and beautiful women in the afterlife when he wanted them now.
933. Dalley (ed.), 99-102, 149-50.
934. Eliade, 284.
935. See Standage, 17-20.

philosopher Eratosthenes in the 3rd century BCE.[936] In ancient Athens in particular, the pursuit of truth was epitomized by the symposium, where philosophers came together to drink and talk of philosophy and literature. Yet it was essential that the wine that was drunk there should be tempered with water. This, the Athenians felt, was what distinguished them from barbarians such as the Scythians and Thracians, who drank unmixed wine and behaved like brutes: only Dionysus could take his wine neat. In charge of the symposium, therefore, was a *symposiarch*, whose task was to maintain the delicate balance between sobriety and drunkenness, fostering free speech and frankness while steering clear of vulgarity and violence. Inevitably, he was not always successful, and some symposia descended into dissolution. In the eyes of the Greek philosophers of the time, the mixture of water and wine thus became a potent metaphor for the mixture of the good and bad in human nature in general.[937]

The Greek tradition of drinking parties at which the wine was mixed with water as a mark of "civilization" was perpetuated in the Roman *convivium*. Christianity, by contrast, has tended to dilute its inebriation into a *spiritualized* form. The image of spiritual drunkenness became a commonplace of Christian mysticism from the writings of Philo the Jew and Gregory of Nyssa through to Erasmus, who compared the ecstatic madness of the Apostles to a state of inebriation.[938] Yet such spiritual inebriation has had to be watered down by simile (it is *like* drunkenness) or by oxymoron: at issue, insists Erasmus, is *sobria ebrietas*, a sober drunkenness, a mere appearance of intoxication to the unknowing. Though frequent among mystical thinkers, rapture or ecstasy has tended to represent a threat to orthodoxy, coming too close for comfort to Dionysian or pagan spiritual possession.

Particularly heady is the imagery of mystical union developed by the 14th-century German mystic Henry Suso (Heinrich Seuse) in his *Book of Truth*:

> it is like an ineffable inebriation in which the spirit forgets itself, ceases to be itself, and has un-become [*entworden*] itself, having passed into God and become wholly one with him. For just as a tiny drop of water poured into a cask of wine un-becomes itself as it takes on the wine's

936. Quoted in ibid., 62. On the Greek symposium, see 56-66.
937. Ibid., 62.
938. See Screech, *Erasmus: Ecstasy and the Praise of Folly*, 72-75.

taste and colour, so it happens with those who are in complete possession of bliss that all human desire falls away, in some ineffable way, and they flow out of themselves and are taken up into the divine will.[939]

In fact, this use of the image of a drop of water in a vat of wine as a way of describing mystical union with God went back to the ultra-orthodox monastic reformer Bernard of Clairvaux in the 12th century, whose words are closely followed by Suso. Unlike Suso, however, Bernard was referring not to earthly union, but the deification of the human spirit in heaven. And Bernard was quick to point out that the soul and God do not *actually* become one substance (this just *seems to* happen).[940] It was perhaps through its association with Suso's mentor, the great mystic Meister Eckhart, that the image of water in wine achieved special notoriety. For Eckhart, the union between the soul and God "is far closer than when someone pours a drop of water into a barrel of wine: the latter would be water and wine, whereas the former are so united with each other that no creature can find a difference between them."[941] Not only does Eckhart radicalize the image (in that mystical union is *even* more intimate than the merging of liquids), but he applies it to an earthly as opposed to a heavenly transformation. Eckhart's use of the image thus came to be equated with the claims made by the notorious Free Spirit heretics, one of whose main tracts (the *Schwester Katrei* or *Sister Catherine Treatise*) reverses the image for the same purpose, referring to "a drop of wine in the middle of the sea" to portray how the contemplative soul can lose its own being and be converted into God.[942] Associated by orthodoxy with pantheism, antinomianism and sheer megalomania, any such heresy was to be repudiated at all costs.[943]

939. Seuse, *Das Buch der Wahrheit*, 22-23.
940. Even this was potentially explosive. According to a well-known 13th-century anecdote, when Bernard's image was taken up in a sermon by the priest John Polinus one female listener was so overwhelmed that she "bubbled over like new wine in an air-tight container," burst a blood vessel, and died on the spot. See Lerner, "The Image of Mixed Liquids in Late Medieval Mystical Thought," 398.
941. Eckhart, *Selected Writings*, 35.
942. See Lerner, 403.
943. See ibid., esp. 406-9, for an account of the contradictions in attitudes to the water-wine image. One of Eckhart's most orthodox Dominican followers, Johannes Tauler, on one occasion described the human spirit as losing itself en-

The fine, inherently unclear line between inspired rapture and diabolical possession – or between orthodox and heretical self-abdication – echoes the fine line between a symposium where higher truths are attained and one that descends into a free-for-all or orgiastic excess. Where heady concoctions have threatened to become too potent, some form of control or restraint has been felt to be indispensable. The cardinal virtue of temperance is the *right* mixture of water and wine.

$$* \quad * \quad * \quad * \quad *$$

It can be countered, of course, that the whole point of inebriation – even sacred inebriation – is that it should *not* be sober. The divine mode of being involves shedding the shackles of selfhood, restraint and reason: the idea, literally, is to "lose oneself" in God, to "forget oneself," perhaps even to "die" to the world so as to return renewed. This may be induced by the wine of Dionysianism or the soma or *haoma* of ancient Indo-Iranian thought, which is presumed to have been some form of hallucinogenic plant or mushroom.[944] Even so, some have seen narcotic intoxication itself as a derived or even decadent form of inebriation when compared with other, time-honoured mystical and shamanic techniques of ecstasy.[945] From this point of view, true inebriation really is spiritual. Control is of

---

tirely in the divine essence "just as a drop of water is lost in a great vat of wine," while in another sermon he claimed that anyone who takes the image literally has succumbed to an "evil, false heresy." Tauler was himself attacked for being a Beghard (i.e. a Free Spirit heretic). The later mystic Jean Gerson explicitly repudiated even Bernard's use of the simile.

944. See, for example, McKenna, *Food of the Gods: The Search for the Original Tree of Knowledge*, 97-120.

945. See Eliade, *Shamanism: Archaic Techniques of Ecstasy*, 401, referring to the techniques of shamanic intoxication: "Narcotics are only a vulgar substitute for 'pure' trance." Cf. 477: "Mystical ecstasy being assimilated to a temporary 'death' or to leaving the body, all intoxications that produced the same result were given a place among the techniques of ecstasy. But closer study of the problem gives the impression that the use of narcotics is, rather, indicative of the decadence of a technique of ecstasy." Traditional methods involve drumming, ritual dancing, fasting and ordeals, breath-control and sexual abstinence.

the essence, and as we shall see below, water too may play its part.

To the extent that narcotic intoxication is an end in itself, however, water has traditionally taken on the role of the spoilsport, killjoy or party pooper. In a context of secular hedonism, temperance is generally considered out of place, the water-drinker is a persona non grata, and the whole *point* of partying is that it should get (at least a bit) out of hand. The Spanish term for a killjoy, *aguafiestas*, says it all. The occasional drink of water may have its uses, postponing the onset of drivelling embarrassment or oblivion, or subsequently replacing the water that our brain cells have sacrificed to flush toxins from the body. But it should keep a low profile. At a good party there should be no suggestion that restraint or temperance is called for.

Cultural and other contextual factors play an important role. Montaigne, who claimed to drink about a pint and a half of diluted wine a day (generally mixed half and half, sometimes one third water), wrote that he could no more bear to see Germans water their wine than Frenchmen drink it neat: common usage was what mattered.[946] Yet minor regional or national differences apart, it is water's apparent abundance and ensuing familiarity that have tended to breed contempt: bread and water are prison fare,[947] covering our barest needs rather than pandering to our pleasures. In general, contempt for water is a privilege of affluent societies that *have* water and by and large waste it. It is reasonable to assume that the more than one billion people on the planet without access to safe drinking water are less contemptuous. "When the well's dry," said Benjamin Franklin, "we know the worth of water."[948]

The German aphorist Lichtenberg recognized that water would taste better if it were a sin to drink it,[949] and a foolish voice in the Bible announces that "stolen water is sweet, and bread eaten in secret is pleasant" (Proverbs, 9:17). The very legality of water renders it plain and charmless. The vine, by contrast, still retains something of the forbidden fruit.[950] Yet recent years have seen a shift in emphasis. Today the question of fashion

946. Montaigne, "On Experience," 1253-54.
947. Rupp, 56.
948. Quoted in *Water* (National Geographic Special Edition, vol. 184, no. 5A, 1993), 1.
949. Lichtenberg, *Sudelbücher*, 284 (F669): *Es ist schade daß es keine Sünde ist Wasser zu trinken, rief ein Italiener, wie gut würde es schmecken.* For some reason Lichtenberg puts his aphorism in the mouth of an Italian.
950. Though perhaps not much. It may be pretty tame stuff for those in pursuit of weirder kinds of kicks. As Lux Interior of *The Cramps* and others have sung: "Some folks like water, / Some folks like wine. / But I like the taste / Of straight strychnine." In this case, the poisonous nux vomica is the forbidden fruit.

pulls virtually as much weight as sin, and the rise of the over-priced plastic water bottle as a lifestyle accessory has made it perfectly acceptable, even in public, to indulge in a drink that tastes of nothing and should be free. Another factor has been the emergence of MDMA, or ecstasy, as a party drug and the associated use of water to maintain fluid intake during dancing.[951] In some party culture at least, the serious water-drinker has become less of a social pariah.

More generally, however, wine has been associated with wit, and water with temperance and dullness. The ancient Romans and Greeks considered not drinking wine at all to be as deviant as drinking it neat, the teetotaller as undesirable as the barbarian. In his comedy *The Wineflask* (which defeated Aristophanes's *The Clouds* at the Athenian drama festival in 423 BCE), the poet Cratinus wrote that "a water-drinker never gives birth to anything ingenious." The poet and satirist Horace claimed that "no verse can give pleasure for long, nor last, that is written by drinkers of water."[952] While water-drinkers have been viewed as surly and witless, the wisdom and wit of wine has been a timeless theme of popular and comic lore, running through the drinking-songs of the *Carmina Burana*, the wise folly of Shakespeare's toper Falstaff, and the convivial and inspired narrative inebriation of Rabelais.[953] In late-19th-century Paris, the literary club known as the *Hydropathes*, one of the precursors of the Symbolist movement, sought not only to celebrate literary and poetic creativity but also – as its name suggests – to denigrate water in favour of wine or more

951. Indeed, the principal cause of the relatively few deaths resulting from ecstasy use has been hyperhydration, or water intoxication, which can also result from water-drinking contests or from long periods of intense exercise (during which too much salt is sweated out, too much sodium lost, and too much water then drunk).
952. See Rupp, 56. For Horace (*Epistles*, xix, 1), see also *The Oxford Dictionary of Quotations*, 258.
953. See, for example, Falstaff's praise of sack, a dry white wine (*vin sec*) or sherry: "A good sherris-sack ... ascends me into the brain, dries me there all the foolish and dull and crudy vapours which environ it, makes it apprehensive, quick, forgetive, full of nimble, fiery, and delectable shapes, which delivered o'er to the voice, the tongue, which is the birth, becomes excellent wit. ... If I had a thousand sons, the first human principle I would teach them should be to forswear thin potations, and to addict themselves to sack" (*2 Henry IV*, 4.3.94-100, 121-23).

potent potions such as absinthe.[954] If the bohemian circle around Henry Murger some 30 years earlier had called themselves *Les Buveurs d'Eau* (the Water Drinkers), this was because they were too hard up to afford anything else.

Yet the converse has also been claimed. Friedrich Nietzsche despised the boorishness of indiscriminate beer-swilling and the false pleasures of artificial stimulants. In the *Gay Science*, he associates drunkenness with a dulling of the senses and the mental stupor of the mediocre: "you rush through life as if you were drunk," he warns his readers, "now and again falling downstairs. Thanks to your inebriation, however, you do not break your limbs: your muscles are too slack and your head too dull for you to find the stone stairs as hard as the rest of us do. For us, life is a greater danger."[955] And while wine may be associated with witlessness, water has been intrinsically linked with creativity. The Muses of classical literature, the proverbial embodiments of poetic inspiration begotten from the union of Zeus with watery Mnemosyne, were initially thought of as mountain and water nymphs and associated in particular with springs such as the Hippocrene on Mount Helicon and Castalia on Mount Parnassus ("One drink from her waters," it was said of Castalia, "and the poet sings"[956]).

It may sometimes seem as though water and wine are opposites or complements in the same way that fire and water appear to be, each with its advocates and each with its detractors. Yet this is only superficially the case. For there is an important sense in which both wine and beer are *unthinkable* without water: ultimately indeed, like most of the liquids we encounter in everyday life, they are just "tainted water, full of dissolved or suspended substances."[957] In this respect, water is *prior* to wine; it is the precondition for its very existence. It takes roughly 250 litres of water merely to grow the crops required for a glass of wine or a pint of beer, and as much as 2,000 litres for a glass of brandy.[958] At the same time, both

---

954. The name *Hydropathes* also playfully alludes to the name of the founder, Émile Goudeau (*goût d'eau* meaning a taste of water). Any link with hydropathy – the then popular term for water therapy – can be taken as ironic.

955. Nietzsche, *Die Fröhliche Wissenschaft*, 133 (3.154).

956. Biedermann, 232.

957. Ball, *H₂O*, 154.

958. See Pearce, 22. This water is known by economists and environmentalists as "virtual water," in that we are not directly aware of its use when we consume the crop in question. In this sense, of course, water is *prior* to most things. Pearce provides a wealth of examples: a kilo of sugar takes 3,000 litres of water to produce, a kilo of coffee no less than 20,000 litres. See ibid., 22-25, on virtual water.

beer and wine won their spurs amongst other things as *forms* of purified water, providing humankind with a drink that was safer than many natural water-sources, vulnerable as these were to contamination by human and animal waste. It continues to be at least in part for this reason that many rural societies brew beer or other liquors based on fermented grain, fruit or vegetable.

Traditionally, moreover, the concept of "water" has extended to incorporate even headier concoctions than mere wine or beer. When distilled wines came to be developed, first in the 8th century by Arab alchemist-scholars such as the great Jabir ibn Hayyan (known in the West as Geber) and then a few centuries later in Europe by the Catalan mystics Arnald of Villanova and Ramon Llull (Raymond Lully),[959] these distillations naturally assumed the magical properties of the wines from which they were derived. By the late 13th century, they were being acclaimed in Latin medical treatises as the "water of life," endowed with miraculous therapeutic qualities. The Christian symbolic framework resonates in Arnald's instructions for the process of distillation, dating from around 1300: "The true water of life will come over in precious drops, which, being rectified by three or four successive distillations, will afford the wonderful quintessence of wine," he explained. "We call it aqua vitae, and this name is remarkably suitable, since it is really a water of immortality." Yet the effects were very much of this world: "it prolongs life, clears away ill-humors, revives the heart, and maintains youth."[960] The advocates of aqua vitae saw it as a panacea that not only preserved youth but could cure no end of physical ailments.

Initially based on the distillation of wine, the concept of "water of life" – denoting a concentrated aqueous solution of alcohol – rapidly spread to other types of distillate. The terms for the originally Scottish or Irish beer distillates "whisky" or "whiskey" have their etymological roots in the Gaelic renditions of aqua vitae, *uisge-beatha* or *uisce-beathadh* (via usquebaugh). Other such life-giving waters are the French eau de vie and the Scandinavian aquavit. In some contexts, spirits are simply referred to as water: Russian vodka, for example, is "little water" (*voda* being water). Equally revivifying – if not more so – is *agua de Valencia* or "water of Valencia," a cocktail comprising cava, Cointreau, orange juice and sugar.

959. It is believed that rice beer (saké) was being distilled by the Chinese considerably earlier, possibly as early as 800 BCE, but it was not until the Arabs that the distillation of wine was pursued more methodically.
960. Quoted in Standage, 98-99.

That such spirits were not only inflammable but also produced a burning effect when imbibed gave rise to the term *aqua ardens* or "burning water," which lives on in the Spanish *aguardiente*. Not surprisingly, such fiery waters would soon develop infernal associations to counter their original status as life-renewing panaceas. Derived from the fermentation of sugar cane, rum was thus known in its early days as "kill-devil," a designation that was gradually replaced by the slang term "rumbullion," meaning "a brawl or violent commotion." A 17th-century visitor to Barbados described the drink as a "hot, hellish and terrible liquor."[961]

*   *   *   *   *

The highly intoxicating "waters of life" make it clear once more that "water" is much too protean to be confined to either side of a simple, binary opposition between sobriety and inebriation. Yet water's powers of intoxication manifest themselves not only when we swallow it, but when it swallows us.

The liberating sense of erotic transgression associated with swimming and bathing was a commonplace of the Romantic imagination: a deep fascination with water was shared by Shelley and Swinburne, Byron and Poe, Goethe and Valéry. Freedom from the shackles of convention and social respectability, freedom from the limitations of selfhood and individuality, freedom from the physical bonds of time and gravity, all combined to intoxicate and enrapture the Romantic swimmer. This intoxication took a variety of forms. In the case of Shelley, who never learnt to swim (and who almost only ever drank water, wine being too much of a stimulant for his brain), the love affair with water inclined him to sink rather than swim: his repeated indifference to drowning expressed an aquatic death-wish, a willingness or yearning to surrender to the

---

961. Ibid., 107, and in general, 105-11. When rum replaced beer as the staple drink on Royal Navy ships in the Caribbean, it was decreed that half a pint of rum should be mixed with two pints of water. The subsequent inclusion of lime juice in this "grog" was to do wonders for the health of the British navy.

"water's kiss."[962] Swinburne echoed Shelley's ecstatic relationship with water, but was a good swimmer who was only interested in dangerous coasts and was bored by the Mediterranean. Byron, certainly not an avid water-drinker, was an extremely strong swimmer, as was Poe.

The element of sexuality was central. Another Romantic, Novalis, saw water as the embodiment of love and voluptuous sensuality, a manifestation of the *Urflüssige*, the primordial fluidity. How few are those, says one of the voices in his uncompleted philosophical novel *Die Lehrlinge zu Sais* (*The Novices at Sais*), who have "immersed themselves in the mysteries of fluidity." The intoxication of those who do so is a form of *Zerfliessen*, a flowing or melting away, or flux: "The inebriated feel only too well the heavenly bliss of fluidity, and in the end all pleasant sensations in us are manifold fluxes [*Zerfliessungen*], movements of those primal waters in us." Sleep itself – a paradigm of narcosis – is "but the flood tide of that invisible ocean"; waking is its subsequent ebbing.[963]

If Novalis's point was that sensual rapture is a heightened state of wateriness, others have stressed watery immersion as a route to erotic delectation. For Swinburne, being pounded and mauled by heavy waters was a source of masochistic pleasure that was closely associated with the delights of flagellation: "I am dying for it," he wrote, "there is no lust or appetite comparable." His was a "craving (ultra Sapphic and plusquam Sadic) lust after the sea."[964] For Goethe the nakedness of a cold bathe represented an invigorating revolt against repressive convention and the dictates of propriety. As a boy, Byron wanton'd on the breakers. For Valéry swimming was a form of *fornication avec l'onde*: "My body becomes the direct instrument of my mind, the author of its ideas," he wrote in his journal. "To plunge into water, to move one's whole body, from head to toe, in its wild and graceful beauty; to twist about in its pure depths, this is

---

962. See Sprawson, 75-82.
963. Novalis, *Werke*, 122. Tellingly, Novalis judged the ideal of philosophy (which was Fichtean philosophy) to be an activity akin to swimming without having learnt how to do so beforehand. This did not entail drowning à la Shelley, but something more like learning by doing: "Fichte's call for simultaneously thinking, acting and observing is the ideal of philosophizing – and by seeking to achieve this – I begin to realize the ideal. Most people do not want to swim until they know how to" (ibid., 475). The message for would-be philosophers was to go ahead and take the plunge, to dive in at the deep end.
964. See Sprawson, 90, and in general on Swinburne, 88-99.

for me a delight only comparable to love."[965] There is something orgiastic about immersion in water: a loss of self, a transcending of boundaries, a regression to chaos, followed by revitalization and new life.[966] As the link with baptism suggests, bathing has thus often tended to hover ambiguously between hedonism and a "higher," purer spirituality. Of course, the contradiction only exists to the extent that spirituality is seen as being *in opposition to* pleasure, euphoria and ecstasy.[967]

The euphoric associations of water have various physiological foundations. These come to light particularly clearly in the case of the *cold* bath, with its "heady rush of endorphins," natural opioids that anaesthetize the body against the cold and induce a general sensation of well-being. In the course of his beautifully recounted swim through the British Isles, Roger Deakin experiences several such moments of cold shock. On the island of Jura in the Hebrides, for example, he encountered the sort of water "that sends your blood surging and crams every capillary with a belt of adrenalin, despatching endorphins to seep into the seats of pleasure in body and brain, so that your soul goes soaring, and never quite settles all day." For Deakin, the cold-water swim is inseparable from ecstasy in its original sense of being outside one's own body.[968]

In certain Romantics, swimming came to be associated with opium dreams, reflecting and intensifying the strange form of self-absorbed autism to which they tended to be prone, their detachment from ordinary life and people, their feeling of exclusion or difference. The expansion of time,

965. Quoted in ibid., 101.
966. Eliade also draws a parallel between orgy and immersion in water: "For a time man goes back to the amorphous, nocturnal state of chaos that he may be reborn, more vigorous than ever in his daylight self. Like immersion in water ..., the orgy destroys creation while at the same time regenerating it" (*Patterns*, 359). The parallel finds concrete expression in the orgiastic debauchery commonly associated with bathhouses, which have often served as houses of assignation or doubled as bawdy houses. Modern-day gay bathhouses perpetuate the image.
967. Iris Murdoch, herself a passionate river swimmer, describes this tension in her novel *The Philosopher's Pupil*: the local baths in the spring town of Ennistone on the one hand appealed to a "lofty conception of the spiritual utility of swimming" while on the other they were viewed as a "temple of hedonism." A visiting evangelist once caused a stir when he exclaimed, "You have dethroned Christ and worship water instead" (30, 32).
968. See Deakin, 211, 244, 307.

the elation and weightlessness, the sharpening of the senses, were all part of this dream-like otherness. Metaphorical links between water and the effects of opium-taking pervade de Quincey's *Confessions of an English Opium Eater*. "I have often been asked," he begins in a passage that was subsequently deleted, "how it was, and through what series of steps, that I became an opium-eater. Was it gradually, tentatively, mistrustingly, as one goes down a shelving beach into a deepening sea?"[969] Many of his visions are of lakes and "silvery expanses of water," of seas and oceans, which could at times assume a nightmarish quality.[970] Unable to move in one dream, he felt "the weight of twenty Atlantics" upon him; he lay powerless and motionless, "deeper than ever plummet sounded."[971] He also draws parallels between Coleridge's and his own "baptismal initiation into the use of that mighty drug": the two of them were "embarked in the self-same boat."[972] Religious images of paradise and celestial pleasure colour his account, as well as imagery of life, death and rejuvenation. Approvingly citing Bacon's conjecture that birth may be as painful as death, he portrays himself as having "the torments of a man passing out of one mode of existence into another. The issue was not death, but a sort of physical regeneration."[973]

That such opiate reveries need not imply actual immersion, however, becomes clear in *Moby Dick*, where the ocean is shown to be intrinsically wedded to meditation and freedom and depth of thought. The "thought-engendering altitude" of the masthead is especially conducive to a state of pantheistic harmony and wellbeing: take the humorous description of the "absent-minded young philosophers" often put on lookout, who remain blissfully oblivious to the passing whales:

---

969. De Quincey, *Confessions of an English Opium Eater*, 139. In fact, he insists, it was simply a response to acute pain.
970. Ibid., 107-8: "now it was that upon the rocking waters of the ocean the human face began to appear: the sea appeared paved with innumerable faces, upturned to the heavens: faces, imploring, wrathful, despairing, surged upwards by thousands, by myriads, by generations, by centuries: – my agitation was infinite, – my mind tossed – and surged with the ocean." This is Proteus transposed into the realm of the surreal grotesque.
971. Ibid., 112-13.
972. Ibid., 142.
973. Ibid., 115.

lulled into such an opium-like listlessness of vacant, unconscious reverie is this absent-minded youth by the blending cadence of waves with thoughts, that at last he loses his identity; takes the mystic ocean at his feet for the visible image of that deep, blue, bottomless soul, pervading mankind and nature; ... . In this enchanted mood, thy spirit ebbs away to whence it came; becomes diffused through time and space.

In such a state of sublime reverie, of course, actual immersion can ensue all too easily. It only takes a tiny slip of the foot for one's identity to come rushing back "in horror": "Over Descartian vortices you hover. And perhaps, at mid-day, in the fairest weather, with one half-throttled shriek you drop through that transparent air into the summer sea, no more to rise for ever. Heed it well, ye Pantheists!"[974]

Even more than the opiate pleasures of swimming or masthead reverie, it is diving that affords some of the most intense opportunities for aquatic inebriation. Tim Ecott describes "neutral buoyancy" – the sensation of near weightlessness to which scuba divers aspire – as "liberation from gravity's tiresome pull [which] frees not just the body, but also the mind." By contrast with the outer space experienced by astronauts, to divers the ocean represents what they like to call "inner space," an immersion in one's own thoughts and reactions that is also a sort of mental release and an escape from the terrestrial.[975]

Yet diving for fun is a recent invention. It was above all the development of the scuba, or self-contained underwater breathing apparatus, by pioneers such as Jacques Cousteau and Hans Hass in the mid-20th century that liberated divers from the enormous risks and difficulties previously associated with venturing underwater to any considerable depth or for any considerable time. The scuba system unfettered divers from the cumbersome equipment and above all from the fragile air-line on which they had relied for a constant supply of air from the surface, in the process turning deep-sea diving into a recreational pastime available to more or less anyone with money, health and the inclination. One of the key figures in this development was the French inventor Yves Le Prieur, who had the brainwave of attaching a diver's mouthpiece to one of the bottles of compressed air being developed by the Michelin Company to inflate tyres. Together with his colleague and friend Jean Painlevé, he in 1934 founded the world's first diving club at St Raphael on the French

---

974. Melville, 162-63.
975. Ecott, 103.

Riviera. It was known informally as the *Club des "sous l'eau"*, which means "underwater" but is also a slang term for drunkards.[976] The link with inebriation was already forged.

This link was reinforced in the 1940s when Cousteau and his companions started to test how deep they could dive with the aqualung system they had designed on the basis of Le Prieur's original invention. Returning after a then-record descent of 210 feet, one of them, Frédéric Dumas, reported that below a depth of 100 feet he had experienced a sensation of light-headed tipsiness.[977] Immediately baptized "rapture of the deep" by Cousteau and his colleagues, the condition is now known as nitrogen narcosis, and along with the bends and oxygen poisoning it represents one of the major risks associated with diving with compressed air: in the early days it claimed numerous lives as attempts were consistently made to dive to ever greater depths. The precise mechanisms are not fully understood, but what is clear is that breathing nitrogen under pressure produces effects similar to alcoholic intoxication, eventually leading to irrational behaviour and a silent death.[978]

However, there is more to deep-sea intoxication than just nitrogen narcosis and oxygen poisoning. Neal Watson, who in 1968 set a new record when he dived to a depth of just over 437 feet using compressed air, describes his feeling in the depths as an experience of what he calls "enlightenment"; it was "a spiritual feeling … like being given the key to the universe." Not merely an effect of the nitrogen or oxygen, he believes, it was something more like a "near-death experience."[979]

Equally intense feelings may be produced by free diving, which has the advantage of reducing to a minimum the diving equipment – and the risk of its failure – and eliminating the threat of narcosis and the bends. In this case, the physical exhilaration is a product, at least in part,

---

976. See ibid., 110.
977. Ibid., 123-24.
978. On nitrogen narcosis and oxygen poisoning, see ibid., 123-35. Nitrogen begins to affect a diver's mental processes below a depth of roughly 75 feet, whereas oxygen does not become toxic until a depth of more than 175 feet. Using oxygen on its own does not solve the problem. Even at the surface, breathing pure oxygen is harmful if done for more than a short time. Under pressure, pure oxygen can cause seizures at considerably lesser depths than when it is mixed with nitrogen. The best solution to the problem of nitrogen narcosis is to mix oxygen with helium instead of nitrogen, since helium is less soluble in the blood. It too can cause narcosis, but not until much greater depths.
979. Ibid., 131.

of extreme breath-control, and has been compared to the sexual practice known as auto-erotic asphyxiation, the intensification of sexual pleasure by means of strangulation, which can likewise produce a sense of giddy elation and on occasion result in death. Both auto-eroticist and diver are believed to be provoking the condition known as cerebral hypoxia, or oxygen deprivation. Whatever the precise causes of free-diving euphoria, the effects are well-documented. Legendary free-diver Umberto Pelizzari, the first man to attain a depth of 150 metres on a "no limits" dive, has said that at extreme depths he forgets his body and is conscious only of his soul.[980] Other free divers have spoken of elation so intense that the temptation is to stay below for good.

As in the case of the scuba-diver Neal Watson, who was well-versed in the techniques of Zen meditation, such feats call for an extreme degree of physical fitness and control. Holding his breath for over seven minutes and slowing his heartbeat to eight pulses a minute, Umberto Pelizzari finds a sort of inner calm "best compared to a mystic trance, like an Eastern yogi."[981] The euphoria that results may seem to have little in common with the lawlessness and indiscipline of wine-induced roistering. Yet as in other forms of inebriation, imagery of immersion and renewal re-emerges in the context of apnoea. As Ecott puts it, "the joy of the free diver is internalized, and carried within as a lasting tranquillity. The symbolism of rebirth, the re-entry to the air world after a brief sojourn in the maternal element of seawater, strikes a chord with many."[982]

4

Trick or Treacle?

Among divers there is a widespread belief that regular immersion in sea water is something akin to an elixir of youth.[983] For habitual bathers and swimmers such as Roger Deakin or the 19th-century Romantics, the encounter with water offers union and communion with Mother Nature,

---

980. See ibid., 297; on free diving in general, see 297-326.
981. Ibid., 302.
982. Ibid., 322.
983. See ibid., 276.

and with it the possibility of self-transcendence and a release from oppressive selfhood. The effect is to soothe, uplift or perhaps unfetter spirits weighed down by terrestrial gravity, and to ward off despondency and gloom. As Deakin writes, "I can dive in with a long face and what feels like a terminal case of depression, and come out a whistling idiot."[984] In the 19th century, the cold-water treatment known as hydrotherapy was commonly prescribed for people prone to depression, including Tennyson and Charles Darwin. Another famous advocate was Charles Dickens, a sufferer of bipolar disorder, who had an improvised douche-bath specially installed in his home and described his cold shower as a "positive necessary of life."[985] The holy Narmada is thought to "dispel the malevolent effects of Saturn," as a result of which "all manner of epileptics, depressives and other unfortunates rush to her banks."[986] To go to sea may have a similar effect, providing an escape from life on land and its attendant melancholy. Melville's narrator Ishmael explains his calling as a sailor as a way of "driving off the spleen, and regulating the circulation. ... With a philosophical flourish Cato throws himself upon his sword; I quietly take to the ship."[987]

Yet the curative attributes of water have been seen to apply not only to afflictions of the soul, but also bodily ailments. The timeless mythology of the fountain of eternal youth is the most potent manifestation of water's powers of regeneration, yet this capacity to counter age and decrepitude in general is inseparable from an ability to counter specific maladies. According to the practical wisdom of the ancient Indian *Atharva Veda*, "the waters are indeed healers; the waters drive away and cure all illnesses."[988] Holy wells, springs and lakes embody water's divine life-giving and life-preserving qualities. One common metaphorical association links such

---

984. Deakin, 4.
985. See Ashenburg, 161-63, on Dickens.
986. Mehta, 145.
987. Melville, 21. Of course, the simple pleasures of maritime existence may be countered or outweighed by the sheer monotony of cramped conditions and an unchanging seascape. This seems to have been the case with Darwin himself. "What are the boasted glories of the illimitable ocean?" he asks. "A tedious waste, a desert of water, as the Arabian calls it." (quoted in Farber, 100).
988. Quoted in Eliade, *Patterns*, 188.

waters to the human *eye*,[989] each combining a reflective surface with profundity or depth. This has led to a special focus on ocular ailments.[990] As described by Peter Ackroyd, the Thames – along with the 26 healing springs found in its vicinity – has nurtured an intrinsic connection with the healing of eyes. It is a tradition that goes back to Augustine's miracles near the river at Cricklade, where he persuaded the blind to see, and to the ophthalmological marvels attributed to the 7th-century princess Frideswide at the well at Binsey near Oxford.[991] This was the well that was transformed by Lewis Carroll into the "treacle well" in *Alice's Adventures in Wonderland*: treacle was an old term – derived from the Latin theriac – meaning a medicine or antidote to poison.[992]

The thermal springs at Bath were the place of worship for the mother goddess Sulis, who was identified with the Roman Minerva as a patron of wisdom and healing. Other maternal deities too have been intimately connected with rivers and their therapeutic powers. In and beyond Egypt, much-revered river-goddesses such as Isis and Hathor were linked both with fertility and motherhood and with medicine and magic. Just as Isis restored to life the mutilated body of her brother-husband Osiris, Hathor restored the sight of their son Horus, whose eyes had been ripped out

989. See Thoreau's description of lakes (such as the one at Walden) as "the landscape's most beautiful and expressive feature." A lake, he writes, "is the earth's eye; looking into which the beholder measures the depth of his own nature." The lakeside trees are its eyelashes, the wooded hills its brows (*Walden*, 233). In the freezing winter, moreover, "like the marmots in the surrounding hills, it closes its eye-lids and becomes dormant for three months or more" (331).
990. Glaucoma, for example, was popularly known as "water of the eye" (see Ackroyd, 287). The disease is caused by increased pressure within the eyeball as a result of a blockage in the flow of aqueous humour. The word shares its etymological roots with Glaucus, one of the shape-shifting sea-gods of the Greeks, and "glaucous" means bluish-green, the colour of the sea.
991. See ibid., 287-90.
992. See ibid., 289; also 413. In the tale told by the Dormouse, three little sisters dwelled at the bottom of a treacle well, where they lived on treacle and learnt to draw ... treacle (and why not, if water can be drawn from a water well?). Alice rightly objects that if they were *in* the well (well in, as the Dormouse concurs), they would not be able to draw treacle *from* the well. But everyone is starting to lose interest by this stage (Carroll, *Alice's Adventures in Wonderland*, 65-67). The popular humorous notion of "treacle mining" has its roots in similar wordplay.

by Seth. In more everyday contexts too, Isis was invoked to treat minor ailments with saliva and urine (i.e. with "the Nile flood between [her] thighs"), while the sick would also travel to Dendera, Hathor's cult centre, to be cleansed and cured by the waters of the Nile.[993] Their powers of maternal protection and healing resonated far and wide through time and space. In 16th-century England, a false etymology that derived the ancient name Tamesis from a confluence or conjunction of the male Thame and the female Isis at Dorchester led to a deep association between the River Thames and the tutelary figure of Isis, whose popularity had lasted right through the Greek and Roman empires: even today the Thames is known as Isis as it passes through Oxford.[994]

Another modern-day demonstration of the magic of water is Lake Baikal in southern Siberia, the oldest and deepest lake on the planet, which holds a fifth of the world's fresh water (in excess of 23,000 cubic kilometres, i.e. more than all North America's Great Lakes combined). It is thought to contain more than a thousand endemic species, including the nerpa, the world's only freshwater seal, as well as a legendary giant sturgeon – the Baikal Monster – that preys on them. Known as the Blue Eye or the Pearl of Siberia and famed for its vertiginous limpidity, its waters are held to be life-enhancing. Locals claim that you can add a year to your life by dipping a toe in, five years for a hand, and an extra 25 if you risk a swim.[995]

By contrast with wells, springs, lakes and rivers in a natural and public environment, the household baths that rose to prominence in the course of the 19th century contained waters that were domesticated, privatized and stripped of their role in human interaction and communication. This was the period, moreover, in which cleanliness came to be "next to godliness" among the expanding middle classes, while the "great unwashed" were despised and considered unpresentable.[996] Here too the link with health was maintained, as it became more generally accepted

---

993. See Scott Littleton, 42-45.
994. On the origins of this misattribution see Ackroyd, 26-29.
995. On Lake Baikal, see Caldecott, 101; Marks, 26-29. See also Chris Moss, "The Lake That Turned Putin Green," in *The Guardian*, 28 April 2006.
996. It was John Wesley, the founder of Methodism and a keen advocate of cold-water bathing, who first placed "cleanliness" next to "godliness," adapting an older Hebrew proverb in a sermon delivered in 1791. The concept of "the great unwashed" originated in William Makepeace Thackeray's novel *Pendennis*, dating from 1849 (see Ashenburg, 130-31, 170).

that people who kept clean were likelier to keep well, and the public health movement brought the connection between dirt and disease increasingly to public notice. In his *Family Cyclopaedia* (1821), James Jennings provided his middle-class readership with a whole A-to-Z of useful advice on such domestic know-how. "Personal cleanliness of the person and of the dress is not only becoming in our intercourse with society," he expostulated, "but is absolutely necessary if we desire that invaluable blessing good health." The immersion could be either "partial" or "general," and there was no objection to the use of soap.[997] According to a distinction drawn in Thomas Webster's *Domestic Encyclopaedia* (1844), baths could be classified either as curative (the "therapeutic" bath) or preventative (the "hygeian" bath). By the end of the Victorian era, the bath had become an indispensable fixture of middle-class domestic decency, and the bathroom was a sine qua non – unless, of course, you happened to be one of the great unwashed.[998]

One central distinction drawn in Victorian times – and recurrently throughout history – was between the hot and the cold bath. Webster wrote that the early-morning cold bath, and in particular the cold shower, "strengthens the digestive organs," while according to Jennings the sudden contact with cold water had proved beneficial not only in the treatment of fevers but also in cases of tetanus, epilepsy, rabies and insanity.[999] In particular, its bracing effects made it an essential component of the character-building of the nation's young men, and it was widely adopted in public schools. The Duke of Wellington's cold immersion was regarded as providing a telling contrast with the leisurely – generally two-hour-long – hot soak indulged in by Napoleon.[1000] The tepid or warm bath, it was held, was for women, weaklings and infants. Such baths, wrote J. H. Walsh in *A Manual of Domestic Economy* (1857), "soothe the general nervous system and are of great use in spasms of any kind as well as in convulsions of young children." Hot baths were potentially dangerous. They were, said Walsh, "by no means a class of agents to be trifled with, and in medical cases where there is time to obtain it, regular advice should

997. Quoted in Eveleigh, 63.
998. Due to a cocktail of economic and practical factors, as well as the prejudice that pervaded all levels of society, baths were not adopted by the majority of the British population until the mid 20th century. See ibid., 159-68.
999. Ibid., 64.
1000. Rupp, 69-70; Ashenburg, 154.

be had recourse to before using them."[1001]

Though of unquestioned value in relieving pain, easing sprains and muscular fatigue, improving the circulation, relaxing spasms, inducing sleep and calming hyperactive or agitated patients, warm baths have traditionally been associated with enervation and dissolution. As early as 5th-century-BCE Athens, the hot bath was identified with effeminacy and the effete,[1002] and the sybaritic Romans in particular turned it into an indispensable part of the good life. As one 1st-century epitaph suggests,[1003] "baths, wine and sex" were the sex, drugs and rock 'n' roll of Roman times. The debauchery, decadence and ultimate downfall of the Roman Empire have commonly been attributed to their addiction to hot-water bathing, whence also the hearty aversion to the habit generally displayed by Christians, ascetics and moralists.

The association of warm or hot water with sensuality and sexual licence is given a further twist by a bawdy metaphor found in Shakespeare's sonnets and taken up with relish in Iris Murdoch's novel *The Philosopher's Pupil*. Here the fictional spa-town of Ennistone has a "copious hot spring" which is said to be endowed with medical and aphrodisiacal qualities and allegedly inspired Shakespeare's Sonnet 153. According to this verse (as well as Sonnet 154), the heat of the spring derives from Cupid's "fiery" (i.e. passionate, syphilitic) weapon, which was dipped in the waters by a mischievous nymph in order to cool down but which in fact functioned more like an immersion heater. Ever since then, the spring's steamy waters have been said to cure the "'sad distempers' and 'strange maladies' which

---

1001. Quoted in Eveleigh, 64-65.
1002. In Aristophanes's *The Clouds* (ll. 835-40), for example, Strepsiades is won over by philosophers such as Socrates because of their frugality: "they never do extravagant things like getting their hair cut or putting on oil, and they would never dream of taking a hot bath." As Right puts it in the formal debate with Wrong, "hot baths cause cowardice" (see Aristophanes, 146-47, 155).
1003. "Baths, wine and sex ruin our bodies, but they are the essence of life – baths, wine and sex," as written on the tombstone of Titus Claudius Secundus, quoted in Ashenburg, 28. A correspondence between baths and rock 'n' rock as the third element of the triad is perhaps reflected in the timeless attraction of bath-time yodelling. Witness the *Satyricon* of Petronius, in which Trimalchio claims that there is "nothing better than a private bath": "Then he sat down as though tired, and being tempted by the acoustics of the bath, with his drunken mouth gaping at the ceiling, he began murdering some songs by Menecrates…" (*Satyricon*, 84).

attend imprudent love."[1004] The warmth of water, the ardour of love, the heat of passion and the fire of the pox – the painful burning of venereal disease – are humorously conjoined in the bawdy heat of a thermal spring.

Cold baths, of course, have a very different set of connotations. Yet though they were imposed on public school-boys with a few to extinguishing youthful passion and dampening the excesses of libido, they probably had the opposite effect. Recent tests[1005] have shown that daily cold baths not only reduce blood pressure and cholesterol, enhance the body's resistance to heart-attacks and strokes, and strengthen the immune system, but also lead to increases in testosterone production in men and oestrogen and progesterone production in women, thus heightening fertility and boosting the libido. This comes on top of the instantaneous rush of natural opioids and adrenaline and the closely attendant feelings of well-being. For a water-romantic such as Goethe, a cold bathe in the open would transmute bourgeois sensual lassitude into freshness and vigour, providing bodily renewal and liberation from the fetters of convention. Goethe was certainly not after some sort of bromide effect.

Therapeutic bathing goes back at least to ancient Greek times. At the temples of Asclepius, the Greek god of medicine, bathing was an essential feature of the regimen, and Hippocrates, who was said to be descended from Asclepius, employed both hot and cold immersions to treat many kinds of ailment. Modern medicine is in turn said to be descended from Hippocrates. It was the 18th and 19th centuries that were to be the heyday of hydrotherapy, or hydropathy as it was commonly known. As early as 1702, Sir John Floyer and Dr Edward Baynard had together published a successful treatise entitled *Psychrolousia: Or, the History of Cold Bathing: both Ancient and Modern*. In the first part, written by Floyer, the salutary effects of cold baths are ascribed to the "Terror and Surprize" they produce, which "contracts the Nervous Membrane and Tubes, in which the aerial Spirits are contained," enhancing sensation, reinvigorating the mind and dispelling stupor. Cold water, according to Floyer, would thus cure "most Infirmities of the Brain" and was of great benefit in treating the "Distempers of the Eyes."[1006] For his part, Baynard pointed out that, contrary to received opinion, cold immersions were *not* effective as a

1004. Murdoch, 25.
1005. See Deakin, 102-3.
1006. Floyer and Baynard, *Psychrolousia*, 69-70.

remedy for concupiscence, but quite the contrary.[1007] *Psychrolousia* was subsequently to exert a major influence on the first German hydrotherapist, Johann Siegmund Hahn, who in 1738 published his own book on water cures.[1008] John Wesley's manual of folk wisdom *Primitive Physick: or, an Easy and Natural Method of Curing Most Diseases*, published in 1747, reinforced the therapeutic status of cold water (again citing blindness as one of the conditions it was known to cure).[1009] And in the final decade of the century Dr James Currie wrote his highly popular *Medical Reports on the Effects of Water, Cold and Warm, as a Remedy in Fevers and other Febrile Diseases*, which not only offered practical advice on the hydrotherapeutic treatment of fever but also espoused the sprinkling of water as a cure for typhoid and smallpox.[1010]

The two most important figures in 19th-century hydropathy, Vincenz Priessnitz (1799-1851) and Sebastian Kneipp (1821-1897), were both from German-speaking Europe and had themselves been saved by water's curative powers. Born in Gräfenberg in Austrian Silesia, the 18-year-old Priessnitz[1011] had been run over by a heavy hay cart and told by doctors that he would be crippled for life. Yet by drinking copious amounts of water and applying compresses soaked in cold spring water – so it is said – he was up and about within a couple of weeks. Priessnitz went on to develop his own nature-based and holistic water cure programme, adapting the family farmstead to accommodate the ailing flocks attracted by the growing fame of his cold water therapy. His methods included the wet compress, a variety of indoor and outdoor cold baths and douches, the wet-sheet body wrap, the use of sweating, and the imbibing of abundant quantities (20 to 30 glasses a day!) of refreshing spring water. This was compounded with a strict diet, plenty of fresh air and exercise, and a healthily spartan way of life (involving bedtime at half past nine and getting up at four). It has perhaps not been everyone's cup of tea: disgruntled patients have tried to blow the place up. Yet it did represent a

1007. Ibid., 267. See also Ashenburg, 129-30. In the words of one contemporary ditty: "Cold bathing has this Good alone, / It makes Old John to hug Old Joan. / And gives a sort of Resurrection / To buried Joys, through lost Erection."
1008. *Lesson on the Powers and Effect of fresh Water on People's Bodies, in particular of the Sick, when applied internally and externally …*
1009. Ashenburg, 130-31.
1010. See Marks, 217-19.
1011. On Priessnitz, see Marks, 220-22; Deakin, 100-2.

step forward compared with much medicine of the time.[1012] Known as "the Water University," Priessnitz's sanatorium is still in existence.

Even more spectacular was the success story of Sebastian Kneipp, the internationally renowned "Water Doctor" from Germany. Diagnosed with terminal tuberculosis in his twenties and given just one month to live, Kneipp chanced upon Hahn's book on hydropathy and lost no time in putting it into practice. Every day throughout the cold winter months, he would go jogging down to the freezing waters of the Danube, strip off for his daily bathe, and then run home again. By the spring he was healthier than ever. Encouraged by the success of Priessnitz, Kneipp set about refining his water-cure methods, and his holistic techniques became increasingly famous. At his death, the small spa town of Bad Wörishofen in Bavaria, where he resided in the Dominican monastery, was attracting tens of thousands of visitors. Kneipp had written bestsellers such as *My Water Cure* and *How You Should Live* and been appointed papal chamberlain by Pope Leo XIII. Today the German association of over 600 Kneipp clubs or *Kneippvereine*, which seeks to further his holistic water teachings, has more than 100,000 members.

Both Priessnitz and Kneipp were viewed with scepticism and mistrust by mainstream medicine on account of their fame, success and an enviable knack of making a profit. Priessnitz was taken to court by the doctors of his day, but won his case thanks to the testimonies of satisfied customers. The spa at Bad Wörishofen too suffered a number of arson attacks by opponents. As the concept of "taking the waters" grew in popularity, a whole industry developed around trips to spas and watering-holes, laying itself open to charges of faddism, fashion-mongering and sheer quackery. On the basis of Priessnitz's work, hydropathy was introduced to Malvern, Ilkley and Matlock. By the 1850s there were some 62 water-cure establishments in the United States, as well as a twice-monthly *Water-Cure Journal* with more than 100,000 subscribers. Yet things could go wrong. It was considered necessary to warn inexperienced self-help hydropaths against the dangers of the so-called "Electric Bath," where the bathwater was infused with an electric current.[1013] And there were cases,

1012. See Farber, 92-93, writing about hydropathy in the United States, which "must be weighed against conventional medicine, which then practiced blood-letting, and held that women were hampered by menstrual problems and intellectually inferior to men. Hydropathy, by contrast, saw women's physiology as normal, opposed drastic remedies, and prescribed rest, changes in diet, temperance, and exercise."
1013. Rupp, 68, cites R. B. D. Wells's *Water, and How to Apply It, in Health and Disease*, which "includes several cautionary anecdotes about patients who foolishly felt competent enough to prepare their own baths. Some barely survived the experience..."

predictably enough, in which water-cure advocates – themselves taken ill – refused the conventional treatment that might have saved their life. Such obstinacy did for Kneipp himself.

The spartan lifestyle of a strict hydropathic regimen contrasts with the more hedonistic or orgiastic spirit of other bathing places. In the course of his stay at Bath, Smollett's satirically-minded hypochondriac Matthew Bramble observed "that this place, which Nature and Providence seem to have intended as a resource from distemper and disquiet, is become the very centre of racket and dissipation," while his rather less jaundiced young niece Lydia was struck by the "gayety, good-humour, and diversion" and her maid Winifred noted "such dressing, and fidling, and dancing, and gadding, and courting, and plotting" that it was a good job God had endowed her with a "good stock of discretion."[1014] Charlie Chaplin's brilliant early short film *The Cure* (1917) satirizes and subverts the apparent stuffiness of water-cure institutions by introducing a hardened dipsomaniac into a chastely water-drinking environment. Chaplin's inebriate naturally has absolutely no truck with anything as insipid as spa water – at least until his own private supply of liquor inadvertently finds its way into it. Then the water suddenly becomes rather more appealing to everyone, and the whole establishment lapses into drunken anarchy.

In the course of the 19th century, the spas in England had in fact suffered a marked decrease in popularity as the burgeoning system of railways made the seaside an increasingly accessible alternative. Sea-bathing too, as we have seen, was viewed as deeply salubrious in effect. So much so, in fact, that in her unfinished novel *Sanditon* Jane Austen caricatured the craze in the figure of the seaside property developer Mr Parker, who couldn't stop banging on about its benefits:

> The Sea air and Sea Bathing together were nearly infallible [he said], one or the other of them being a match for every Disorder, of the Stomach, the Lungs or the Blood; They were anti-spasmodic, anti-pulmonary, anti-sceptic, anti-bilious and anti-rheumatic. Nobody could catch cold by the Sea, Nobody wanted Appetite by the Sea, Nobody wanted Spirits, Nobody wanted Strength. – They were healing, softing, relaxing – fortifying and bracing – seemingly just as was wanted – sometimes one, sometimes the other. – If the Sea breeze failed, the Sea-Bath was the certain corrective; – and where Bathing disagreed, the Sea Breeze alone was evidently designed by Nature for the cure.[1015]

1014. Smollett, *Humphry Clinker*, 34, 39, 42.
1015. Austen, 302.

Even more than spas, the seaside came to be associated with a carnival atmosphere of freedom and fun. By the early 20th century, the "Brighton weekend" had become a form of popular entertainment, a release from the drudgery of working life and buttoned-up Victorianism. It acquired a saucy naughty-but-niceness that was laughingly endorsed by music-hall comedians: "Bathing strengthens the interlect, braces the body, clears the system, puts new life in the bloods, old heads onto young shoulders, fills the pockets, drives away care, cures corns, warts, bunions, Pilgrim's progresses, water on the brain, *new*-ralgia, *old*-ralgia....."[1016]

* * * * *

On top of the bathing, Priessnitz had wanted his patients to drink an inordinate quantity of water each day, while some doctors even recommended that sea-water should be taken internally. The benefits of water have been judged to operate inside as well as outside the body. Yet just as the benefits of hot and cold bathing have on occasion been attributed to the heat and the cold rather than the water itself, which is given a purely passive role,[1017] the salutary properties of drinking-water have often been ascribed to the dissolved minerals it contains, its own health-sustaining attributes relegated to mere contingency.

This is clearly misguided. For like all land organisms, human beings must constantly confront the unremitting threat of drying out. Without our sap – our blood, our lymph, our cytoplasm – we would be a shrivelled bag of bones (and even our bones are 33 per cent water), and it is vital we should regularly replace the waste-bearing waters we eliminate from our body. However, our undoubted dependence on periodic refilling

1016. See Staveacre, 144; 142-45.
1017. The 1911 *Encyclopaedia Britannica*, for example, took exception to the term hydrotherapy, preferring thermotherapeutics or thermotherapy. Water, it claimed, was a mere "vehicle" for the heat or cold. The linguistic quibble clearly failed to have much effect, however, as the 2008 version of the encyclopaedia had an entry for "hydrotherapy" but not for its thermo- variants. Yet it still insists: the "primary value" of hydrotherapy "is as a medium for application or reduction of heat" ("hydrotherapy." *Encyclopaedia Britannica 2008 Ultimate Reference Suite*. Chicago: Encyclopaedia Britannica, 2008).

to maintain an inner equilibrium has recently served as the basis for a new "water myth,"[1018] fomented by large-scale commercial interests, a boom in marketing, an obsession with personal health, and our addiction to handy solutions. We are told we should drink at least eight glasses, or two and a half litres, of water per day, yet most of what our body requires is contained in foods. While it is undoubtedly true that dehydration may produce adverse effects such as headaches, depression and a loss of concentration and even promote obesity when thirst is mistaken for hunger, the idea that continuous hydration is necessary for health and we should always have a plastic water bottle to hand – that bottled water is a new panacea – is a very recent one. In the words of Anne Hardy, historian of modern medicine, people "have taught themselves to need water."[1019] Even though good hydration certainly fosters the transport of nutrients and the elimination of toxins and is vital for healthy joints, kidneys and skin, the recent phenomenon of potomania – compulsive drinking – and the resulting over-hydration can just as easily stress the kidneys and result in a loss of magnesium and potassium.

This conception of drinking-water as a cure-all or panacea is lent additional weight by an understanding of life – and death – as a gradual process of drying out. It may seem rather obvious. Traditional African belief systems view life as a progression from the "wetness" of newborn babies to the "dryness" of the aged, wizened and wrinkly,[1020] and the idea is corroborated not only by the common-sense observation that we wither and shrivel as time passes, but by the statistical evidence showing a reduction in body water as a percentage of total human weight from 97 per cent at the embryonic stage to 60 per cent and on occasion considerably less in adulthood.[1021] Yet it also naturally fosters the belief that water itself might in some way check, slow or even stop the otherwise

1018. See "Six Scientific Myths Exploded," *The Week*, 12 Jan 2008, 17, which summarizes conclusions published in the *British Medical Journal*. See Shapiro, 224, on the "veritably biblical style" of the ubiquitous exhortation to drink eight glasses of water a day. It has been described as "the first commandment of good health and is supported by a number of excessive claims. More than half of the population is permanently dehydrated, we are told; you can be dangerously dehydrated without even knowing it; and you can only properly rehydrate with pure water and not by drinking other drinks like tea, coffee, soft drinks or alcohol."
1019. Quoted in "Think Before You Drink," *The Guardian*, 13 July 2006.
1020. See Black, *Water, Life Force*, 100.
1021. Robert Gardner, quoted in Marks, 186.

relentless process of age-related desiccation. This not only underscores the widespread attraction of fountains of eternal youth and sacred springs whose waters bestow immortality, but also helps account for the instinctive appeal of the water-cure treatment offered by modern-day water doctors such as Fereydoon Batmanghelidj. For Batmanghelidj and his acolytes, "chronic dehydration" is the cause of most modern ailments, physical and psychological alike. "You are not sick, you are thirsty," he proclaimed; his remedy, an intake of ordinary water that would prevent and cure depression, asthma, arthritis, back pain, migraines, allergies, high blood pressure, constipation, diabetes, multiple sclerosis, and much much more.[1022]

Batmanghelidj's work has come under constant attack for its lack of scientific rigour: his claim that water provides the brain with "hydroelectric" energy by splitting into hydrogen and oxygen has elicited a collective wince of pain in scientific circles. Yet despite the inevitable allegations of quackery, the value of his work resides in what is in fact a time-honoured mistrust of professional medicine, its drugs and its jargon. When he writes that modern medicine is "routinely treating symptoms, signs and complications of drought in the body with toxic chemicals that kill more rapidly than the dehydration itself,"[1023] he is perpetuating a line of anti-medical polemic that finds its most eloquent expression in Montaigne (and its most comic expression in Molière).[1024]

According to Montaigne, indeed, there is no-one "more quickly ill nor more slowly well than those who are under the jurisdiction of medicine," whereas the approach he advocates is nature-based, holistic

---

1022. For an account of his life, see the obituary in the *Washington Post*, 20 Nov. 2004. Batmanghelidj's self-help book *Your Body's Many Cries for Water* (1992) was translated into 15 languages. For an adherent's view, see Liz Hodgkinson, *The Drinking Water Cure.*

1023. This quotation is taken from Batmanghelidj's online article "Cure Pain and Prevent Disease by Drinking Water." According to Liz Hodgkinson, "we must assume that we were designed by nature to function without complicated medication, and that the body has many self-righting mechanisms. It is designed to work without outside interference," (*The Drinking Water Cure*, 44).

1024. For Montaigne's hearty dislike of medical charlatanry, see in particular "On the resemblance of children to their fathers," in *The Complete Essays*, 858-88. Paracelsus too criticized physicians and apothecaries for their ignorance, incompetence and dishonesty, himself advocating minimal intervention, keeping wounds clean, and trusting, where possible, in the healing power of nature. Not surprisingly, he was ostracized by the medical profession (see Ball, *The Devil's Doctor*, 168-76).

and homeopathic.[1025] Today, Montaigne's humanistic common sense would almost certainly target the behemoths of the pharmaceutical industry rather than the medical profession itself, and perhaps with an even greater sense of moral outrage.[1026] Spa water itself, he writes,

> is in the first place not inimical to my taste; secondly it is both natural and simple and so, at the very least, not dangerous even if it does no good. ... Although I have never seen any miraculous or extraordinary cures there – on the contrary whenever I have bothered to investigate a little more carefully than is usual I have found all the rumours of cures which are scattered about such places to be ill-founded and false ... – nevertheless I have also hardly met anyone who was made worse by taking the waters; and you cannot honestly deny that they stimulate the appetite, help the digestion and liven us up a bit. ... They cannot rebuild massy ruins but they can shore up a tottering wall or forestall the threat of something worse.

Montaigne's conclusion? That taking the waters is the "least artificial" branch of medicine, though it still has "its fair share of the confusion and uncertainty you see everywhere else in that Art."[1027]

Of course, drinking-water itself – even the most limpid spring-water fresh from the source – retains its mercurial ambivalence. Water

---

1025. Ibid., 866, 867: "We set about disturbing and activating our illnesses by fighting them with contraries: yet it ought to be our way of life which gently reduces them and brings them to an end."

1026. The criticism levelled at the pharmaceutical industry is that it seeks to prolong or even "invent" illness – in order to sell more drugs – rather than curing it. In practice, this "pharmacologization" of human health results in a greater interest in marketing and advertising than in research and development. In *Suck ers* (33-34, 165-68), Rose Shapiro shows that certain criticisms of "Big Pharma" can quickly degenerate into paranoia and conspiracy theories. Given the nature of capitalism, however, it is anything but paranoid to suggest that over-powerful pharmaceutical transnationals on occasion put the (financial) interests of their share-holders above the (medical) interests of the planet's sick and poor.

1027. Ibid., 877-78. While Montaigne is rather lukewarm in his approval of drinking-water (it is more to his taste when mixed with wine), his endorsement is whole-hearted when it comes to bathing: "I reckon that bathing in general is salubrious and I believe that our health has suffered several quite serious inconveniences since we lost the habit ... of washing our bodies every day; I can only think that we are all the worse for having our limbs encrusted and our pores blocked up with filth" (ibid., 877).

may bear either man-made or naturally occurring toxins, and drinking-water scares have constantly shadowed our dealings with the freshwater on which we depend.[1028] With the development of agriculture and a sedentary lifestyle over the last 10,000 years, this dependence has been reshaped and transformed by the apparition of new beverages such as beer and wine, which have above all provided forms of water that are more or less *safe to drink*. These new beverages in turn came to be endowed with medicinal qualities in their own right. As Tom Standage recounts, both the Mesopotamians and the Egyptians used beer for medicinal purposes. A cuneiform tablet from Sumer dating from the third millennium BCE contains a pharmacopoeia based on beer, while an ancient Egyptian medical text from ca. 1550 BCE (the "Ebers Papyrus") includes beer-based herbal remedies for constipation, indigestion and labour pains.[1029] In the 2nd century CE Galen used wine for disinfecting wounds and regulating the humours, and insisted that the emperor Marcus Aurelius should use the very best Falernian wine to wash down his daily dose of the cure-all theriac, the ur-treacle designed to keep him alive for as long as possible.[1030]

It is the history of the now universal drink by the name of Coca-Cola that provides perhaps the best illustration of the perpetual moral ambiguity of water-based beverages: a would-be panacea in its origins, an infinitely manipulable commercial brand in its modern manifestation, the very essence of global capitalism.[1031] For like all other artificially carbonated soft drinks, Coca-Cola is a direct descendant of soda water, i.e. water impregnated with what is now known as carbon dioxide, first produced by Joseph Priestley in the 1760s. Convinced of its potential usefulness (in the treatment, for example, of "putrid fevers, dysentery, bilious vomitings, etc."[1032]), the chemist and apothecary Thomas Henry was soon marketing artificially carbonated water as a medicine, and by the early years of the following century scientists and entrepreneurs such as

---

1028. Such scares are as mutable as water itself. One of the latest is the threat of extremely powerful "cytotoxic" drugs in our water supply. It is thought, for example, that the anti-cancer drugs used in increasing quantity in chemotherapy – which are discharged unaltered into the sewerage system in the urine of cancer patients – may be resistant to conventional water-treatment techniques. See Steve Connor, "Tests for Drugs in Tap Water," *The Independent*, 29 September, 2008.
1029. Standage, 38.
1030. See ibid., 82-84.
1031. The following account is indebted to ibid., 223-49.
1032. Ibid., 227.

Jacob Schweppe and Benjamin Silliman had successfully spread the drink across Europe and into the United States. Generically known as soda water because of the sodium bicarbonate often used in its preparation, the new drink started out as a strictly medical product, and in the United States the soda fountain soon came to be a regular feature of the apothecary's shop. Particularly in the USA, however, it also became increasingly popular as a refreshment, albeit one with impeccable medical credentials. As well as being taken on its own, it could be used to make sparkling lemonade or flavoured with special syrups made from berries or other fruits. By the 1870s the soda-water business had become big business, mass-produced and industrialized. It was perceived as incarnating a specifically American spirit of democracy: "the millionaire may drink champagne while the poor man drinks beer," wrote a commentator in *Harper's Weekly* in 1891, "but they both drink soda water."[1033]

Yet just a few years earlier, a whole new dimension had been added to the archetypally American syrupy soda water by the pharmacist John Pemberton, an old hand in concocting the patent medicines that were so popular at the time: quack remedies and nostrums generally marketed through newspaper advertisements and often incorporating substantial quantities of alcohol, caffeine, cocaine, opium or morphine. Having originally experimented with an elixir comprising French wine infused with coca leaves together with kola extract, Pemberton responded to a two-year, county-wide trial ban on alcohol by dispensing with the wine and adding sugar to mask the bitterness. This new drink was a "temperance drink," a medicinal soda water flavoured with a syrup of coca, kola and sugar, which Pemberton intended to commercialize as both a soda-water flavouring and a patent medicine. The wording on the label heralded "not only a delicious, exhilarating, refreshing and invigorating Beverage ..., but a valuable Brain Tonic, and a cure for all nervous affections – Sick Head-Ache, Neuralgia, Hysteria, Melancholy, etc."[1034] The drink was launched in 1886, but Pemberton died of cancer just two years later. Coca-Cola was taken over by Asa Candler, another patent-medicine pusher, who pushed this new one so successfully that by the end of 1895 more than 76,000 gallons were being sold each year, throughout the USA. This was the year, moreover, in which it ceased to be marketed as a medicinal beverage – as a

1033. Quoted in ibid., 232.
1034. Quoted in ibid., 238-39.

"Sovereign Remedy for Headache"[1035] – and was transformed into a thirst-quenching refreshment with universal appeal.

And universal it has certainly proved to be. Having conquered the United States, since the Second World War it has taken over the world. Today, the Coca-Cola Company supplies some three per cent of humankind's global liquid intake, and the drink has come to be indelibly associated with the hegemony of the United States and the free-market capitalism it embodies. Resentful cold-war communists in Europe coined the term *Coca-Colonization*, suggesting that the drink was detrimental to the health and would infest the moral landscape with US-American cultural values. It was claimed that the drink led to impotence, infertility and cancer.[1036] Even today it is associated by many with a chronically unhealthy lifestyle. Yet those who have sought to staunch the flood have generally underestimated the power of capitalism and of souped-up soda water. To symbolize anything as shapeless as capitalism, after all, is to symbolize everything and nothing at all. It is water at its most slippery, protean and seemingly invincible.

* * * * *

Coca-Cola is a panacea that symbolizes a certain conception of "freedom" and rots your teeth. It has been phenomenally successful, especially since handily ditching its medicinal pretensions at the end of the 19th century. No other water-based "treacle" has thrived to the same extent, although some – operating on or around the margins of mainstream medical science – have been highly influential.

One of the best known and most controversial cases is homeopathy, which traces its origins back to the work of Dresden-born Samuel Hahnemann at the turn of the 19th century. Disillusioned with the ham-handed medical practices of his time, Hahnemann formulated what is known as the "law of similars" (or the principle that "like cures like"), an idea prefigured by the Paracelsian notion that "the dose makes the poison" or "what makes a man ill also cures him," as well as by the

1035. Quoted in ibid., 242.
1036. Ibid., 256-61.

medieval Christian doctrine of "signatures."[1037] According to Hahnemann's law, small amounts of a substance that would otherwise provoke certain symptoms in a healthy patient could be administered to alleviate those same symptoms in a patient suffering their effects. Some of the substances involved, such as arsenic and mercury, were highly toxic, so Hahnemann resorted to dilution in water in order to minimize the dangers, which led to his second main principle: the more dilute the preparation, the greater its effect. Most remarkably of all, and unlike Paracelsus, Hahnemann ended up using what are known as "infinitesimal" dilutions or dosages, theoretically containing absolutely negligible quantities of the active ingredient and leaving just the solvent.[1038]

Hahnemann cannot be dismissed as a quack. His focus on a good diet, fresh air and exercise and on the emotional well-being of his patients was humane, enlightened and a welcome antidote to the purging, bleeding and bungling pharmaceutics of the day. By the standards of the time, the fact that he attributed his homeopathic observations to a "vital force" was by no means unreasonable. Within the framework of modern-day orthodox science, however, recourse to vitalism or to a non-material force as an explanatory principle is tantamount to an admission of non-knowledge. Accordingly, homeopathy today faces two principal charges: the first is that we do not know how it works (which is perhaps part of its interest); the second, more serious

---

1037. Paracelsus himself puts it thus: "In all things there is a poison, and there is nothing without a poison. It depends only upon the dose whether a poison is poison or not" (quoted in Ball, *The Devil's Doctor*, 237). The doctrine of signatures claimed that for every ailment God had provided a remedy which could be recognized by His "signature." For example, the white spotted leaves of lungwort, which looked like consumptive lungs, were taken to be a cure for tuberculosis, while the maidenhair fern was a treatment for baldness. On Hahnemann and homeopathy in general, see Shapiro, 79-87, also Ball, H_2O, 292-95.

1038. Successive dilutions tend to be by a factor of 100, mixing one part of the active ingredient with 99 of the solvent. This is repeated up to thirty times. As *The Family Encyclopaedia of Homeopathic Medicine* (ed. Eric Meyer and J. P. LeGrand) explains, "somewhere between the seventh and ninth dilution, ... all traces of the original homeopathic substance disappear" (40). Just *how* dilute such dilutions end up is shown amusingly in Shapiro, 83-88: at a potency of 13c (which equals 13 dilutions of one-in-a-hundred), we are left with the equivalent of "one drop of remedy in three quarters of the earth's oceans"; by 19c, it is one drop of remedy "in ten spheres with the same diameter as our solar system"; the standard homeopathic dilution of 30c is equivalent to one drop "in nearly a hundred million galaxy-sized balls of water."

one is that it does not in fact work anyway (which, if it can be unequivocally demonstrated, presumably spells the end of the story).[1039]

Our ignorance of how it works is something many homeopaths are perfectly willing to admit. According to one prominent consultant, "there is no real doubt that homeopathic medicines above the 12th centesimal dilution can contain only water. If, therefore, they do have a measurable effect, we have to conclude that in some unexplained way the substance they originally contained has somehow impressed itself on the water. ... Unfortunately it is very difficult to imagine how water could preserve traces of the original substance in the way I have suggested."[1040] Notions of "subtle information" have been invoked[1041] – where "subtle," again, is an admission of ignorance, conjuring a spirit of alchemy rather than orthodox science. The idea is that the active ingredient "somehow"[1042] imprints a memory on the water, allowing its biological activity to persist in its absence. As one advocate puts it, "if water does consist of a subtle but complex arrangement of a vast number of molecules, this means that information could be 'written onto' water by very slightly [subtly] changing the nature of this arrangement. ... Within the body this information might be 'read' by the cells and used to bring about active changes in the whole body."[1043]

Homeopathy received an unexpected boost in 1988 when the French immunologist Jacques Benveniste and his team published a paper in the prestigious journal *Nature* claiming to provide experimental proof that

1039. A further path, perhaps, is to argue that though it works no better than a placebo, it does work better – given a positive therapeutic relationship and a goodly dose of self-deception – than nothing at all. As a placebo, it also has the advantage of being harmless and non-invasive. A study in *The Lancet* in 2005 took the apparent lack of distinction between homeopathy and placebo to signal "the end of homeopathy," but was forced to admit that "the more dilute the evidence for homeopathy becomes, the greater seems its popularity" (see Shapiro, 76). Around a quarter of Europeans currently use it.
1040. Anthony Campbell, quoted in Ball, H_2O, 295-96.
1041. Peat, 138.
1042. The explanation usually involves the peculiarities of water's structure, in particular the hydrogen bonding, which can cause stable, highly structured configurations of water molecules (known as hydration shells) to form around the biomolecule, functioning rather like templates or moulds of the substance in question – and possibly persisting even after the molecule itself has gone.
1043. Peat, 139.

water did indeed have a memory.[1044] Needless to say, the scientific world threw its toys out of the pram. Despite the most rigorous tests imposed by the journal and its explicit "editorial reservation," there was no evidence either of fraud or of glaring incompetence – yet the claims are generally still regarded as unsubstantiated. Some scientists have dismissed the whole episode as what Irving Langmuir famously called "pathological science": in other words, the phenomena are barely detectable; the magnitude of the effect seems independent of that of the cause; great observational accuracy is claimed; the explanation offered is usually fantastic; and criticisms are answered with ad hoc excuses.[1045] Among other arguments, Philip Ball also presents a *reductio ad absurdum* of the conception of "memory" that is implied: "if this kind of templating ... takes place," he reasons, "why doesn't it happen all the time? Why isn't the cytoplasm of our cells for ever getting clogged up with the ghosts of the proteins they contain? ... How is it that we can ever dilute any solution, that orange juice does not keep tasting of oranges however much water we add to it because the flavoursome molecules have been templated?"[1046] If water has such a phenomenal memory, how does any particular drop know *what* to remember? Perhaps there are some gadabout water molecules dispersed across the oceans that recall sharing a tub of suds with Cleopatra, being imbibed by Boadicea, retained by a premenstrual Helen of Troy, passed by Hildegard of Bingen. Or perhaps, remembering everything, such water would end up remembering nothing.

Water's ambiguous relationship with "memory" is notoriously difficult to pin down. Ball cites the highly dynamic nature of water's structure, as each specific hydrogen-bonded structure breaks and re-forms roughly every billionth of a second, relentlessly randomizing the arrangement of its molecules. Indeed, while homeopathy depends on water "remembering" the pattern of some healing substance it once contained, water is commonly regarded as the very antithesis of memory,

1044. For an account of Benveniste's controversial work on the memory of water, see Ball, *H2O*, 287-310.
1045. See the discussion of "pathological science" in Wolpert, 137-42.
1046. Ball, *H2O*, 302-3. Ball likewise applies the concept of pathological science to the spectacular rumpus in the late 1960s concerning "anomalous" water or polywater, which for a while was believed (by some) to be a new, possibly polymerized form of water with different properties from ordinary water (properties subsequently shown to have been caused by ionic contaminants). See ibid., 258-71.

removing all traces and stains, washing away the past, and dissolving all structure in its all-embracing yet productive chaos. At the same time, even non-pathological science acknowledges that water is endowed with *some* memory in the form of its capacity to "retain the mark of past environments."[1047] The idea of water as the planetary *unconscious* itself suggests memory that is lost or hidden, i.e. a characteristic tension of memory and oblivion.

So who is to be preferred, Mnemosyne or Lethe? Given that scientists themselves are willing to admit that "of all the known liquids, water is probably the most studied and least understood,"[1048] our choice perhaps reflects our attitude to our own ignorance. For some, this very mystery and inscrutability is part of what generates water's incomparable mythological power, and water remains a timeless source of pre-scientific wonder: the power of homeopathy is akin to the power of poetry.[1049] Others, such as Rose Shapiro, are less indulgent: "all this talk of poetry and beauty and pictures and metaphysics must be quite soothing when there is nothing seriously wrong with you," she argues, "or if you've got something from which you will recover regardless."[1050] But it won't do much good if you have just been run over by a lorry or need your appendix removing.

Homeopathy is not alone in its unscientific stance and the constant charges of wilful quackery or dewy-eyed hogwash to which it is subject. With its capacity to dissolve or contain stuff and its symbolic association with vitality and spirit, water has repeatedly lent itself to notions that it can harbour and transmit hidden, invisible or perhaps "subtle" energies and forces, or that it can somehow impart auras or vibes. Such cures go back to the "magnetised water" used by the Austrian doctor Franz Mesmer in the late 18th century. Mesmerizing his gullible patients (and possibly

---

1047. See Kandel, 124-31, who attributes "memory" not only to the earth's ice, but also to its aquifers and even, in limited measure, to the depths of the oceans.
1048. Felix Franks, an expert in the chemistry and physics of water, quoted in Ball, *H₂O*, 141. As D. H. Lawrence expresses it in his poem "The Third Thing": "Water is H₂O, hydrogen two parts, oxygen one, / but there is also a third thing, that makes it water / and nobody knows what that is" (Lawrence, 428).
1049. Wolpert himself seems to suspect that the "pathological" episode of Benveniste's claims about water memory is not over yet. It may "quietly disappear" like other examples of pathological science, but "more likely it will burst forth again with equally unpersuasive evidence" (Wolpert, 142).
1050. Shapiro, 96-97.

himself) with his charismatic presence, hypnotic movements and good old-fashioned hocus-pocus, Mesmer claimed that his healing powers were transmitted through vessels or bowls full of allegedly magnetised water. Even today such water is available – at a substantial cost – as a special treat for pets: "given the choice," dog-owners are told, "your dog will always choose magnetised water."[1051] In a similar spirit, though more harmful, were the radium-water drinks marketed for a while following the discovery of radioactive substances around the turn of the 20th century: five glasses a day of this "liquid sunshine," it was claimed, would renew energy and dispel the nervous disorder then known as neurasthenia. In fact, the subtle waterborne energies claimed a number of unsuspecting victims before the drink was taken off the market.[1052]

Modern forms of water-based alternative medicine include a range of products sold as Indigo Essences and the water remedies known as Bach flower essences. Marketed as "good vibes in a bottle," the former are manufactured by dipping rocks in water, diluting that water, bottling the resulting dilution, labelling the bottle "Confidence," "Champion" or "Happy" and adding a price tag. First, of course, the rocks themselves have to be prepared, again using a bowl of water: "the spirit of the rock is healed and cleaned," explains the inventor, "so that only its most pure and healing vibration goes into the water during the essence making process." The result is "a kind of first aid kit for feelings."[1053] Bach flower remedies are produced by exposing flower buds to the sun in a bowl of spring water, diluting the resultant solution, and adding alcohol as a preservative, and are likewise generally administered for spiritual or emotional maladies such as anxiety, stress or depression. According to "bestselling" author Masaru Emoto, whose books espouse his own version of *hado* medicine, "the energy and vibration of flowers is transferred to water, and by drinking this water, the patient receives both physical and mental healing benefits. You might postulate that during the transferring process, it is the actual components of the flower that are dissolved in the water, but actually it is only the vibration that gets transferred. Therefore, a chemical analysis of flower essence will detect only water."[1054] Shapiro describes the product as "watered-down

1051. Quoted in Shapiro, 119; on magnetic water, 115-20. In fact, no such thing exists: magnets do not "magnetise" water, which is very slightly repelled by a magnetic field.
1052. See ibid., 111-12.
1053. Quoted in ibid., 217-18.
1054. Emoto, *The Secret Life of Water*, 54.

brandy at £399 per litre."[1055] A list published by the Dr Edward Bach Centre includes remedies such as honeysuckle (for "living in the past"), hornbeam (for "procrastination"), aspen (for the "fear of unknown things"), vervain (for "over-enthusiasm") and centaury (for an "inability to say 'no'").[1056]

Flower essences have been interpreted as a perpetuation of the ancient reverence for dew, which goes back both to the Judaeo-Christian symbolic association of dew with divine grace (the gift of the Holy Spirit that renews parched souls)[1057] and the alchemical conception of heavenly dew as a representation of the philosopher's stone in embryo. For Pliny the Elder the morning dew was a gift from heaven for treating eyes, ulcers, and intestines.[1058] Equally venerable – and equally vulnerable to scepticism – is the ancient tradition of urine-therapy, described by one water-cure advocate as "the oldest water cure of all: drinking your own water"[1059] and by Martin Gardner in the *Skeptical Inquirer* as a crazy theory "currently bamboozling gullible persons captivated by alternative medicines."[1060] Such remedies are an important and much-used component of Ayurvedic medicine, according to which urine is the "water of life." Well-known apologists for therapeutic piss-taking include Pliny the Elder, Arnald of Villanova, and the great natural philosopher Robert Boyle, who wrote that "the medical virtues of man's urine, both inwardly given, and outwardly applied, would require rather a whole book, than a part of an essay, to enumerate and insist on."[1061] Pierre Fauchard, commonly regarded as the father of modern dentistry, recommended the use of human urine in the treatment of caries. The remedy has pedigree, for the custom of brushing the teeth with urine dates from Roman times, and Erasmus noted it amongst the Spanish.[1062] One more recent book on urine-therapy claims that it will cure cancer, multiple sclerosis, malaria, arthritis, AIDS, gonorrhoea, jaundice, ringworm, tuberculosis, migraine, hepatitis, whooping cough,

---

1055. Shapiro, 101; 99-103. There now also exists an alcohol-free variant: i.e. "a tiny phial of 'no-taste' water" sold for roughly the same price.
1056. See http://bachcentre.com/centre/remedies.htm
1057. Describing the seventh heaven, the *midrash* refers to "the dew with which God will revive the dead on the resurrection day" (Ginzberg, I.10; cf. I.354).
1058. See Biedermann, 95, 375.
1059. Hodgkinson, 170.
1060. Martin Gardner, "Urine therapy," *Skeptical Inquirer*, 1 May 1999.
1061. Quoted in ibid.
1062. Erasmus, "On Good Manners for Boys," cited in Ashenburg, 75. Urea has antiseptic and other medical qualities, although it is not usually derived from urine.

hay fever, depression, prostrate trouble and diabetes.[1063]

It is the protean nature of water that allows it to assume whatever imaginative shape the human mind projects onto it. Just as the sea thus came to embody not only humankind's fears and anxieties (in the form of formidable leviathans) but also its hopes and aspirations (as in St Brendan's intrepid naval quest for utopia), on a smaller scale too water seems to invite fantasies as a cure-all and panacea, potentially at least. There has long been a tendency to divide water wholesale into water that is "bad" (a product of humankind's disharmonious relationship with nature) and water that is "good" (vital, living, healthy, freely flowing and natural). Good water implies a good world, a restoration of harmony and order. Subtle vibrations and hidden information are often at play. According to Emoto, "water carries information. The information can be positive or negative. Since we are water, our body surely responds to the information carried by the water we drink. When we get positive information from water, we become healthier. When we get negative information, we get sick."[1064] The relationship is bilateral. We shouldn't swear at water, but tell it we love it and be nice to it. We should not play it heavy metal or punk.

For Schauberger too, when water is treated in a way that is disrespectful or insensitive, it loses its vitality and becomes "anti-life." Degenerate modern culture and technology give rise to water that has lost its energy and its ability to "resonate" or communicate. According to Theodor and Wolfram Schwenk, living, flowing waters are open to benevolent cosmic influences, whereas bad waters – despoiled by human mistreatment – are "as though deaf" and "apathetically insensitive" to the healing celestial rays: "When, misusing water, we ruin it and render it insensitive to cosmic influences, we close not only ourselves, but the whole world with all its life-realms, to the cosmic life-source. Then devastation is apparent, in and around us."[1065]

Schauberger and the Schwenks at times yield to a rather disconcerting anthropomorphism. With their veneration for water as a vital flow rather than a static or stagnant phenomenon, their practical and acutely observed appreciation of the swirling, rolling eddies and vortices of water in motion, and their resulting sense of this flow as something that *wants to realize itself,* they clearly stray onto non-scientific territory. Water, of course, does not "want" to do anything (any more than it "wants" Emoto to gaze at it lovingly and play it classical music). Yet the capacity of flowing water for self-organization (as

1063. See Gardner.
1064. Emoto, *The True Power of Water*, 43.
1065. Schwenk and Schwenk, 233-34.

well as self-cleansing) lends itself naturally to metaphors of "volition." Both Schauberger and Theodor Schwenk were imbued with a poetical mysticism which equated the spirit of nature with the spirit of water, a spirit they were desperate to defend from the implacable threat of industrial technology and pollution. Though mindful of the charge of anthropomorphism, they were also painfully aware – at a time when "water-consciousness" was anything but fashionable and rivers such as the Rhine and the Thames were biologically dead – that scientific-technological thinking was not necessarily the best way to save the rivers they loved and revered.[1066]

For Schauberger and Schwenk, water was not only the victim of a destructive, technology-fixated society, but offered itself as a natural solution to the ills it brought. On occasion, water has also been seen as providing a scientific-technological solution. Even Schauberger is said to have claimed: "More energy is encapsulated in every drop of good spring water than an average power station is able to produce."[1067] Of course, there was hydroelectric power, the "white coal" fervently championed in the early 20th century, when it was seen as offering a powerful, cheap, renewable and inexhaustible alternative to coal and oil: in the words of one German engineer, this was the "true Rhine Gold."[1068] Yet white coal was anathema to thinkers such as Schauberger and Schwenk, who abhorred the "shackling" of water in dams and reservoirs and were aware of the risks and drawbacks.

Of equal interest to both pathological and non-pathological science has been the idea of "unlocking" the energy water is believed to harbour within its chemical structure. The notion of water as a panacea for the ills of humanity – what Philip Ball has called the "myth of water as saviour"[1069] – thus extends to its function as a fuel, embodied in the persistent dream of "splitting" water and in the process releasing combustible hydrogen.[1070] It is a dream that goes back to the origins of

1066. See ibid., 12: "this may sound like anthropomorphism," writes Theodor Schwenk. "But there is a practical aspect to the statement..." Schwenk himself saw water as a mediator or bridge between a mechanistic, reductionistic, analytic understanding of the world and a holistic, teleological approach (ibid., 23). Most scientists would nonetheless insist that Schwenk's writings are under no circumstances to be mistaken for science.
1067. Quoted in Bartholomew, 73, no source given.
1068. See Blackbourn, 206-10; quotation, 209.
1069. Ball, *H$_2$O*, 273. On water as a potential fuel see 272-87.
1070. Water can be split by a process called electrolysis, yet breaking the chemical bonds between the oxygen and hydrogen atoms in a molecule of water itself

research into nuclear fusion. By 1919 the Nobel-Prize-winning chemist Francis Aston was already speculating about how changing "the hydrogen in a glass of water into helium would release enough energy to drive the 'Queen Mary' across the Atlantic and back at full speed."[1071] It is a dream that has also strayed into the realm of pathological science, most famously in the "cold fusion" controversy sparked in the late 1980s when two chemists from the University of Utah claimed to have fused the deuterium atoms in a solution of heavy water (D_2O), forming helium and generating nuclear energy in the process.[1072]

In fact, water is not so much a fuel as an exhaust from the combustion of fuel. It is "spent fuel."[1073] It is what is *given off* by burning – in the presence of oxygen – either hydrogen, hydrocarbon fuels (as in the heat- and light-generating combustion of coal or oil), or carbohydrates such as glucose (as in the energy-producing process of cellular respiration). Attempts to provide carbon-free energy in the future are likely to involve the use of a sort of battery known as a "fuel cell" to harness the electrochemical energy generated by the recombination of hydrogen and oxygen, again producing water as the exhaust.[1074] Yet we should not forget the capacity of water to bear or contain other "stuff" within itself – stuff which *may* be combustible. This includes the possibility of sewage-powered or microbial fuel cells, which harvest the electricity generated through the catabolism of wastewater by micro-organisms. Though not yet commercially viable, the generation of electricity from the water we pass – as a future part of an integrated water-treatment process – is certainly not to be sniffed at.[1075]

---

takes too much energy for it to be economically viable. Water is also split by the natural process of photosynthesis, which uses sunlight to produce combustible carbohydrates, in the process releasing oxygen.

1071. Quoted in Ball, *H₂O*, 273.

1072. In fact, extreme heat and pressure are required to unfetter the reaction, as in the thermonuclear fusion produced by the so-called "hydrogen" bomb. The nuclear fusion announced by the Utah chemists, by contrast, involved the electrolysis of heavy water in a test tube at room temperature, i.e. "cold fusion." For an account of the storm in the cold-fusion teacup, see Ball, *H₂O*, 278ff.

1073. Ibid., 273.

1074. At present, the holy grail of hydrogen-powered vehicles is still in its infancy, owing to the difficulties of storing enough hydrogen gas for anything but a short journey. Yet much work is being done, for example, on "packing" the hydrogen atoms into a solid material, to be released as required.

1075. See Carter, 222-24, on the work being carried out at Pennsylvania State University.

Conclusion

In answer to the question "What is Zen?" one well-known compilation of Zen wisdom includes the Hindu story of a fish who went to the queen fish and said "I have always heard about the sea, but what is this sea? Where is it?" The queen fish answered: "You live, move, and have your being in the sea. The sea is within you and without you, and you are made of sea, and you will end in sea. The sea surrounds you as your own being."[1076] According to the Zen master Hakuin (1685-1768), "not knowing how near the Truth is, people seek it far away – what a disaster! They are like one who, in the middle of a lake, cries out in thirst imploringly."[1077]

Hakuin here uses our relationship to water as a way of explaining the experience of Zen. Conversely, the wisdom of Zen can be taken as a metaphor for our relationship to water. At issue is a form of awareness that sees what we have stopped seeing and that defamiliarizes what we have come to take for granted. Such awareness may be mystical, scientific, philosophical or aesthetic. It may also be ecological: there is a very real sense in which if we persist in the collective blindness we now display

---

1076. Reps, ed., *Zen Flesh, Zen Bones*, 165. In a speech given to a graduating class at Kenyon College, Ohio, the writer David Foster Wallace gave his own version of the anecdote: "There are these two young fish swimming along, and they happen to meet an older fish swimming the other way, who nods at them and says, 'Morning, boys, how's the water?' And the two young fish swim on for a bit, and then eventually one of them looks over at the other and goes, 'What the hell is water?'" Wallace stresses that the point he is making is not about morality, religion, dogma or life after death. It is, he says, about "life before death." It is about "simple awareness – awareness of what is so real and essential, so hidden in plain sight all around us, that we have to keep reminding ourselves, over and over: 'This is water, this is water.'" Quoted in an abridgement of this speech published in *The Guardian Review*, 20 Sept., 2008, pp. 2-4, just over a week after his death.
1077. Bowker (ed.), 1066.

towards water – if we continue to fill our natural waters with agricultural, industrial and domestic wastes, with phosphates, heavy metals and miscellaneous toxins – then soon we may indeed find ourselves in the middle of a lake crying out for thirst.

Such a renewal of vision or re-apprehension of what is familiar is apt to generate wonder or awe. In purely phenomenal terms, the awe-struck observer is reawakened to the sheer *weirdness* of water, the mind-bogglingly complex hydrodynamics of a drop from a tap, the physical and chemical anomalies that make the Earth a life-bearing planet, as well as our human dependence on clean freshwater and the sheer misery of those deprived of a reliable supply of it. To be in awe of water is to be alive to the sublimity of the oceans, their immensity, power and deep unknowability, the timeless temporality of rivers, symbols of the eternal present or the dialectic of constancy and change. The ancient Greek sea-god Thaumas, born of Pontus and Gaia and father of the rainbow, was a god of wonder.

In unthinking everyday life, of course, the wealthy western world has come to take water for granted. In one sense, this is a sign of good fortune. The fact that it is available "on tap" to meet our daily needs relieves us of the anxiety of dehydration, in principle *the* existential threat for terrestrial creatures such as we are.[1078] The fact that it is flushed away after we've dirtied it ensures that it is quickly put out of sight and mind (unless the plumbing malfunctions). While occasional voices may warn us that we shall know the worth of water once the well has run dry or that water is like good health in that we ignore it as long as we have it,[1079] the

1078. Water-romantics who lament the "lifeless ubiquity" (Deakin, 180) of piped chlorinated water certainly have a point, often motivated by a deep veneration for the substance in its natural context. Yet two counterpoints should also be borne in mind: a) that it is still at least a life-*sustaining* ubiquity; and b) that this "ubiquity" only holds for a privileged part of the world population anyway. While a domestic tap may not satisfy our aesthetic sensibility in the same way as a well, a spring or a babbling brook, safe piped water too is a miracle of nature and worthy of wonder. Idyllic dreams of pre-industrial riverbank life are one thing; a ten-mile hike to the nearest well (in practice generally left to the women and girls) to fetch a pitcher-full of water laced with faecal coliform bacteria is quite another. As ever, water is too protean to tolerate an easy disjunction of living versus lifeless varieties.

1079. Benjamin Franklin's "well" quotation is cited in the National Geographic Special Edition on *Water* (vol. 184, no. 5A, 1993), page 1. The "good health" analogy is from ibid., 8. See also Kinnersley, 166-68, on the need to counter what he calls the "flush and forget" attitude, a product of both distaste and habit.

consensus seems to be that the well has not yet (quite) run dry, while our collective or planetary ill-health is masked by indifference and collective self-deception. Chronic waterlessness is the problem of the planet's poor, the voiceless and the invisible.

The loss of wonder in our relationship to water takes the form not only of unseeing or unthinking indifference, but on occasion even active distaste and aversion. Whereas in traditional agrarian societies rain was a blessing from above and drought a signal of divine disfavour, modern-day industrial and post-industrial culture tends to be ungrateful for precipitation and cloud. Names with "lowly" bodily connotations are used for the phenomenon: in England it pisses down, and it spits too for that matter, generally as a prelude to unleashing something more gratifyingly torrential; the French word for drizzle, *crachin*, also implies a spitting; the German *nieseln*, a little sneeze; the Spanish *calabobos* somehow only soaks idiots. Rain is viewed as something that keeps us indoors (watching bad television), blights bank holiday weekends, ruins outdoor functions and causes devastating floods, rather than as a source of fertility and abundance and an instrument of atmospheric cleansing. Whereas in parched Iran to have "your sky always filled with clouds" is a symbol of good fortune,[1080] in the western world clouds are associated with seasonal affective disorder (SAD) and prolonged melancholy. A "cloud on the horizon" betokens the end of blue-sky happiness, but stoically we cheer ourselves up with the thought that "every cloud has a silver lining." In England at least, rain-clouds are rarely invoked except after protracted periods of drought or on the fifth day of cricket matches against Australia. People are sick of the sight of them.

Despite the grotesque success of over-priced water in plastic bottles, water – in its "straight" form at least – enjoys mixed fortunes as a beverage too, associated as it is with workaday fluid-replacement rather than stimulation of the taste-buds, roistering or inebriation. The lament of Coleridge's Ancient Mariner can equally well apply to parties where the alcohol has run out. Chaplin's dipsomaniac in *The Cure* can hardly bring himself to put the stuff to his lips (until it is unwittingly mixed with his own preferred restorative). In general water is felt to be tasteless or insipid, and if it does have any taste this is thanks to the minerals that "happen" to be dissolved in it. The common perception is that water is the *Drink without Qualities* and as such neutral, colourless and even valueless.

1080. See Pretor-Pinney, 167, 77-78. Pretor-Pinney's eloquent critique of "blue-sky thinking" is a timely antidote to nephophobia.

Yet the other side of this coin is water's ever-recurrent proteanism, its mercurial many-sidedness, and the impossibility of pinning it down. Leonardo, for one, was fascinated by water's protean nature: "It has nothing of its own but seizes hold on everything, changing into as many different natures as there are different places on its course, acting just like the mirror which takes in as many images as there are things passing in front of it. So it changes continually, now as regards place, now as regards colour, now it absorbs new smells or tastes, now it detains new substances or qualities, now it brings death, now health…"[1081]

This negativity applies both to the substance in itself (its taste-lessness, formlessness, odourlessness, its colourlessness or transparency) and to its manifestations in nature (the boundlessness of the ocean, the timelessness of rivers, the unknowability of the depths). Given the impossibility of capturing its essence except by saying what it is *not* (a strategy known in theology as the *via negativa*), it is not surprising that water has been described as an evocation of "the elusive Nothingness"[1082] and become something akin to mystical divinity. Like the god of the mystics,[1083] water is featureless, omnipresent, beyond words or concepts, and in this sense ineffable. Like the divine nothingness, it is also the matrix from which "something" (or "life") emerges, while it may equally be the very embodiment of death, on a whim engulfing its creations within its gargantuan maw. This, perhaps, is part of the problem with using excessively anthropomorphic imagery to characterize water and its many states: e.g. describing water as "alive" or "angry" or attributing volition to it. More appropriate for water are "theomorphic" concepts, such as "transcendence," "ineffability," "immensity" or "origin." By using such terms, aqueous creatures such as we are can be awakened to the divinity in us. It is a soggy, water-logged form of divinity, more a divine splash or a splodge than a spark. Most importantly, it is a form of divinity we share with everyone else, past, present and future, and with the whole of the biosphere.

However, the unfathomability of watery nothingness may also provoke less favourable responses. It is telling that Sartre should have chosen an ultimately nautical term – nausea (from the Greek *naus*, ship)

1081. Leonardo da Vinci, 47.
1082. Farber, 103.
1083. Eckhart, for example, referred to the Godhead as a "fathomless ocean" into which the noble soul was to throw himself (*Selected Writings*, 248). It was also ineffable, nameless, Nothing.

– to describe human experience of the contingency or groundlessness of existence. In these terms, Sartre's existential sea-sickness denotes an elementary discomfort produced by the relationship of a conscious being to the sea of contingency in which it is adrift, betraying a landlubber's yearning for underlying grounds or foundations.[1084] It has its roots in a schizoid dualism or split between the self (as consciousness) and a watery world that includes the body[1085]: as a consequence of this split, our relationship to the wetness that constitutes us is deeply ambivalent (and in Sartre this forms the basis for our nausea).[1086] From a dualistic perspective, the human body – with its intrinsic wateriness – tends to constitute a self that is unfathomable in the sense of being an unconscious or "lower" self.

Of course, such dichotomies between our lower and our higher functions – between water and mind – are anything but watertight. For a start, as Sartre himself acknowledged, water's fluidity makes it a perfect metaphor for mind. The high-low dichotomy is equally leaky where water

1084. On nausea, see Sartre, *Being and Nothingness*, 338-39.
1085. Ibid.: "A dull and inescapable nausea perpetually reveals my body to my consciousness. ... We must not take the term *nausea* as a metaphor derived from our physiological disgust. On the contrary, we must realize that it is on the foundation of this nausea that all concrete and empirical nauseas (nausea caused by spoiled meat, fresh blood, excrement, etc.) are produced and make us vomit." Attempting to resolve this split, Sartre in fact recognizes that consciousness is itself bodily (or, as he puts it, that consciousness "exists" its body [cf. ibid., 329]). At the same time, this body is both me and not-me: "I *am* my body to the extent that I *am*; *I am not* my body to the extent that I am not what I am" (ibid., 326).
1086. Not surprisingly, Sartre himself did not elaborate on the nautical implications of his concept of nausea and is unlikely to have endorsed a reading of it in terms of water. In fact, given his fondness for the metaphor of "viscosity" to describe the nature of the world, it might seem as though the sea of contingency that causes his nausea has more in common with a sea of treacle. *Being and Nothingness* incorporates a detailed comparison of the symbolic value of water and the viscous, analysing how a drop of water instantly transforms itself into the body of water it hits whereas the viscous sluggishly melts into itself. The symbol of the body of water, writes Sartre, lends itself to "the construction of pantheistic systems": the viscous "is the agony of water" (607). The idea of himself being transformed into water does not disturb Sartre, "because water is the symbol of consciousness" on account of "its movement, its fluidity, its deceptive appearance of being solid, its perpetual flight," whereas "the viscous offers a horrible image. ... A consciousness which became viscous would be transformed by the thick stickiness of its ideas" (610) (I have slightly changed the translation, using "viscous" rather than "slimy" to render *le visqueux*).

is concerned. The US activist and social reformer John W. Gardner (1912-2002) hit the nail on the head when he declared: "The society which scorns excellence in plumbing because plumbing is a humble activity, and tolerates shoddiness in philosophy because philosophy is an exalted activity, will have neither good plumbing nor good philosophy. Neither its pipes nor its theories will hold water."[1087] The British philosopher Mary Midgley has even portrayed philosophy as a *form* of plumbing, as something that remains unnoticed (again like health) until it malfunctions: "Then suddenly we become aware of some bad smells, and we have to take up the floorboards and look at the concepts of even the most ordinary piece of thinking."[1088] There are important parallels between the well-being of our ideas and our domestic water-installations.

Like water, philosophy is too protean to be pinned down by metaphors of place or position. While a lineage of philosophers including Socrates, Bruno and Nietzsche has aspired to the soaring heights, Wittgenstein – as we have seen – recognized the risk of vaporousness or vapidity and preferred his wisdom as precipitation rather than clouds. In another context, he advocated plumbing the depths, drawing an analogy between philosophical thinking and diving beneath the surface when swimming: "just as one's body has a natural tendency towards the surface and one has to make an *exertion* to get to the *bottom* – so it is with thinking."[1089] The still waters that run deep are usually taken to be *wise* waters.

Too often, however, water's negativity has been transposed into moral terms, denoting what is base, lawless, uncivilized and – by extension – alien. Like "Nature" considered refractory, water has thus been repressed or consigned to a form of collective unconscious. It is something to be "tamed" or "shackled." It is banished to subterranean pipes. It is bottled in plastic containers to be sold to those who can afford it. Streams and brooks are concreted over to provide space for car parks and supermarkets, and rivers are dammed so their energy can be harnessed and deserts made to bloom. Wetlands are drained and dyked. The hidden heritage of ancient

1087. Quoted as the epigraph to Carter, no page number.
1088. From L. Else, "Mary, Mary, quite contrary," interview in *New Scientist*, 3 Nov 2001. See the essay "Philosophical Plumbing," in Midgley, *Utopias, Dolphins and Computers*, 1-14.
1089. Malcolm, *Ludwig Wittgenstein: A Memoir*, 55.

aquifers is plundered with no thought of future generations.[1090] Rivers are turned into conduits for our effluent, with the seas as the final dumping ground. Where the human craving for mastery over nature fails to impose itself (as with the mighty oceans), it turns hostile, destroying what it cannot control: the "lawlessness" of nature is exploited as a pretext for a lawless free-for-all. The seas are pillaged relentlessly, human ignorance and indifference coinciding with a will to wanton devastation and a traditional animosity towards the creatures that inhabit the depths. The freedom conventionally associated with the oceans has in practice amounted to a freedom to violate and despoil, the freedom of blind rapacity and short-term gratification. It is the freedom of a collective id where a nature-despising "super-ego" (endorsed by religious and philosophical dualisms) has decided to join in the carnage.

The human, social and environmental costs and risks associated with such repression[1091] – in particular with the construction of mega-dams and the taming of rivers – are well documented. While such projects may often be genuinely humanitarian in intention, in practice they have tended to serve as vehicles for technocratic ostentation or totalitarian megalomania. Ultimately, the issue is to shift from working *against* nature or water (an act of conquest) to working *with* it (an act of participation and cooperation); it is also to shift from mega-projects imposed from outside or above by profit-greedy transnationals and despotic states to local "water democracies" governed by the people whose livelihoods are at stake. Flexibility rather than dogma is vital. This is crucial to what experts are calling a new "water ethic" or "water culture" based not on mastery and subjugation but veneration and wonder.[1092]

At the heart of any such ethic lies an egalitarianism underwritten by water itself. Our own watery nature bonds us with all other humans

---

1090. See Pearce, 346: "We are already living on borrowed time by mining the aquifers. ... We will live to regret this; and if we don't, our children will. Up to a billion people are today eating food grown using underground water that is not being replaced."

1091. That it is a form of repression is made particularly clear by the Spanish language, in which *represar* means both "to repress" (also *reprimir*) and "to dam," and *represión* has a meaning in the fields of both psychoanalysis and dam-construction.

1092. Some speak of renewing our sense of the sacredness or sanctity of water, although this may upset dogmatic atheists.

and with life in general.[1093] Not only is there just one ocean, but there is ultimately just one hydrological cycle, and we are all a part of it. Water's protean fluidity means that unlike land it naturally resists appropriation. In the words of David Kinnersley, one of the co-founders of the charity WaterAid: "Because it is fixed and stable, land can be divided by hedges and walls. ... Thus land has the potential to be held in common or to become, as it has done in many countries, the foundation of private property, personal wealth and inheritance. By contrast, water has to be a communal asset because it will not stay still. For thousands of years, legal systems across the world have accepted and insisted that there can be no ownership of running water."[1094] If access to water is tied to market forces and the law of scarcity, moreover, it is poor and marginalised communities – as opposed to the manufacturing, agribusiness and leisure industries – that are first to suffer when the prices hit the ceiling. The basic human right to clean, safe drinking water and sanitation is unconditional: any system that fails in this respect – as ours does at present – can only be called unethical.

However, water's traditional status as a natural commons or communal asset may itself run the risk of breeding familiarity (and thus contempt). It has been argued that the most effective way of protecting water is in fact to "commodify" it, bestowing it with an economic value and thus a price. Only by costing water, according to some, is it possible to discourage wastage and foster the respect we all have for things we have to pay for. According to a statement appearing in *Fortune* magazine in 2000, "water promises to be to the 21st century what oil was to the 20th century: the precious commodity that determines the wealth of nations."[1095] But doesn't the commodification of water in turn run the risk of de-sacralising it? Transforming it into just another good: low in value if abundant, exclusive and discriminative if scarce? Market mechanisms cannot be trusted to protect the interests either of the poor, the rest of the biosphere, or future generations, all of whom lack a "voice" within such a

1093. The relationship of this bond – our aqueous nature – to ethics is of course symbolic. There would be no a priori reason to employ any different ethical criteria in our behaviour towards a *non-water-based* life-form, if such a thing were known to exist. The deeper foundation of ethics is a capacity for suffering.
1094. Kinnersley, 1. Kinnersley mentions a well-developed code of water law dating from the time of the 6th-century Emperor Justinian, which stipulates that flowing water cannot be owned (ibid., 36).
1095. Quoted in Black, *The No-Nonsense Guide to Water*, 75.

system. Some form of regulation is clearly required.

In fact, regulation is imperative for the protection of natural commons, and the disastrous effects of its absence are well documented. In early industrial society, for example, commodities such as water (or air) did not enter the market pricing mechanism, but were treated as goods that were inexhaustible in supply and freely available to all. As there was nothing to stop companies dumping effluent into rivers (or spewing fumes into the air), they took full advantage of their impunity while they could. In this sense the prices they charged did not reflect the true costs – which were borne by a population lumbered with water that was no longer fit either for drinking, fishing or recreation (as well as air unfit for breathing).[1096] This "problem of the commons" – or what Clive Ponting has termed the problem of "open access regimes"[1097] – was also responsible for the hunting to extinction or near-extinction of the creatures of the seas. Countless species of whales, seals and fish were virtually wiped off the map as hunters competed with one another to exploit dwindling resources before they ran out. Again, it was a question of maximizing short-term individual gains, with complete disregard for the medium and long-term collective well-being. In the absence of regulation, the individual hunters acted not only against the animals' interests, but also their own.

There is evidently a need for some sort of control, countering the drive for short-term gratification with a rational and ethical perspective that seeks not only to combat inequality and provide universal safe water, sanitation and waste treatment, but also (for example) to prevent the over-extraction of groundwater, manage water conflicts or international river basin disputes, protect the oceans from whaling, bottom trawling, over-fishing and pollution, and establish a network of marine reserves. Global regulation is also clearly necessary to curb anthropogenic carbon dioxide emissions, which are likely not only to provoke higher temperatures, de-glaciation, rising sea-levels and the massive inundation of coastal regions, but are also in the process of turning the ocean waters

---

1096. Economists use the term "externalities" to describe situations such as these, where costs are transferred away from the activities that generate them and instead borne by people or communities who have done nothing to incur them. They represent a market failure to the extent that costs are not correctly reflected in market prices. On externalities, see Kinnersley, 153-56.

1097. Ponting, 150; see in particular 150-70 for a sobering account of mankind's brainless destruction of sea-creatures, as well as the over-hunting of fur-bearing animals. On the problem of the commons see also Pearce, 63.

acidic, with incalculable consequences.[1098] Public awareness, education and debate is vital. Conceptual tools such as "virtual water"[1099] help make the water in agricultural and industrial use more *visible*, alerting consumers to the staggering quantities of water required to grow crops and manufacture products: almost three tons for a cotton T-shirt, one ton for a kilo of wheat, five litres of virtual water just to produce the plastic used in a one-litre water-bottle. Such a concept helps draw attention to the perversity of exporting virtual water when this is based on the cultivation of water-guzzling crops (such as cotton) in arid regions – achieved by over-exploiting "invisible" underground water reserves or reducing major rivers to a trickle. It is a way of quantifying water's invisible essentiality, the protean presence without which everything else is unthinkable.

Such a "water ethic" is not to be confused – though it may overlap – with the ethic of "being like water" or even "being water," which goes back to the ancient wisdom of Taoism and was catapulted into the realm of cliché (in Spain at least) when Bruce Lee's words "be water (my friend)" were used by BMW to market a car. Advocating a flexible, non-formalized fighting technique ("if you put water into a cup, it becomes the cup; if you put water into a bottle it becomes the bottle..." and so on), Bruce Lee doubtless knew what he was talking about – and Proteus would have certainly acquiesced. As an existential strategy, the fluidity and adaptability championed by Lao Tzu and Chuang-tzu likewise has a great deal to be said for it. Yet its cynical use as a marketing slogan serves to underscore a certain vacuity: "Be water!" says the wise man. "I am!" answers the pedant, "70 per cent!" The advice is as empty as telling someone: "be what you are!" or "be yourself!" It may be useful for the repressed (which includes almost everyone in some way or other), but in itself it can never provide any "concrete" ethical guidance.

Yet the wisdom of "being (like) water" also has other connotations. It may be taken as an injunction to self-knowledge meaning "remember that you *are* water" (don't disparage your bodily functions, they are you too). To be aware of one's wateriness is to achieve a certain sort of (limited) self-knowledge and recognise the oneness of body and mind: this muddy

---

1098. The massive absorption of carbon dioxide by the oceans – some 500 billion tons since the start of the industrial revolution – has so far helped curb global warming, but in the process turned the surface waters into dilute carbonic acid.
1099. On virtual water see Pearce, 21-25; Caldecott, 147-48. Worldwide, the virtual water trade is currently thought to total about a thousand cubic kilometres a year.

materialism contrasts sharply with the schizoid disunity of Cartesian mind-body dualism. Water-like fluidity and flexibility may also imply an ability to transcend dogma and the rigidity of doctrine. To be like water in one's thinking is to flow beyond static ideas or concepts and be open to what is new or unfamiliar. It may also imply a more environmentally harmonious mode of existence, one that – like water – adapts to the form of its medium (the environment, nature, the world), co-existing rather than clashing with what is around it. Julian Caldecott has drawn a distinction between the Confucian and the Taoist sides of our minds (and their respective approaches to water and ecosystem management). Whereas the former embodies an imperialistic, top-down, mechanistic, hierarchical approach ("hard" thinking), the latter is flexible, holistic, egalitarian and "soft": it is associated with "a much more organic approach to the world, one that accepts its complexity and subtlety, that values diversity and the individual lives of all its citizens more-or-less equally, even if they don't happen to be human."[1100] These two approaches correspond to what Caldecott conceives as the terrestrial and the aquatic ape within us.

Caldecott is aware of the need for a "balancing of these two approaches."[1101] Indeed, the image of water and flow has important limitations as an ethical principle.[1102] Going with the flow may imply not merely an easy-going nature, but an inclination to go for the easy option or quiet life when *taking a stance* is what is called for: moral laziness. At times there is good reason to go *against* the current or tide. Metaphors of fluidity or liquidity are commonly applied to humankind's postmodern condition as well as to the unsustainable capitalist system itself, which is the very epitome of "flow." To be (like) water, some might say, is to be cool, adaptable and postmodern (whatever that is supposed to mean) and very much a part – a fluid part – of the ethically questionable capitalist system. So be a salmon, my friend.

The alchemists of old knew that truth comprised a marriage of water and fire, moon and sun. We are not *just* water. But nor, for that matter, is water, which is very rarely, if ever, "itself." By the same token, we are not purely aquatic creatures. In fact, we are neither aquatic nor terrestrial, neither fish nor flesh nor good red herring, but something in between: terrestrial creatures who nonetheless maintain the essence of the (salty and thermally stable) sea internalised *within ourselves*, possibly

1100. Caldecott, 51; see 50-52.
1101. Ibid., 205.
1102. Perhaps the idea is that it is not really a principle.

slightly nauseous wherever we are, ill at ease on dry land and unable to survive in the amniotic waters of the deep. This double nature of ours – as water that is not water – finds a further echo in the double nature of water, which can symbolize both the unconscious (what is unfathomable, lowly or bodily) and consciousness itself (its ever-changing fluidity, its reflective transparency). And this in turn mirrors our own duality as self-observing beings, i.e. as both subject and object. So while we may be just a drop in a seemingly infinite ocean or cycle of water, there is also a sense in which the ocean itself exists *within us* as living, sentient and occasionally thinking beings. To adapt an insight from the German philosopher Schelling, it is through mind that water opens its eyes and notices that it exists. We are water bursting into self-visibility.

Bibliography

Ackroyd, Peter. *Thames: Sacred River*. London: Chatto & Windus, 2007.

Andersen, Hans Christian. *Fairy Tales*. Translated by Pat Iverson. London: Penguin, 1994.

Arabian Nights: *Tales from the Thousand and One Nights*. Translated by N. J. Dawood. Rev. ed. Harmondsworth: Penguin, 1973.

Ariosto, Ludovico. *Orlando Furioso*. Translated by Guido Waldman. Oxford: Oxford University Press, 1974.

Aristotle. *Meteorologica*. Translated by E. W. Webster. In: *Works. Vol. 3*. Edited by W. D. Ross. Oxford: Clarendon Press, 1931.

Aristotle. *Poetics I*. Translated by Richard Janko. Cambridge: Hackett Publishing Company, 1987.

Aristophanes. *Lysistrata. The Acharnians. The Clouds*. Translated by Alan H. Sommerstein. Harmondsworth: Penguin, 1973.

Arrojo, Pedro. *El Reto Ético de la Nueva Cultura del Agua: Funciones, valores y derechos en juego*. Barcelona: Paidós, 2006.

Ashenburg, Katherine. *Clean: An Unsanitized History of Washing*. London: Profile Books, 2008.

Ashokamitran. *Water*. Translated by Lakshmi Holmström. Oxford: Heinemann, 1993.

Auden, W. H. *Selected Poems*. Edited by Edward Mendelson. London: Faber and Faber, 1978.

Austen, Jane. *Northanger Abbey. Lady Susan. The Watsons. Sanditon*. Edited by James Kinsley and John Davie and with an introduction by Claudia L. Johnson. Oxford: Oxford University Press, 2003.

Bacon, Francis. *Sylva Sylvarum: Or a Natural History in Ten Centuries*. Montana: Kessinger Publishing Co., 1996.

Ball, Philip. *The Devil's Doctor. Paracelsus and the World of Renaissance Magic and Science*. London: Arrow Books, 2007.

Ball, Philip. *H₂O: A Biography of Water*. London: Phoenix, 2000.

Ballard, J. G. *The Drowned World*. 1962; London: Harper Perennial, 2006.

Barber, Peter, ed. *The Map Book*. London: Weidenfeld & Nicolson, 2005.

Barnes, Jonathan, trans. *Early Greek Philosophy*. Harmondsworth: Penguin, 1987.

Barrow, John D., and Frank J. Tipler. *The Anthropic Cosmological Principle*. Oxford: Clarendon Press, 1982.

Bartholomew, Alick. *Hidden Nature: The Startling Insights of Viktor Schauberger*. Edinburgh: Floris Books, 2003.

Baudelaire, Charles. *Les fleurs du mal et autres poèmes*. Paris: Garnier-Flammarion, 1964.

Bergson, Henri. *Creative Evolution*. Translated by Arthur Mitchell. London: Macmillan and Co., 1911.

Biedermann, Hans. *Dictionary of Symbolism: Cultural Icons and the Meanings behind them*. Translated by James Hulbert. New York: Meridian, 1994.

Black, Maggie. *The No-Nonsense Guide to Water*. Oxford / London: New Internationalist / Verso, 2004.

Black, Maggie. *Water, Life Force*. Oxford: New Internationalist Publications, 2004.

Blackbourn, David. *The Conquest of Nature: Water, Landscape and the Making of Modern Germany*. London: Pimlico, 2007.

Blumenberg, Hans. *Das Lachen der Thrakerin. Eine Urgeschichte der Theorie*. Frankfurt-am-Main: Suhrkamp, 1973.

Borges, Jorge Luis. *Selected Poems*. Bilingual ed. Edited by Alexander Coleman. Harmondsworth: Penguin, 2000.

Bowen, E. G. *Britain and the Western Seaways*. London: Thames and Hudson, 1972.

Bowker, John, ed. *The Oxford Dictionary of World Religions*. Oxford / New York: Oxford University Press, 1997.

Broad, William, J. *The Universe Below: Discovering the Secrets of the Deep Sea*. New York: Simon & Schuster, 1997.

Brown, Lloyd A. *The Story of Maps*. 1949; New York: Dover Publications, 1979.

Bryson, Bill. *A Short History of Nearly Everything*. London: Black Swan, 2004.

Buckingham, George Villiers, 2nd duke of. *The Rehearsal*. In *Three Restoration Comedies*. Edited by G. G. Falle. New York: St Martin's Press, 1964.

Bürger, G. A. *Wunderbare Reisen zu Wasser und zu Lande, Feldzüge und lustige Abenteuer des Freiherrn von Münchhausen*. Frankfurt-am-Main: Insel, 1976.

Burke, Edmund. *A Philosophical Enquiry into the Origin of our Ideas of the Sublime and Beautiful.* Edited by Adam Phillips. Oxford / New York: Oxford University Press, 1990.

Burnet, John. *Early Greek Philosophy.* 2nd ed. London: Adam and Charles Black, 1908.

Burnet, Thomas. *The Sacred Theory of the Earth.* 1684; Carbondale: Southern Illinois University Press, 1965.

Byron, George Gordon. *Complete Poetical Works.* Edited by John D. Jump. Rev. ed. Oxford: Oxford University Press, 1970.

Caldecott, Julian. *Water: Life in Every Drop.* London: Virgin Books, 2007.

Calvino, Italo. *Cosmicomics.* Translated by William Weaver. London: Sphere / Abacus, 1982.

Carpentier, Alejo. *Narrativa completa.* Vol. 1. Barcelona: RBA, 2006.

Carroll, Lewis. *Alice's Adventures in Wonderland and Through the Looking-Glass.* Edited by Roger Lancelyn Green. Rev. ed. Oxford: Oxford University Press, 1982.

Carter, W. Hodding. *Flushed. How the Plumber Saved Civilization.* New York: Atria Books, 2007.

Chuang-tzu. *The Seven Inner Chapters and other writings from the book Chuang-tzu.* Translated by A. C. Graham. London: George Allen & Unwin, 1981.

The Cloud of Unknowing. Edited by Evelyn Underhill. New York: Dover Publications, 2003.

Coleman, Loren, and Patrick Huyghe. *The Field Guide to Lake Monsters, Sea Serpents, and Other Mystery Denizens of the Deep.* New York: Jeremy P. Tarcher / Penguin, 2003.

Coleridge, Samuel Taylor. *The Complete Poems.* Edited by William Keach. Harmondsworth: Penguin, 1997.

Conway Morris, Simon. *The Crucible of Creation: The Burgess Shale and the Rise of Animals.* Oxford: Oxford University Press, 1998.

Cornford, F. M. *The Origin of Attic Comedy.* Edited by T. H. Gaster. 1914; New York: Doubleday, 1961.

Cowley, Abraham. *The Works of Mr. A. Cowley.* Vol. 3. London: John Sharpe, 1809.

Dalley, Stephanie, trans. *Myths from Mesopotamia: Creation, The Flood, Gilgamesh, and Others.* Rev. ed. Oxford: Oxford University Press, 2000.

Davies, Paul. *The Mind of God. Science and the Search for Ultimate*

Meaning. Harmondsworth: Penguin, 1993.

Deakin, Roger. *Waterlog. A Swimmer's Journey through Britain.* London: Vintage, 2000.

De Quincey, Thomas. *Confessions of an English Opium Eater.* Edited by Alethea Hayter. Harmondsworth: Penguin, 1986.

Descartes, René. *Discourse on Method, and other writings.* Translated by Arthur Wollaston. Harmondsworth: Penguin, 1960.

Diamond, Jared. *Guns, Germs and Steel: a Short History of Everybody for the Last 13,000 Years.* London: Vintage, 1998.

Dickens, Charles. *Our Mutual Friend.* Edited by Adrian Poole. Harmondsworth: Penguin, 1997.

Dickinson, Emily. *The Complete Poems of Emily Dickinson.* Edited by Thomas H. Johnson. London: Faber and Faber, 1970.

Diogenes Laertius. *Lives of Eminent Philosophers.* With an English translation by R. D. Hicks. 2 vols. London: William Heinemann, 1925 (Loeb Classical Library).

Donne, John. *A Selection of His Poetry.* Edited by John Hayward. Harmondsworth: Penguin, 1950.

Douglas, Mary. *Purity and Danger: an Analysis of Concepts of Pollution and Taboo.* 1966; London and New York: Routledge Classics, 2002.

Eckhart, Meister. *Selected Writings.* Translated by Oliver Davies. Harmondsworth: Penguin, 1994.

Ecott, Tim. *Neutral Buoyancy: Adventures in a Liquid World.* London: Penguin, 2002.

Eliade, Mircea. *Patterns in Comparative Religion.* Translated by Rosemary Sheed. 1958; Lincoln and London: University of Nebraska Press, 1996.

Eliade, Mircea. *Shamanism. Archaic Techniques of Ecstasy.* Translated by Willard R. Trask. 1964; London: Arkana, 1989.

Elias, Norbert. *The Civilizing Process: Sociogenetic and Psychogenetic Investigations.* Translated by Edmund Jephcott. Rev. ed. Oxford: Blackwell, 2000.

Eliot, Alexander. *The Universal Myths: Heroes, Gods, Tricksters and Others.* New York: Truman Talley Books / Meridian, 1990.

Ellis, Richard. *Sea Dragons: Predators of the Prehistoric Oceans.* Lawrence, Kansas: University Press of Kansas, 2003.

Emoto, Masaru. *The Hidden Messages in Water.* Translated by David A. Thayne. London: Simon & Schuster UK, 2005.

Emoto, Masaru. *The Secret Life of Water*. Translated by David A. Thayne. London: Simon & Schuster UK, 2006.

Emoto, Masaru. *The True Power of Water*. Translated by Noriko Hosoyamada. London: Simon & Schuster UK, 2005.

Eveleigh, David J. *Bogs, Baths and Basins: The Story of Domestic Sanitation*. Phoenix Mill: Sutton Publishing, 2006.

Farber, Thomas. *On Water*. Hopewell, N.J.: The Ecco Press, 1994.

Fernández, Mauro. *Diccionario de Refranes. Antología de refranes populares y cultos de la lengua castellana, explicados y razonados*. Madrid: Alderabán, 1994.

Fielding, Henry. *Completed Works*. 16 vols. Edited by W. E. Henley. London: Heinemann, 1903.

Floyer, John, and Edward Baynard. *Psychrolousia: Or, the History of Cold Bathing: Both Ancient and Modern*. 4th ed. London: William Innys: 1715.

Freud, Sigmund. *Standard Edition*. Vol. 21. *The Future of an Illusion, Civilization and its Discontents,* and *Other Works*. Translated by James Strachey. London: Vintage, 2001.

Frost, Robert. *Robert Frost's Poems*. New York: St Martin's Paperbacks, 2002.

Fry, Iris. *The Emergence of Life on Earth: A Historical and Scientific Overview*. London: Free Association Books, 1999.

García, Marlene, and José Ramón Alonso. *Diccionario Ilustrado de Voces Eróticas Cubanas*. Madrid: Celeste Ediciones, 2001.

Gee, Henry. *Deep Time: Cladistics, The Revolution in Evolution*. London: Fourth Estate, 2000.

Gilchrist, Cherry. *The Elements of Alchemy*. Longmead: Element Books, 1991.

Ginzberg, Louis. *The Legends of the Jews. Volume I. From the Creation to Jacob*. Translated by Henrietta Szold. 1909; Baltimore and London: The Johns Hopkins University Press, 1998.

Glasgow, R. D. V. *The Comedy of Mind: Philosophers Stoned, or the Pursuit of Wisdom*. Lanham: University Press of America, 1999.

Glasgow, R. D. V. *Madness, Masks, and Laughter: An Essay on Comedy*. Madison, N. J.: Fairleigh Dickinson University Press, 1995.

Glasgow, R. D. V. *Split Down the Sides: On the Subject of Laughter*. Lanham: University Press of America, 1997.

Goethe, Johann Wolfgang von. *The Sorrows of Young Werther*. Translated by Michael Hulse. Rev. ed. Harmondsworth: Penguin, 1989.

Goodall, Jane (with Gary McAvoy and Gail Hudson). *Harvest for Hope: A Guide to Mindful Eating*. New York: Warner Wellness, 2006.

Gould, Stephen Jay. *Leonardo's Mountain of Clams and the Diet of Worms: Essays on Natural History*. London: Vintage, 1999.

Gould, Stephen Jay. *Wonderful Life: The Burgess Shale and the Nature of History*. Harmondsworth: Penguin, 1991.

Graves, Robert. *The Greek Myths*. Rev. ed. 2 vols. Harmondsworth: Penguin, 1960.

Green, Jonathon. *The Cassell Dictionary of Slang*. London: Cassell, 1998.

Gribbin, John. *In the Beginning. The Birth of the Living Universe*. Harmondsworth: Penguin, 1994.

Grimm, Jacob and Wilhelm. *Complete Fairy Tales*. London: Routledge, 2002.

Halliday, F. E. *A History of Cornwall*. 2nd ed. London: Duckworth, 1975.

Hegel, G. W. F. *Werke*. 20 vols. Edited by E. Moldenhauer and K. M. Michel. Frankfurt-am-Main: Suhrkamp, 1986.

Heine, Heinrich. *Selected Poems*. Translated by David Cram and T. J. Reed. London: J. M. Dent, 1997.

Hemingway, Ernest. *The Old Man and the Sea*. 1952; London: Arrow Books, 2004.

Hesse, Hermann. *Siddhartha*. Translated by Hilda Rosner. London: Picador, 1973.

Hobbes, Thomas. *Leviathan*. Edited by C. B. Macpherson. Harmondsworth: Penguin, 1968.

Hodgkinson, Liz. *The Drinking Water Cure*. London: Carnell, 1996.

Homer. *The Odyssey*. Translated by E. V. Rieu. Harmondsworth: Penguin, 1946.

Hume, David. *A Treatise of Human Nature. Book One*. Edited by D. G. C. Macnabb. London: Fontana, 1962.

Illich, Ivan. *H$_2$O and the Waters of Forgetfulness: Reflections of the Historicity of "Stuff"*. Dallas: The Dallas Institute of Humanities and Culture, 1985.

James, William. *The Principles of Psychology. Vol. 1*. 1890; New York: Cosimo, 2007.

Johnson, Paul. *A History of the Jews*. 1987; London: Phoenix, 2001.

Joyce, James. *Finnegans Wake*. 1939; London: Faber & Faber, 1960.

Kandel, Robert. *Water from Heaven. The Story of Water from the Big*

Bang to the Rise of Civilization, and Beyond. New York: Columbia University Press, 2003.

Kant, Immanuel. *Anthropologie in pragmatischer Hinsicht.* Edited by Wolfgang Becker. Stuttgart: Reclam. 1983.

Kant, Immanuel. *Kritik der Urteilskraft.* Edited by Gerhard Lehmann. Stuttgart: Reclam, 1963.

Keats, John. *Letters of John Keats.* Edited by Robert Gittings. Oxford: Oxford University Press, 1970.

Kennedy, Paul. *The Rise and Fall of the Great Powers: Economic Change and Military Conflict from 1500 to 2000.* London: Fontana Press, 1989.

Kinnersley, David. *Troubled Water: Rivers, Politics and Pollution.* London: Hilary Shipman, 1988.

Koestler, Arthur. *The Act of Creation.* 1964; London: Arkana, 1989.

Kunzig, Robert. *Mapping the Deep: The Extraordinary Story of Ocean Science.* London: Sort of Books, 2000.

Kurlansky, Mark. *Salt. A World History.* London: Vintage Books, 2003.

Lao Tzu. *Tao Te Ching.* Translated by D. C. Lau. Harmondsworth: Penguin, 1963.

Lawrence, D. H. *The Complete Poems of D. H. Lawrence.* Edited by David Ellis. Ware: Wordsworth Editions, 2002.

Leonardo da Vinci. *The Notebooks of Leonardo da Vinci.* Edited by Irma A. Richter. Oxford: Oxford University Press, 1952.

Lerner, Robert E. "The Image of Mixed Liquids in Late Medieval Mystical Thought." In: *Church History,* Vol. 40, No. 4 (Dec. 1971), pp. 397-411.

Leslie, Jacques. *Deep Water: The Epic Struggle over Dams, Displaced People, and the Environment.* New York: Picador / Farrar, Straus and Giroux, 2005.

Levinson, David, and Karen Christensen, eds. *Encyclopaedia of World Sport. From Ancient Times to the Present.* Oxford: Abc-Clio, 1996.

Lewis, C. S. *The Lion, the Witch and the Wardrobe.* Harmondsworth: Penguin, 1959.

Lichtenberg, Georg Christoph. *Sudelbücher.* Edited by Franz H. Mautner. Frankfurt-am-Main: Insel, 1984.

Logan, William Bryant. *Dirt: the Ecstatic Skin of the Earth.* New York and London: W. W. Norton & Company, 2007.

Macdougall, Doug. *Frozen Earth: The Once and Future Story of Ice Ages.* Berkeley, Los Angeles and London: University of California Press, 2006.

Macfarlane, Robert. *Mountains of the Mind. A History of a Fascination.* London: Granta Books, 2004.

McKenna, Terence. *Food of the Gods: the Search for the Original Tree of Knowledge.* London: Rider, 1992.

Machiavelli, Niccolò. *The Prince.* Translated by George Bull. Rev. ed. London: Penguin, 2003.

Malcolm, Norman. *Ludwig Wittgenstein: A Memoir.* London: Oxford University Press, 1958.

Marcus Aurelius. *Meditations.* Translated by Meric Casaubon. London: J. M. Dent & Sons, 1906.

Marks, William E. *The Holy Order of Water: Healing Earth's Waters and Ourselves.* Great Barrington, MA: Bell Pond Books, 2001.

Marshall, Peter. *The Philosopher's Stone: a Quest for the Secrets of Alchemy.* London: Macmillan, 2001.

Maupassant, Guy de. *La Maison Tellier.* Rev. ed. Paris: Gallimard-Jeunesse, 1995.

Mehta, Gita. *A River Sutra.* London: Vintage Books, 2007.

Melville, Herman. *Moby Dick.* 1851; London: Penguin, 1994.

Meyer, Eric, and J. P. LeGrand, eds. *The Family Encyclopaedia of Homeopathic Medicine.* Bodywell Publishing, 1999.

Midgley, Mary. *Beast and Man: The Roots of Human Nature.* London: Methuen, 1980.

Midgley, Mary. *Science as Salvation: A Modern Myth and its Meaning.* London: Routledge, 1992.

Midgley, Mary. *Utopias, Dolphins and Computers: Problems of Philosophical Plumbing.* London and New York: Routledge, 1996.

Milne, A. A. *Winnie-the-Pooh's Little Book of Wisdom (The Wisdom of Pooh).* London: Methuen, 1999.

Montaigne, Michel de. *The Complete Essays.* Translated by M. A. Screech. Harmondsworth: Penguin, 1991.

Morgenstern, Christian. *Alle Galgenlieder.* Zurich: Diogenes, 1981.

Morris, Desmond. *The Naked Woman: A Study of the Female Body.* London: Vintage, 2005.

Munda, Guiseppe. "Social Multi-Criteria Evaluation: Methodological foundations and operational consequences." In: *European Journal of Operational Research,* 158 (2004), pp. 662-77.

Murdoch, Iris. *The Philosopher's Pupil.* Harmondsworth: Penguin, 1984.

Murray, John. *John Dory.* Hexham: Flambard Press, 2001.

Nagel, Thomas. "What Is It Like to Be a Bat?" In: Hofstadter, Douglas R., and Daniel C. Dennett, eds. *The Mind's I: Fantasies and Reflections on Self and Soul*. Harmondsworth: Penguin, 1982.

Nagle, Garrett. *Rivers and Water Management*. London: Hodder & Stoughton, 2003.

Nash, Elizabeth. *Madrid: A Cultural and Literary History*. London: Signal Books, 2001.

Nietzsche, Friedrich. *Die Fröhliche Wissenschaft*. Edited by Peter Pütz. Goldmann Verlag, 1987.

Nouvian, Claire. *The Deep. The Extraordinary Creatures of the Abyss*. Chicago and London: University of Chicago Press, 2007.

Novalis (Friedrich von Hardenberg). *Werke*. Edited by Gerhard Schulz. Rev. ed. Munich: C. H. Beck, 2001.

The Oxford Dictionary of Humorous Quotations. Edited by Ned Sherrin. Oxford: Oxford University Press, 1995.

The Oxford Dictionary of Quotations. 3rd ed. Oxford: Oxford University Press, 1980.

Pagels, Elaine. *The Gnostic Gospels*. London: Penguin, 1990.

Palmer, D. J., ed. *Comedy: Developments in Criticism*. London: Macmillan, 1984.

Passig, Kathrin, and Aleks Scholz. *Lexikon des Unwissens. Worauf es bisher keine Antwort gibt*. Berlin: Rowohlt, 2007.

Pavel, Ota. *Wie ich den Fischen begegnete. Erzählungen*. Translated from Czech into German by Elisabeth Borchardt. Berlin: Phileas, 2005.

Paxman, Jeremy, ed. *Fish, Fishing and the Meaning of Life*. London: Penguin, 1995.

Pearce, Fred. *When the Rivers Run Dry: What happens when our water runs out?* London: Eden Project Books, 2006.

Peat, F. David. *Blackfoot Physics: a Journey into the Native American Universe*. London: Fourth Estate, 1995.

Pelikan, Jaroslav. *Mary through the Centuries. Her Place in the History of Culture*. New Haven and London: Yale University Press, 1996.

Pernetta, John. *Philip's Guide to the Oceans*. London: Philip's, 2004.

Petronius. *The Satyricon*. And Seneca. *The Apocolocyntosis*. Translated by J. P. Sullivan. Harmondsworth: Penguin, 1977.

Philo. *The Works of Philo: Complete and Unabridged, New Updated Edition*. Translated by C. D. Yonge. Edited by David M. Scholer. Peabody, Mass.: Hendrickson, 1993.

Plato. *Theaetetus. Sophist*. With an English translation by H. N. Fowler.

London: Heinemann, 1921 (Loeb Classical Library).

Plato. *Timaeus. Critias. Cleitophon. Menexenus. Epistles*. With an English translation by R. G. Bury. London: Heinemann, 1929 (Loeb Classical Library).

[Plutarch]. "Whether Water or Fire Be Most Useful." In: Plutarch. *The Morals. Vol. 5*. Translated by William W. Goodwin. Boston: Little, Brown, and Co., 1878.

Ponting, Clive. *A New Green History of the World. The Environment and the Collapse of Great Civilisations*. Rev. ed. London: Vintage Books, 2007.

Pope, Alexander. *Collected Poems*. Edited by Bonamy Dobrée. London: J. M. Dent & Sons, 1924.

Popol Vuh. The Mayan Book of the Dawn of Life. Translated by Dennis Tedlock. Rev. ed. New York: Touchstone, 1996.

Pretor-Pinney, Gavin. *The Cloudspotter's Guide*. London: Hodder & Stoughton, 2006.

Prigogine, Ilya, and Isabelle Stengers. *Order out of Chaos. Man's New Dialogue with Nature*. London: Flamingo, 1985.

Rabelais, François. *Oeuvres complètes*. Edited by Guy Demerson et al. Paris: Seuil, 1973.

Renfrew, Colin. *Before Civilization: the Radiocarbon Revolution and Prehistoric Europe*. Harmondsworth: Penguin, 1978.

Reps, Paul, ed. *Zen Flesh, Zen Bones*. 1957; London: Arkana, 1991.

The Rig Veda. An Anthology. Translated by Wendy Doniger O'Flaherty. Harmondsworth: Penguin, 1981.

Roman, Joe. *Whale*. London: Reaktion Books, 2006.

Roob, Alexander. *The Hermetic Museum: Alchemy and Mysticism*. Translated by Shaun Whiteside. Cologne: Taschen, 2001.

Roy, Arundhati. *The Cost of Living: The Greater Common Good* and *The End of Imagination*. London: Flamingo, 1999.

The Ruba'iyat of Omar Khayyam. Translated by Peter Avery and John Heath-Stubbs. London: Allen Lane, 1979.

Rudolph, Kurt. *Gnosis: the Nature and History of Gnosticism*. Translated by P. W. Coxon, K. H. Kuhn and R. McL. Wilson. Rev ed. New York: Harper & Row, 1987.

Rupp, Rebecca. *Four Elements: Water, Air, Fire, Earth*. London: Profile Books, 2005.

Russell, Bertrand. *History of Western Philosophy and its Connection with Political and Social Circumstances from the Earliest Times to the*

Present Day. London: George Allen and Unwin, 1946.

Said, Edward W. *Representations of the Intellectual*. London: Vintage, 1994.

Sartre, Jean-Paul. *Being and Nothingness: an Essay on Phenomenological Ontology*. Translated by Hazel E. Barnes. 1958; London: Routledge, 1991.

Schechner Genuth, Sara. *Comets, Popular Culture, and the Birth of Modern Cosmology*. Princeton, NJ: Princeton University Press, 1997.

Schiller, Friedrich. *Sämtliche Gedichte und Balladen*. Edited by Georg Kurscheidt. 2nd ed. Frankfurt-am-Main: Insel, 2004.

Schopenhauer, Arthur. *Sämtliche Werke*. 5 vols. Edited by W. F. von Löhneysen. Frankfurt-am-Main: Suhrkamp, 1986.

Schrödinger, E. *What is Life?* Cambridge: Cambridge University Press, 1946.

Schwenk, Theodor and Wolfram Schwenk. *Water: the Element of Life: Essays*. Translated by Marjorie Spock. Anthroposophic Press, 1989.

Scott Littleton, C. *Mythology: the Illustrated Anthology of World Myth and Storytelling*. London: Duncan Baird Publishers, 2002.

Screech, M. A. *Erasmus: Ecstasy and the Praise of Folly*. Harmondsworth: Penguin, 1988.

Screech, M. A. *Montaigne and Melancholy. The Wisdom of the* Essays. Harmondsworth: Penguin, 1991.

The Scriblerus Club [Jonathan Swift, Alexander Pope, John Gay et al.]. *Memoirs of the Extraordinary Life, Works, and Discoveries of Martinus Scriblerus* [1741]. Edited by C. Kerby-Miller. New York: Russell & Russell, 1966.

Seuse, Heinrich. *Das Buch der Wahrheit*. Edited by Loris Sturlese and Rüdiger Blumrich. Translated by Rüdiger Blumrich. Hamburg: Felix Meiner Verlag, 1993.

Shakespeare, William. *The Complete Works*. Edited by Stanley Wells and Gary Taylor. Oxford: Clarendon Press, 1986.

Shapiro, Rose. *Suckers: How Alternative Medicine Makes Fools of Us All*. London: Harvill Secker, 2008.

Sharma, Chandradhar. *A Critical Survey of Indian Philosophy*. London: Rider, 1960.

Shubin, Neil. *Your Inner Fish: A Journey into the 3.5-Billion-Year History of the Human Body*. London: Allen Lane, 2008.

Singer, Peter. *Animal Liberation*. 2nd ed. London: Pimlico, 1995.

Smith, Margaret. *Rabi'a the Mystic and her Fellow-Saints*. 1928;

Cambridge: Cambridge University Press, 1984.

Smollett, Tobias. *The Adventures of Peregrine Pickle*. Montana: Kessinger Publishing Co., 2004.

Smollett, Tobias. *The Expedition of Humphry Clinker*. Edited by Lewis M. Knapp. Rev. ed. Oxford: Oxford University Press, 1984.

Sobel, Dava. *Longitude. The True Story of a Lone Genius Who Solved the Greatest Scientific Problem of His Time*. London: Harper Perennial, 2005.

Speaking of Siva. Translated by A. K. Ramanujan. Harmondsworth: Penguin, 1973.

Sprawson, Charles. *Haunts of the Black Masseur: The Swimmer as Hero*. 1992; Minneapolis: University of Minnesota Press, 2000.

Standage, Tom. *A History of the World in Six Glasses*. London: Atlantic Books, 2007.

Staveacre, Tony. *Slapstick: the Illustrated Story of Knockabout Comedy*. London: Angus & Robertson, 1987.

Stone, Brian, ed. *Medieval English Verse*. Rev. ed. London: Penguin, 1971.

Swift, Jonathan. *Gulliver's Travels*. Edited by Paul Turner. Oxford: Oxford University Press, 1986.

Thomas, Keith. *Religion and the Decline of Magic. Studies in Popular Beliefs in Sixteenth- and Seventeenth-Century England*. 1971; Harmondsworth: Penguin, 1991.

Thoreau, Henry David. *Walden* and *Civil Disobedience*. Edited by Michael Meyer. London: Penguin, 1986.

Turner, Alice K. *The History of Hell*. London: Robert Hale Ltd, 1996.

Verne, Jules. *Journey to the Centre of the Earth*. London: Penguin, 1994.

Verne, Jules. *Twenty Thousand Leagues under the Sea*. Translated by Mendor T. Brunetti. London: Penguin, 1994.

Veyne, Paul, ed. *A History of Private Life: I. From Pagan Rome to Byzantium*. Translated by Arthur Goldhammer. Cambridge, Mass., and London: Harvard University Press, 1992.

Von Düffel, John. *Wasser*. Munich: Deutscher Taschenbuch Verlag, 2000.

Warner, Marina. *From the Beast to the Blonde: On Fairy Tales and their Tellers*. London: Vintage, 1995.

Water: The Power, Promise, and Turmoil of North America's Fresh Water. National Geographic Special Edition, vol. 184, no. 5A, 1993.

Weightman, Gavin. *The Frozen Water Trade: How Ice from New England Lakes Kept the World Cool.* London: HarperCollins, 2003.
Wittgenstein, Ludwig. *Werkausgabe.* 8 vols. Frankfurt-am-Main: Suhrkamp, 1984.
Wolpert, Lewis. *The Unnatural Nature of Science.* London: Faber and Faber, 1993.
Wordsworth, William. *The Prelude: The Four Texts (1798, 1799, 1805, 1850).* Edited by Jonathan Wordsworth. Harmondsworth: Penguin, 1995.

Lightning Source UK Ltd.
Milton Keynes UK
UKOW05f0203161014

240178UK00007B/260/P